MISSING PERSONS AND MISTAKEN IDENTITIES

OVERTURES TO BIBLICAL THEOLOGY

EDITORS

MISSING PERSONS
AND
MISTAKEN IDENTITIES

WOMEN AND GENDER
IN ANCIENT ISRAEL

Phyllis A. Bird

FORTRESS PRESS
MINNEAPOLIS

MISSING PERSONS AND MISTAKEN IDENTITIES
Women and Gender in Ancient Israel

Grateful acknowledement is made for permission to reprint the following articles in this volume: "'Male and Female He Created Them': Gen 1:27b in the Context of the Priestly Account of Creation" by Phyllis A. Bird appeared in volume 74 (1981) of the *Harvard Theological Review*, copyright © 1981 by the President and Fellows of Harvard College. Reprinted by permission. "Genesis 1–3 as a Source for Contemporary Theology of Sexuality" appeared in *Ex Auditu* III (1987) 31–44. "The Harlot as Heroine: Narrative Art and Social Presupposition in Three Old Testmament Texts" appeared in *Semeia* 46 (1989) 119–139. "Translating Sexist Language as a Theological and Cultural Problem" appeared in *Union Seminary Quarterly Review* 42 (1988) 89–95. "Poor Man or Poor Woman: Gendering the Poor in Prophetic Texts" was previously published by E. J. Brill. "Israelite Religion and the Faith of Israel's Daughters: Reflections on Gender and Religious Definition," appeared in *The Bible and the Politics of Exegesis: Essays in Honor of Norman K. Gottwald on His Sixty-Fifth Birthday,* David Jobling, Peggy L. Day, and Gerald T. Sheppard, eds., Pilgrim Press. "Biblical Authority Reappraised" was previously published by CMBC Publications, used by permission of Canadian Mennonite Bible College. "Genesis 3 in Modern Biblical Scholarship" is an English translation of "Genesis 3 in der gegenwärtigen biblischen Forschung," which previously appeared in *Jahrbuch für Biblische Theologie* 9 (1994) 4–24, published by Neukirchener Verlag. Extract from "Women (OT)" from *The Anchor Bible Dictionary* (ed. David Noel Freedman, 1992) is courtesy of Doubleday, a division of Bantam Doubleday Dell Publishing Group, Inc. Used by permission.

Cover and book design by Joseph Bonyata.

Cover art: *Venus of Menton,* Limestone, Austria. Courtesy of Musée des Antiquités Nationales, St-Germain-en-Laye, France. Used by permission. Author photo: Evanston Photographic Studios.

Library of Congress Cataloging-in-Publication Data

Bird, Phyllis A. (Phyllis Ann), 1934–
    Missing persons and mistaken identities : women and gender in
ancient Israel / Phyllis A. Bird.
       p.   cm. — (Overtures to biblical theology)
    Includes bibliographical references.
    ISBN 0-8006-3128-5 (alk. paper)
    1. Women in the Bible. 2. Bible. O.T.—Criticism,
interpretation, etc. 3. Bible. O.T.—Feminist criticism,
I. Title. II. Series.
BS1199.W7B57 1997
221.6'082—dc21

                                     97-27404
                                        CIP

Manufactured in the U.S.A.   AF /-3128

01   00   99   98   97   1   2   3   4   5   6   7   8   9   10

CONTENTS

FOREWORD

THE GAINS IN FEMINIST INTERPRETATION IN RECENT YEARS ARE immense. Indeed, since the publication of *God and the Rhetoric of Sexuality* by Phyllis Trible in Overtures in 1978, feminist practices in Scripture interpretation have become well established as inescapable and welcome perspectives in the midst of more general interpretive theory and practice. Few, if any, have contributed more to the effectiveness and cruciality of this fresh interpretive angle than Phyllis Bird. The present volume attests to her steadfastness in such an enterprise. Because this collection of essays stretches over the long period of her research, a longitudinal range evidences not only her maturing sensitivity about the issues but also her development and growing sophistication in hermeneutics more generally. Indeed, Bird can speak of the "interpretive legacy of representatives of the first generation" of feminist scholars. And while she stands in continuity and solidarity with their work, she has pursued her own quite distinctive course of study to our great gain.

It is now a commonplace to observe that patriarchal habits have dominated both the text and the history of interpretation. There is no doubt, moreover, that correction of such unfortunate perspectives has required determined and sustained advocacy. While Bird has shared the concern of feminist advocates, her work is of another sort, surely in the long run more durable and more persuasive than frontal advocacy. For along with her acute theological sensitivity, Bird is a discerning historian who proceeds by a study of the sociopolitical environment in which texts are placed, offering an account of the context that decisively impinges upon the voice of the text. Thus Bird is precisely the sort of scholar who can help most in facing texts that are ideologically tilted, combining the discipline of a critical historian and the sensitivity of a knowing theologian. Her several essays presented here make clear that moving beyond conventional ideological reading requires sustained attentiveness and technical competence along with a good deal of courage.

Theological exposition cannot simply read across the top of the text, nor can it simply be a shrill echo of our contemporary wishes. As much as anyone I know, Bird models the toughness and delicacy that are needed for a rereading of these holy texts that may contribute to a redefining of social reality informed by resolved faith. For all of these reasons, it is a source of great satisfaction that these essays are now made available in this accessible form. The collection exhibits how theology must attend to the detail in the text, the power of environment, the force of ideology, and the possibility of fresh discernment. Bird is a champion of the dialogical perspective that she here advocates.

Walter Brueggemann
Columbia Theological Seminary

ABBREVIATIONS

AARAS	American Academy of Religion Academy Series
AB	Anchor Bible
ABD	D. N. Freedman, ed., *Anchor Bible Dictionary*
ABL	R. F. Harper, *Assyrian and Babylonian Letters*
Adam and Eve	*Books of Adam and Eve*
AfO	*Archiv für Orientforschung*
AHW	W. von Soden, *Akkadisches Handwörterbuch*
Akk.	Akkadian
AnBib	Analecta biblica
ANEP	J. B. Pritchard, ed., *Ancient Near East in Pictures*
ANET	J. B. Pritchard, ed., *Ancient Near Eastern Texts*
AOAT	Alter Orient und Altes Testament
AOS	American Oriental Series
Ass. Code	Assyrian [Law] Code
ATD	Das Alte Testament Deutsch
AUSS	*Andrews University Seminary Studies*
BASOR	*Bulletin of the American Schools of Oriental Research*
BDB	F. Brown, S. R. Driver, and C. A. Briggs, *Hebrew and English Lexicon of the Old Testament*
BHS	*Biblia hebraica stuttgartensia*
BibOr	Biblica et orientalia
BJRL	*Bulletin of the John Rylands University Library of Manchester*
BJS	Brown Judaic Studies
BK	*Bibel und Kirche*
BKAT	Biblischer Kommentar: Altes Testament
BZAW	Beihefte zur *ZAW*
CAD	*The Assyrian Dictionary of the Oriental Institute of the University of Chicago*
CBQ	*Catholic Biblical Quarterly*
CD	K. Barth, *Church Dogmatics*

CT	Cuneiform Texts from Babylonian Tablets
De civ.	Augustine, *De civitate Dei*
De opif. mundi	Philo, *De opificio mundi*
DN	Deity's name
2 Enoch	*Slavonic Enoch*
EvQ	*Evangelical Quarterly*
ExpTim	*Expository Times*
HALAT	W. Baumgartner et al., *Hebräisches und aramäisches Lexikon zum Alten Testament*
HAT	Handbuch zum Alten Testament
Hatch-Redpath	E. Hatch and H. A. Redpath, *Concordance to the Septuagint and Other Greek Versions of the Old Testament*
HSM	Harvard Semitic Monographs
HTR	*Harvard Theological Review*
HUCA	*Hebrew Union College Annual*
ICC	International Critical Commentary
IDB	G. A. Buttrick, ed., *Interpreter's Dictionary of the Bible*
IDBSup	Supplementary volume to *IDB*
Int	*Interpretation*
JAAR	*Journal of the American Academy of Religion*
JB	Jerusalem Bible
JBL	*Journal of Biblical Literature*
JBTh	*Jahrbuch für biblische Theologie*
JCS	*Journal of Cuneiform Studies*
JEN	Joint Expedition with the Iraq Museum at Nuzi
JSOT	*Journal for the Study of the Old Testament*
JSOTSup	Journal for the Study of the Old Testament Supplement Series
JTS	*Journal of Theological Studies*
KAI	H. Donner and W. Röllig, *Kanaanäische und aramäische Inschriften*
KAV	Keilschrifttexte aus Assur verschiedenen Inhalts
KB	L. Koehler and W. Baumgartner, *Lexicon in Veteris Testamenti libros*
KD	K. Barth, *Kirchliche Dogmatik*
KJV	King James Version
KN	King's name
LSJ	Liddell-Scott-Jones, *Greek-English Lexicon*
LXX	Septuagint
MA	Middle Assyrian
MAOG	*Mitteilungen der altorientalischen Gesellschaft*

MT	Masoretic Text
NA	Neo-Assyrian
NAB	New American Bible
NB	Neo-Babylonian
NCB	New Century Bible
NEB	New English Bible
NJV	New Jewish Version
NRSV	New Revised Standard Version
OBO	Orbis biblicus et orientalis
OBT	Overtures to Biblical Theology
OLZ	*Orientalistische Literaturzeitung*
OTL	Old Testament Library
PN	Personal name
RB	*Revue biblique*
RelS	*Religious Studies*
RSV	Revised Standard Version
SB	Standard Babylonian
SBB	Stuttgarter biblische Beiträge
SBH	G. A. Reisner, *Sumerisch-babylonische Hymnen nach Thontafeln griechischer Zeit*
SBLDS	Society of Biblical Literature Dissertation Series
Sib. Or.	*Sibylline Oracles*
ST	*Studia theologica*
TDNT	G. Kittel and G. Friedrich, eds., *Theological Dictionary of the New Testament*
TDOT	G. J. Botterweck and H. Ringgren, eds., *Theological Dictionary of the Old Testament*
THAT	E. Jenni and C. Westermann, eds., *Theologisches Handwörterbuch zum Alten Testament*
ThZ	*Theologische Zeitschrift*
TS	*Theological Studies*
TToday	*Theology Today*
UF	*Ugarit-Forschungen*
USQR	*Union Seminary Quarterly Review*
Vg	Vulgate
VT	*Vetus Testamentum*
VTSup	Vetus Testamentum, Supplements
WMANT	Wissenschaftliche Monographien zum Alten und Neuen Testament
ZA	*Zeitschrift für Assyriologie*
ZAW	*Zeitschrift für die alttestamentliche Wissenschaft*

PREFACE

THE ARTICLES IN THIS VOLUME WERE WRITTEN OVER A PERIOD OF more than twenty years, a period marked by major changes in biblical studies, seminary education, and the church—as well as the larger society. Reading through these essays has reminded me of some of those changes, leaving me both surprised and embarrassed at some of the things I had written: surprised by ideas I thought newly won that I have rediscovered in earlier writings, embarrassed by dated and discarded ideas and expressions.[1] I would say some things differently today and modify some views (though not many); I have come to see the sexism of the Scriptures as much deeper than I had earlier perceived, and I cringe at the "generic" masculine language I used in 1972. But I have left the articles as originally published,[2] with only minor additions and corrections.[3] Thus they stand

---

1. One of the most significant shifts in terminology during the period has been the wide-scale replacement of "Old Testament" by "Hebrew Bible," a change that acknowledges the specifically Christian character of the older language and the denigrating supercessionist connotations it carries for some. Although I welcome the new usage for nonconfessional and interfaith discourse, I have resisted its adoption when writing and speaking in a Christian context or from a Christian theological perspective. While I reject the notion of inferiority associated by some with the designation "Old," I want to maintain the traditional Christian insistence on a two-part canon of Scripture in which Old and New Testaments are inseparably united as witness to one and the same God. In the Marcionite environment of contemporary Protestantism my battle is with Christians who dismiss the Old Testament as Jewish Scriptures, and therefore (in their understanding) not Christian—a view that is reinforced by the term "Hebrew," especially when paired with designation of the New Testament as the "Christian Scriptures."

2. The article on Genesis 3 (= chap. 8 in this volume) was originally published in German as "Genesis 3 in der gegenwärtigen biblischen Forschung," *JBTh* 9 (1994) 3–24. It appears here for the first time in English.

3. These include updating of publication data, correction of typographical and minor errors, and occasional retraction or qualification of an earlier view (by means of a supplementary note). No attempt has been made to update bibliographies, some of which are now woefully inadequate or superseded by the enormous growth of literature in such fields as women's and gender studies and feminist criticism. See below for an explanation of changes in this volume.

as historical witnesses to a changing world and a changing discipline, and to my involvement in both.

Most of the articles reprinted here were written in response to requests for contributions on particular topics or for particular occasions. As a result, there is considerable overlap in the content of some articles, as research on a particular text or subject was related to different contemporary questions or addressed to different audiences. That is especially true of the articles on Genesis 1–3, where attention to such distinct but related issues as gender and the image of God, the theological meaning of sexual differentiation and sexuality, and the origins of sin and the role of woman in the "fall" led to multiple recastings and couplings of the same exegetical arguments. Although some proposed articles have been eliminated in an effort to reduce duplication,[4] substantial overlap remains, and readers are advised to read selectively, looking for what is new or distinctive in articles treating the same texts or subject matter.

The articles are presented here by topical, rather than chronological, arrangement. As an aid to understanding them in the social and intellectual contexts in which they arose, I offer the following sketch of the major currents and concerns behind the texts.

Twenty-five years ago, as I was beginning my first year of teaching, and completing my dissertation, I was asked to write a chapter on "the image of woman in the Old Testament" for a volume of essays on "images of woman in the Jewish and Christian traditions." The volume was designed, according to its editor, Rosemary Ruether, to "fill a growing need for a more exact idea of the role of religion . . . in shaping the traditional [Western] cultural images that have degraded and suppressed women."[5] Ruether observed that much of the literature of the women's movement at the time had been written by women who were alienated from religion and had little historical or doctrinal information about the church's role in this history of repression. She sought to fill the gap in information about the history of religion and sexism in Western culture by asking representatives of the first generation of women scholars in religion to write

4. "'Bone of My Bone and Flesh of My Flesh,'" *TToday* 50 (1994) 521–34 (on the general question of Old Testament theological anthropology); "Sexual Differentiation and Divine Image in the Genesis Creation Texts," in Kari Børresen, ed., *Image of God and Gender Models in Judeo-Christian Tradition* (Oslo: Solum, 1991) 11–34; republished as *Image of God: Gender Models in Judeo-Christian Tradition* (Minneapolis: Fortress Press, 1995) 5–28; and "Women in the Ancient Mediterranean World: Ancient Israel," *Biblical Research* 39 (1994) 33–64 (a "state-of-the-question" article with review of literature).

5. Rosemary Radford Ruether, "Preface," in idem, ed., *Religion and Sexism: Images of Woman in the Jewish and Christian Traditions* (New York: Simon and Schuster, 1974) 9. My chapter appeared as "Images of Women in the Old Testament," ibid., 41–88 (= chap. 1 in this volume).

articles on their fields of specialization.[6] I recall this beginning to explain how one who considered herself neither a feminist nor a scholar at the time became engaged in a multifaceted project of historical and theological research and writing exemplified, at least in part, by the essays in the present volume.

I agreed to write the essay on the image of woman in the Old Testament because at the time (1971) I was totally ignorant of the subject, and uneasy about current use of the term "patriarchal" to describe a wide range of cultural and religious phenomena, past and present. A background in anthropology and comparative institutions made me wary of such undifferentiated characterization and its attendant assumptions, and curious to explore the primary data in my own field—widely regarded as the seedbed of Western misogyny. I also agreed to the assignment because I thought it a "safe" project on which to risk exposing my ignorance. The fact that the article was intended for a popular audience, coupled with my thesis adviser's warning not to get distracted by "women's lib," assured me that the results of my first effort at publication would never be exposed to the scrutiny of my academic mentors and peers. How wrong I was! But I was not alone. The women's movement of the seventies and eighties has affected us all, male and female. We have been led in directions we never planned to go, and we have arrived at places we could not have imagined when we began our journeys. The essays in this volume are markers along my own unanticipated way.

That first project lay completely outside anything I had ever done or planned to do, and I did not regard it as a scholarly publication. It was a response to a current social and religious need, which I was beginning to feel in personal terms as I entered the then all-male realm of seminary teaching.[7] It was also impelled by curiosity, which has always drawn me to explore unknown, and uncongenial, practices and beliefs.[8] But what began as a project outside my scholarly training and interests represented an area of concern that would eventually be drawn within the arena of recognized scholarly investigation in the disciplines of biblical studies and

6. There were forerunners to the ten women who contributed to that volume, but they were few and mostly no longer active. There was also one male author, a reminder that men have been allies in the new feminist revolution from the beginning.

7. One of the notable exceptions to the all-male rule was Nelle Morton at Drew University School of Theology, where I began my own teaching. Because she was in the field of Christian Education, however, a field traditionally associated with women, her presence did not fundamentally challenge the all-male ethos that continued to dominate the "classical" disciplines, in both the seminaries and the professional societies—especially in the biblical field.

8. My dissertation grew out of interest in the Old Testament conquest traditions, an interest prompted by my pacifist upbringing and inclinations.

theology. In that changing arena and climate of scholarship I would de-vote a considerable amount of my research and writing efforts to the un-finished agenda left by my first preliminary sketch of the Old Testament image of woman.

My initial investigation proceeded in a simple and superficial manner: reading through the RSV and noting every reference to a woman, named or unnamed; then analyzing the references for patterns. I was aided by a group of female students and student spouses, who gathered weekly for supper in my tiny basement apartment on the Drew University campus. Together we discussed findings, exchanged impressions, and speculated about the world behind the biblical text. It was an exciting time of discov-ery as we explored a largely unknown past, attempting to disentangle it from an interpretive legacy of narrow and oppressive stereotypes. But it was only a beginning, an opening of the door, and a record of first impres-sions. One of the things I have attempted to do in subsequent work is to give greater attention to underlying structures of relationships and related values. Thus my 1992 article in the *Anchor Bible Dictionary* highlights family organization as critical for understanding women's roles and status.[9]

Publication deadlines for the original article and the need to limit the scope of the investigation led me to exclude the prophetic corpus on grounds that relatively few women appear in its pages. Some years later, on my first sabbatical, I began reading through the Latter Prophets in Hebrew to remedy the earlier omission. I was soon struck by the promi-nence of metaphorical references to women or the feminine, which I had not considered previously. Out of this reading came an interest in the figure of the harlot, both as reflecting a social role in Israelite society and as a theological metaphor for apostate Israel. The close association of the harlot with the hierodule ("consecrated woman")[10] in a number of bib-lical—but no extrabiblical—texts, and the common interchange or con-fusion of the categories in secondary literature, has led me to study both biblical and ancient Near Eastern texts relating to these two marginal classes of women. That study, reflected in a number of limited and prelim-inary publications,[11] involves complex historical and hermeneutical issues and is still in progress.

---

9. "Women (OT)," *ABD* 6:951–57 (= chap. 2 in this volume).

10. Heb. *qĕdēšâ*. Although the Greek term which I have used to designate this class of women (and men) means simply "temple servant/slave" and describes a class of persons dedicated to a temple or deity, modern usage has tended to equate it, unjustifiably, with "sacred prostitute."

11. See especially "The Harlot as Heroine: Narrative Art and Social Presupposition in Three Old Testament Texts," in Miri Amihai, George W. Coats, and Anne M. Solomon, eds.,

Thus one immediate consequence of that first writing assigment was a continuing and broadening interest in the status, roles, and activities of women in ancient Israel in relation to its ancient Near Eastern neighbors, and ultimately a more general interest in the role of gender in ancient Israelite and Near Eastern society and religion.[12] A focus on religion emerged as a consequence of an invitation to write an essay on "The Place of Women in the Israelite Cultus." The assigned formulation of the topic led me to ask about women's own religious practice and experience, not only within the male-defined cultus but also outside it.[13] Focusing on women's religious lives in relation to the "general" religious practice described in the Old Testament raised further questions concerning the role of gender in defining religion and religious practice, and reflection on the differing ways in which men and women may view the boundaries and the relationships between the religious and the "secular" spheres, as evidenced in cross-cultural studies.[14]

These branching paths of inquiry, which attempt to bring the largely invisible women of the Hebrew Scriptures into focus and locate them in the social and religious world of ancient Israel, represent an effort at historical reconstruction informed by cross-cultural study and anchored in literary analysis.[15] However new the questions or eclectic the methodology, it is still fundamentally historical-critical study, and its sole aim is to give a more adequate account of the social and conceptual world of ancient Israel and its Scriptures—an account that will be intelligible to criti-

Narrative Research on the Hebrew Bible (*Semeia* 46; Atlanta: Scholars Press, 1989) 119–39 (= chap. 9 in this volume); "'To Play the Harlot': An Inquiry into an Old Testament Metaphor," in Peggy L. Day, ed., *Gender and Difference in Ancient Israel* (Minneapolis: Fortress Press, 1989) 75–94 (= chap. 10 in this volume); and "The End of the Male Cult Prostitute: A Literary-Historical and Sociological Analysis of Hebrew *qādēš-qĕdēšîm*," in John A. Emerton, ed., *Congress Volume: Cambridge, 1995* (VTSup; Leiden: Brill, forthcoming).

12. Exemplified in the following articles: "Israelite Religion and the Faith of Israel's Daughters: Reflections on Gender and Religious Definition," in David Jobling, Peggy L. Day, and Gerald T. Sheppard, eds., *The Bible and the Politics of Exegesis* (Cleveland: Pilgrim, 1991) 97–108 (= chap. 5 in this volume); "'Bone of My Bone'" (n. 4 above); and "Poor Man or Poor Woman? Gendering the Poor in Prophetic Texts," in Bob Becking and Meindert Dijkstra, eds., *On Reading Prophetic Texts: Gender-Specific and Related Studies in Memory of Fokkelien van Dijk-Hemmes* (Leiden: Brill, 1996) 37–51 (= chap. 3 in this volume).

13. "The Place of Women in the Israelite Cultus," in Patrick D. Miller, Jr., Paul D. Hanson, and S. Dean McBride, eds., *Ancient Israelite Religion: Essays in Honor of Frank Moore Cross* (Philadelphia: Fortress Press, 1987) 397–419 (= chap. 4 in this volume).

14. These issues are explored in "Israelite Religion and the Faith of Israel's Daughters" (n. 11 above).

15. Since access to the social and symbolic world of ancient Israel is primarily through the preserved text of the Hebrew Bible, literary analysis is the indispensable first step in all historical reconstruction. On the use of cross-cultural data in reconstruction, see Bird, "Place of Women," 400–401 [* 85–87].

cal readers of disparate religious sympathies and commitments, or of no
religious orientation. But the historical study has implications that extend
beyond the realm of history to affect both meaning and faith. The absence
of women, and women's voices, from most of the Hebrew Scriptures raises
questions about the ability of the Scriptures to speak either about the human condition or about the divine nature and will. The cultural captivity
of the Bible is exposed in a new and more radical way, and fundamental
issues of truth, meaning, and authority are raised.

In most of the writings represented in this volume, the theological issues are formulated in historical and descriptive terms, and hermeneutical
reflection on current theological and ethical issues is minimal. Despite the
absence of explicit connections between ancient text and current contexts,
however, these historical studies play an essential role in my *theological*
approach to Scripture. Because I understand the divine self-disclosure in
Scripture as essentially incarnational, I understand the testimony of Scripture as historically and culturally conditioned—and therefore as limited
and changing. The Eternal is revealed only in time, and temporality is a
defining characteristic of scriptural revelation. Anchored in time, it extends through time, bearing the indelible marks of its journey through
ancient and alien cultures. The Bible's ability to speak a contemporary
word does not require it to shed its foreign garb or accent, but it does
require bilingual and bicultural interpreters.

Reading the Bible is always an exercise in cross-cultural understanding,
and it is aided by knowledge of the writers' and compilers' world(s). Readers will attempt to reconstruct the world of the text, with or without instruction, and in the absence of historical knowledge will imagine a world
like their own, or like the biblical world portrayed by their tradition. My
concern has been to offer a critical reconstruction of the world of the text
that will clarify the meaning of reported actions and sentiments and
honor the integrity of the ancient writers. I have not sought to discover
views or practices congenial to my own, but have aimed to identify interpretations that distort the ancient writer's understanding or intention,[16]
whether to "negative" or "positive" effect. I seek dialogue with the ancient
author, not agreement, and I believe that dialogue requires an initial act

---

16. I understand the text as the product of an author who spoke or wrote with some
audience in mind (however general) and with an intention to communicate something to
that audience. The fact that I may never be able to know with certainty who that audience
was or what the author's intention was and the fact that each preserved communication has
been recontextualized, and often reinterpreted, for subsequent audiences, who may also
elude identification, does not alter my search for the ancient rhetorical contexts implied in
these communicative acts, nor does it relieve me of my sense of obligation to the ancient
author for as attentive and sympathetic a hearing as I wish for my own speaking and writing.

of attentive listening. My historical work aims to sharpen the hearing; my hermeneutical work engages the dialogue.

Dialogue as a mode of reception and response to the word of Scripture corresponds to the form of Scripture's own message. The Bible as a collection of writings is irreducibly multivocalic and pluriform, not only in its canonical form but in many of its constituent parts. In its plurality of voices it presents readers with a conversation that extends over time, encompassing reformulations and revocations of earlier words, diverse and contending theologies, new visions and new judgments. It represents the conversation of a community about the source and meaning of its life, and its message is grasped only by entering into that conversation.[17] Modern interpretation extends that dialogue into the present, but now with more diverse participants and a greatly expanded realm of discourse.

In the new interpretive realm of contemporary Bible reading and scholarship two issues have particularly engaged my hermeneutical interest: the use of the Bible for contemporary understanding of sexual roles and relationships, and the nature of biblical authority. Although they originally presented themselves to me in unrelated contexts, I have come to see them as deeply interconnected. I have already noted how broader issues of gender arose from my study of women in the Old Testament. In a similar development, issues of sexual ethics emerged as I attempted to relate historical exegesis to contemporary belief and practice. In my 1981 article on Gen 1:27,[18] I had sought to interpret the Bible's first statement on human sexual differentiation in its own literary and historical context—against a backdrop of theological speculation that had taken a course of its own, apart from biblical studies, and a contemporary feminist search for an egalitarian biblical foundation. In arguing for a minimal, procreation-oriented understanding of the text in its original context, I countered both ancient and modern theological appropriations without proposing an alternative constructive approach. In 1987, however, in the context of a symposium on theological interpretation of Scripture, I attempted to spell out the implications of my historical understanding of the two creation accounts for a contemporary theology of sexuality.[19]

That effort to sketch a path from historical analysis to constructive theology had consequences for other contemporary debates on sexuality and

17. See Bird, *The Bible as the Church's Book* (Philadelphia: Westminster, 1982), esp. 67–79.

18. "'Male and Female He Created Them': Genesis 1:27b in the Context of the Priestly Account of Creation," *HTR* 74 (1981) 129–59 (= chap. 6 in this volume).

19. "Genesis 1–3 as a Source for a Contemporary Theology of Sexuality," originally presented at the Second Annual Frederick Neumann Symposium on Theological Interpretation of Scripture, Princeton Theological Seminary, October 16–19, 1987, and subsequently published in *Ex Auditu* 3 (1987) 31–44 (= chap. 7 in this volume).

sexual ethics, and led to involvement in ecclesiastical deliberations concerning homosexuality—where I have found myself once again maintaining that the commonly cited texts have been abused by both "sides" in the debate, or too readily dismissed. I note this involvement, because the church, in its local and ecumenical manifestations, has been the primary locus of my hermeneutical reflection and provided the primary occasions and vehicles for that effort. The places where I have engaged in creative theological encounter with the biblical text have been the pulpit, church Bible study, pastors' school or clergy retreat, seminary classroom, guest lectureship, and church study commission. Little of this interpretive work has found its way into publication,[20] because it is highly context-oriented and situation-dependent. It forges connections between specific contemporary questions and specific texts, themes, trajectories—or the whole biblical tradition—as circumstances (and the Spirit) dictate. And while the historically interpreted Bible has an essential word in these encounters, it does not have the final word. It serves rather to point to the living Word, which must be heard afresh in the language and experience of contemporary hearers, generating reformulations, and new formulations, of the truth mediated through Scripture.

Some examples of more confessionally oriented and hermeneutically reflective interpretation are included in this volume, especially as they relate to the questions of feminist critique of Scripture and the authority of the Bible. The latter question was already present in the small book for laity that I wrote on the "doctrine of the Bible" in a series on Christian doctrines[21]—the result of another publishing request for which I had no prior credentials, and which set me on a wholly new path of discovery and inquiry. As a United Methodist, from an experientially oriented tradition, I was an unlikely candidate to author such a book. The resulting research gave me a new appreciation for the history of the biblical canon and its interpretation and led me to place the emerging question of biblical authority in a historical framework. It is only in the last decade, however, that the issue of authority has become a topic of major concern,

---

20. Some of the lectures formed the basis of later publications (see below). A contribution to current debate on homosexual ethics will be published in a collection of papers from a recent ecumenical symposium ("The Bible and Sexual Ethics," chaired by David Balch, Brite Divinity School/Texas Christian University, September 27–29, 1996). My preferred form of constructive biblical interpretation is preaching, where the freedom, and constraints, of attending to the word of God in a particular time and for a particular audience demand creative yet faithful response to the text. These sermons, preached over decades, represent an ongoing conversation with the Bible through changing circumstances of life (including changing social and political circumstances), and changing climate of the soul.

21. *The Bible as the Church's Book* (n. 16 above).

emerging now at a point of convergence with the stream of feminist inquiry that has hitherto claimed my primary attention.

Feminist critique of the Bible has seen it as a primary source and legitimator of patriarchal religion, and feminist biblical interpreters, including myself, have found the Bible to be more deeply and pervasively androcentric than earlier critics recognized. The consequences of this analysis are now being addressed in every branch of theology, but they have particular bearing on the question of biblical authority, because they concern the truth of the Bible's testimony concerning the nature of our humanity and of the God in whose image we are created. Feminist critique of the Bible as a distorted account of our nature and history constitutes, I believe, the most radical challenge to the claim of biblical authority for contemporary faith and practice. Thus a contemporary understanding and affirmation of the Bible's authority must be framed with this critique in mind. My article in *The New Interpreter's Bible* is meant as a general and comprehensive statement, but it incorporates considerations of feminist critique.[22] More pointed attention to the intersection of modern biblical interpretation and the crisis of biblical authority with the modern feminist movement is found in a series of lectures on the topic "Feminism and the Bible,"[23] whose concluding lecture is published here.[24]

A final area of interest represented in this volume grows out of my work on the translation committee for the New Revised Standard Version of the Bible. It concerns the translation of sexist language and the translator's dual responsibility to ancient authors and modern audiences in a context that demands, but limits, interpretive commentary.[25] Here again I am concerned with larger issues of biblical interpretation that are focused by attention to feminist sensitivities, and here again I am committed to maintaining the integrity of the ancient witness while serving the modern reader.

22. "The Authority of the Bible," in Leander Keck, ed., *The New Interpreter's Bible* (Nashville: Abingdon, 1994) 1:33–64.

23. *Feminism and the Bible: A Critical and Constructive Encounter: The 1993 J. J. Theissen Lectures* (Winnipeg: CMBC Publications, 1994). These lectures, delivered at Canadian Mennonite Biblical College, October 19–20, 1993, profited from earlier exploration of the issues in the Francis B. Denio Lectures on the Bible at Bangor Theological Seminary, January 20–21, 1992 (given under the general title of "Biblical Authority in Crisis"); and a series of five lectures on the topic "Feminist Theology and the Bible" at the Triennial Translators Workshop of the United Bible Societies, Victoria Falls, Zimbabwe, May 15–20, 1991.

24. Originally entitled "Living Waters: Biblical Authority Reappraised" (in *Feminism and the Bible*, 68–87), it is reprinted here as "Biblical Authority in the Light of Feminist Critique" (= chap. 12).

25. "Translating Sexist Language as a Theological and Cultural Problem," *USQR* 42 (1988) 89–95 (= chap. 11 in this volume).

I have attempted in these comments to explain how my historical scholarship relates to my theological concerns and how both have been shaped, in unexpected ways, by the modern feminist movement. I want to conclude by thanking those who have accompanied me on the journey represented by these writings, often opening doors for me on which I had not knocked and pointing me in directions I would never have considered, prodding me, arguing with me, encouraging me, believing me, and patiently enduring the flood of arguments that inundated any hapless acquaintance whenever I was working on some new project or idea—which was most of the time. Those who have earned my gratitude include colleagues, students, pastors, and parishioners—too numerous to mention. But it is editors and publishers who have finally made this work possible, so I will name only the last in this series. I am grateful to Fortress Press for making this collection of often hard to locate writings available to a wider public; to Cynthia Thompson, who prodded it into completion; and above all to Walter Brueggemann, who suggested the idea in the first place.

Note on Additions and Changes in this Edition

Additions required to indicate significant changes in opinion or subsequent publication of works referred to originally in unpublished form or superseded publications are signaled by square brackets [ ] in the text, which also identify supplementary footnotes. Demand for uniform style necessitated minor changes in bibliographical references, footnote style, and the rendering of Hebrew citations. In the case of articles originally published in the "social science style," new footnotes have been created for bibliographical references previously included in the text. As a result, the footnote numbers in this edition do not correspond to those of the original publications. As an aid to locating cross-references to other articles appearing in this volume as well as page numbers within articles published here, the corresponding page numbers in this volume (identified by an asterisk) have been added in square brackets following the original page numbers (thus [*]).

I

WOMEN IN
ANCIENT ISRAEL

1

IMAGES OF WOMEN IN
THE OLD TESTAMENT

FOR MOST OF US THE IMAGE OF WOMAN IN THE OLD TESTAMENT is the image of Eve, augmented perhaps by a handful of Bible-storybook "heroines," or villianesses, as the case may be (Sarah, Deborah, Ruth, Esther, Jezebel, Delilah). Some may also perceive in the background the indistinct shapes of a host of unnamed mothers, who, silent and unacknowledged, bear all the endless genealogies of males. But it is the named women, by and large, the exceptional women, who supply the primary images for the usual portrait of the Old Testament woman. These few great women together with the first woman (curiously incompatible figures in most interpretations) fill the void that looms when we consider the image of woman in the Old Testament. For the Old Testament is a man's "book," where women appear for the most part simply as adjuncts of men, significant only in the context of men's activities.

This perception is fundamental, for it describes the terms of all Old Testament speech about women. The Old Testament is a collection of writings by males from a society dominated by males.[1] These writings portray a man's world. They speak of events and activities engaged in pri-

Originally published in Rosemary R. Ruether, ed., *Religion and Sexism: Images of Woman in the Jewish and Christian Traditions* (New York: Simon and Schuster, 1974) 44–88. For the genesis of this article during my first year of teaching in 1971–72, see above, pp. 2–4.

1. The term "patriarchy" is appropriate to designate such a society, but it is avoided here because of the fact that widespread indiscriminate use of the term has led to the blurring of significant social and cultural distinctions among various "patriarchal" societies. Whatever the terms employed, however, the characterization of ancient Israel as a male-centered and male-dominated society is meant as a descriptive statement. The aim of this essay is not to decry or to advocate but simply to record the perceptions of women found in the Old Testament writings and to analyze them in terms of their sources and consequences in ancient Israelite society and religion. Speculation concerning origins is renounced, and *Nachgeschichte* (the subsequent history of the ideas) is left to students of more recent periods in the tradition.

marily or exclusively by males (war, cult, and government) and of a jealously singular God, who is described and addressed in terms normally used for males.[2]

But women appear in these pages more frequently than memory commonly allows—and in more diverse roles and estimations.[3] In some texts the woman of ancient Israel is portrayed simply as a class of property. In others she is depicted as possessing a measure of freedom, initiative, power, and respect that contemporary American women might well envy. This essay attempts to examine that full range of Old Testament images of women, with attention to the contexts in which they were formed and formulated and the meaning given to them by the various "authors."

Only a reading of the Old Testament can give an adequate impression of the variety of viewpoints and expression represented in its words about women and also expose the common threads that run through them. Here we can do no more than sample that literature. The short selections offered below aim only to suggest the compass of the evidence upon which the following analysis is based.

> Most blessed of women be Jael
>   the wife of Heber, the Kenite,
>   of tent-dwelling women most blessed.
> . . . .
> She put her hand to the tent peg
>   and her right hand to the workman's mallet;
> she struck Sisera a blow,
>   she crushed his head,
>   she shattered and pierced his temple.
> (Judg 5:24, 26)[4]

> I brought you up from the land of Egypt,
>   and redeemed you from the house of bondage;
> and I sent before you Moses, Aaron, and Miriam.
> (Mic 6:4)

2. Exceptions to this latter rule are invariably deemed noteworthy by commentators. The extent and the meaning of gynomorphic language applied to the Deity has still to be assessed. See Phyllis Trible, "Depatriarchalizing in Biblical Interpretation," *JAAR* 41 (1973) 31–34. Whether the Old Testament use of feminine metaphors for God (always "mother" images, never "wife") is the product of Israelite monotheism or is a more general characteristic of language about certain types of deities (e.g., creator gods or tutelary deities) also needs to be explored.

3. See Edith Deen, *All the Women of the Bible* (New York: Harper, 1955).

4. All citations are from the Revised Standard Version of the Bible (RSV) unless otherwise noted.

Now when the queen of Sheba heard of the fame of Solomon concerning the name of the Lord, she came to test him with hard questions. She came to Jerusalem with a very great retinue, with camels bearing spices, and very much gold, and precious stones. (1 Kgs 10:1-2)

So Bathsheba went to King Solomon, to speak to him on behalf of Adonijah. And the king rose to meet her, and bowed down to her; then he . . . had a seat brought . . . and she sat on his right. (1 Kgs 2:19)

Everyone who curses his father or his mother
shall be put to death. (Lev 20:9)

The peasantry grew plump in Israel,
    they grew plump on booty
When you arose, O Deborah,
    arose, a mother in Israel.
(Judg 5:7)[5]

Out of the window she peered,
    the mother of Sisera gazed through the lattice:
"Why is his chariot so long in coming?
    Why tarry the hoofbeats of his chariots?"
Her wisest ladies make answer,
    nay, she gives answer to herself,
"Are they not finding and dividing the spoil?—
    A maiden [lit. womb] or two for every man."
(Judg 5:28-30)

Now King David was old and advanced in years; and although they covered him with clothes, he could not get warm. Therefore his servants said to him, "Let a young maiden be sought for my lord the king . . . let her lie in your bosom, that my lord the king may be warm." So they sought for a beautiful maiden throughout all the territory of Israel, and found Abishag the Shunammite, and brought her to the king. (1 Kgs 1:1-4)

The men of the city, base fellows, beset the house round about, beating on the door; and they said to the old man, the master of the house, "Bring out the man who came into your house, that we may know him." And the man, the master of the house, went out to them

5. The translation is that of Marvin Chaney in "Israel's Earliest Poetry" (Ph.D. diss., Harvard, 1974), based on a new understanding of the Hebrew; used by permission of the author.

and said to them, "No, my brethren, do not act so wickedly . . . here are my virgin daughter and his concubine; let me bring them out now. Ravish them and do with them what seems good to you, but against this man do not do so vile a thing." (Judg 19:22-24)

When you go to war against your enemies . . . and you take them captive, and see among the captives a beautiful woman, and you have desire for her and would take her for yourself as a wife, then you shall . . . [permit her to] bewail her father and mother a full month; after that you may go in to her and be her husband, and she shall be your wife. Then, if you have no delight in her, you shall let her go where she will; but you shall not sell her for money, you shall not treat her as a slave, since you have humiliated her. (Deut 21:10-14)

When Rachel saw that she bore Jacob no children, she envied her sister; and she said to Jacob, "Give me children, or I shall die!" . . . Then God remembered Rachel, and God hearkened to her and opened her womb. She conceived and bore a son, and said, "God has taken away my reproach." (Gen 30:1, 22-23)

If a woman conceives and bears a male child she shall be unclean seven days. . . . But if she bears a female child, then she shall be unclean two weeks. (Lev 12:2, 5)

A certain woman threw an upper millstone upon Abimelech's head, and crushed his skull. Then he called hastily to the young man his armor-bearer, and said to him, "Draw your sword and kill me, lest men say of me, 'A woman killed him.'" (Judg 9:53-54)

My people—children are their oppressors,
    and women rule over them.
O my people, your leaders mislead you,
    and confuse the course of your paths.
(Isa 3:12)

Now when Athaliah the mother of Ahaziah saw that
her son was dead, she arose and destroyed all the
royal family . . . [and she] reigned over the land
for seven years. (2 Kgs 11:1, 3)

The Lord has created a new thing on earth:
    a woman protects [lit. encompasses] a man.
(Jer 31:22)

A good wife
. . . .
She considers a field and buys it;
    with the fruit of her hands she plants a vineyard.
She girds her loins with strength
    and makes her arms strong.
She perceives that her merchandise is profitable.
(Prov 31:10, 16-18)

Rejoice in the wife of your youth,
    a lovely hind, a graceful doe.
Let her affection fill you at all times with delight,
    be infatuated always with her love.
(Prov 5:18-19)

A continual dripping on a rainy day
    and a contentious woman are alike.
(Prov 27:15)

The daughters of Zion are haughty
    and walk with outstretched necks,
    glancing wantonly with their eyes,
mincing along as they go,
    tinkling with their feet.
(Isa 3:16)

The lips of a loose woman drip honey,
    and her speech is smoother than oil;
but in the end she is bitter as wormwood,
    sharp as a two-edged sword.
(Prov 5:3-4)

How fair and pleasant you are,
    O loved one, delectable maiden!
You are stately as a palm tree,
    and your breasts are like its clusters.
I say I will climb the palm tree
    and lay hold of its branches
Oh, may your breasts be like clusters of the vine
    and the scent of your breath like apples,
and your kisses like the best wine. . . .
(Cant 7:6-9)

I found him whom my soul loves.
I held him, and would not let him go

until I had brought him into my mother's house,
and into the chamber of her that conceived me.
(Cant 3:4)

The daughter of any priest, if she profanes herself by playing the
harlot, profanes her father; she shall be burned with fire. (Lev 21:9)

I will not punish your daughters
    when they play the harlot,
nor your brides when they commit adultery;
for the men themselves go aside with harlots,
    and sacrifice with cult prostitutes.
(Hos 4:14)

So God created man in his own image,
    in the image of God he created him;
male and female he created them.
(Gen 1:27)

The variety of images apparent even in this limited selection of texts
suggests that no single statement can be formulated concerning *the* image
of woman in the Old Testament. At the same time an attempt must be
made to discover what unity and coherence may exist within this plurality
of conceptions. This process cannot be short-circuited by simply focusing
upon the image of woman presented in the creation narratives. While
those accounts have been rightly recognized to contain statements of primary importance concerning the nature of man and woman, their place
within the total Old Testament literature has been virtually ignored. The
task of this essay—to present the *Old Testament*'s view—requires that an
effort be made to locate the creation accounts within the larger testimony
of the Old Testament.

One consequence of such an effort must be the recognition that Eve—
or the first woman—is nowhere referred to in the Hebrew Old Testament
outside the accounts of origins found in Genesis 1–4.[6] Because of this limited context of reflection upon the original woman, these too familiar passages are treated last in this essay, after a picture of woman has been

6. Two references occur in later writings contained in the Greek canon: Tob 8:6 and Sir
25:24; cf. 2 Cor 11:3; 1 Tim 2:13; and numerous references in the Pseudepigrapha (see index
to R. H. Charles, ed., *The Apocrypha and Pseudepigrapha of the Old Testament in English*, vol.
2, *Pseudepigrapha* [Oxford: Clarendon, 1913]). References to Adam are more frequent, but
only Job 31:33, in the Hebrew Old Testament, refers to him apart from genealogies and the
original creation stories.

formed from references contained in the legal, didactic, historical, and prophetic writings.

The diversity in the Old Testament conceptions of women may be attributed in part to differences in the time of composition of the writings and in part to differences in socioreligious context. The texts span close to a millennium in their dates of composition (twelfth to third century B.C.E.), while particular themes, motifs, images, and language may derive from even earlier periods and cultures. However, since the "prehistory" of these texts can be assessed only by speculation that moves beyond adequate controls and scholarly consensus, they must be judged in their present form as products of that society known to us as Israel and as reflecting primarily the beliefs and practices of the period of their composition.[7]

That millennium saw enormous changes in the social, economic, political, and religious life of Israel. The texts on which this study is based reflect social patterns and images of seminomadic tribal society and of settled peasant agriculturalists. They mirror the modest and homogeneous life of the village, but also the cosmopolitan and stratified society of the capital and major cities. They embody the religious and cultural heritage of Mesopotamia and of Canaan and presuppose the differing political organization of autonomous clans, tribal league, independent monarchies, and the exile communities and subject provinces of a series of foreign imperial states. With these political changes went changes in the economic and religious life. New forms of social and religious organization emerged, new offices, new roles, new classes, new ideas and definitions—of man, and woman, of God, and of his people. Some of the differences in the Old Testament conceptions of women must be attributed to these changes.

They may also be related to the individual authors, to the nature of the literature in which they are found, and to the particular situations they address. Thus prescriptive statements must be distinguished from descriptive, and attention must be given to the fact that different literary genres (e.g., myths, proverbs, admonitions and instruction, hymns, law, history, tales, sermons, and prophetic discourse) follow rules of their own and reflect in different ways and different paces the changing images of the society. Hence the references considered below have been roughly grouped by literary types.[8]

---

7. Thus all speculation concerning an "original" matriarchy is rejected in this essay as inconsequential for the period and the society under consideration.

8. A chronological arrangement, while desirable, has not proved feasible, because of the frequent impossibility of determining dates for individual texts. Of the four groupings created for this study (laws, proverbs, "historical" texts, and accounts of origins) the third is,

The Image of Woman in the Old Testament Laws

Though the laws of the Old Testament give only a partial view of the norms of ancient Israel, they are nevertheless a primary source for reconstructing the ideals and practices of that society. They are preserved, for the most part, in several large "codes," or collections, ranging in date from premonarchic (before 1000 B.C.E.) to postexilic (500–400 B.C.E.) times.[9] Each collection, however, in its own prehistory has taken up material of different ages, and each combines laws of different types, including both "secular" law (the "law of the [city] gate"—where deliberation of cases took place) and religious law (the law of the sanctuary or religious assembly). Despite this variety, however, none of the "codes" can be considered comprehensive. All are samplers of one kind or another. All presuppose the current existence of a system which they seek not to formulate but to preserve from dissolution and destruction. Thus the laws frequently deal with areas in which changes have occurred or threaten, while the common assumptions of the society are left unspoken and must often be inferred from the special cases treated in the collections.

In many respects Israelite law differs little from that of ancient Mesopotamia and Syria. It is testimony to Israel's participation in a common ancient Near Eastern social and cultural milieu. Salient features of this shared culture revealed in Israel's laws are patriarchy (together with patrilineal descent and patrilocal residence as the usual norm), a more or less extended family, polygyny, concubinage,[10] slavery (under certain conditions), and the thoroughgoing institutionalization of the double standard. Israel's laws differ most notably from other known law codes in their unusual severity in the field of sexual transgression and in the severity of the religious laws that prescribe and seek to preserve the exclusive and undefiled worship of Yahweh, the national deity. These two unique features are interrelated,[11] and both had significant consequences for women in ancient Israel.

---

unfortunately, too omnibus. Based primarily upon references in the historical books, it incorporates some material from the prophetic writings, which have received no separate treatment because of limitations of time and space. The third section of the canon, apart from the book of Proverbs, has also suffered neglect for the same reasons, though occasional references from that corpus have found their way into the discussion at places. These omissions are acknowledged with regret.

9. Martin Noth, *The Laws in the Pentateuch and Other Studies* (trans. D. R. Ap-Thomas; Philadelphia: Fortress Press, 1966) 8.

10. Polygyny and concubinage appear to have been more common in early Israel and are not mentioned in later texts, except in connection with the royal household.

11. Israel's view of the proper place of sex and the harsh penalties laid upon sexual offenders presumably reflect a deliberate antithesis to the practices of the surrounding peoples (specifically Canaanites), but they may also be rooted in Israel's peculiar understand-

The majority of the laws, especially those formulated in the direct-address style of the so-called apodictic law (the style used primarily for the statement of religious obligations), address the community *through its male members.*[12] Thus the key verbal form in the apodictic sentence is the second person *masculine* singular or plural. That this usage was not meant simply as an inclusive form of address for bisexual reference is indicated by such formulations as the following:

> You shall not covet *your neighbor's wife.* (Exod 20:19)

> You shall not afflict any widow or orphan. If you do . . . then *your wives* shall become widows and your children fatherless. (Exod 22:22-24 [Heb. 21-23])

> You shall be *men* consecrated to me. (Exod 22:31 [Heb. 30])

Similarly, the typical casuistic law (case law) begins with the formula, "If a *man* does x. . . ." The term used for "man" in this formulation is not the generic term, *'ādām,* but the specifically and exclusively masculine term, *'îš.* Even if one argues that these laws were understood to apply by extension to the whole community, it must be noted that the masculine formulation was apparently found inadequate in some circumstances. Thus *'ādām* is substituted for *'îš,* or the terms "man" and "woman" (*'îš, 'iššâ*) are used side by side where it is important to indicate that the legislation is intended to be inclusive in its reference.[13]

The basic presupposition of all the laws, though modified to some extent in the later period, is a society in which full membership is limited to males, in which only a male is judged a responsible person. He is responsible not only for his own acts, but for those of his dependents as well. These include wife, children, and even livestock, in the extended and fluid

---

ing of herself as a "holy people." Sexual offenses are religious offenses in Israel. They are not private matters, but matters of vital concern to the whole community. See Noth, *Laws,* 55.

12. The whole community was bound by the law, however, sometimes explicitly and sometimes implicitly. E.g., the absence of any mention of the wife in the Sabbath law (Exod 20:10; Deut 5:14), though sons and daughters and male and female slaves are listed, suggests that the wife was treated as one person with the man ("you," second person masculine singular), who is addressed by the law. (Whatever the interpretation, she is clearly not an independent person in this formulation.) In the postexilic community the inclusive reference is made explicit; the assembly (*qāhāl*) convened to hear the reading of the law is described as consisting of "both men and women and all who could hear with understanding" (Neh 8:2-3). In this late period the concept of the religious assembly itself has apparently been broadened to include women.

13. Compare Lev 13:9 (*'ādām*) and Lev 13:38 (*'îš, 'iššâ*) with Lev 13:40 (*'îš*). See also Num 6:2 (*'îš, 'iššâ*).

understanding of household/property that pertained in ancient Israel (Exod 20:17; 21:28-29). The law addresses heads of families (the family is called appropriately a "father's house" in the Hebrew idiom), for it is the family, not the individual, that is the basic unit of society in old Israel.[14]

But this definition of society as an aggregate of male-dominated households was modified in Israel by a concept of the society as a religious community, a religious community composed in the first instance exclusively of males or, perhaps originally, all adult males.[15] This is the understanding of the covenant congregation or of the "people" (*'am*), Israel, addressed by Moses on Sinai:

> So Moses went down from the mountain to the people (*'am*). . . .
> And he said to the people (*'am*), "Be ready by the third day; do not go near a woman." (Exod 19:14-15)[16]

It also coincides with the understanding of the "people" (*'am*) as the warriors of the community, a usage illustrated in certain texts pertaining to the premonarchic period.[17]

> The Lord said to Gideon, "The people (*'am*) are too many for me to give the Midianites into their hand." (Judg 7:2)

> Sisera called out all his chariots . . . and all the men (*'am*) who were with him. . . . (Judg 4:13)

14. Compare the idea, familiar even in contemporary Western society, of the citizen as property owner and/or family head. On the family and the place of the family in ancient Israel see Johannes Pedersen, *Israel*, I–II (Copenhagen: Branner og Korch, 1926; London: Oxford University Press, photo reprint, 1964) 46–96. See also Roland de Vaux, *Ancient Israel: Its Life and Institutions* (New York: McGraw-Hill, 1961) 19–40, 53ff. Israelite family life and institutions are illuminated by references to recent and contemporary Middle East families in Raphael Patai, *Sex and Family in the Bible and in the Middle East* (Garden City, N.Y.: Doubleday, 1959).

15. Circumcision as the sign of the covenant (Genesis 17; Lev 12:3; cf. Exod 12:48) makes this explicit. This practice is in other societies a "rite of passage," performed at puberty and signaling the initiate's entry into the tribe as a full, adult member with all attendant privileges and duties, including marriage. See Exod 4:26 and Josh 5:2-7.

16. I.e., the men are to keep themselves "holy." Sexual intercourse was considered defiling in Israel. See Lev 15:18; 1 Sam 21:4-5; 2 Sam 11:11.

17. The *'am* is first and foremost a kinship group—in a patriarchal society, "the sons of PN." It may be used in an inclusive sense as a designation for the whole community, including women (Judg 16:30), or it may be restricted to the men, the community at worship and at war (Pedersen, *Israel*, I–II, 54–56).

In both cult and war the "true" nature of Israel manifested itself.[18]

The coincidence in Israel of these two male-oriented and male-dominated systems (the sociopolitical and the religious) created a double liability for women, enforcing upon them the status of dependents in the religious as well as the political and economic spheres. Discrimination against women was inherent in the socioreligious organization of Israel. It was a function of the system. And though this systemic discrimination need not be represented as a plot to subjugate women—and thereby liberate the male ego—the system did enforce and perpetuate the dependence of women and an image of the female as inferior to the male.

This is illustrated in the legal material by laws dealing with inheritance, divorce, sexual trangressions, religious vows, cultic observances, and ritual purity. One of the chief aims of Israelite law is to assure the integrity, stability, and economic viability of the family as the basic unit of society. In this legislation, however, the interests of the family are commonly identified with those of its male head. His rights and duties are described with respect to other men and their property. The laws focus mainly upon external threats to the man's authority, honor, and property, though they may occasionally serve to define and protect his rights in relation to members of his own household (slaves: Exod 21:20-21; children: Deut 21:18-22; wife: Num 5:11-31). Only in rare cases, however, are the laws concerned with the rights of dependents (Exod 21:26-27; Deut 21:10-14, 15-17; 22:13-21).[19]

The wife's primary contribution to the family was her sexuality, which was regarded as the exclusive property of her husband, in respect to both its pleasure and its fruit. Her duty was to "build up" his "house"—and his alone. This service was essential to the man in order for him to fulfill his primary role as paterfamilias. It was as a consequence jealously guarded. Adultery involving a married woman was a crime of first magnitude in Israelite law (Lev 20:10; Exod 20:14), ranking with murder and major religious offenses as a transgression demanding the death penalty—for both offenders.[20] The issue was not simply one of extramarital

18. See the evolutionary interpretation given to this phenomenon by Herbert Richardson, *Nun, Witch, Playmate* (New York: Harper & Row, 1971) 14: "What happened in ancient Israel was that the male group displaced the tribe as the primary social institution. It displaced the tribal family into a secondary position so that the family existed within the male group rather than vice versa."

19. The laws of Num 27:1-11 and 36:1-9 are not concerned with the daughter's rights but with the father's, while the prohibition of Lev 19:29 is a cultic proscription, not a defense of a minor's rights.

20. See Lev 18:20. Martin Noth (*Leviticus* [trans. J. E. Anderson; OTL; Philadelphia: Westminster, 1965] 150) sees the reference to the woman in 20:10 as an addition to the older law,

sex (which was openly tolerated in certain circumstances). The issue was one of property and authority. Adultery was a violation of the fundamental and exclusive right of a man to the sexuality of his wife. It was an attack upon his authority in the family and consequently upon the solidarity and integrity of the family itself.[21] The adulterer robbed the husband of his essential honor, while the unfaithful wife defied his authority, offering to another man that which belonged only to him—and that which constituted her primary responsibility toward him.

The corollary of the unwritten law that a wife's sexuality belongs exclusively to her husband is the law that demands virginity of the bride.[22] The wife found guilty of fornication is, like the adulteress, sentenced to death. In this case, however, the crime is not simply against her husband, but against her father as well.

Extramarital sex is treated quite differently where a husband's rights are not involved. The man who violates an unmarried girl must simply marry her, making the proper marriage gift (*mōhar*) to her father. The only penalty he suffers is that he may not divorce her (Deut 22:28-29).[23] Prostitution seems to have been tolerated at all periods as a licit outlet for male sexual energies, though the prostitute was a social outcast, occupying at best a marginal place in the society. Hebrew fathers were enjoined not to "profane" their daughters by giving them up to prostitution, and the prophets used the figure of harlotry to condemn Israel's "affairs" with other gods.[24]

Taken together, the various laws that treat of extramarital sex evidence a strong feeling in Israel that sexual intercourse should properly be con-

---

representing a later interpretation, namely, that the woman is to be viewed not only as the object but as a fellow subject in the proceedings for breach of marriage. The actual practice and presuppositions reflected in historical, prophetic, and proverb texts point to a milder punishment, at least in the periods represented by those texts. See Jer 3:8 and Hos 2:2-7.

21. Incestuous sexual relationships, which were judged with equal severity (Lev 18:6-18 and 22:10-21), may have been understood in a similar way as threatening the complex relationship of rights and authority within the extended family, and thus the order and stability of the family. See Pedersen (*Israel*, I–II, 65), who stresses the psychological aspect of these offenses. For another explanation, see below, p. 25.

22. Likewise unwritten, but implied in Deut 22:13-21.

23. See Exod 22:16-17 and 2 Sam 13:11-16. Gen 34:1-7, 25-27 expresses a more severe attitude toward rape. In no case, however, are the girl's interests regarded by the law.

24. See below, p. 40 and n. 69. There is considerable fluidity in the metaphorical use of the terms for adultery and prostitution to describe idolatrous worship and "idolatrous" political relationships (see Hos 2:2; Jer 3:8-9; Ezek 16:30-35). Israel's relationships with other gods and nations are usually described as harlotry, thus emphasizing the brazen and habitual character of the act. This figure presumes that the "marriage" bond with Yahweh has long been broken or disregarded. The figure of the adulteress lays more stress upon the "marital" relationship and the exclusive nature of its claim.

fined to marriage,[25] of which it was the essence (Gen 2:24) and the principal sign.[26] Thus the victim of rape, the slave girl, or the female captive taken for sexual pleasure must become, or must be treated as, a wife (Exod 21:7-11; Deut 21:10-14). Polygny was a concession to the man's desire for more than one sexual partner, with concubinage a modification or extension of this.[27] Perhaps prostitution was tolerated as a poor man's substitute. It must certainly have been strengthened by the increasing institution of monogamous marriage as the general norm.

The laws dealing with sexual transgressions represent a strong statement of support for the family. But they are all formulated from the male's point of view, the point of view of a man who jealously guards what is essential to the fulfillment of his role in the family. Thus a jealous husband who suspects his wife of infidelity, but has no proof of it, may require her to submit to an ordeal. If she is "proved" innocent by this procedure, the husband incurs no penalty for his false accusation (Num 5:12-31).[28] Infidelity by the husband is not recognized as a crime.

Divorce was recognized in ancient Israel and regulated by law, at least in the later period of the monarchy. The extent of the practice and the circumstances in which it was sanctioned remain unclear; there is no doubt, however, that it was an exclusively male prerogative. Some scholars have interpreted the "indecency" (*'erwâ*) given as the ground for divorce in the law of Deut 24:1-4 as a reference to sexual infidelity.[29] If so, it would

25. The common ancient Near Eastern understanding of the sexual act as holy (or at least potentially so) was emphatically rejected by Israel, though the Canaanite terms *qĕdēšîm* (masc.) and *qĕdēšôt* (fem.) ("holy/consecrated ones") were used to refer to illicit cult prostitutes.* Sex in Israel belonged to the order of the profane, not the holy. Its proper uses included both enjoyment and procreation. Emphasis upon the former accounts for literature such as the Song of Songs and also explains Israel's concession (in the male interest) to prostitution. For the most part, however, extramarital sex was discouraged for practical, moral, and religious reasons. [*The once common understanding represented here is disputed by current scholarship. For my own investigation of the assumed institutions and practices see above, p. 4.]

26. Sexual union as the sign of marriage is suggested by the designation of the wife as her husband's "nakedness" (Lev 18:7, 14, 16). See Pedersen, *Israel,* I–II, 65.

27. In some circumstances concubines were treated much as wives (Judg 19:2-9), though they did not have the full rights of free persons. There is some indication that the king's concubines were inherited by his successor, at least in the early days of the monarchy (2 Sam 16:21-22; see also 2 Sam 3:7-8 and 1 Kgs 2:13-22), but this practice (which may have extended to all the king's wives on occasion [2 Sam 12:8]) was probably a special feature of the royal household. See Patai, *Sex and Family,* 41–43.

28. See the later law of Deut 22:13-21, however, where the husband who slanders his wife with a false accusation of unchastity incurs a double penalty—corporal punishment and a fine.

29. See Patai, *Sex and Family,* 120 (citing Hos 2:4ff.; Isa 50:1; and Jer 3:8—all prophetic similes); and Gerhard von Rad, *Deuteronomy* (trans. Dorothea Barton; OTL; Philadelphia: Westminster, 1966) 150.

represent a modification of the more severe law of adultery found in Leviticus 20. Others have suggested barrenness.[30] The Israelite man must commonly have understood his conjugal rights to include the right to progeny, especially male progeny. A wife who did not produce children for her husband was not fulfilling her duty as a wife. In early Israel it was apparently customary for her to offer him a female slave to bear for her (Gen 16:1-3 and 30:1-3); or the husband might simply take another wife (where economically feasible [1 Sam 1:2])—or secure the services of a harlot (?) (Judg 11:1-3). In the monogamous family of the later monarchy divorce must have been a more frequent alternative. All the Old Testament references to divorce are found in sources stemming from this period or later (Deut 24:1-4; Jer 3:8; Isa 50:1; possibly Hos 2:2).

The integrity of the family was also secured by inheritance laws that insured against the alienation of family property, that essential property which assured to each father's house its "place" in Israel. The basic inheritance laws are not contained in the Old Testament legal codes, but can be inferred from extralegal references and from a number of laws dealing with special cases in the transfer of family property (Num 27:1-11 and 36:1-9; Jer 32:6-8; Ruth 4:1-6). Two of these concern the inheritance of daughters. Since a daughter left her father's house at marriage to become a member of her husband's family, she normally received no inheritance. (Neither did the wife, since property was transmitted in the male line.) By special legislation, however, daughters were permitted to inherit where sons were lacking (Num 27:1-11).[31] But they were only placeholders in the male line, which was thereby enabled to continue in their children.[32] The rare institution of the levirate (the marriage of a widow to the brother of her dead husband) may also have been designed to preserve the property of a man to his name—that is, for his male descendants.

---

30. Pedersen thought this to be the most common reason for divorce, but could only refer to Gen 29:34 as evidence (*Israel*, I–II, 71). Patai (*Sex and Family*, 120) notes that divorce for barrenness is never mentioned, but argues that the emphasis on procreation and the insecurity of the childless woman indicated in the patriarchal stories make barrenness a most probable cause for dismissal. In this connection it should be noted that the several conspicuously barren wives of the Old Testament all bear eventually (e.g., Sarah, Samson's mother, Hannah, and the "great" woman of Shunem). Their barrenness is a literary device that retards the action of the story, heightens anticipation and suspense, and gives a miraculous character to the birth. In most cases the real interest of the story is in the child that is finally born. Attention is focused upon him through this device. His existence is made to depend upon a special act of God in opening his mother's womb.

31. This special provision for female inheritance was further modified in the interests of tribal solidarity and the preservation of tribal land by a specification that the inheriting daughter marry within her father's tribe (Num 31:1-9). From this it is clear that the daughter's husband was regarded as the real heir.

32. The property would otherwise pass to the father's nearest male relative and thus be lost to his name.

In the patriarchal family system of Israel a woman had only a limited possibility of owning property, though responsibility for managing it may have been assumed with some frequency.[33] Normally, however, a woman was dependent for support upon her father before marriage and her husband after marriage. As a consequence, the plight of a widow without sons might be desperate. Her husband's property would pass to the nearest male relative, who was apparently under no obligation to maintain his kinsman's wife. She would be expected to return to her own family. The frequent impossibility of this solution, however, is suggested by the special plea for defense of the widow that occurs repeatedly in the ethical injunctions of the Old Testament (e.g., Isa 1:17; Jer 7:6 and 22:3; Zech 7:10; Exod 22:22 [Heb. 21]).

The laws also illustrate, both explicitly and implicitly, disabilities of women in the religious sphere. As noted above, the oldest religious law was addressed only to men, while the sign of membership in the religious community was circumcision, the male initiation rite. Only males were required by the law of Deut 16:16 to attend the three annual pilgrim feasts, the primary communal religious acts of later Israel.[34] Consonant with this bias was the assumption of the cultic law that only males might serve as priests (eventually restricted to the "sons of Aaron"). However, in keeping with the understanding of the family as the basic social unit, the priest's whole household shared in the holiness of his office and in the obligations imposed by it. Thus a priest's daughter who "defiled" herself by fornication incurred the sentence of death, since she had also defiled her father by her act (Lev 21:9: see also 22:10-14).

Women also suffered religious disability that was only indirectly sex-determined. Israelite religion, following widespread ancient practice, excluded from cultic participation all persons in a state of impurity or uncleanness—that is, in a profane or unholy state. Various circumstances were understood to signal such a state, during which time (usually limited) it was considered unsafe to engage in cultic activity or have contact with the cult. Israel's laws recognized leprosy and certain other skin diseases, contact with a corpse, bodily emissions of all types (both regular

33. Von Rad (*Deuteronomy*, 107) notes that the "updating" in Deut 15:12-17 of the old law of the Hebrew slave (Exod 21:1-11) presupposes that the woman has in the meantime become capable of owning landed property and is thus able to sell herself into slavery for debt just as a male. Cf. 2 Kgs 8:3-6 (though in this case the property claimed by the widow might possibly belong to her minor son).

34. Women may have been excused from this obligation in view of their more highly deemed—and confining—services to home and children. But the fact that they were dispensable in the practice of the cult would support any notion of their inferiority in that realm. Note, however, that against the law of Deut 16:16, the custom of a single annual visit to a local sanctuary is described in 1 Sam 1:3-8 (from the period of the judges), in which the man was regularly accompanied by his wife or wives. Only the man sacrificed, however (v. 4).

and irregular, in members of both sexes), sexual intercourse, and child-birth as among those factors that caused uncleanness (Leviticus 12–15). The frequent and regular recurrence of this cultically proscribed state in women of childbearing age must have seriously affected their ability to function in the cult.

An explicitly discriminatory expression—or "extension"—of the idea of ritual uncleanness is found in the law determining the period of impu-rity occasioned by childbirth (Lev 12:1-5). Seven days are prescribed for a mother who has borne a son, but fourteen for the mother of a female child. Another cultic law that gives explicit statement to the differential values placed upon males and females is the law of Lev 27:2-8, which de-termines monetary equivalents for vows of persons to cultic service. Ac-cording to this reckoning the vow of a male aged twenty to sixty years was valued at 50 shekels, while that of a woman in the same age bracket was worth only 30 shekels.[35] Thus it appears that a male of any age was more highly valued than a female.[36]

The reason for this differential valuation must have been in large part economic, though a psychological factor is also evident. As in most pre-modern, labor-intensive societies, a large family was prized, since it offered a superior labor supply and flexibility and sustaining power when faced with serious threats to its existence. The large family carried more weight in the community and assured honor to its head—and to his spouse.[37] Many descendants also assured the continuity of the father's house and name. But only males could perform this task, and only males remained as primary economic contributors. On both economic (labor value) and psychological grounds the significant size of the family was reckoned in terms of males.[38] Females were necessary as child bearers and child rearers, but they always had to be obtained from outside the fam-ily—and at a price. A man's own daughters left his house to build up

35. Further gradations by age and sex make it clear that it was labor value that was reckoned by this table of equivalents.

36. See Neh 5:1-5, in which the impoverished Jews complain that in order to pay their debts they are being forced to sell their sons and daughters into slavery—and that some of their *daughters* have *already* been enslaved. The relatively greater expendability of females may also have found expression in female infanticide by abandonment, a practice attested among contemporary peoples of the Middle East and suggested for the Old Testament pe-riod by the image of the female foundling in Ezekiel 16 (Patai, *Sex and Family*, 136).

37. See the blessing of Gen 24:60: "[May you] be the mother of thousands of ten thou-sands."

38. See, for example, Gen 46:8-27, in which wives are explicitly omitted from the tally given in v. 26, and only one daughter is included among the seventy persons counted! See also Neh 7:6-37, in which the number of persons returning from the exile is counted by families of men only.

another man's family. Thus an excess of female dependents was a luxury or a liability.

The picture sketched above is not a complete portrait of woman in ancient Israel; nevertheless it does present the essential features. Additions and qualifications are necessary at many points. Most stem from sources outside the legal material and are treated later; but a few, explicit or implicit in the laws themselves, must be noted here.

The ancient command to honor one's parents (Exod 20:12; Deut 5:16) recognizes the female as the equal of the male in her role as mother. It places the highest possible value upon this role, in which her essential function in the society was represented—the reproductive function.[39] The welfare of family and society and the status of the husband depended upon her performance of that task. Consequently she was rewarded for it by honor and protected in it by law and custom, which "exempted" her (indirectly) from military service and "excused" her from certain religious and civic obligations.

Laws of this type, though positive (or compensatory) in their discrimination, may be classed together with those that discriminate negatively as laws in which the sociobiological role of the individual or his/her social value (= productivity) is a significant factor in the legal formulation. In a society in which roles and occupations are primarily sexually determined, sexual discrimination is bound to be incorporated in the laws. At the same time, however, laws that do not regard the person, but only acts or states, may be "egalitarian" in their conception.[40] This is illustrated in the old laws of Exod 21:26 and 21:28, which assess penalties on the basis of injury suffered, without regard to the sex of the injured person. Egalitarianism, or nondiscrimination, is characteristic of most of the laws concerning ritual impurity and is a consistent feature of the laws dealing with major ethical, moral, and cultic infractions. Thus illegitimate association with the supernatural incurred the same penalty, whether the practitioner was male or female (Lev 20:27; Deut 17:2-7), and cult prostitutes of both sexes were equally proscribed (Deut 23:17). Illicit types of sexual intercourse, with their equal and severe penalty (death) for both offenders, may also have been viewed as belonging to this category of offenses—that is, as practices of the surrounding peoples, abhorrent to Yahweh (Lev 18:6-18; 20:10-21; Deut 22:30).[41]

The only statements of equal "rights" in Old Testament law are indirect

---

39. Cf. Gen 3:20, in which Eve's name is interpreted to mean "mother of all living."

40. It must be noted, however, that inequality of opportunity may make equal responsibility discriminatory in effect.

41. For a different interpretation, see n. 21 above.

and qualified. They too pertain to the cultic sphere. The laws of Num 6:2ff. and 30:3-15 (both belonging to the latest of the law codes) indicate that women, as well as men, might undertake on their own initiative binding obligations of a religious nature. Num 30:3-15 qualifies this, however, by upholding—but limiting—the right of a husband or father to annul a vow made by his wife or daughter (thereby allowing the interests of family to take precedence over the interests of the cult).[42]

The picture of woman obtained from the Old Testament laws can be summarized in the first instance as that of a legal nonperson; where she does become visible it is as a dependent, and usually an inferior, in a male-centered and male-dominated society. The laws, by and large, do not address her; most do not even acknowledge her existence. She comes to view only in situations (a) where males are lacking in essential socioeconomic roles (the female heir); (b) where she requires special protection (the widow); (c) where sexual offenses involving women are treated; and (d) where sexually defined or sexually differentiated states, roles, and/or occupations are dealt with (the female slave or captive as wife, the woman as mother, and the sorceress). Where ranking occurs she is always inferior to the male. Only in her role as mother is she accorded status and honor equivalent to a man's. Nevertheless, she is always subject to the authority of some male (father, husband, or brother), except when widowed or divorced—an existentially precarious type of independence in Israel.[43]

The Image of Woman in Proverbs

References to women in the book of Proverbs are limited and stereotyped. Three major types dominate: (1) the mother, (2) the wife, and (3) the "other/foreign" woman.

The mother is portrayed in Proverbs as a teacher, whose instruction a son is commended to heed. In this role she is typically ranked alongside the father (in the normal parallelism, "father ... mother" [1:8; 6:20]), though in the instruction of 31:1-9 it is the mother alone who is mentioned as author of the advice. Elsewhere mother and father together represent the parents, who take delight in a wise son (10:1; 15:20; 23:24-25) and to whom honor is due (20:20; see also Exod 20:12). In Proverbs, as in the laws, the mother is described in positive terms only. But here it is clear that the term "mother" does not refer primarily to her reproductive func-

42. The widow and the divorcée are alone free to make binding vows, since they alone bear no immediate responsibility to a male whose interests might be hurt by the action (v. 9).

43. The prostitute, as a pariah, existed for the most part outside the primary authority structures of the society.

tion, but to her role in the nurture and education of the child. She is not merely the womb that bears a man, but a source of wisdom essential to life.

The wife is depicted in a more varied and ambivalent light. The "good" wife, or "woman of quality," is described as the crown of her husband (lit. "master") and is contrasted with the wife "who brings shame," that is, who degrades rather than enhances her *husband's* reputation (12:4). She is also described as prudent (19:14) and gracious (11:16), with honor as her gain (11:16). Obtaining such a wife is deemed a gift from God (18:22; 19:14).

A detailed list of the activities and skills of the "wife of quality" is found in the acrostic poem of Prov 31:10-31. Here we see a woman of the upper class, presumably from the time of the monarchy. She is manager of the household, directing the work of servants and seeing to it by industriousness and foresight that her family is well provided for in food and clothing. She engages in business transactions, apparently on her own initiative, buying land, setting out a vineyard with the profits reaped from her undertakings, and manufacturing clothing. She is generous and ready to help the poor and needy, possesses strength and dignity, is a wise and kind teacher. In consequence of her good character and her provision for her household, her husband is "known in the gates." He trusts her and profits by her. Recognizing his good fortune ("a good wife is far more precious than jewels" [v. 10]), he praises her in company with his children. In this portrait the sexual attributes of the wife are not mentioned. She is characterized in wholly nonsexual terms as provisioner of home and husband, toward whom all her talents and energies appear to be directed. In this role "she does him good" (v. 12).

A "bad" wife is also described in Proverbs, but not as a general type. She is identified primarily in terms of a single trait—contentiousness. The contentious woman is likened to a "continual dripping on a rainy day" (19:13; 27:15). It is better to live in a desert land or in the "attic" than to share a house with her (21:9, 19; 25:24). The bad wife is characterized as "one who causes shame" (12:4); she disgraces not only herself but her husband—which is the main point of the admonition.

In only one passage in Proverbs is the wife described as a sexual partner. The counsel to fidelity in 5:15-19 contrasts the "wife of your youth" with the "loose woman," advising the husband to "drink water from [his] own cistern" and not to let his streams flow for others (vv. 15-16; cf. Sir 26:19-21). He should let her breasts delight him and be intoxicated always (and only) by her love. The ideal portrayed here is that of sexual pleasure identified with marriage; and it is monogamous marriage that is presumed.

This counsel to fidelity is paralleled by the admonition to beware the seductions of the "other/foreign" woman—the most common word concerning women found in the instruction literature (2:16; 5:3-6; 5:20; 6:24; 7:5; 22:14; 23:27-28; cf. 31:3; Eccl 7:26; "harlot": 7:10-23, 29:3). Characterized by the RSV translation as a "loose woman" or "adventuress,"[44] she is depicted as luring men to destruction (her house/path leads to death: 2:16; 5:3; cf. 7:22; 9:18; 22:14; 23:28) by her "smooth talk" (2:16; 5:3; 6:24; 7:5; cf. 7:21). She accosts her victim in the squares and marketplace and lies in wait at the street corners to entice him into her house (7:12; 9:14-15).

The loose woman in Proverbs personifies "folly" and is contrasted with the "wise woman," or "wisdom" personified (9:1-6, 13-18), while association with harlots and love of wisdom describe antithetical behavior (29:3). But wisdom is not simply the antithesis of the folly characterized by the loose woman; it is the antidote. Throughout these admonitions runs the idea that wisdom will protect a man from the disaster she portends.

As the counsel to fidelity shows, the condemnation of the "strange" woman and her ways is not a condemnation of erotic love, but of its abuse—its employment as the tool of an unscrupulous woman, out of the man's control.[45] In Proverbs sex is subordinated to wisdom. It is not extolled, like wisdom, as a good in itself, but is praised and appreciated only when channeled and controlled within the confines of marriage. The control essential to its enjoyment (in this view) must be exercised by the man, to whom the words of advice are directed.[46]

Two references are made to an adulteress. In 6:26 she is compared with the harlot; while the latter takes a man's money ("may be hired for a loaf of bread"), the former may cost him his life. The thought, which is ampli-

44. The Hebrew word used in most of these passages means simply a "stranger" or "foreigner"; only in 7:10-22 and 29:3 is the professional term "harlot" (zônâ) employed. Scholars dispute whether the woman in question was actually a foreigner or simply a woman whose mores made her a social outcast and therefore an "outsider" (see William McKane, *Proverbs* [OTL; Philadelphia: Westminster, 1970] 285, 287). Some see in the descriptions of her a reference to a devotee of a foreign cult and thus a cult prostitute (ibid., 284, 287). For the discussion here it is sufficient simply to designate her as the "other" woman, contrasting her with the wife. The admonitions against association with her are not religious or ethical, but "practical." "She'll be the death of you," they predict.
45. See Brevard Childs, *Biblical Theology in Crisis* (Philadelphia: Westminster, 1970) 186-90.
46. Ibid. In striking contrast to Proverbs, the Song of Songs extols erotic love for itself as the most prized of human possessions. Its power and beauty are expressed in a relationship of complete mutuality, controlled neither by the man nor by the woman and therefore (necessarily) apart from the marriage relationship with its structure of male domination and female subordination. In the Song the lovers alternate in initiating acts of lovemaking. There the woman is portrayed as seeking out her beloved in the very same language used by Proverbs to describe the aggressive enticement of the harlot—but with no hint of condemnation. For further comparison of the parallel passages in Proverbs and Song of Songs, see Childs, ibid., 190-96. See also Trible, "Depatriarchalizing in Biblical Interpretation," 42-47.

fied in the following verses, is that adultery constitutes theft, and the wronged husband will avenge himself upon the adulterer. In 30:20 the adulteress is portrayed as an amoral woman who refuses to acknowledge her guilt: "she eats, wipes her mouth, and says, 'I have done no wrong.'"

The wisdom sayings and instruction literature of Proverbs give a somewhat different picture from that of the laws. A more homogeneous social milieu is assumed here: urban, monogamous, and relatively comfortable. It is a literature of the upper class predominantly; and it addresses men exclusively. A man's success depends upon heeding his parents' instruction and obtaining a good wife. His fortune is seen as determined in large measure by his relationships with women, relationships determined both by accident (providence) and choice. Practical and moral suasion are employed here to guide that choice. The evils he is warned to recognize and avoid apparently carry no legal penalties. Adultery is redressed only by a husband's jealousy, and prostitution, conceived as the primary threat to a man, appears to flourish unsanctioned. Women are not chattel in Proverbs, nor are they simply sexual objects; they are persons of intelligence and will, who, from the male's point of view expressed here, either make or break a man. The man must learn to recognize the two types and abstain from harmful relationships. He does so by means of wisdom, wisdom gained first and foremost from his parents—of both sexes.

The Image of Woman in the Historical Writings

The historical writings amplify greatly the picture of woman obtained from the laws and proverbs. The descriptions they offer of the women of their day and of the legendary figures of times past add richness of color and detail to the outline already sketched, confirming in many instances the initial broad strokes, but demanding reassessment and redrawing of some features. The composite portrait contained in these writings displays variety and ambiguity in the image and status of women not apparent in the laws.

Despite the quantity and diversity of the references and despite occasionally vivid and individualistic portrayals, the great majority of women referred to in the historical writings appear in reality more as types than as "real," historical individuals. Even where a woman—or a woman's name—has attained legendary stature, where force of character or peculiarity of vocation or position has procured a unique place for her, or where an author, following his own sympathies or artistic aims, has lingered over a particular female figure, the roles played by women in these writings are almost exclusively subordinate and/or supporting roles.

Women are adjuncts to the men: they are the minor (occasionally, major) characters necessary to a plot that revolves about males. They are the mothers and nurses and saviors of men;[47] temptresses, seducers, and destroyers of men;[48] objects or recipients of miracles performed by and for men;[49] confessors of the power, wisdom, and divine designation of men.[50] They are necessary to the drama and may even steal the spotlight occasionally; but the story is rarely about them.[51]

Only Deborah and Jezebel stand on their own feet—possibly also Miriam and Huldah. But far too little evidence survives about them to assess their actual position in Israelite society or their representativeness. The queen of Sheba also appears as an independent figure, but this legendary foreigner cannot be placed within the context of Israelite society; she is introduced only as an exotic rival of Solomon in wisdom and wealth, a figure who must have the status of an equal or near equal in order to test him and acknowledge his superiority (1 Kgs 10:6-9).

The two most common images of woman in the historical writings are those of wife and mother, frequently combined where the woman is portrayed as a historical individual. Other types, such as the barren woman, the foreign woman, and the widow, represent subtypes or modifications of these two. Identification of women by occupation or profession other than wife-mother is found in a small though significant group of references.

The primary characteristics of the mother in the historical writings are compassion, solicitousness, and jealousy for her children; she also appears (indirectly) as a teacher or determiner of character and as a figure of authority and respect—usually in conjunction with the father (i.e., as co-parent; see 1 Kgs 19:20; 1 Sam 22:3-4; Judg 14:2-3, 16). The special feeling of the mother for her child—and for a son in particular—is given frequent and varied expression: the mother of Sisera suppressing her premonition of disaster with self-assuring visions of the scenes of victory (Judg 5:28-30); Rachel weeping inconsolably for her children (Jer 31:15); Rizpah in mourning vigil over the bodies of her dead sons, moving both heavens and king to acts of sympathy (2 Sam 21:8-14); the "true" mother in Solomon's famous test revealing herself by her willingness to give up her own

47. E.g., Jehosheba (2 Kgs 11:2), Rahab (Josh 2:1-21), Moses' mother and sister and Pharaoh's daughter (Exod 2:2-10).

48. E.g., Delilah, Jael, the woman of Thebez (Judg 9:53), Jezebel.

49. E.g., the widow of Zarephath (1 Kgs 17:8-24; see also 2 Kgs 4:1-7), the "great" woman of Shunem (2 Kgs 4:8-37), Sarah, Samson's mother (Judg 13:2-3).

50. E.g., Rahab (Josh 2:8-13), Abigail (1 Sam 25:28-29), the queen of Sheba.

51. The exceptions, Ruth and Esther, are both encountered in works of a distinct literary genre, the novella, in which they are the central figures.

child to another woman in order to save his life (1 Kgs 3:16-27); the wealthy woman of Shunem cradling her dying child in her lap (2 Kgs 4:18-20).[52] These adumbrations of the pietà show no distinctions of social status. Queen mother (Judges 5), concubine (2 Samuel 21) and harlot (1 Kings 3) all exhibit in these representations a common maternal feeling, a special and enduring bond with the fruit of their womb that makes the loss of a child a woman's greatest loss. In this bereavement all women are alike, and all are equal.

Suffering also marks the other primary image of the mother, the image that predominates in the prophetic writings. It is the woman in childbirth (Isa 13:8; 21:3; 26:17; Jer 4:31; 30:6; 48:41; Mic 4:9-10, etc.) that has fixed the poet's attention. Her pangs represent for him the greatest anguish known to man, and their vivid portrayal expresses the deep pain and turmoil of all persons in extremity. The male writer sees in them not only pain, but helplessness and fear, so that he contrasts the woman in childbirth with the warrior, strong and courageous, and mocks the fearful army by calling them women (Nah 3:13; see also Jer 30:6).

Socioeconomic factors certainly played a role in Israelite attitudes toward children and toward motherhood. The loss, or threatened loss, of an only child, especially when the woman was a widow, might be an occasion of panic as well as pathos, for the mother's life and/or welfare might depend upon the life of the child (2 Sam 14:2-17; 2 Kgs 4:18-25). The barren woman shared with the woman made childless by bereavement the same precarious future. In addition, however, she suffered immediate social and psychological deprivation for her failure to achieve motherhood.

Barrenness was a shame and a reproach in Israel (Gen 30:1-2, 22-23; 1 Sam 1:3-7, 11); it was interpreted as divine punishment or at least a sign of divine displeasure (Gen 16:2; 20:18; 30:26; 1 Sam 1:5; 2 Sam 6:20-23). It brought gloating derision from other women, especially from co-wives who had proved their fertility (1 Sam 1:6; cf. Gen 30:1, 8 and 16:4), and it threatened the woman's status as a wife (Gen 30:1-2, 15-20). The barren woman was deprived of the honor attached to motherhood—the only position of honor generally available to women, representing the highest status a woman might normally achieve. Consequently, the expression "a mother in Israel" could be used metaphorically to describe a woman or a city (grammatically feminine) of special veneration[53] (Judg 5:7; 2 Sam 20:19), and the reversal of a woman's fortunes might be depicted in the

---

52. See also Hannah in her yearly visits to the child she had vowed to the service of Yahweh (1 Sam 2:19) and Moses' mother boldly trusting in the compassion of another woman to save the life of her own son (Exod 2:1-10).

53. Or, perhaps, one who protects, saves, or succors. Cf. Isa 22:21 and Job 29:16.

image of a barren woman giving birth to seven sons (1 Sam 2:5). But motherhood brought more than honor, more than security and approval of husband and society. It brought authority. It offered the woman her only opportunity to exercise legitimate power over another person.[54] In the hierarchically organized patriarchal family, in which women of every age and status were subject to the authority of a male superior, this must have been a significant factor in a woman's desire for children. The only relationship in which dominance by the woman was sanctioned was the mother-child relationship.

The authority of the mother over her children is illustrated by relatively few examples, most of which pair the woman in this role with the father (Hebrew has no common term for "parents"). Her influence on the character of the child is indicated only indirectly in the historical writings.[55] Direct power and influence over the life of the child may be seen in a mother's dedication of a child to cultic service (1 Sam 1:11), in her efforts to effect the choice of a son's wife (Gen 27:46—28:2; cf. Judg 14:3), and in attempts to have her own son (in a polygynous family) or a favorite son declared principal heir (Gen 21:10; 1 Kgs 1:15-20).

The interests of a mother in the fortunes of her son are especially apparent where he is a potential heir to the throne, since his ascension elevates her to the honored position of queen mother. This position appears to have been a recognized institution, at least in the Judaean monarchy, where the queen mother was referred to by the title "(great) lady" (*gĕbîrâ*), and her name included in the regnal formulas of each king.[56] The deference accorded the queen mother is illustrated in the account of Bathsheba's reception by her own son, King Solomon (1 Kgs 2:19). The potential power inherent in the position is evidenced in Athaliah's successful seizure of the throne (and six-year reign) on the death of her son, King Ahaziah (2 Kgs 11:1-3).

54. Indirect or "underhanded" means of exercising power are the devices commonly employed by women in patriarchal societies. See Pedersen, *Israel*, I–II, 69.

55. In a rare acknowledgment of a woman's effect upon the political and moral life of the nation, the Deuteronomic historian judges the sibling kings, Ahaziah and Joram, in terms of the (evil) example of *both* parents, Ahab and Jezebel (1 Kgs 22:52; 2 Kgs 3:2, 13; see also 2 Kgs 9:22ff.). The widespread practice of cursing a man by cursing his mother may also be an acknowledgment of the mother's influence on the child. Compare Saul's reproach of Jonathan in 2 Sam 20:30, "you son of a perverse, rebellious [= possibly "runaway"] woman," with the English deprecations "s.o.b." and "bastard."

56. The name of the queen mother is omitted from the formulas of two southern kings, Ahaz (2 Kgs 16:2) and Jehoram (2 Kgs 8:16-18). Jehoram's *wife's* name is given, however, which is unique in these records (she was the daughter of the notorious northern king Ahab). Normally the king's wives were of no interest to the official chroniclers or to the Deuteronomic historian. Only David's wives are known, because of the roles they played in the extended biographical history of David's rise and reign.

The primary category to which all these women belong is that of wife. It is the comprehensive category that describes the destiny of every female in Israel.[57] Yet the image of the wife is an elusive one. As wife alone she is all but invisible. Neither eulogized nor deprecated, she rarely appears, unless thrust forward by some peculiarity of family, character, position, or deed or unless required to link two male figures (1 Kgs 3:1; 4:11; 2 Kgs 8:18; 1 Sam 18:20-27; 2 Sam 3:13ff.) or two generations of males.[58] Wives figure most prominently in the patriarchal narratives, primarily because they are by their nature *family stories,* created and/or employed for the purpose of creating a history based upon a genealogical scheme. In these tales the wives are seen primarily, though not exclusively, as mothers, while daughters appear only as wives—accounting for external relations.[59] Wives also figure in the tales incorporated into the books of Judges, Samuel, and Kings and play significant parts in the court narrative of David, which also partakes of the story genre. But they are almost totally lacking in the "political" history of Joshua—Kings, except for an occasional word of warning about the danger of foreign wives—or of marriage with foreigners in general.

Hebrew has no special term for "wife," but uses the common word for "woman" (*'iššâ*) in genitive "construct" with the name of the husband ("woman of NN")—a formula that can be applied to a concubine (*pilegeš*) as well as a full wife. There is also no specific term for "husband," though the relational term *ba'al* ("master") was frequently used in the corresponding genitival construction instead of the general word for man (*'iš*) ("man/master of NN"). This usage is indicative of the nature of the husband-wife relationship in Israel. It suggests why the marriage relationship was appropriated as a metaphor for the covenant relationship of Yahweh to Israel, a relationship characterized by intimacy—and subordination.

The Hebrew wife has often been characterized as essentially chattel. And in some respects this view is justified. Wives, children, slaves, and livestock described a man's major possessions (Exod 20:17). Wives, or simply "women," are found in lists of booty commonly taken in war (Deut 20:14; cf. Deut 21:10-14; 1 Sam 30:2, 5, 22; 1 Kgs 20:3, 5, 7; 2 Kgs 24:15), and wives are counted—along with concubines, silver, and gold—as an index

57. Exceptions only confirm the rule. See Judg 11:37-40.

58. Rachel and Leah, together with their servants, Bilhah and Zilpah, are in the first instance simply mothers of the twelve "sons of Israel," and are only secondarily fleshed out with individual characteristics as wives of Jacob. See Martin Noth, *Das System der zwölf Stämme Israels* (Stuttgart: Kohlhammer, 1930) 7.

59. See Genesis 34 (Dinah and Shechem—though the relationship failed to result in marriage, according to this account).

of a man's wealth (1 Kgs 10:14-11:8).[60] In these and other references where mention of a wife serves simply to complete a reference to family, household, or possessions, she is usually anonymous and is not formally distinguished from other property.

Despite legal, economic, and social subordination, however, wives were not simply property. They could not be bought and sold, and it is doubtful that they could be divorced without substantial cause. Later law required a formal writ of divorce (Jer 3:8; Isa 50:1; see also Deut 24:1-4).[61] But the rights of concubine and wife were not fixed by contract (as in later Jewish practice) or by any surviving law. They were presumably customary and negotiated by agreements between the husband and the wife's family. A wife's rights and freedom within the marriage would depend in large measure upon the ability of her family to support and defend her demands. Thus the daughter of a rich and powerful man could expect better treatment as a wife. Her status as a wife would reflect the status of her family.

The wives depicted in the historical writings exhibit a wide variety of characteristics, yet a coherent picture is not difficult to obtain. The good (ideal) wife is well illustrated by Abigail, wife of Nabal (and later of David) (1 Sam 25:2-42), with supplementary traits drawn from other examples. She is intelligent, beautiful, discreet, and loyal to her husband (despite his stupidity and boorish character in the case of Nabal; see Jer 2:2). Prudent, quick-witted, and resourceful, she is capable of independent action, but always acts in her husband's behalf. The good wife does not attempt to rule her husband, nor does she openly oppose him. She defers to him in speech and action, obeys his wish as his command, and puts his welfare first. She employs her sexual gifts for his pleasure alone and raises up children to his name.[62]

The Old Testament historical texts portray the woman as intelligent, strong-willed, and capable, and especially endowed with the gift of persuasion (see 2 Sam 14:1-20; 2 Sam 20:16-22; 1 Kgs 1:11-31). As a consequence, she was also potentially dangerous to the man, since, if she wished, she could use her sexual and intellectual gifts to undo him or to gain her own ends at his expense. Against this female power not even the strongest man

60. Despite the moralistic interpretation given by the editor, the enumeration of Solomon's wives and concubines was certainly intended to suggest his great means as well as his great appetite.

61. Even concubines and female prisoners of war taken as wives had limited rights, by virtue of their sexual union with the master, that distinguished them from ordinary slaves— or other property.

62. A case of extreme loyalty in this respect is exemplified by Tamar, who in desperation to fulfill her duty to her dead husband lures her father-in-law to impregnate her (Genesis 38). See Pedersen, *Israel*, I–II, 79.

could stand (Judg 16:4-21). The danger presented by the woman to the man was greatest where the relationship was most intimate, namely, in marriage. And there the threat had a second root. For the wife was always to some degree a stranger in her husband's household, an outsider who maintained bonds of loyalty to her father's house and who might consequently be used by her kinsmen. This danger from the wife's external connections was magnified if she was a foreigner, a fact that is reflected in a demonstrated preference for in-group marriage (Gen 24:1-4; 26:34-35 and 27:46—28:5; Judg 14:1-3)[63] and in numerous laws, preachments, and "case histories" that warn against the disastrous consequences of marriage with foreigners (Judg 3:5-6; Ezra 9–10, esp. 9:1-2; Num 31:15-16; see 1 Kgs 11:1-8).

The historical writings rarely portray the wife as a sexual partner or lover, though they assume (as ideal) a high correspondence between love and marriage.[64] In general they give too little information about the marriage relationship to permit substantial conclusions. Israelite marriage was essentially an arrangement between two families, usually initiated by the man or his parents (Judg 14:1-2; Gen 34:1-4, 8; Genesis 24). This male locus of the initiative is illustrated by the verbs and the actions that commonly describe the incorporation of the woman into the new household: she is "given," "taken," "sent for," "captured"—and even purchased, in the case of a slave wife. Some texts suggest, however, that the woman's role was not wholly passive or lacking in initiative (2 Sam 11:2-5; 1 Sam 18:20),[65] that she could refuse an "offer" (Gen 24:5, 57-58) and make demands of her own (Judg 1:15). Though a woman could not divorce her husband, the mistreated wife might simply return to her father's house (Judg 19:2).[66]

Polygyny is a recurrent feature in the narratives of the premonarchic period, and efforts to assure equal rights to multiple wives (and/or their children) are evidenced in both the laws and the narratives (Gen 30:15; Deut 21:15; cf. Gen 29:30-31).[67] By the eighth century B.C.E., however, and probably a good deal earlier, monogamous marriage was clearly the norm and the ideal.[68] It is presupposed by Hosea's use of the marriage analogy

---

63. Even half-sibling marriage seems to have been tolerated in David's time (2 Sam 13:13), though later law prohibits it (Lev 18:9; 20:17). See Pedersen, *Israel*, I–II, 64–65.

64. Compare Judg 16:1ff. and 16:4ff. A man "goes in to" or "lies with" a harlot, but he is expected to take the woman he "loves" as a wife. Where he does not, the relationship is clearly an abnormal one (2 Sam 13:1ff. and 15-16). The major exception to this rule is found in the Song of Songs, where love is extolled without thought of marriage.

65. In this case Michal's obvious love for David is exploited by her father, Saul, who makes an exorbitant demand as the bride-price.

66. But a father might also step into the marriage and give a neglected daughter to another man (Judg 15:1-2; 1 Sam 25:44).

67. See Patai, *Sex and Family*, 44.

68. The major exception is the royal family (2 Kgs 24:15).

to speak of Yahweh's exclusive and demanding relationship to Israel. This metaphor of Israel as the bride or wife of Yahweh, which is also employed by Jeremiah (2:2; 3:1, 4, 6-10) and Ezekiel (chap. 16), is always found in the context of an indictment of Israel's unfaithfulness. She is described in alternating images as harlot and adulteress, though the language of harlotry predominates.[69] The choice of the latter metaphor may be related to the conspicuous feature of cult prostitution in Canaanite religion,[70] but the fact that it becomes prominent only in the eighth century while dominating later theological language suggests that it should be correlated with the use of the bride/wife motif.

The harlot was the primary symbol of the double standard in Israel. She was in every period a figure of disrepute and shame (Gen 34:31; Judg 11:1; 1 Kgs 22:38; Isa 1:21; Jer 3:3; Ezek 16:30), at best merely ostracized, at worst (in circumstances involving infidelity and defilement) subjected to punishment of death (Gen 38:24; see also Lev 21:9). But the harlot was also tolerated in every period by men who incurred no legal penalties— or even censure—for the enjoyment of her services (Gen 38:15ff.).[71] Her status and image gained nothing, however, from this tolerance. The two best-known stories of harlots (Rahab, who saved the spies of Joshua [Josh 2:1-21], and the two harlots who presented their case to Solomon for judgment [1 Kgs 3:16-27]), often cited as evidence of their acceptance in Israelite society, also presuppose their low repute. In both accounts the harlot heroines are made to demonstrate in their words and actions faith, courage, and love that would scarcely be expected of the average upright citizen and thus are all the more astonishing and compelling as the response of a harlot—that member of society from whom one would least expect religious and moral sensitivity. They serve the storyteller's purpose in much the same way as the poor widow—that member of society whose existence is most precarious and who is consequently a favorite for depicting great faith and generosity.

69. See p. 24 and n. 43 above. The harlot as a metaphor for Israel is found in Isaiah, Hosea, Micah, Jeremiah, Ezekiel, and Nahum. The verb *zānâ* ("to play the harlot") is used to speak of apostasy in Judg 2:17; 8:27, 33; Exod 34:15-16; Deut 31:16; Leviticus passim; Num 15:39; 25:1; Hos 1:2; 4:12, 15; 9:1; Jeremiah 2 and 3 (4 times); Ezekiel (15 times); Ps 106:39; 1 Chr 5:25.

70. Note, however, that our chief source of information is the highly biased accounts of Hebrew prophets and theologians, who frequently describe all non-Yahwistic worship as simply prostitution.

71. See Patai, *Sex and Family,* 147. Patai argues that attitudes toward harlotry became more lenient in the later period of the monarchy, by which time harlots were an accepted part of urban society (1 Kgs 22:38; Isa 23:16; Exod 16:24-25; Jer 3:2; 5:7; Prov 2:16; 5:3, 8; 6:24-25; 7:5, 10, 11, 12; 9:14, 15; Sir 9:3-9; 19:2; 26:9). His argument that later Hebrew attitudes toward prostitution involved no essentially moral judgment is supported only by citations from Proverbs and Sirach, both of which represent a genre of literature characterized by practical rather than moral judgments.

In addition to the primary roles of wife and mother, women appear in the historical writings in a number of other, more specialized roles, occupations, and professions. Except in the case of the harlot, these are normally not alternatives to the wife-mother role, but represent complementary or supplementary activities. Foremost among these is the prophetess, of which the Old Testament canon knows three by name:[72] Deborah (Judg 4:4-16), in the premonarchic period; Huldah (2 Kgs 22:14-20), in the late monarchic period (seventh century B.C.E.); and Noadiah (Neh 6:14), in the postexilic period (fifth century B.C.E.). Too little is known about any of them to speak confidently or in detail about women in this role. But some general statements are possible. None of the authors who introduce these figures into their writings gives special attention to the fact that these prophets are women—in contrast to Old Testament commentators, who repeatedly marvel at the fact.[73] Despite some compounding in the traditions relating to Deborah and consequent difficulty in interpreting her role(s), the descriptions of the words and activities of the three named prophetesses coincide closely with those of their male contemporaries in the same profession. There is no evidence to suggest that they were considered unusual in this role.

But if female prophets were accepted in Israel, they were also rare. No collections of their words have survived among the prophetic books of the Old Testament—at least none identified by a woman's name. Discrimination might be argued, discrimination that was broken through only in the periods of national crisis, when the three known prophetesses emerged. But Israel knew other crises when no women arose to prophesy. Most likely, female prophets were always few in number, and presumably not associated with guilds and disciples who might have collected and preserved their oracles. Their exercise of their calling must have been at best part-time, at least during child-rearing years, and may not even have begun until later in life.[74] For the Israelite woman such a profession could only have been a second vocation. Early marriage, with its demand upon women of a primary vocation as wife and mother, would have excluded the early cultivation of the gift of prophecy.[75] But its authenticity was not

72. The enigmatic unnamed prophetess (*hannĕbîʾâ*) of Isa 8:3 is excluded from this analysis since nothing is known about her *prophetic* activity and her identity and role are disputed.

73. "Why did a chief priest inquire of a woman? And who was she? The question has been asked since at least Kimchi's day" (James A. Montgomery, *A Critical and Exegetical Commentary on the Books of Kings* [Edinburgh: T. & T. Clark, 1951] 525).

74. Deborah and Huldah are both referred to as married women; it is generally assumed that all women of marriageable age and condition were married.

75. This pattern may be contrasted with that of the prophet Jeremiah, who knew himself to have been called as a "youth" (Jer 1:7) and whose vocation obliged him to renounce normal family life (16:2). Other male prophets are known to have been married. But marriage

subject to doubt on the basis of sex. Prophecy was a charismatic gift, and as such, no respecter of persons. The person who had a message from God would be sought out, heeded, and accorded recognition if his/her message was understood to have validity. The message authenticated the messenger. The Old Testament accounts of female prophets are testimony to Israel's recognition that God could and did communicate with females as with males, entrusting to them messages of vital concern to the whole community.

Prophecy may be contrasted with cultic service as the only religious profession generally open to women throughout Israel's history. There are some suggestions that women did function in the cult of the earlier period: the portrayal of Miriam alongside the priestly figure of Aaron in Num 12:1-2,[76] and reference to "serving women" in the tent of meeting (Exod 38:8; cf. 1 Sam 2:22). But any early openness to women in the cult seems to have been foreclosed by a strong reaction during the period of the monarchy to the religious practices of Canaan, especially to fertility rites which involved female cult personnel. Thus the women referred to in association with the cult of the monarchic period are all described as illicit practitioners of non-Israelite rites.[77] Reference to female (temple) singers is found in works of the postexilic period (Ezra 2:65; Neh 7:67; 1 Chr 25:5), though they are associated there with the preexilic (and exilic) cult. This service, performed both by males and females, was in any case clearly auxiliary to the main cultic office.

Women were also recognized as practitioners of occult arts ("mediums" and "sorceresses"), though they were banned in Israel together with

---

was never considered a vocation for males, as it was for females, and would generally have interfered far less with their "choice" and exercise of a profession.

76. Her "punishment" (vv. 9-14), in which she is made cultically unclean and excluded from the holy camp, also suggests a cultic interpretation of her role. In Exod 15:20 she is described as a prophetess, but the meaning of the term for this early period is disputed. See Mic 6:4.

77. These included the qĕdēšâ ("holy/consecrated" woman) (Deut 23:18 [Heb.; Eng.: v. 17]; Hos 4:14; cf. Gen 38:21, 22) and devotees of the Canaanite mother goddess, Asherah* (2 Kgs 23:7). In addition to cult personnel, women are also singled out as worshipers of foreign gods in Ezek 8:14 (women weeping for Tammuz, a Sumerian god, whose death was annually lamented by women) and Jer 7:18; 44:17-19 (women making offerings to the Queen of Heaven, a female deity of Assyro-Babylonian or Canaanite provenance). It is significant that the syncretistic rites with which Israelite women were explicitly connected are associated solely with female deities or with deities whose cult was predominantly female. See Thorkild Jacobsen, *Toward the Image of Tammuz and Other Essays on Mesopotamian History and Culture* (Cambridge: Harvard University Press, 1970) 29, 73–101. Compare also the practice of Elephantine Jews, whose cult included a female deity. See Raphael Patai, *The Hebrew Goddess* (New York: Ktav, 1967); and W. F. Albright, *Archaeology and the Religion of Israel* (2d ed.; Baltimore: Johns Hopkins University Press, 1946). [*Recent discoveries and a growing literature during the past two decades make this characterization of Asherah as a "mother goddess" inadequate and suggest that she was also an Israelite goddess.]

their male counterparts (1 Sam 28:7; Exod 22:18; cf. Deut 18:10; 2 Chr 33:6).[78] The functioning of women in this capacity is analogous to that of the prophetess; the profession was in both cases based upon the exercise of a special "gift."[79] A related specialization of women, though less distinctly "professional," is illustrated by the "wise woman" (2 Sam 14:2; 20:16). The women so designated seem to have been noted especially for astute counsel, persuasiveness, and tact.[80] Their reputation, built upon demonstrated skill or the efficacy of their words, might extend well beyond the boundaries of their own towns (2 Sam 14:2). Thus wisdom was recognized as a gift that, like prophecy, was in no way restricted to men. It was honored and sought out wherever it manifested itself.

Other professional specializations of women (all part-time) were more closely related to the primary roles played by women in the society. These include professional mourners, or "keening women" (Jer 9:17), midwives (Gen 35:17; 38:28; Exod 1:15-21), and nurses (Ruth 4:16; 2 Sam 4:4; Gen 24:59; 35:8; Exod 2:7; 2 Kgs 11:2; 2 Chr 22:11). Female slaves or servants, particularly those of the king's household, were apparently trained in a variety of specialties, as "perfumers," bakers, and cooks (1 Sam 8:13). In addition to these, female singers are mentioned as entertainers in 2 Sam 19:35 and Eccl 2:8.

The hundreds of references to women in the historical and prophetic books present many and varied images. Central to most, however, and underlying all are the images of wife and mother (or wife-mother), with the harlot as a kind of wife surrogate or antiwife image. These two primary roles defined most women's lives, though in varying degrees and

78. The old law of Exod 22:18 refers to "sorcery" alone of the magic arts, citing it along with bestiality and sacrifice to other gods (vv. 19-20) as practices demanding death. The clause concerning sorcery stands out from the rest by its feminine formulation ("you shall not permit a sorceress to live"). The practice was presumably considered a female specialty at that time. The later list of seven proscribed types of magic or divination in Deut 18:10 is entirely masculine in its formulation (and probably inclusive in its intended reference). By this time, at least, sorcery and necromancy were clearly not regarded as exclusively female arts. See Isaac Mendelsohn, "Magic, Magician," *IDB* 3:223–25; "Familiar Spirit," *IDB* 2:237–38; and "Divination," *IDB* 1:856–58.

79. See Mendelsohn, "Magic," 224. The "gift" employed by the magicians consisted largely of special techniques, knowledge, or talismans that could be learned or acquired and passed on. As a consequence, sociological factors, including sexual distinctions, might be expected to play a larger role in the identification and classification of these manipulative artists than of the charismatics (prophets).

80. The adjective "wise" as applied to both men and women covers a wide variety of meanings and usages. While it frequently designates a class of counselors found in the court (see Judg 5:29, where it describes the ladies who counsel the queen mother of Sisera), it may also be used of persons skilled in various arts and crafts (such as the keening women of Jer 9:17 or the spinners of Exod 35:25), and may be used in an even broader sense of one who is prudent, discerning, capable in solving problems and in counseling profitable action. See Sheldon H. Blank, "Wisdom," *IDB* 4:852–61.

with varying meaning depending on the size, structure, function, and status of the particular family. That is, for most women the sexually determined roles of wife and mother also described their *work*, since the division of labor was based almost exclusively on sex. In the limited roles open to her, however, the ancient Israelite woman contributed more substantially and more significantly to the welfare of family and society than the modern Western woman in the same role. She was not simply a consumer, but a primary producer or manufacturer of much of the essential goods required by the household; in addition, she had charge of the basic education of the children. She apparently had considerable power, authority, and freedom of decision in this important realm that she managed,[81] and she could make significant decisions about her own life and that of her children (by religious vows, specifically)—though her husband (or father) was granted veto power in some cases.

While in certain limited circumstances a woman might be thought of only as a sexual object (Judg 5:30; 1 Kgs 1:2-4; see also Gen 19:8; Judg 19:24), nonsexual attributes predominate in most Old Testament references to women; in particular, intelligence, prudence, wisdom, tact, practical sense, and religious discernment recur in numerous characterizations of women, often replacing or preceding descriptions of physical appeal. The women of these texts are not depicted as silly or frivolous, except perhaps in the prophetic caricatures of the harlot or of the pampered ladies of the upper class (Isa 3:16—4:1; Amos 4:1). Women may be portrayed as unscrupulous, but they are rarely, if ever, characterized as foolish.

Despite the family locus of most of the woman's activity, the knowledge and abilities of women were not confined to the family circle or limited to expression in strictly female activities. The possession of special gifts and powers beneficial to the larger community was recognized and acknowledged in women as well as men, with the result that some professional specialization was possible for a few women along with their primary occupation of wife and mother. Most of these involved the exercise or employment of special kinds of knowledge: practical wisdom (the "wise women" of Tekoa and Abel); ability in deciding legal disputes (Deborah as judge); power to receive divine communications (Deborah as prophetess, Miriam, Huldah, and possibly Noadiah); and ability to call up spirits from the dead (the medium of Endor).

Judged by economic criteria or in terms of interest in continuity of house and name, the woman of the Old Testament was deemed inferior

---

81. As a consequence, it is women who are the saviors of men when the threat is felt within the house or living quarters, the woman's province (see Exod 1:15—2:10; Josh 2:1-7, 15-16; 1 Sam 19:11-17; 2 Sam 17:17-20; 2 Kgs 11:1-3). But the home can also be a battlefield if the woman chooses (Judg 4:18-21; 5:24-27; see also Judg 16:4-22).

to the man. In the realm of the cult her activity was restricted. And from the viewpoint of the law she was a minor and a dependent, whose rights were rarely acknowledged or protected. These several systems in which woman's roles and status have been described represent in large measure cultural givens, which cannot be ignored. They mark the baseline for any discussion of the image of Old Testament woman; but they do not describe all situations or all points of view.[82] In many situations the woman was in fact and/or in theory an equal, despite manifold and combined pressures to treat her as an inferior.[83] She was recognized as equal (or superior) in the possession and employment of certain kinds of knowledge and in religious sensibility and sensitivity. In love she might also be an equal,[84] and could exploit (Judg 16:4-22) as well as suffer exploitation. She was in general charged with the same religious and moral obligations as men, and she was held responsible for her acts.[85] Man in the Old Testament recognizes woman as one essentially like him, as a partner in pleasure and labor, one whom he needs, and one who can spell him weal or woe. From his point of view—the only point of view of the Old Testament texts—the woman is a helper, whose work as wife and mother is essential and complementary to his own. In a sense, she completes him—but as one with a life and character of her own. She is his opposite and equal.

The Image of Woman in the Accounts of Creation

Against the multitude of Old Testament references to women, actual and ideal, contemporary and past, the Bible has set two accounts of the first

82. Notably absent from all these references to women is any conscious reflection upon woman's place and being in society, including any theological interpretation of her purpose and portion.

83. The actual status of women is exceedingly difficult to judge in a patriarchal and patrilineal society, where systematic bias in favor of the male characterizes language, laws, and most formal structures and relationships. The compensation that necessarily exists in such a system is rarely visible in formal documents and is hard to assess. Whether formalized or informal, it generally serves to reinforce the system by making it bearable for those discriminated against. Thus the honoring of the mother is a necessary compensation, since the mother's role is an essential one to the maintenance of the society. Informal compensation is represented in the "underhanded" tactics used by women to get their way. But significant attempts were also made in Israel, against prevailing cultural norms, to recognize women as equals in the covenant community. Glimpses of this can be seen in some of the laws and especially in prophetic judgments (Hos 4:14) and prophetic eschatology (Joel 2:28-29 and Jer 31:32).

84. See especially the Song of Songs. Phyllis Trible ("Depatriarchalizing in Biblical Interpretation," 47) sees in these poems an expression of paradise regained, of the possibility of nonexploitative male-female relationship.

85. See, for example, the nondiscriminating laws and Isa 3:16—4:1; 32:9-12; Amos 4:1-3; Jer 44:20-30.

woman. Each belongs to a larger creation "story," and each shares many common features with similar accounts from the ancient Near East. In the mythopoeic world that was Israel's cradle accounts of origins did not simply explain what happened in the beginning; they were statements about the nature of things as they "are" (or as they should be). In the recitation or reenactment of the myth the original drama of creation was repeated and the present order of the world maintained through re-creation. Thus the Babylonian account of the creation of the world was a central feature in the liturgy of the New Year celebration, serving to insure that the forces of order (the created, present order) would prevail for another year over the forces of chaos (associated especially with the spring floods), and the account of the creation of mankind was the text of an incantation, recited by a midwife to assure a good birth.[86] The primary concern of a myth is not with the past but the present.

Israel's accounts of creation draw heavily upon the myths current at their times of composition. The same basic themes occur, the same developments—even the same language is used in some cases. But the meaning of the biblical accounts differs radically from that of their prototypes, because the context of their employment is different. The Genesis accounts are no longer myth, but history—or a prologue to history. Creation has become the first of a series of events that extend on down to the writer's own day. That intervening period is never wholly collapsed in the biblical view. Creation stands always and only at the beginning—remote, complete, unrepeatable, the first of God's works. The God who performed that work continues to labor and to act, but in new ways. History is the drama of the interaction of God and the world which he created, the world to which he gave a life and a will of its own. The creation stories tell of man's place in that created world of nature and of his-her essential character. This is spelled out in Genesis 3 by an account of the first acts taken by that autonomous creation.

While the two creation accounts of Genesis differ markedly in language, style, date, and traditions employed, their basic statements about woman are essentially the same: woman is, along with man, the direct and intentional creation of God and the crown of his creation. Man and woman were made for each other. Together they constitute humankind, which is in its full and essential nature bisexual.

The well-known word of the Priestly writer (P) in Gen 1:27 is eloquent and enigmatic in its terseness: "God created mankind ('ādām) in his own image . . . male (zākār) and female (nĕqēbâ) he created them." Two essen-

---

86. The text as it has been transmitted is complete with rubrics addressed to the midwife and the pregnant woman.

tial statements and that is all. No exposition is given, no consequences stated, only the prefatory statement in verse 26 proclaiming the intentionality of this creation. The first statement has as its primary point the assertion that the human animal is distinguished from all others in being modeled or patterned after God himself ("in his image" is an adverbial clause describing the process of fashioning). In contrast to the other creatures, man's primary bond is with God and not with the earth; man's purpose in creation is to rule the earth. The second major statement is an expansion and a specification of the first. It does not relate a subsequent act of creation, but only a subsequent thought of the narrator; and it does not explicate the meaning of the image. It simply makes the essential point that the species, ʾādām, is bisexual in its created nature.[87] There is no androgynous original creation in P.

The older, Yahwistic (J) account of creation in Genesis 2–3 is of a wholly different genre—a narrative. Here the art of the storyteller is seen in a work of great beauty and pathos, a narrative of beguiling simplicity, filled with yearning, compassion, and dramatic tension—the "soul" version of creation, in contrast to the cool cerebral account of the Priestly writer. In J's account the creation of man (ʾādām, deliberately ambiguous here)[88] is the beginning and the end of the story, with all of God's other creative acts bracketed in between. Here God's primary creation remains incomplete until, by a process of trial and error which populates the earth with creatures, that one is finally found for whom the man has waited and longed, namely, woman. With the creation of woman, man is finally his true self, a sexual and social being (ʾîš). J's account is a drama of the realization of the divine intention in creation.

The man in this creation drama recognizes the woman as his equal, as a "helper fit for him" (2:18). She is emphatically not his servant. "Helper" (ʿēzer) carries no status connotations, while the Hebrew expression translated "fit for" means basically "opposite" or "corresponding to." The statement simply expresses the man's recognition (the story is told from his point of view exclusively) that he needs her and that she is essentially like him. She is the "thou" that confronts him and the other that completes

87. The P formulation implies an essential equality of the two sexes. But its implications were only partially perceived by the Priestly writer, whose own culturally determined ideas concerning appropriate roles and activities of men and women generally fail to reflect this insight. Thus male genealogies and an exclusively male priesthood dominate the rest of his work.

88. ʾādām in Genesis 2 is both the species and the first individual, who appears as male and not androgynous, though the woman is formed from him. That he is conceived as a man in this naive version is clear from the statement concerning his loneliness (2:18); but he is not yet sexually aware. His true nature as a sexual being is manifest only as he is confronted by the woman. Thus he is at once truly male and truly [hu]man when joined by woman.

him. The story represents her as derived but not inferior. The fact that she is formed directly from the man is meant to emphasize the essential identity of man and woman. Woman is not a separate order of creation like the animals, each of which was created, like ʾādām, from the earth. The scientific and symmetrical language of P, with his concept of one species (ʾādām) in two sexes ("male" and "female"), is not used here, but the same idea is expressed in dynamic and dramatic language. The essential oneness of the two distinct persons (identified by the sociosexual terms "man" and "woman") is proclaimed in the man's recognition of and emotional response to the fact: "This one at last is bone of my bones and flesh of my flesh!"[89]

In J's work the drama of creation forms part of a larger story of origins. The Yahwist's word about man and woman in their essential nature is not finished with the simple statement of their existence or of the "original" state of their existence; it is spelled out, as the account of creation itself, in the language of events. The true nature or character of man and woman is revealed only as they begin to interact with each other and with their environment, as feeling, rational, and responsible beings. In this action/ interaction their latent capacity for judgment, for disobedience, and for self-interest is actualized, and the pain and frustration that the author knows as a mark of human existence becomes a part of the history of the first couple and of mankind.

The author of this well-known and often misinterpreted account shared the age-old notion that misery is a sign of sin or guilt. Mankind's suffering was therefore conceived as punishment. The crime that the Yahwist depicts is the crime of disobedience, a crime committed by both man and woman.[90] The order of their transgressing is unimportant for the question of their guilt; the consequences of their acts (knowledge, shame—and pain) are described only when *both* have eaten the forbidden fruit.[91] The manner and the explanation of the responses of the pair are

89. Gen 2:23; see also v. 24. In J's view the sexual act that unites man and woman is the sign of an intended and original union. The man and the woman do not simply exist alongside one another, as partners in work—though they are that; nor is their sexuality created primarily for procreation (as in P). They are created *for* each other, to complete each other. Their union in "one flesh" is a reunion. The fact that this is expressed by a man from his point of view should not obscure the basic intention and significance of the statement.

90. The crime is devoid of malicious intent, and is "softened" still further by the introduction of an instigator external to the man and woman. The serpent is the seducer, and he is made to bear the blame and punishment for the seduction. But the pair who succumbed to his tempting must pay the consequences of their common sin, the sin of disobeying the divine command.

91. The sequence of events in the narrative and the roles of the man and woman in it derive, presumably, from a much older story, whose basic characters and meaning have been radically transformed in this Israelite appropriation of it. See John S. Bailey, "Initiation and the Primal Woman in Gilgamesh and Genesis 2–3," *JBL* 89 (1970) 137–50.

also inconsequential for the question of their guilt and punishment. Each individually and knowingly disobeys the divine command. But the way in which their response is portrayed may be understood to indicate something of the author's—or the tradition's—view of the character of man and woman. The woman in this portrait responds to the object of temptation intellectually and reflectively, employing both practical and aesthetic judgment. The man, on the other hand, passively and unquestioningly accepts what the woman offers him.[92]

In their common act of disobedience the man and woman become fully human, identifiable with men and women of the author's own day. Losing their original innocence, they become knowledgeable, responsible, and subject to pain and the contradictions of life. The "punishment" described in the poem of 3:14-19 simply represents the characteristic burdens and pain of man and woman as traditionally perceived in Israelite society. Ample testimony is offered by other Old Testament texts that the pangs of childbirth were viewed as the most common and acute pain suffered by women. They were at the same time indicative of the woman's primary and essential work in the society—procreation. By no means an inclusive definition of her work, it was nevertheless that to which all other work and all other roles were subordinated. The man's pain is described analogously as related to his work—gaining a living from the soil. The work of the pair is here simply described as the work of survival, biological (the work of the female) and material (the work of the male). But it is not simply the pain of toil that the author describes, it is the pain of alienation in that toil. The ground, the source of the man's life and work, has become his antagonist rather than his helper, and the man, the source of the woman's life and work, has become her ruler rather than her friend.[93]

The words of Genesis 3 are descriptive, not prescriptive. J's story of the

---

92. In Trible's characterization ("Depatriarchalizing in Biblical Interpretation," 13) the man's one act is "belly-oriented," while the response of the woman is that of a theologian. I doubt that the minimal description given here of the man's response can support substantial inferences concerning the character of the man. According to Trible, "the man is passive, brutish, and inept," in contrast to the woman, who is "intelligent, sensitive, and ingenious" (ibid.). The man acts here in his normal role at mealtime: he accepts the food offered to him by his wife. No qualification is necessary of the general rule of male dominance in a patriarchal society. More important, however, is the fuller description of the woman's response. It, too, presents a picture that is consonant with the portrait of woman found in other Old Testament sources, where she is indeed "intelligent, sensitive, and ingenious."

93. The ambiguity in human existence and the interrelatedness of pleasure and pain are more clearly shown in the case of the woman, since her work is described in relational terms. That definition is given in the culture and the tradition with which the author had to work. The focus of this passage is upon the couple's work, not upon the male-female relationship. Consequently, the asymmetry in the description of the man's and the woman's lot should not be overinterpreted. The man's desire for the woman is quite as prominent in this author's mind (2:23-24) as the woman's desire for the man (3:16).

first couple is heavily etiological; it offers an explanation for the primary characteristics of the human situation as Israel knew it. And this minimal statement shows substantial agreement with the fuller account gleaned from other Old Testament writings. But it is not normative. Israel did not use this legend to justify the existing order or to argue for woman's subordination. She did not need to. She understood the states described— for both man and woman—as givens. J's view was larger than the common one, however, and marked by a profound sense of the wrongness of this order: given, but not willed, the tragic consequence of man's exercise of his-her God-given reason and will. This was also not J's final word about the human situation. In its present setting the story has lost much of its etiological significance, for it is no longer simply a description of things as they are but is the first act in a world-historical drama that the historian has created as the context for Israel's history. For J, the central figure in that drama is Yahweh, God, who continues to will, to act, and to create. Adam and Eve are the beginning of his works, not the end. Yahweh goes on in a play of many acts to create a new people and to enter into a new relationship with them.

It is with that same understanding of the dynamic character of history that the prophets speak of God's continued action in their own day, an action portrayed typically as judgment upon a people who had replaced theological norms with sociological ones (security, status, wealth, etc.). Neither the prophets nor the theologians, such as J and P, succeeded in wholly escaping the culturally determined understanding of male and female roles that they had inherited. And their greater egalitarianism should not be too sharply contrasted with the overtly discriminatory laws and practices recorded in other Old Testament literature, since there, too, male-dominated language and structures disguised to a considerable degree the actual power, freedom, and respect of women in the society— respect based largely, though not solely, upon complementarity of roles. But distinctions of all types lend themselves to exploitation and to the creation of differential ethical standards. The historians of the Old Testament look behind the present state of division and alienation to an original and intended equality and harmony in creation, while the prophets focus upon the existing state of inequality and exploitation, addressing it with a concept of justice manifested in judgment—justice understood as a new act that God will perform to purge his creation, an act of retribution and rectification. The proud will be abased (Isa 4:17), and the "men of distinction" will head the exile train (Amos 6:4-7); but she who is now an outcast in men's eyes will not be punished for her sin (Hos 4:14).

Some among the prophets saw beyond the present day, beyond the present order and the impending judgment. They looked to a new act of

God in creation, to a new order with new possibilities for human existence, radical possibilities that would abolish the present alienation and exploitation based on distinctions of species, age, sex, and social status. These prophetic visions speak of the knowledge of God in every heart, requiring no class of teachers to expound it (Jer 31:31-34); of God's spirit free to all, so that old and young, male and female, bond and free shall prophesy (Joel 2:28-29); of lion and lamb, wild beast and helpless child living together in harmony and without fear (Isa 11:6-9); and the reversal of the prevailing sexual roles: "a woman protects a man" (Jer 31:22).[94]

The statements concerning the first man and woman must be read together with the statements of God's interaction with the world of his creation, his promises and his demands, his sending of saviors and spokesmen (both male and female), his judgments, his forgiveness, and his new creation. Israel's best statements about woman recognize her as an equal with man, and with him jointly responsible to God and to cohumanity. That Israel rarely lived up to this vision is all too apparent, but the vision should not be denied.

94. Literally, "a woman encompasses a man." See William L. Holladay, "Jer. 31:22b Reconsidered: 'The Woman Encompasses the Man,'" *VT* 16 (1966) 236–39.

2

WOMEN
(OLD TESTAMENT)

Terminology

THE COMMON HEBREW TERM FOR "WOMAN" IS *'iššâ* (CONSTRUCT *'ēšet*), which may also be translated "wife" (the corresponding masculine term, *'îš*, "man," is used analogously for "husband," along with *ba'al*, "master," "lord"). Women characterized by particular attributes are designated by descriptive nouns, adjectives, or participles, used either alone or as a qualifier to *'iššâ*: for example, (*'iššâ*) *zônâ*, "prostitute," *hôrâ*, "pregnant woman," *'iššâ ḥăkāmâ*, "wise woman," (*'iššâ*) *zārâ*, "strange/foreign woman," *zĕqēnôt*, "old women," *mĕyallĕdôt*, "midwives" (lit. "birthing women"). Other nouns describing women of particular age, state, or position include *bat*, "daughter"; *kallâ*, "daughter-in-law," "bride"; *'āḥôt*, "sister"; *'ēm*, "mother"; *bĕtûlâ*, "young woman," "virgin"; *'almâ*, "young woman"; *na'ărâ*, "young woman," "girl"; *'āmâ* and *šipḥâ*, "female servant or slave"; *malkâ*, "queen"; *gĕbîrâ*, "lady," "queen mother." The term for the female of human as well as animal species is *nĕqēbâ* (typically paired with *zākār*, "male," as in Gen 1:27).

Methodological Considerations

In the Hebrew Bible women appear for the most part as minor or subordinate figures; yet they play an essential role in the record of Israel's faith

---

Originally published in *ABD* 6:951–57. Bibliographical references originally included in the text of the article have been transferred to footnotes in this edition, with the result that the footnote numbers no longer correspond to those of the original publication. Items in the bibliography appended to the original article but not cited in footnotes are listed as "Supplementary Bibliography" at the end of this article. Cross-references to articles that are reprinted in this volume are indicated by an asterisk in square brackets following the original page number.

and include some of the best-remembered actors in the biblical story. The names of Sarah, Rebekah, Rachel, Miriam, Deborah, and Ruth are indispensable to the rehearsal of that story, as are Jezebel, Esther, and Eve. Behind these, however, stand thousands of unnamed, and unnoted, women who have engaged the attention of recent biblical scholarship. Through new literary and sociological analyses attempts are being made to reconstruct Israel's history and reinterpret its literature with an aim to restoring a glimpse of the missing women and reassessing the surviving portraits.

Key to understanding the roles, images, and limited appearances of women in the Old Testament literature is the patrilineal and patriarchal organization of Israelite society and its family-centered economy. Although the patriarchal character of the society has long been recognized, recent scholarhip has given new insight into the economic, social, and psychological dimensions of gender relations in patriarchal societies and, more specifically, into women's lives in premodern agrarian and pastoral societies, bringing a new comparative perspective to the biblical data.[1]

The Old Testament is the product of a patriarchal world, and more specifically, of a literate, urban elite of male religious specialists. Whatever the ultimate origin of its traditions in family worship, clan wisdom, popular tales, or the songs of women, the present form of the Hebrew Bible is the work of male authors and editors, whose views created or reflect the dominant theological perspectives. Women in the biblical texts are presented through male eyes, for purposes determined by male authors. This does not mean that women are necessarily suppressed in the account or portrayed unsympathetically. It does mean, however, that women are not heard directly in the biblical text, in their own voices; the Old Testament gives no unmediated access to the lives and thought of Israelite women.[2]

Women in the biblical text provide the primary clues to women behind the text. But interpretation of these clues requires knowledge of women's lives in comparable societies, ancient and modern, where fuller documentation of the private and economic spheres offers a broader view of

---

1. Summarized in Carol Meyers, *Discovering Eve: Ancient Israelite Women in Context* (New York and Oxford: Oxford University Press, 1988) 3–46.

2. For implications and strategies in interpreting androcentric texts see Letty M. Russell, ed., *Feminist Interpretation of the Bible* (Philadelphia: Westminster, 1985); Mary Ann Tolbert, "Defining the Problem: The Bible and Feminist Hermeneutics," in idem, ed., *The Bible and Feminist Hermeneutics* (*Semeia* 28; Chico, Calif.: Scholars Press, 1983) 113–26; Adela Yarbro Collins, ed., *Feminist Perspectives on Biblical Scholarship* (Chico, Calif.: Scholars Press, 1985); Katharine Doob Sakenfeld, "Feminist Perspectives on Bible and Theology: An Introduction to Selected Issues and Literature," *Int* 42 (1988) 5–18; idem, "Feminist Biblical Interpretation," *TToday* 46 (1989) 154–68; Phyllis Trible, "Five Loaves and Two Fishes: Feminist Hermeneutics and Biblical Theology," *TS* 50 (1989) 279–95; and Peggy L. Day, ed., *Gender and Difference in Ancient Israel* (Minneapolis: Fortress Press, 1989).

women's roles and activities within the context of the larger society. New archaeological investigation focusing on family and village life (size and arrangement of dwelling, density of settlement, diet, mortality rates, etc.)[3] together with documents from surrounding cultures relating to the domestic realm (e.g., personal letters, marriage and adoption contracts, inheritance stipulations, and other economic and legal documents)[4] enable construction of a more adequate picture of women's roles, activities, and authority within ancient Near Eastern patriarchal society and, more particularly, within the family, which is the primary sphere of women's activity.

To these data from the social world of ancient Israel comparative anthropology brings a cross-cultural perspective of gender roles and relationships that correlates patterns of gender interactions with techno-economic and sociopolitical variables, such as differences between pastoral and agrarian societies, between intensive irrigation agriculture in lowland plains and cultivation of new or marginal upland areas, and between tribal federations and centralized monarchic states. Such differences within the broad category of patriarchal societies are reflected in differing demands for women's productive and reproductive labor and differences in the value of women's services, range of activity outside the home, and authority within the family.[5] Anthropological study of gender reveals complex patterns of male-female relationships within patriarchal societies, involving distinctions of formal and informal power and recognition of spheres of influence and authority, which require qualification of many commonly held views of women's lives in ancient Israel.

The Old Testament does not yield a single portrait of women in ancient Israel. Its millennium-spanning traditions and the differing purposes and perspectives of its authors have produced a kaleidoscopic image, whose distinct components require note. A common status or lifestyle cannot be assumed for the woman of an Early Iron Age pioneer settlement, the wife of a wealthy merchant or large landowner in Samaria or Jerusalem, the daughter of an indebted eighth-century peasant, the foreign wife of a returned exile, a priest's daughter, queen mother, palace servant, childless widow, or prostitute. Nor can one expect a common portrait from narra-

---

3. Lawrence A. Stager, "The Archaeology of the Family in Ancient Israel," *BASOR* 260 (1985) 1–36; Meyers, *Discovering Eve*, 47–71.

4. Barbara S. Lesko, ed., *Women's Earliest Records: From Ancient Egypt and Western Asia*, Proceedings of the Conference on Women in the Ancient Near East, Brown University, Providence, Rhode Island, November 5–7, 1987 (BJS 166; Atlanta: Scholars Press, 1989); Jean-Marie Durand, ed., *Les Femmes dans le Proche Orient Antique*, XXVIIIe Rencontre Assyriologique Internationale, Paris, 1986 (Paris: Éditions Recherche sur les Civilisations, 1987).

5. Martin K. Whyte, *The Status of Women in Preindustrial Societies* (Princeton: Princeton University Press, 1978); Meyers, *Discovering Eve*, 24–26, 189–94.

tive compositions, proverbial sentences, prophetic oracles, and legal stipulations.

Behind the disparate images and distinct life histories, however, lies a common set of expectations and values that govern the life of every Israelite woman of every period and circumstance. These are rooted in the need for women's labor in the domestic sphere, and more specifically in childbearing and nurture, broadly described as "reproductive" work. To this primary work, which was the expectation of every woman, are joined the major tasks of household management and provision. The importance of this work in a society in which the family, rather than the individual, was the basic social, economic, and religious unit (at least during significant periods of Israelite history), is evidenced in the honor and authority given to women in their role as mother. Fulfillment of that socially demanded, and rewarded, role also meant self-fulfillment for most women, for whom barrenness was a bitter deprivation.

It is the woman's primary and essential role within the family, with its multiple demands of time and skill, that accounts for her highest personal and social reward—but also for her restriction in roles and activities outside the family and her hiddenness in documents from the public sphere. It also accounts for changes in women's status and roles over the course of Israel's history as the size, autonomy, and economic status of the family changed. And it provides clues to the interpretation of women's roles and activities outside the family, which may be understood in large measure as extensions or adaptations of women's primary roles within the family.

The Israelite Family

The Israelite family was in all periods a male-headed household (called *bêt ʾāb*, "house of the father"), in which descent and transmission of property (in particular, the patrimonial land, *naḥălâ*, "inheritance") were reckoned through males. In early Israel, family associations (lineages, or "clans") and tribes based on patrilineal descent exercised primary political as well as social functions. Although the monarchy deprived the lineage system of most of its political power, the Israelite family continued to function as the basic social and economic unit and to bear a patrilineal and patriarchal stamp, exhibited in patterns of organization and authority, marriage, place of residence, and inheritance.

One consequence of patrilineal organization is that women are to some extent either aliens or transients within their family of residence. Married women are outsiders in the household of their husband and sons, while daughters are prepared from birth to leave their father's household and transfer loyalty to a husband's house and lineage. Preference for endogamy seems to have operated in certain periods as a means of reducing the strains associated with the "alien" wife (Gen 24:4; 28:1-2). When the woman was a foreigner, the strain might be perceived as a threat, as seen in the repeated condemnations of foreign marriages (Deut 7:3; Ezra 9:12; 10:2). Underlying this attack is the assumption that the foreign wife will maintain her alien ways, and more particularly her religion, undermining the religious ethos and solidarity of the family and the nation (Exod 34:16; Num 25:1-2; Deut 7:4; Judg 3:5-6; Neh 13:23-27).[6]

The Old Testament attack on foreign wives is indirect testimony to the independence and power of women within the family sphere despite the formal structures and symbols of patriarchal power. It reflects the power of influence that wives may exert over husbands (Judg 14:17; 1 Kgs 1:15-21) as well as the important educational role of the mother in transmitting basic religious values and wisdom essential for life (Prov 1:8; 31:1). It also reflects fear of foreigners, and more particularly the foreign woman ('iššâ zārâ, nokrîyâ), who in Proverbs becomes a symbol for the immoral, seductive, and predatory woman, an embodiment of evil.[7] Admonitions against intermarriage with foreigners may include reference to sons as well as daughters, but only the foreign daughter is described as a threat (Deut 7:3-4; cf. Ezra 9:2).

Another consequence of patrilineal family organization is that women do not normally inherit land. Exceptions treat daughters as placeholders in the absence of sons (Num 27:1-11), bridging the gap between the generations until their sons can resume the paternal line and legacy (insured, according to Num 36:6-9, by requiring the daughter to marry within her father's tribe). Similar concern for the preservation of the patrimony appears to underlie the institution of levirate marriage, which obligated a man to marry the wife of a deceased brother (Deut 25:5-10; Gen 38:8) or close kinsman (Ruth 2:20; 4:5-6) in order to continue the brother's "name."

The importance of patrilineal organization in ancient Israel may be seen in the prominence of genealogies and genealogical narratives in the Old Testament. The genealogies, which serve a variety of social, political, and literary functions, account for the majority of personal names recorded in the Old Testament and for the great preponderance of male over female names (1212:108, approximately 12:1). As lists of those who "counted" in the society, these normally all-male lists provide dramatic testimony to the androcentrism that characterizes the formal structures of patriarchal societies. A different picture is obtained, however, by com-

---

6. Meyers, *Discovering Eve*, 185.
7. Gale A. Yee, "'I Have Perfumed My Bed with Myrrh': The Foreign Woman ('iššâ zārâ) in Proverbs 1–9," *JSOT* 43 (1989) 53–68.

paring the common nouns for "man" (*'îš*) and "woman" (*'iššâ*), whose ratio of occurrences is 2160:775,[8] or roughly 3:1. Excluding the many generic uses of *'îš* (as, e.g., in Ps 1:1, "Blessed is the one [*'îš*] who walks . . .") increases the relative weight of references to women, suggesting the importance of women as a social category, if not as named individuals.

A characteristic feature of patriarchal societies, illustrated by the disparity of ratios between named and unnamed men and women, is asymmetry of gender roles and symbols, including language. Male genealogies, male-oriented legal codes and cultic stipulations, masculine forms for generic speech, and the predominance of males in historical records and recollections all reflect the male dominance of Israel's public life and formal structures. The primary social and economic unit, however, which provided the basis for life in the public sphere, was the family, in which women exercised significant formal and informal power, at times equaling or even exceeding that of men, according to some scholars.[9] Even in its reduced economic role under the monarchy, the family continued to play a dominant role in socialization.

Asymmetry between male and female-centered spheres of life may be seen in the fact that the family was represented in the public sphere by its male head or adult male members—and it is this male-dominated sphere that is the locus of the major overarching and integrating institutions of the society. Here women are to some degree always outsiders, characterized by temporary appearances (e.g., marketing, legal process, payment of vows) or marginal roles (e.g., prostitutes and cult attendants). At the same time, men are given legal authority over women, even in the sphere of women's primary activity, the family. Moreover, since the legal and religious institutions that give expression to the society's values and attempt to regulate behavior belong to the public sphere and are designed and governed by men, the values they articulate and seek to enforce are essentially male values, though formulated in general or universal terms. Thus asymmetry between the primary spheres of male and female activity has the character of encapsulation and penetration of the domestic sphere by the public sphere.

Primary Roles and Images

Wife and Mother

The life and work of the Israelite woman centered in the home and duties to family. The ideal portrait of the adult female depicts her as the mother

8. *HALAT,* 1:41, 90.
9. Meyers, *Discovering Eve,* 181, 187.

of many children (or sons; Heb. *bānîm* [pl. of *bēn*, "son"] may have either meaning) and the wise and industrious manager of the household, providing for the welfare of husband and children (Prov 31:10-29). This latter image, which gives rare attention to the role of wife, is the product of wisdom reflection designed to counsel men concerning the path of success in life, in which knowledge of women and their ways plays a critical role. Thus the book of Proverbs warns against the loose or foreign woman and especially the adulteress, who can cost a man his life (Prov 5:3-5; 6:24-35; 9:13-19), while counseling fidelity (5:15-19) and extolling the "woman of worth" (*'ēšet ḥayil*) in detailed and extended commendation (Prov 31:10-29). Such a wife will "do him good, and not harm" (v. 12). Emphasis in this portrait is on skill, resourcefulness, industry, wisdom, and charity, rather than fertility or beauty (the latter characterized in v. 30 as "deceitful" and "vain").

The role of wife is rarely separated from the dominant role of mother, appearing outside the wisdom literature primarily in tales of courtship, conflict, and conquest (Judges 14; 1 Sam 18:20-27; Genesis 34). Here sexual attraction plays a role, but also wit and will (1 Samuel 25)—and often family or ethnic ties. Behind many scenes of courtship lies a genealogical theme, which points to an ultimate role of mother. The woman as wife also describes a fundamental biosocial category, designating the one who provides the essential sexual and social complement to the man, creating the pair that represents the species (Gen 1:27; 2:18-23) and assures its continuity (thus Noah and his sons [named] enter the ark together with his wife and sons' wives [unnamed], Gen 7:13). Here, too, the wife is usually a mother.

The role of mother dominates Old Testament references to women. Motherhood was expected and honored, reflecting social need (Judg 21:16-17) and divine sanction (Gen 1:28). Desire for many children, and especially sons, is a prominent Old Testament theme (1 Sam 2:7; Gen 30:1; Pss 127:3-5; 128:3-4), attributed to women as well as to men, despite the pain and dangers of childbirth. Rooted in the economic needs of subsistence agriculture and social need for perpetuation of the lineage, the demand for childbearing was rewarded with security and prestige (Deut 5:16; 27:16). As a consequence, women identified children with status (Gen 30:20; 1 Sam 1:2-8) and sometimes vied with one another in childbearing (Gen 30:1-24).

Barrenness was viewed as the ultimate disgrace, understood as a sign of divine disfavor (Gen 30:23; 2 Sam 6:20-23). (The literary theme of the barren wife—who subsequently bears—assumes this negative expectation in order to reverse it.) The barren, or childless, woman suffered not only lack of esteem, but also threat of divorce or expulsion from her husband's household at his death. Unable to continue his line, she cannot claim his inheritance, and she has no sons to support her in old age.

The role of mother included primary care of children of both sexes at least until the time of weaning (about age three), the education and disciplining of older children, and provision of food and clothing for the entire household. The latter requires arduous and time-consuming labor: sorting, cleaning, parching, and grinding grain, as well as kneading and baking bread; drawing water and collecting fuel (a task of both sexes); cleaning and butchering small animals; milking, churning butter, and making cheese and yogurt; tending vegetable gardens and fruit trees; and preserving fruits and meat for storage. Women may also have produced at least some of the common ceramic ware, as suggested by cross-cultural study of ceramic production.[10] If so, Old Testament references to male potters (Jer 18:2-4; 1 Chr 4:23) may be seen as an example of a widely attested pattern of male professional specialization of crafts originally practiced exclusively by women. Such crafts may continue as female occupations within the domestic context while men dominate commercial production (e.g., weaving, sewing/tailoring, cooking and baking).

Clothing the family involved not only spinning, weaving, tailoring, and sewing, but also preparation of raw wool or flax fibers (Prov 31:13). Spinning and weaving are identified throughout the ancient Mediterranean world as symbolic of female domestic activity and skill, so that even queens and wealthy women are depicted holding a spindle[11] (Prov 31:13, 19; Judg 16:14; cf. English "spinster" and "distaff side"). The mother, together with other females of the household, also bore the burden of washing and cleaning.

The mother's role in the socialization and moral instruction of small children was critical for both sexes, but her instruction seems also to have had a more formal and extended character, even in the education of sons, as attested in the wisdom literature (Prov 1:8; 31:1).[12] An extension of the mother's role as teacher and counselor may be seen in the "wise woman," whose skill (in negotiation and persuasion) commands public recognition (2 Sam 14:1-20; 20:16-22). The mother also had a special role in educating daughters in the traits and competencies expected of the adult woman (wife), as well as in specialized female skills.

Among the features that make up the Old Testament's portrait of women there appears to be a primary cluster of attributes and images that derive ultimately from association with birthing and nurture, or womb

10. Ibid., 148.
11. *ANEP*, 43 pl. 144.
12. Meyers, *Discovering Eve*, 151–52.

and breasts[13] (Luke 11:27; 23:27). The pain and danger of childbirth has stamped itself on the consciousness of the Old Testament's male narrators and poets, who employ images of women in labor as symbols of anguish and helplessness (Isa 13:8; 21:3; Jer 48:41; Mic 4:9-10). A different type of maternal pain is associated with the death of a child, formalized in the ritual wailing of women at funerals and in the specialized female profession of keener, performer, and composer of dirges (Jer 9:16, 19 [Eng. 9:17, 20]). The mother's bond with the fruit of her womb is understood as deep and persisting (Isa 49:15), overriding self-interest (1 Kgs 3:16-27) and extending even beyond death, as exemplified in Rizpah's vigil over her slain sons (2 Sam 21:8-14), protecting them in death (a female role) as she could not do in life (a male role). It is also evidenced in the customary roles of women in preparing the dead for burial and in visits to tombs (Mark 16:1; cf. Luke 23:55—24:1).

Care for the dead may be seen as an extension of the mother's primary role in care for the living, initiated in the nursing of infants (1 Sam 1:22; cf. Num 11:12; Isa 45:15) and continued in nursing of the sick and infirm (2 Sam 13:5; 1 Kgs 1:2; 2 Kgs 4:18-30). If the feeling of tenderness toward the weak expressed as "compassion" or "pity" is attributed to fathers (e.g., Ps 103:13) as well as mothers, the Hebrew etymology of the term identifies it as "womb-feeling" (raḥămîm; verb rāḥam < reḥem, "womb").

As the female head of a household or family unit within an extended household, the mother supervised the work of dependent females, including daughters, daughters-in-law, and servants. Although there is no direct evidence for the way in which multiple wives shared responsibilities of household management (narrative and legal texts focus on rivalry and favoritism: Deut 21:15-17; Gen 29:30-31; 1 Sam 1:6; cf. Exod 21:10), some form of seniority system may be assumed, especially where a second wife had the status of a concubine. Each woman, however, would have control over her own children. Normally a woman gained authority with age, together with a measure of freedom and leisure, although there is no recognized role for women comparable to that of the male "elders." It is likely that many of the specialized roles and activities of women outside the home or involving public recognition and action (prophets, mediums, wise women, keeners, midwives) were performed by older women no longer burdened by the care of small children (e.g., the wise woman of Tekoa plausibly presents herself as a widow with grown children [2 Sam 14:4-7]). Cross-cultural studies attest increased religious activity and authority, including new religious roles, on the part of postmenopausal women or women with grown children.

13. Cf. *ANEP*, 162 pl. 469.

Virgin Daughter or Bride

Alongside the image of the mother is another image that represents both a prior state and an alternative or complementary ideal of the feminine, viz., the virgin daughter or bride. In this portrait female sexuality is described in erotic rather than maternal terms. The subject is the young woman who is sexually ripe and ready for love, who may be designated *bĕtûlâ*, "virgin," *'almâ*, "young woman," "maiden," *kallâ*, "bride," or, in the conventions of ancient Near Eastern love poetry, *'āḥôt*, "sister" (Cant 4:9). She may be a young wife or an unmarried woman. She is described as the object of male desire (Canticles 4), but also as one who seeks a man's embrace (Cant 3:1-4). The ultimate tragedy of the death of Jephthah's daughter is expressed in the notice that "she had never known a man" (Judg 11:39). The bride is praised for her beauty (Gen 12:11, 15; 24:16; 1 Sam 25:3; Cant 4:1-5), fragrance, and adornment (Cant 4:10-11; Isa 61:10; cf. 3:16, 18-24), in which she also takes delight (Cant 2:1-2; Jer 2:32). Although little of the rich erotic metaphor of the love songs is found in the restrained language of the courtship narratives, both share the ideal of the virgin bride as ripe and unblemished fruit, or fair and chaste (Cant 4:10-13, 16; Gen 24:16). The same ideal viewed from the perspective of male control underlies the legal stipulations regarding women's sexuality.

In the love poetry of the Song of Songs sex is free and freely given; but in Israelite society, as every society, it was not free. Patrilineal and patriarchal interests demanded exclusive right for men to their wives' sexuality. A woman's sexuality was consequently guarded before marriage by her father (Deut 22:13-21, 28-29; cf. Gen 34:5-7) and after marriage by her husband (Num 5:11-31). Adultery was the most serious of women's crimes, though both partners received the same sentence—death (Lev 20:10; Deut 22:22). Proverbs identifies the adulteress with the evil/dangerous woman (Prov 5:24; 7:10-23)[14]—while the adulterer is portrayed as a weak and foolish victim, succumbing to her advances (Prov 6:32; 7:7-13, 21-27; 9:13-18). In prophetic metaphor the promiscuous bride, likened at times to a professional prostitute, becomes a symbol of apostate Israel (Hos 1–3; 4:10, 12, 17-18; Jer 3:1-3; Ezekiel 16; 23).

Prostitution in ancient Israel (Gen 38:13-26; 1 Kgs 3:16-27; Amos 7:17; Prov 23:27) is characterized by the same ambivalence attested in other cultures.[15] It exemplifies the asymmetry of sexual relations in patriarchal societies, also exhibited in the "double standard" respecting premarital sex

14. Yee, "I Have Perfumed My Bed," 61.
15. Phyllis A. Bird, "The Harlot as Heroine: Narrative Art and Social Presupposition in Three Old Testament Texts," in Miri Amihai, George W. Coats, and Anne M. Solomon, eds., *Narrative Research on the Hebrew Bible* (*Semeia* 46; Atlanta: Scholars Press, 1989) 121–22, 131–33 [*201–02].

(Deut 23:28-29) and the male prerogative of divorce (Deut 24:1). Prostitution allows men to maintain exclusive control of their wives' sexuality while providing opportunity for sexual relations with other women without violating another man's rights. The prostitute, who supplies this service for her livelihood, is a social outcast, who is generally forced into the profession by destitution or loss of parents or spouse.[16]

Roles and Activities outside the Family

Women's roles and activities outside their household-centered work were of two types, assistance in the basic tasks of production (agriculture and animal husbandry), and specialized professions and services. Women's contribution to the primary work of production is difficult to determine; it fluctuated not only in relation to seasonal need, but also to geographic, demographic, technological, and political factors (e.g., drought, war, and disease). Meyers argues that the peculiar ecological conditions of a frontier society demanded intensification of female labor in both productive and reproductive tasks during the early settlement period—with corresponding heightening of female status.[17] Radically altered circumstances in later periods will have produced different patterns of participation and reward. Scanty data for all periods, however, make inferences hazardous. There is textual evidence for women's involvement in harvesting (Ruth 2, where male and female workers form distinct groups) and in tending flocks (Gen 29:9; Exod 2:16).

Women's work in clothing their households or in other types of domestic production may lead to limited commercial development in manufacture for sale (Prov 31:24); women's cottage industry may be associated with urban growth. Specialized female labor was also employed by the palace, whose workforce of female slaves or impressed servants included perfumers, cooks, and bakers (1 Sam 8:13). One well-attested type of professional specialization is service to other women, best exemplified by the midwife (Exod 1:15-21), who in other ancient Near Eastern cultures was a religious specialist as well as a medical technician.

Religious Life

Little is known of women's religious life in ancient Israel, except what is depicted in conjunction with men's activities (1 Sam 1:13-18) or high-

---

16. Bird, ibid., 120–22, 129–33 [*199–202].
17. Meyers, *Discovering Eve*, 50–63.

lighted by explicit mention of women in collective references (Neh 8:2; cf. Deut 16:11, 13, where the wife is assumed in the masculine singular address to the male household). Inferred participation of women in activities ascribed to the "people" or "congregation" or formulated in "generic" masculine terms expands the picture, but may not represent women's actual participation, which may be limited or peripheral. Women's religious activity may also take other forms hidden from the communal record.[18] One area of women's lives given explicit ritual attention is that related to procreation, with prescriptions for purification following menstruation and childbirth (Lev 15:25-30; 12:1-8).

Evidence of women's magic, or devotion, is seen by many scholars in the small clay plaques or figurines of a naked female found throughout Iron Age excavations. Interpreted either as amulets to aid in conception or birth (especially those depicting a pregnant woman) or as representations of a "mother goddess," these mass-produced images appear in both domestic and (peripheral) cultic sites. Although generally identified with women's practice, their precise meaning and use remain uncertain, due to the variety of forms, changing styles, and lack of clear correspondence to objects mentioned in the biblical text.[19]

Within the sphere of public religious practice women specialists are attested in several roles, especially in sources for the premonarchic period. They include women who ministered at the entrance to the tent of meeting (Exod 38:8; 1 Sam 2:22); prophets, of whom three are named: Deborah (Judg 4:4-16), Huldah (2 Kgs 22:14-20), and Noadiah (Neh 6:14); and "consecrated women" (qĕdēšôt), usually described as "cultic prostitutes" and associated with Canaanite-type cultic practices (Hos 4:14; Deut 23:19-20). Miriam, though identified as a prophet in Exod 15:20, appears to have exercised some form of cultic leadership.[20]

18. Phyllis A. Bird, "The Place of Women in the Israelite Cultus," in Patrick D. Miller, Jr., Paul D. Hanson, and S. Dean McBride, eds., *Ancient Israelite Religion: Essays in Honor of Frank Moore Cross* (Philadelphia: Fortress Press, 1987) 408–10 [*99–101].

19. James B. Pritchard, *Palestinian Figurines in Relation to Certain Goddesses Known through Literature* (AOS 24; New Haven: American Oriental Society, 1943); M. D. Fowler, "Excavated Figurines: A Case for Identifying a Site as Sacred?" *ZAW* 97 (1985) 333–44; James S. Holladay, Jr., "Religion in Israel and Judah under the Monarchy: An Explicitly Archaeological Approach," in Miller, Hanson, and McBride, *Ancient Israelite Religion,* 275–80; Urs Winter, *Frau und Göttin: Exegetische und ikonographische Studien zum weiblichen Gottesbild im Alten Israel und in dessen Umwelt* (OBO 53; Freiburg: Universitäts Verlag; Göttingen: Vandenhoeck & Ruprecht, 1983) 96–134.

20. Rita J. Burns, *Has the Lord Indeed Spoken Only through Moses? A Study of the Biblical Portrait of Miriam* (SBLDS 84; Atlanta: Scholars Press, 1987) 39–79.

Legal Status

Women's legal status is a function of the larger system of social values and needs, and it cannot be isolated or absolutized. As it can be inferred from the Old Testament's disparate and partial sources, it may be characterized as generally subordinate to that of males. This is evidenced in women's "hiddenness" as legal persons behind the male citizen or husband addressed by the law (Exod 20:3-17; Deut 16:4); in indirect (third person) reference to women within masculine-formulated direct address (Exod 20:17), or in literary subordination to a male subject (Exod 21:3; Jer 44:25); in limitation of women's right in conflicts of interest (Num 30:3-8), and in generally circumscribed rights and duties in the public sphere. Apart from the treatment of vows and suspected adultery (both cases involving extrafamilial interests), Old Testament laws do not generally treat intrafamilial relationships. Parental authority over unruly children was invested in both parents (Deut 21:18-20) and also, apparently, responsibility for a daughter's chastity (Deut 22:15)—though the father alone represents his daughter "in court." As a general rule, women within the family were subject to male authority, as either daughters or wives. Only widows, divorced women (Num 30:9), and prostitutes (Josh 6:22) had legal status unmediated and unqualified by males. Although wives, together with children, slaves, and livestock, were counted among a man's possessions (Exod 20:17; cf. Deut 5:21), neither wives nor children were understood as property.

Literary and Symbolic Representation

While legal subordination reflects the formal structures of power, it is an inadequate measure of women's actual power or even recognized authority. Hints of the wider influence and power exercised by women in Israelite life may be seen in the Old Testament's literary presentation of women, which depicts them as more complex and forceful than their legal status suggests and gives them leading roles in some of the critical biblical dramas (e.g., Sarah and Hagar, Rahab, Deborah, Jezebel, Huldah, Esther). The expanded role of women in literature, however, especially in family sagas and novellas, reflects artistic need as well as lived reality. Behind this need is a more general pattern of gender symbolization, exhibited in linguistic as well as literary forms.

Woman as symbol plays an important role in the Old Testament literature and must be distinguished, at least conceptually, from woman in history or society. Important examples of female symbolization in the Old Testament include the female as goddess or symbol of divinity (most prominently exhibited in Asherah and the *ʾăšērîm*), representation of the capital city or nation as virgin, mother, or bride (Amos 5:2; Isa 40:2; Jer 31:21; Hosea 1–2), and the hypostatization of Wisdom in Proverbs 8. The negative symbolization of woman is represented in Dame Folly (Prov 9:13-18), apostate Israel (Hosea 1–2; Jer 2:20; 3:2; 4:30; Ezekiel 16; 23), and fallen Tyre (Isa 23:15-18; cf. Rev 17:4-5), all portrayed as a harlot or adulteress.

Conclusion: Hermeneutical Considerations

Within the Old Testament, viewed as either canonical text or historical testimony, the women who emerge as actors testify to the essential and active role of women in the formation and transmission of Israel's faith. Despite its overwhelmingly androcentric and patriarchal orientation, Israelite faith was a woman's faith—cherished, defended, and exemplified by women. But the text also exhibits a tension between the statement made by the leading female figures and that made by the nameless and voiceless women "offstage." Acknowledging their presence and incorporating their voices into the message of the Old Testament is part of the new hermeneutical task, requiring new interpretive strategies and techniques.

Various forms of literary criticism (including rhetorical and structuralist approaches) have provided feminist interpreters with a tool for representing the women of the Old Testament in relation to contemporary concerns. As a counter or complement to historical exegesis, such interpretation focuses on the received form of the text, tracing the sexual dynamics of its narrative portraits and inviting identification with its female subjects. Depicted according to contemporary norms as victims (Jephthah's daughter)—and challengers (the Hebrew midwives; Ruth and Naomi)—of patriarchal ideology and power, or simply as survivors in a man's world, the women of the ancient text reflect and prefigure modern struggles and ideals. While interpreters such as Phyllis Trible,[21] Mieke Bal,[22] Cheryl Exum,[23] and Esther Fuchs[24] represent differing aims and approaches to the patriarchal text, they share a common reader orienta-

21. Phyllis Trible, *God and the Rhetoric of Sexuality* (OBT; Philadelphia: Fortress Press, 1978); idem, *Texts of Terror: Literary and Feminist Readings of Biblical Narratives* (OBT; Philadelphia: Fortress Press, 1984).

22. Mieke Bal, *Lethal Love: Feminist Literary Readings of Biblical Love Stories* (Bloomington: Indiana University Press, 1987); idem, *Death and Dissymmetry: The Politics of Coherence in the Book of Judges* (Chicago: University of Chicago Press, 1988).

23. Cheryl Exum, "You Shall Let Every Daughter Live: A Study of Ex. 1:8—2:10," in Tolbert, *The Bible and Feminist Hermeneutics,* 63–82.

24. Esther Fuchs, "The Literary Characterization of Mothers and Sexual Politics in the Hebrew Bible," in Collins, *Feminist Perspectives,* 117–36.

tion that invokes response to their retold tales: celebration for unsung triumphs, mourning and rage for unlamented victims and unnamed crimes. These literary-constructive readings present the mothers and daughters of ancient Israel as sisters "heard into speech" by modern feminist interpretation.

Supplementary Bibliography

Bird, Phyllis A. "Images of Women in the Old Testament." In Rosemary R. Ruether, ed., *Religion and Sexism: Images of Woman in the Jewish and Christian Traditions,* 44–88. New York: Simon and Schuster, 1974.

Brenner, Athalya. *The Israelite Woman: Social Role and Literary Type in Biblical Narrative.* Sheffield: JSOT Press, 1985.

Camp, Claudia V. *Wisdom and the Feminine in the Book of Proverbs.* Bible and Literature Series 11. Sheffield: JSOT Press, 1983.

Emmerson, Grace I. "Women in Ancient Israel." In Ronald E. Clements, ed., *The World of Ancient Israel: Sociological, Anthropological and Political Perspectives,* 371–94. Cambridge: Cambridge University Press, 1989.

Hackett, JoAnn A. "In the Days of Jael: Reclaiming the History of Women in Ancient Israel." In Clarissa W. Atkinson, Constance H. Buchanan, and Margaret R. Miles, eds., *Immaculate and Powerful: The Female in Sacred Image and Social Reality,* 15–38. Boston: Beacon, 1985.

————. "Women's Studies and the Hebrew Bible." In Richard E. Friedman and Hugh Godfrey Maturin, eds., *The Future of Biblical Studies: The Hebrew Scriptures,* 141–64. Atlanta: Scholars Press, 1987.

Locher, C. *Die Ehre einer Frau in Israel: Exegetische und rechtsvergleichende Studien zu Deuteronium 22, 13-21.* OBO 70. Freiburg and Göttingen: Vandenhoeck & Ruprecht, 1986.

Otwell, John H. *And Sarah Laughed: The Status of Women in the Old Testament.* Philadelphia: Westminster, 1977.

3

POOR MAN OR
POOR WOMAN?

Gendering the Poor in Prophetic Texts

R ECENT STUDIES OF POVERTY IN CONTEMPORARY SOCIETY HAVE
alerted us to the fact that men and women join the ranks of the
poor in different ways and numbers, and experience the consequences
of poverty differently. Female poverty was long underestimated because
women did not, for the most part, show up in the ranks of the unem-
ployed. It is only recently that we have begun to get an adequate count,
and portrait, of poor women—a portrait that is being amplified and
differentiated by studies of women in the Third World.[1] What is apparent
from these modern studies is that the very indexes used to identify and
measure poverty have been biased with respect to gender.[2] That appears
also to be the case in biblical studies of the poor. Poverty in ancient Israel
has presented an almost exclusively male face in most studies, with virtually no recognition of the gender bias in the portrait.

Most biblical treatments of poverty or the poor consist primarily of
word studies, though these may include broader analysis of the social circumstances and attitudes related to poverty.[3] A recent example is the

Originally published in Bob Becking and Meindert Dijkstra, eds., *On Reading Prophetic
Texts: Gender-Specific and Related Studies in Memory of Fokkelien van Dijk-Hemmes* (Leiden:
Brill, 1996) 37–51.

1. The invisibility of female poverty is signaled by the title of a recent book by Pamela
Brubaker, *Women Don't Count: The Challenge of Women's Poverty to Christian Ethics* (AARAS
87; Atlanta: Scholars Press, 1994).

2. Ibid., 23–42.

3. Leslie J. Hoppe, *Being Poor: A Biblical Study* (Good News Studies 20; Wilmington,
Del.: Michael Glazier, 1987), and R. N. Whybray, *Wealth and Poverty in the Book of Proverbs*
(JSOTSup 99; Sheffield: Sheffield Academic Press, 1990), are examples of studies that have a
considerably broader base.

article by J. David Pleins,[4] which is organized as a study of nine Hebrew words, treated alphabetically. Six of these describe individuals, with a total of 239 occurrences: *'ebyôn* (61), *dal* (48), *miskēn* (4), *'ānî* (80), *'ănāwîm* (24), and *rāš* (22).[5] Of these only two are grammatically feminine, both forms of *'ānî* used in reference to personified Jerusalem (Isa 51:21 and 54:11).[6] This usage conforms to Deutero-Isaiah's general practice of employing *'ānî* to characterize the entire exile population as "poor" or "afflicted," and neither reference reveals a distinctively feminine face of poverty or helps us to understand the poor woman. But how are the masculine terms to be understood? Do they refer only, or primarily, to males? May they include women? Are they defined by male activities, roles, or circumstances of life? In this short essay, intended to honor the pioneering work of Fokkelien van-Dijk Hemmes in "gendering" texts of the Hebrew Bible,[7] I can examine only a few cases and must invariably raise more questions than I can answer.

The primary terms translated by the English word "poor" are distributed unevenly through the Hebrew Bible, with concentrations in prophetic and legal texts, the Psalms, and wisdom literature, most notably Proverbs and Job.[8] The same word may have different meanings and associations in different social and literary contexts, and these may change over time. Attitudes differ toward those so designated, as do analyses of the cause(s) of their condition.

The most common term for the economically destitute or distressed is *'ebyôn*, occurring 61 times (17 in the prophetic corpus). Pleins describes the *'ebyônîm* as "the beggarly poor," characterized by severe economic deprivation, which may involve homelessness and dependence on alms.[9] The term *dal*, with 48 occurrences (12 in the prophetic corpus), has the general sense of "poor, weak, inferior, lacking." Pleins characterizes the *dal* as "the beleaguered peasant farmer," one step above the landless *'ebyôn*. This term is the preferred word for the poor in the sentential literature of Proverbs, occurring 15 times in chapters 10–29.[10] Two other terms,

4. J. David Pleins, "Poor, Poverty: Old Testament," *ABD* 5:402–14.

5. Pleins also included *maḥsôr* (13), the collective noun *dallâ* (5), and *miskĕnût* (1).

6. With the exception of *'ănāwîm*, which appears only as a masculine plural noun, all of the terms translated "poor" are adjectives, or participles (*rāš*), which could conceivably have feminine inflections.

7. My great regret is that I shall miss the sympathetic and energetic critique that Fokkelien would have given this essay.

8. I have chosen a word-study approach, since this characterizes the existing literature. In the course of the study the limits of this procedure will become apparent, as well as the bias in the analysis.

9. Pleins, "Poor, Poverty," 403–4.

10. Ibid., 405–6.

rāš and *miskēn,* are concentrated in the wisdom literature and do not occur in the Pentateuch or prophetic writings.[11]

The most frequent and widely distributed term for "poor" in the Hebrew Bible is *ʿānî* with 80 occurrences. In addition to describing economic distress, it frequently carries a sense of being oppressed, exploited, afflicted, suffering. It is the dominant term in the prophetic literature (25 times), where it describes victims of unjust economic and legal practices and, in Deutero-Isaiah, Israel as a whole as the victim of political oppression.[12] The plural noun *ʿănāwîm* occurs only in the Psalms (13 times, mainly in laments), the prophetic corpus (7 times), and wisdom texts (3 times in Proverbs and once in Job). Many scholars see a merger of the ideas of poverty and piety in this term.[13] Pleins views it as a plural form of *ʿānî,* arguing that its semantic range corresponds to that of the other words for poverty.[14]

Pleins's treatment of the vocabulary of poverty is gender neutral and emphasizes a variety of circumstances and associations. His opening paragraph highlights that variety: "The poor constituted a diverse body of social actors: small farmers, day laborers, construction workers, beggars, debt slaves, village dwellers."[15] Despite inclusive language, however, the terms of this summary betray a male image. "Village dwellers" is too encompassing and "beggars" would appear to admit of female representation, but the remaining descriptive categories certainly suggest male subjects from what we know of ancient Israelite society.[16] Thus, even if we admit the possibility that terms which appear only in masculine form may conceal females through collective or "representative" uses, we must still ask whether we are likely to find women in the circumstances assumed by analysis of contexts. We must also ask whether there was a distinctive vocabulary for the female poor.

The Vocabulary of Poverty in the Book of Amos

The opening lines of the first words addressed to Israel indict the nation for its crimes against the poor (Amos 2:6-7).[17] The indictment combines

11. Ibid., 407.
12. Ibid., 408–9.
13. Ibid., 411. Cf. Norbert Lohfink, "Poverty in the Laws of the Ancient Near East and of the Bible," *TS* 52 (1991) 34–50.
14. Pleins, "Poor, Poverty," 411, 413.
15. Ibid., 402.
16. On the possible exception of debt slavery, see below.
17. I had originally intended to treat all occurrences of the commonlly recognized terms for "poor" in the prophetic texts, but restrictions of space made this impossible. Because the prophetic usage tends to be very general, formulaic, and emotionally charged, little new is

all three of the terms for poor used elsewhere in the book (4:1; 5:11-12; 8:4, 6), introducing them with a fourth term, *saddîq*. Although the oracle expands to include religious as well as social crimes and incorporate other themes of the book in its redactional form, these opening words serve as a summary of the eighth-century prophet's message of social justice. Introduced by the same formula that announces God's judgment on the surrounding nations, the oracle grounds the judgment with the following accusations:

(6b) because they sell the *saddîq* for silver
    and the *'ebyôn* for a pair of sandals
(7a) those who trample the head of the *dallîm* upon the dust of
    the earth,
    and turn aside the way of the *'ănāwîm*

The translation of v. 7a is disputed at several points, and opinions differ on the degree to which legal as well as economic abuses may be targeted by the whole.[18] What is clear, however, is that together the two bicola summarize a variety of abuses of power directed against weak members of the society. The piling up of all of the primary terms used to designate the poor in the prophetic (and prescriptive) literature suggests a comprehensive intention in this fourfold accusation, while the placement of *saddîq* at the head of the series indicates the perspective by which all are to be viewed, viz., as innocent, or "in the right."[19]

Who are these that are "sold," "trampled," and "pushed aside," and how are we to understand the actions by which they are deprived of their rights? The language of v. 7a is general, and in v. 7aα, at least, metaphorical; it does not allow us to see the mechanisms of abuse or particular cases. We cannot get behind the class terms to see individuals and their circumstances. This passage at least offers little evidence that might reveal the gender of the victims.

We might argue that the violent image of trampling on the head of the

---

learned from examining additional texts beyond those initially studied, and interpretation must depend heavily on descriptive passages outside the prophetic corpus.

The distribution of terms in the prophetic corpus is as follows: Isaiah: *'ebyôn* (5), *dal* (5), *'ănāwîm* (4)/*'ānî* (10); Jeremiah: *'ebyôn* (4), *dal* (1); Ezekiel: *'ebyôn* (3), *'ānî* (4); Amos: *'ebyôn* (5), *dal* (4), *'ănāwîm* (2); Habakkuk: *'ānî* (1); Zephaniah: *'ānî* (1)/*'ănāwîm* (1); Zechariah: *'ānî* (4[2 *'ăniyê hassō'n*]).

18. James Luther Mays, *Amos: A Commentary* (OTL; Philadelphia: Westminster, 1969) 45–46; J. Alberto Soggin, *The Prophet Amos: A Translation and Commentary* (trans. John Bowden; London: SCM, 1987) 47–48; Shalom M. Paul, *A Commentary on the Book of Amos* (Hermeneia; Minneapolis: Fortress Press, 1991) 77–81; Robert B. Coote, *Amos among the Prophets: Composition and Theology* (Philadelphia: Fortress Press, 1981) 11, 32–33.

19. Soggin, *The Prophet Amos*, 47.

dallîm (if such is the correct interpretation) would not be used to describe abuses against women. Violence against women is typically reported in relation to their sexuality or sexually defined roles: rape (Gen 34:2; Judg 5:30; 19:24-25; 2 Sam 13:14), public humiliation by exposure of genitals (Hos 2:12; Ezek 16:37), ripping open of pregnant women (Amos 1:13; Hos 14:1), sterility or loss of fertility (2 Sam 6:23; Hos 9:14), and the slaughter of mothers alongside their children (Hos 10:14). A similar argument might be made for v. 7aβ—if it describes the action of pushing someone off the road, a scene more likely to involve men (?). If, on the other hand, it refers to perversion of justice, there seems to be no reason for excluding women. It would appear in any case that we must look elsewhere for clues if we are to gender these "poor."

In Amos 8:4-6 the same three terms for poor occur in two lines which appear to be variants of the accusations in 2:6-7. Here, however, they frame, in reverse order, a series of indictments that specifically target unjust market practices.

> (4) Hear this, you that trample the *'ebyôn,*
>   bringing to ruin the *'anwê* [K; Q: *'ănîyê*]-*'āreṣ,*
> (5) saying, "When will the new moon be over
>   so that we may sell grain;
> and the sabbath,
>   that we may offer wheat for sale?"
> making the ephah small and the shekel large,
>   and tilting dishonest scales,
> (6) buying the *dallîm* for silver,
>   and the *'ebyôn* for a pair of sandals.

Here the "trampling" or ruin of the poor is associated with dishonest and greedy traders, who sell grain at high prices to the landless or those who have lost their harvest to drought, debts, or taxes. These same merchants buy at low prices from those forced to sell their produce on the market. Here the accused are buying rather than selling the poor, and *dallîm* has replaced the *ṣaddîq* of 2:6. The object of the "trampling" (8:4a) is now the *'ebyôn* (sg.), creating an *inclusio* with *'ebyôn* in the final colon (8:6b). The order of the accusations suggests that the final consequence, or most extreme example, of the abuse of the poor through unjust trade is trade in the poor themselves, as slaves.[20]

---

20. The two additional passages in Amos containing *dal* and *'ebyôn* (4:1 and 5:11-12) do not add substantially to the evidence or analysis of the texts examined here. In 4:1 the language of abuse is more violent and more general (*'ŠQ,* "oppress" and *RṢṢ,* "crush"), suggesting the complicity of the women in the actions for which their husbands are elsewhere indicted, but without specification of particular actions. Their reported command to their

Two texts shed light on the practice of debt slavery in ancient Israel. In Deut 15:12-17 the old "law of the Hebrew slave" (Exod 21:2-6) is updated in a manner that clearly identifies the subject as a member of the community, a "brother," who has fallen on hard times. The new law seeks to limit the bondage to the maximum term of six years and enable the slave to resume his position within the community of "brothers." It also extends these provisions to women:

> kî yimmākēr lĕkā ʾāḥîkā hāʿibrî ʾô hāʿibrîyâ waʿābādĕkā šēš šānîm
> When your brother, a Hebrew man or a Hebrew woman, sells him-
> self[21] to you, he shall serve you six years. (Deut 15:12)

In contrast to the Covenant Code, Deuteronomic legislation does not recognize a separate category of female slave, or slave-wife (Exod. 21:7-11),[22] but makes the male slave law inclusive.

What are we to make of the inclusion of women in this law? It has been argued on the basis of this text that women must have obtained the right to inherit land, since the law presupposes loss of land required to support oneself. Although this reasoning appears faulty in my judgment (see below), it recognizes that the woman's action envisioned in the law presupposes her right of control over her own person (assuming the interpretation of self-sale holds for the woman as well as the man) and the absence of other means of support. Such a situation could only arise in the case of a woman with no father, husband, brother, or property-owning son to

---

"lords," which completes the two-line indictment, suggests that rather than exploiting the poor directly, they make their husbands the instruments of their desire (Mays, *Amos*, 72). In 5:11-12 the *dal* and ʾ*ebyôn* are once again objects of unjust economic and legal practices. V. 11 accuses wealthy landowners of "trampling" (*bôšaskem*, or "collecting rent"—Soggin, *The Prophet Amos*, 88, who derives the hapax *BŠS* from Akk. *šabāsu*) the *dal* and taking levies of grain. Here the *dal* is clearly the poor peasant farmer. V. 12 concludes the indictment by characterizing the accused as "enemies of the righteous (*ṣaddîq*)" and "takers of bribes," who "push aside (*hiṭṭû*) the ʾ*ebyônîm* in the gate," pointing to injustices in the legal system.

21. Cf. NJV, NRSV "is sold." The reflexive interpretation seems preferable, since the term "brother" suggests an adult, who stands on an equal plane with the one who purchases him and hence acts on his own (cf. Lev 25:39 and Isaac Mendelsohn, "Slavery in the OT," *IDB* 4: 384-85), unlike a child who may be sold by parents (cf. Neh 5:5 and Exod 21:7). Amos characterizes the one who must enter into a bond servant relationship as "sold" by his creditors.

22. Mendelsohn ("Slavery," 384) argues that the sale of the daughter in Exod 21:7-11 was "not a sale into slavery," despite the use of the terms *MKR* and ʾ*āmâ*. The two laws in 21:1-6 and 7-11 are not parallel in construction, and Niels Peter Lemche ("The 'Hebrew Slave': Comments on the Slave Law Ex. xxi 2-11," *VT* 25 [1975] 143) argues that vv. 7-11 are a special case. Nevertheless, the second case is presented as a variant of the first, since it modifies the terms for release in the "basic" law, specifying that the daughter sold as an ʾ*āmâ* "shall not go out like the going out of male slaves (*kĕṣēʾt hāʿābādîm*, v. 7)"—a statement that precedes mention of the special conditions of her service. Note that Hebrew has no gender-inclusive term for "slave," reinforcing the notion that the conditions of service, as well as duties, were distinct for male and female slaves.

support her, a case normally exemplified only by widows (or perhaps an unmarried daughter cast out of her father's house?). It would appear in any case that the number of women who might fall into this category must be very small.

Alternatively, one might view the separate mention of the Hebrew woman as a reformulation of the earlier provisions concerning the male slave's wife. In Deuteronomy all references to a wife (and children) have been eliminated, either as accompanying the man into slavery or as provided by the master. Does Deuteronomy want to suggest that a woman cannot be impressed into servitude for her husband's debts, but must "sell herself" as she finds herself deprived of support? This would in effect establish the principle that each individual (more precisely, adult "citizen") is responsible for his or her own debts—while ignoring the dependence of the woman in a family-based social and economic system.

The extension of the law to include women does not erase its male orientation. It retains the basic structure and language of the old law, qualifying the terms with new provisions and exhortations. The critical change is the identification of the subject as a "brother." The concern of this legislation is to safeguard the rights of members of the community understood as "brothers," that is, as equals. Editorial additions at the beginning and end of the law (vv. 12 and 17) seek to redefine the "brotherhood" to include women, and elimination of references to the slave's wife and children limit consideration to individuals, treated as single and self-determining. What we have here is a statement of principle: women as well as men are full members of the covenant community and are to receive equal protection from return to the conditions of slavery out of which YHWH redeemed Israel. Whether women actually found themselves in the situation described here is impossible to determine, but the inclusive formulation should be understood primarily as an ideological statement rather than as evidence for change in the social or economic status of women.[23]

The other category of woman described in references to forced bond-

---

23. Deuteronomy is first of all a theological treatise. The intention of this law to limit the servitude of a "brother" is shared by Lev 25:39-46, which draws the line even more clearly between the Israelite servant and the foreign slave. In Leviticus the terms describing the Israelite bondsman are exclusively male, suggesting that circumstances in the community have not changed substantially with respect to women's economic or social position. In Leviticus too the defining term is "brother": kî-yāmûk ʾāḥîkā ʿimmāk wĕnimkar-lāk lōʾ-taʿăbōd bô ʿăbōdat ʿābed, "If your brother who is with you (dependent on you) becomes so impoverished that he must sell himself to you, you shall not make him serve as a slave" (Lev 25:39). Here even the term "slave" is rejected; the one who sells himself is to be treated as a hired or bound laborer (kĕśākîr kĕtôšāb yihyeh ʿimmāk, v. 40). Slaves, identified explicitly as male and female (ʿebed wĕʾāmâ, v. 44), may be acquired only from the surrounding nations and from resident aliens (vv. 44-46).

age is the daughter sold by her father or parents. As noted above, Exod 21:7 treats the sale of a daughter by an Israelite as a case distinct from that of a male slave (whose wife, provided by the master, is not accounted for in the existing legislation). In contrast, Neh 5:5 describes the forced servitude of both male and female children as a single statement, although it goes on to highlight the daughters' plight. The account begins with a report of dissension within the community, expressed in "a great outcry of the people and their wives (*hāʿām ûnĕšêhem*) against their Jewish brothers (*ʾăḥêhem hayyĕhûdîm*, 5:1)."[24] Here again we encounter a male-defined community, to which the voices of women (specifically, wives) are added, presumably because the complaints concern conditions that affect the family, including the female members.[25]

The complaints are threefold. Some say, "We are having to give up our sons and our daughters as surety[26] so that we may get grain to eat and stay alive" (v. 2). Others say, "we are having to pledge (*ʿōrĕbîm*) our fields, our vineyards, and our houses in order to get grain during the famine" (v. 3). Still others complain, "we are having to borrow money on our fields and vineyards to pay the king's tax (*lāwînû kesep lĕmiddat hammelek śĕdōtênû ûkĕrāmênû*)" (v. 4). They conclude by pointing to the basis of their complaint and the consequences of their "brothers'" actions:

> Now our flesh is like the flesh of our brothers, our children (*bānênû*) are like their children; yet we are having to subject our sons and daughters as slaves (*ʾănaḥnû kōbĕšîm ʾet-bānênû wĕʾet-bĕnōtênû laʿăbādîm*)—and some of our daughters have already been subjected (*wĕyēš mibbĕnōtênû nikbāšôt*).[27] We are powerless, and our fields and vineyards belong to others. (V. 5)

24. The NJV, NAB, and NEB render *hāʿām* as "the common folk/people." Cf. Joseph Blenkinsopp, *Ezra-Nehemiah: A Commentary* (OTL; Philadelphia: Westminster, 1988) 257.

25. Jacob M. Meyers (*Ezra. Nehemiah* [AB 14; Garden City, N.Y.: Doubleday, 1965] 127) and F. Charles Fensham (*The Books of Ezra and Nehemiah* [New International Commentary on the Old Testament; Grand Rapids: Eerdmans, 1982] 191) see the reference to wives as evidence of the gravity of the situation, but do not connect the mention of the women to the nature of the complaint.

26. Reading *ʿōrĕbîm* "giving in pledge" for MT *rabbîm* (so BHS ed.; cf. NAB, NEB, and Blenkinsopp, *Ezra-Nehemiah*, 253, 254). The first complaint complements the second, which deals with the pledging of property; it names the most serious loss first, viz., the pledging of family members.

27. NRSV translates *nikbāšôt* as "ravished." This interpretation of *KBŠ*, used in the previous clause for both male and female children, introduces an unjustified distinction, which does not fit the circumstances of economic pressure. The use of *KBŠ* in Esth 7:8 in the sense of "subdue" or "force" a woman does not justify an interpretation of rape in this text, nor is it appropriate to the situation of sale as a slave wife (Exod 21:7-11; Fensham, *The Books of Ezra and Nehemiah*, 192; cf. Blenkinsopp, *Ezra-Nehemiah*, 254). The term is a harsh one, but applies equally to sons and daughters. The singling out of the daughters is significant, however. See below.

It appears that economic hardship has forced members of the community to hand over their land and their children to their neighbors as pledges on loans of grain and money. When the debts were not paid, the pledged children were sold as slaves—beginning with the daughters. Mendelsohn understands that the creditors sold the children, against the parents' will.[28] The term *MKR* "sell" is not used by the parents to describe their own actions, presumably because they do not profit from the sale; rather they are "forcing" (*KBŠ*) their children into slavery. This is the crisis that leads to the outcry. The participle (*kōbĕšîm*) suggests an action in progress or about to be undertaken, with some of the daughters already (*wĕyēš*) subjected. It appears that when forced to give up their children into slavery, parents surrendered their daughters first—a reasonable preference in view of the high value placed on sons, especially when the survival of the family is at stake.[29]

Nehemiah responds to the outcry by bringing charges against the "nobles (*ḥōrîm*) and the officials (*sĕgānîm*)," capping his argument with the accusation, "you (would) even sell your own brothers" (*gam-ʾattem timkĕrû ʾet-ʾăḥêkem*, vv. 7-8).[30] Exhorting them to abandon their claims on their brothers, he concludes with the plea: "restore to them, this very day, their fields, their vineyards, their olive orchards, and their houses, and the interest on money, grain, wine, and oil that you have been exacting from them" (v. 11).

Special terminology for the poor is lacking in this text,[31] but the conditions described here are precisely those treated in the pentateuchal legislation concerning the poor[32] and appear to correspond to the conditions alluded to in the prophetic texts under consideration. Thus Nehemiah's summary accusation, "you are selling your brothers" (Neh 5:8), corresponds to Amos's opening indictment of "selling" the *ṣaddîq* and the

---

28. Mendelsohn, "Slavery," 384; cf. Fensham, *The Books of Ezra and Nehemiah*, 192.

29. Fensham (ibid.) thinks the case with daughters was different since they could be taken by the creditor as a second wife. In his view, the creditors do not sell the children to others, but force them to work for them until the debts are paid.

30. The language of "selling" is used only here. It does not occur in the preceding catalog of complaints that culminate with the forced enslavement of children, and specifically daughters. It is set in the context of efforts to redeem Israelites sold into bondage to foreigners. "We have done our best to buy back our Jewish brothers who were sold to the nations," Nehemiah declares, "but you would now sell your own brothers, so that they must be sold [back] to us" (on the difficult final clause, see Blenkinsopp, *Ezra-Nehemiah*, 254–55; cf. Meyers, *Ezra. Nehemiah*, 128–29; and Fensham, *The Books of Ezra and Nehemiah*, 195, 197). The following request, to restore property and interest, suggests that the "selling of brothers" represents an extreme and summary formulation of the end consequences of the various forms of economic oppression recorded in the previous complaints.

31. Perhaps because a substantial segment of the population has fallen into this condition. It is the wealthy exploiters who are identified here by special terminology.

32. Lohfink, "Poverty," 38–50.

ʾebyôn (Amos 2:6). The language of "brothers" in this indictment corresponds to its use in Deuteronomy and Leviticus to describe those targeted by the laws and exhortations concerning sale into slavery, taking of pledges, and conditions of loans.

In view of this explicit orientation toward the male members of the community, it seems likely that the grammatically masculine terms used to describe various classes of the economically weak and exploited in Amos 2:6-7 and 8:4-6 should be understood in their primary sense as designating males. The figure that best represents injustice within the community, understood as violation of covenant norms, is a weak and exploited "brother." Nehemiah 5 suggests that even where women of the community are clearly suffering from the conditions of poverty—and may be singled out for mention—the injustice done to the poor by the rich is formulated with males in mind. Except in the case of children forced into slavery, it is the male Israelite who is the primary object of concern, and even there the summary accusation is formulated in terms of "brothers." The wife remains hidden and unaccounted for in these cases, though she clearly suffers from actions taken against her impoverished spouse. We are permitted to hear her voice in this text, but we cannot distinguish it from the voices of the male speakers, nor can we discern her image as a victim within the afflicted population.

This view of the poor, which understands the terms ʿānî/ʿănāwîm, ʾebyôn, and dal primarily as designating a poor "brother," is reinforced by consideration of other terms that desginate weak or marginal members of the society, especially the widow (ʾalmānâ), the fatherless (yātôm), and the resident alien (gēr). Norbert Lohfink has noted that these terms, which occur as a fixed series throughout Deuteronomy, are combined at times with the slave and the Levite, but never with the ʾebyôn and ʿānî.[33] The reason, he argues, is that they identify persons who do not possess landed property and therefore require special structures of support (such as provisions for gleaning). They are not, however, as a class, "poor."[34] In contrast, the ʾebyôn and ʿānî are landowning members of the community caught in the spiral of debt.[35] They are mentioned only in a cluster of laws in chapters 15 and 24, all of which, Lohfink argues, pertain to the situation of indebtedness.[36]

33. Ibid., 40, 43–44.
34. Ibid., 44.
35. Pleins ("Poor, Poverty," 404) characterizes the ʾebyôn as "landless wage laborers," at least in the legal texts. It appears that the crucial factor in Lohfink's analysis is that, unlike the slave or alien, the ʾebyôn is still considered a full member of the community defined by its landholding members, even though he has "temporarily" lost his land.
36. Lohfink, "Poverty," 45.

The separate treatment of the widow, orphan, and alien in Deuteronomy corresponds to the usage in the prophetic corpus, in which only two texts join references to these classes with the common terms for "poor." Isa 10:1-5 indicts "those who make iniquitous decrees (*ḥiqĕqê-ʾāwen*), who write oppressive statutes" (v. 1), describing the victims and the effects as follows:

> to turn aside the *dallîm* from justice
> and to rob of their right the *ʿănîyê* of my people,
> that widows (*ʾalmānôt*) may be their spoil,
> and fatherless children (*yĕtômîm*) their prey.
> (V. 2)

Here *dal* and *ʿānî* serve to identify those members of the community whose limited possessions and precarious economic position make them especially vulnerable to unjust exactions from the court and wealthy landowners. The second pair of terms describes the legally vulnerable, who have no male protector or advocate to represent their claims in the courts. The text makes it clear that they are also economically vulnerable, but they do not belong to the category of "the poor."[37]

The other prophetic text that links widow and orphan to the poor is Zech 7:10, which adds the alien (*gēr*) in the manner of Deuteronomy. The list appears in a two-part summary of divine commands, which begins with the exhortation to "render true judgment and perform *ḥesed* and *raḥămîm* to one another (*ʾîš ʾet-ʾāḥîw*, 'a man to his brother,')" (v. 9), and continues with the following injunctions: "do not oppress (*ʾal-taʿăšōqû*) a widow, orphan, alien, or *ʿānî* and do not devise evil in your hearts against one another" (v. 10). The special mention of the four named classes appears to be an attempt to represent all of the classes of the socially vulnerable.

The first three are landless and are not attached to a family. They therefore lack legal representation in the community of free citizens/"brothers." The slave is not mentioned because the slave is a member of the household. The "poor (man)," here represented by *ʿānî*, is the poor farmer, who may have had to mortgage his land and is in constant danger of falling

---

37. It is noteworthy that the case of the widow's garment is treated separately from that of the *ʿānî* in the laws concerning pledges in Deuteronomy 24. Deut 24:10-13 contains two provisions concerning pledges: vv. 10-11 prohibit entering the house of a neighbor to take a pledge, and vv. 12-13 prohibit sleeping in a pledged garment "if [the man] is poor (*ʾim-ʾîš ʿānî hûʾ*)." In contrast, a widow's garment may not be taken in pledge at all. But this prohibition is not presented as a further case relating to pledges. It appears rather in a separate section (vv. 17-18) treating the alien, orphan, and widow: "You shall not deprive a *gēr* (and) a *yātôm* of justice; you shall not take the garment of an *ʾalmānâ* in pledge" (v. 17).

into servitude and thereby losing his position within the community. As a householder, his entire family suffers from his economic distress, but they are not identified separately because they fall within the family system. The only class of woman who is generally recognized outside this system is the ʾalmānâ.[38]

The basic social and economic unit of ancient Israel was the male-headed family, and the attention of the Hebrew Scriptures is focused on these male heads, as the main public actors and key to the general welfare of the society. The male focus of legislation and prophetic critique holds not only for the landed citizens, but also, it appears, for the marginal classes. The resident alien, whether single or with family, is recognized as a social category only by a masculine term (gēr). The yātôm likewise appears to be a male-defined category, with no feminine form of the term attested. He is the male child without a male protector, whose (anticipated) place in the community of free males is jeopardized. And the "poor," represented by the terms ʾebyôn, dal, and ʿānî/ʿănāwîm, are those male members of the community whose precarious economic condition puts them in danger of losing their place in the "brotherhood" of free citizens. Prophetic concern for the "poor" should be understood essentially as concern for a poor man, and more particularly a "brother."

38. See Paula S. Hiebert, "'Whence Shall Help Come to Me?': The Biblical Widow," in Peggy L. Day, ed., *Gender and Difference in Ancient Israel* (Minneapolis: Fortress Press, 1989) 125–41.

II

WOMEN IN
ISRAELITE RELIGION

———————————

4

THE PLACE OF
WOMEN IN THE
ISRAELITE CULTUS

DESPITE THE TIMELINESS OF THE QUESTION POSED IN THE TITLE of this essay, it is not a new one in the history of Old Testament scholarship.[1] It occasioned lively debate at the turn of the century, in terms remarkably similar to arguments heard today. A key figure in that early debate was Julius Wellhausen, whose analysis of Israelite religion emphasized its masculine, martial, and aristocratic nature, positing an original coincidence of military, politicolegal, and religious assemblies, in which males alone had full rights and duties of membership.[2] Others argued that women were disqualified from cultic service by reference to an original ancestral cult of the dead which could be maintained only by a male heir.[3] A further argument associated women's disability or disinterest in the Yahweh cult with a special attraction to foreign cults or pre-Yahwistic beliefs and practices involving local numina.[4]

This article was written in 1985–86 as a contribution to a Festschrift honoring my teacher Frank Cross, and was originally published in Patrick D. Miller, Jr., Paul D. Hanson, and S. Dean McBride, eds., *Ancient Israelite Religion: Essays in Honor of Frank Moore Cross* (Philadelphia: Fortress Press, 1987) 397–419. The assigned title, defining the topic, became the subject of reflection in the course of developing the article.

1. This chapter is a preliminary and highly abbreviated form of the introduction to a book-length work (in preparation) on women in Israelite religion.

2. Julius Wellhausen, *Israelitische und jüdische Geschichte* (3d ed.; Berlin: Georg Reimer, 1897) 89–90.

3. Immanuel Benzinger, *Hebräische Archäologie* (Freiburg im Breisgau and Leipzig: J. C. B. Mohr, 1894) 140; and Wilhelm Nowack, *Lehrbuch der hebräischen Archäologie* (Freiburg im Breisgau and Leipzig: J. C. B. Mohr, 1894) 154, 348.

4. See, e.g., Bernhard Stade, *Biblische Theologie des Alten Testaments* (Tübingen: J. C. B. Mohr, 1905) 1:40. Cf. Eduard König, *Geschichte der alttestamentlichen Religion* (Gütersloh: Bertelsmann, 1912) 216 n. 1.

Underlying these arguments and assumptions concerning the marginal or subordinate status of women in the Israelite cultus was a common understanding of early Israel as a kinship-structured society of nomadic origin, whose basic social and religious unit was the patrilineal and patriarchal family.[5] Though it was the agricultural village with its assembly of free landowners that Wellhausen had in mind when he correlated political and religious status, the principle he articulated had broader applicability: "Wer politisch nicht vollberechtigt war, war es auch religiös nicht."[6] Women, who were disenfranchised in the political realm, were disenfranchised in the religious realm as well.

Stated in such terms of disability—or disinterest and disaffection—the widely held view of women's inferior status in the Israelite cultus, exhibited in the critical historiography of the period, elicited vigorous rebuttal in a series of studies aimed at clarifying, and defending, women's position in ancient Israelite religion and society.[7] While the arguments and conclusions of these studies differed, the general outcome was to demonstrate that women's participation in the religious life of ancient Israel was in fact broader and more significant than commonly depicted.[8]

Today many of the same arguments and much of the same evidence put forward in the earlier discussion are being employed once more in a renewed debate over the androcentric and patriarchal character of Israelite religion.[9] This time, however, the discussion appearing in scholarly publications, or in works by biblical scholars, is fueled by a debate arising outside the academy and borne by a literature that is primarily lay-oriented and largely lay-authored, a literature marked by the anger and urgency of profound existential and institutional conflict.[10] Modern femi-

---

5. See, e.g., Benzinger, *Archäologie* (1907), 102; Nowack, *Lehrbuch,* 153–54.

6. Wellhausen, *Geschichte,* 94.

7. The earliest (1898) and most positive in its assessment was that of Ismar Peritz, "Women in the Ancient Hebrew Cult," *JBL* 17 (1898) 111–48. Other major studies include the following: Max Löhr, *Die Stellung des Weibes zur Jahwe-Religion und -Kult* (Leipzig: Hinrichs, 1908); Georg Beer, *Die soziale und religiöse Stellung der Frau im israelitischen Altertum* (Tübingen: J. C. B. Mohr [Paul Siebeck], 1919); and Elizabeth M. Macdonald, *The Position of Women as Reflected in Semitic Codes of Law* (Toronto: University of Toronto Press, 1931).

8. For an excellent review and assessment of the history of scholarship on women in Israelite religion, see chap. 1 of Urs Winter's *Frau und Göttin: Exegetische und ikonographische Studien zum weiblichen Gottesbild im alten Israel und in dessen Umwelt* (Freiburg: Universitäts Verlag; Göttingen: Vandenhoeck & Ruprecht, 1983). Winter's work, which became available to me only after the completion of my initial draft, exhibits substantial parallels to my own approach and significant accord with my analysis.

9. See, e.g., Clarence J. Vos, *Woman in Old Testament Worship* (Delft: Judels & Brinkman, 1968); John Otwell, *And Sarah Laughed: The Status of Women in the Old Testament* (Philadelphia: Westminster, 1977); and Winter, *Frau und Göttin.*

10. By "lay" I mean nonbiblical specialist. This literature, which is a product of, or response to, the modern women's movement, is largely, though by no means exclusively, written by women and is characterized by a high degree of existential involvement and political

nist critique of the Bible as male-centered and male-dominated has elicited widely differing historiographical and hermeneutical responses, ranging from denial of the fact or intent of female subordination to rejection
of the authority of the Scriptures as fundamentally and irredeemably
sexist.

In the current debate, with its heavy charge of personal and theological
interest, the biblical historian has a limited but essential contribution to
make by isolating and clarifying the historical question. The task of Old
Testament historiography must be to determine as accurately as possible
the actual roles and activities of women in Israelite religion throughout
the Old Testament period and the meaning of those roles and activities in
their ancient socioreligious contexts. The question for the historian today
is the same as that addressed to earlier scholars, but it must be answered
in a new way—because of new data, new methods of analysis, and a new
understanding of history. The following is an attempt to set forth a rationale and a plan for that new answer.

The question about the place of women in the Israelite cultus exposes
a defect in traditional historiography—beginning already in Israelite
times. It is a question about a forgotten or neglected element in traditional
conceptions and presentations of Israelite religion, which typically focus
on the activities and offices of males. Where women appear at all in the
standard works, it is in incidental references, as exceptional figures, or in
limited discussion of practices or customs relating especially to women.
This skewed presentation may be explained by the limits of the available
sources and may even be understood as an accurate representation of the
Israelite cultus as a male-constituted or male-dominated institution. But
it can no longer be viewed as an adequate portrait of Israelite religion.
The religion of Israel was the religion of men and women, whose distinctive roles and experience require critical attention, as well as their common activities and obligations. To comprehend Israelite religion as the
religion of a people, rather than the religion of males, women's roles, activities, and experience must be fully represented and fully integrated into
the discussion. What is needed is a new reconstruction of the history of
Israelite religion, not a new chapter on women. Until that is done, the

---

intention (protest and advocacy). In the three decades since the appearance of Simone de
Beauvoir's *The Second Sex* (trans. H. M. Parshley; New York: Alfred A. Knopf, 1953; French
original, 1949), it has swelled to a flood, establishing itself as a major new category in both
religious and secular publishing—and affecting the entire field of publishing in its attention
to gendered language and images. While this literature treats a broad range of social, psychological, and historical issues, a recurring theme, in secular as well as religious writings, is the
legacy of biblical tradition in Western understanding of the nature and status of women.
Recent scholarly attention to women in the biblical world has arisen, in part at least, as an
effort to correct and inform the "popular" discussion (cf. Winter, *Frau und Göttin*, 17).

place of women in the Israelite cultus will remain incomprehensible and inconsequential in its isolation, and our understanding of Israelite religion will remain partial, distorted, and finally unintelligible.

A first step toward this integrated reconstruction must be an attempt to recover the hidden history of women and to view the religion through their eyes, so that women's viewpoint as well as their presence is represented in the final account.[11] The obstacles to that effort are immense, but, I shall argue, not insurmountable. They do, however, require that critical attention be given to methodology before any reconstruction can proceed. That being the case, this chapter can offer no more than a highly provisional sketch of the assigned subject, prefaced by a summary of the methodological study that forms the essential introduction.

Preliminary Methodological Considerations

1. Two fundamental shifts in focus or perspective are necessary to the reconstruction I have proposed: (a) The cultus must be understood in relation to the total religious life in all of its various forms and expressions, "private" as well as public; heterodox, sectarian, and "foreign" as well as officially sanctioned;[12] and (b) religious institutions and activities must be viewed in relation to other social institutions, such as the family, and in the context of the total social, economic, and political life. While both of these shifts are essential to an understanding of Israelite religion as a total complex, they have particular consequence for the understanding of women's place and roles.

2. The information needed to give a fully adequate account of the place of women in Israelite religion, including the cultus, is in large measure

---

11. Cf. Elisabeth Schüssler Fiorenza's groundbreaking work for the New Testament, *In Memory of Her: A Feminist Theological Reconstruction of Christian Origins* (New York: Crossroad, 1983).

12. By cultus I understand the organized, usually public, aspects of religious life centered in a temple, shrine, or other sacred site, maintained by a priesthood and/or other specialized offices and roles, and finding expression in sacrifices, offerings, teaching and oracular pronouncement, feasts, fasts, and other ceremonies and ritual actions. Since our knowledge of Israelite religion is limited almost entirely to the "national" cultus and its several schools of theology or streams of tradition, it is easy to slip from analysis of the cultus to generalizations about the religion. This tendency has been qualified to some extent by the recognition that we have no direct evidence for North Israelite theology and practice and by attempts to recover and reconstruct it from elements surviving within Judaean compositions. It is also being qualified by new attention to local or folk traditions of Israelite Yahwism evidenced in extrabiblical texts. The question about women in the cultus, I shall argue, raises the question about the role of the cultus in the total religious life of Israel in an even broader and more radical way.

unavailable—and unrecoverable—from either biblical or extrabiblical sources. We have at best isolated fragments of evidence, often without clues to context. As a consequence, any reconstruction must be tentative and qualified. The same, however, is true, though in less extreme degree, of our knowledge of men's roles, and demands similar caution and qualification. Our fullest and best information is partial and skewed.

3. A comprehensive and coherent account of Israelite religion and of women's place in it requires the use of an interpretive model, not only to comprehend the available evidence but also to locate, identify, and interpret missing information—which is often the most important.[13] The blanks in the construct are as essential to the final portrait as the areas described by known data. They must be held open (as the boxes in an organizational chart)—or imaginatively filled—if the structure is not to collapse or the picture is not to be rendered inaccurate or unintelligible. The primary means of filling the blanks is imaginative reconstruction informed by analogy.

4. The closest analogies may be found in other ancient Near Eastern societies. They are limited, however, by dependence on written documents, most of which come from the spheres of men's activities and reflect male perspectives.

5. Modern ethnographic studies of individual societies and institutions and cross-cultural studies of women's roles in contemporary non-Western societies can aid the Old Testament historian in formulating questions and constructing models.[14] Such studies are especially valuable for their

---

13. The need for consciously articulated interpretive models has been convincingly argued in recent decades and needs no further defense. It does need reiteration, however, as paucity of evidence intensifies the need. For example, if we assume that the Israelite congregation was composed of all adults, we will picture women as a silent constituent even where no reference is made to their presence. But if we construe the congregation as a body of males, we must give a different account of the missing women—and of the role of the cultus in the society.

14. This is an exceedingly rich and suggestive literature combining descriptive and theoretical interests. It is also expanding so rapidly that it is impossible to list even the most important works. The following is a sample of works I have found useful: Martin K. Whyte, *The Status of Women in Preindustrial Societies* (Princeton: Princeton University Press, 1978); M. Kay Martin and Barbara Voorhies, *Female of the Species* (New York: Columbia University Press, 1975); Michelle Rosaldo and Louise Lamphere, eds., *Woman, Culture, and Society* (Stanford: Stanford University Press, 1974); Nancy A. Falk and Rita M. Gross, eds., *Unspoken Worlds: Women's Religious Lives in Non-Western Cultures* (San Francisco: Harper & Row, 1980); Elizabeth W. Fernea, *Guests of the Sheik: An Ethnography of an Iraqi Village* (Garden City, N.Y.: Doubleday, 1969); E. Bourguignon et al., *A World of Women: Anthropological Studies of Women in the Societies of the World* (New York: Praeger, 1980); and Sharon W. Tiffany, ed., *Women and Society: An Anthropological Reader* (Montreal: Eden Press Women's Publications, 1979).

attempts to view societies as total systems as well as for their attention to features that native historians and lay members of the society may overlook or deem unimportant. Because they do not depend on written records but are based on observation and interview of participants, they give us access to women's roles and experience that is otherwise unavailable.

6. Androcentric bias is a pervasive feature of the ancient sources, their subjects, and their interpreters. It has also characterized most anthropological research and writing until recently.[15]

Summary of Findings of Cross-Cultural Studies

The most important finding of cross-cultural studies for a reconstruction of women's religious roles in ancient Israel is the universal phenomenon of sexual division of labor, which is particularly pronounced in preindustrial agricultural societies.[16] Basic to this division of labor is an understanding of women's primary work as reproductive work, including care of children and associated household tasks, with a consequent identification of the domestic sphere as the female sphere, to which women's activities may be restricted in varying degree.[17] This fundamental sexual division of labor has far-reaching consequences for the status and roles of women in the society as a whole as well as their patterns of activity and

15. For efforts to identify and counter this bias and an introduction to the study of gender as a major new field of anthropological theory, see especially Judith Shapiro, "Anthropology and the Study of Gender," in Elizabeth Langland and Walter Gove, eds., *A Feminist Perspective in the Academy: The Difference It Makes* (Chicago: University of Chicago Press, 1981) 110–29; Naomi Quinn, "Anthropological Studies on Women's Status," *Annual Review of Anthropology* 6 (1977) 182–222; and Sherry B. Ortner and Harriet Whitehead, eds., *Sexual Meanings* (Cambridge: Cambridge University Press, 1981).

16. Michelle Rosaldo, "Woman, Culture, and Society: A Theoretical Overview," in Rosaldo and Lamphere, *Woman*, 18; and Judith K. Brown, "A Note on the Division of Labor by Sex," *American Anthropologist* 72 (1970) 1074–78. Cf. Martin and Voorhies, *Female of the Species*, 276–332; and Whyte, *Status of Women*, esp. 156–73.

17. Rosaldo, "Woman, Culture, and Society," 26–27. See further Hannah Papanek and Gail Minault, eds., *Separate Worlds: Studies of Purdah in South Asia* (Delhi: Chanakya Publications, 1982) esp. 3–53 and 54–78; Fernea, *Guests;* and Martin and Voorhies, *Female of the Species*, 290–95. Women's activities are never completely confined to the home, but sexual division is the rule in both work and play wherever mixed groups are found. See Brown, "A Note"; Peggy R. Sanday, "Female Status in the Public Domain," in Rosaldo and Lamphere, *Woman*, 189–206; and Ernestine Friedl, *Women and Men: An Anthropologist's View* (New York: Holt, Rinehart & Winston, 1975) 8. For Old Testament examples, cf. the young women (*nĕʿārôt*) as distinct from the young men (*nĕʿārîm*) working in Boaz's field (Ruth 2:8, 9; cf. 2:22, 23). Note the sexual division of labor described in 1 Sam 8:11-13. Cf. also OT references to women drawing water (Gen 24:11; 1 Sam 9:11), grinding grain (Job 31:10; cf. Matt 24:41), cooking and baking (1 Sam 8:13; Lev 26:26), and dancing and singing (Exod 15:20; 1 Sam 18:6-7).

participation in the major social institutions. In all the primary institu-tions of the public sphere, which is the male sphere, women have limited or marginal roles, if any. Thus leadership roles in the official cultus are rarely women's roles or occupied by women.[18]

Conversely, however, women's religious activities—and needs—tend to center in the domestic realm and relate to women's sexually determined work. As a consequence, those institutions and activities which appear from public records or male perspective as central may be viewed quite differently by women, who may see them as inaccessible, restricting, irrel-evant, or censuring. Local shrines, saints and spirits, home rituals in the company of other women (often with women ritual leaders), the making and paying of vows (often by holding feasts), life-cycle rites, especially those related to birth and death—these widely attested elements of wom-en's religious practice appear better suited to women's spiritual and emo-tional needs and the patterns of their lives than the rituals of the central sanctuary, the great pilgrimages and assemblies, and the liturgical calen-dar of the agricultural year.[19] But the public sphere with its male-oriented and male-controlled institutions dominates and governs the domestic sphere, with the result that women's activities and beliefs are often viewed by "official" opinion as frivolous, superstitious, subversive, or foreign.[20]

Women in Israelite Religion and Cultus: Observations and Hypotheses

I have argued that an adequate understanding of the place of women in the Israelite cultus requires attention both to the place of the cultus in the total religious and social life of the society and to the place of women in the society—including consideration of the society's understanding of male and female nature, capacities, and inclinations and its organization and assignment of male and female roles, activities, rights, and duties. Despite the efforts of the Israelite cultus to exert a controlling influence over the total life of the society and despite its significant stamp on the culture, the cultus must still be seen as one institution among others, influenced by general social and cultural norms, especially as they define

18. Rosaldo, "Woman, Culture, and Society," 17, 19–21. Cf. Ortner and Whitehead, *Sexual Meanings,* 4 and passim; Peggy R. Sanday, *Female Power and Male Dominance* (Cambridge: Cambridge University Press, 1981); and Shapiro, "Anthropology," 118–22.

19. These generalizations summarize an extensive review of descriptive literature and case studies, which cannot be documented here. For a fuller analysis with examples and references, see my forthcoming work.

20. Cf. I. M. Lewis, *Ecstatic Religion* (New York: Penguin Books, 1971) 86–88, 96–97, 101.

appropriate male and female roles and activities. Consequently, we should expect significant correspondence between women's roles and status in the cultus and in the society as a whole. Three prominent elements of that general understanding of women's nature and duty have direct bearing on women's place in the cultus: (1) the periodic impurity of women during their reproductive years;[21] (2) the legal subordination of women within the family, which places a woman under the male authority of father, husband, or brother, together with a corresponding subordination in the public sphere in which the community is represented by its male members; and (3) an understanding of women's primary work and social duty as family-centered reproductive work in the role of wife-mother.

The effect of each of these determinants is to restrict the sphere of women's activities—spatially, temporally, and functionally. Only roles that were compatible with women's primary domestic-reproductive role and could be exercised in periods or situations free from ritual taboo, or from the requirement of ritual purity, were open to women. While restrictions also existed on men's ability to participate in particular cultic roles and activities (e.g., economic constraints on offering vows and sacrifices and restriction of priestly office to members of priestly families), these did not affect all males as a class. A significant distinction between male and female relationships to the cultus may be seen in the fact that for women, but not for men, conflict between social and cultic obligation is a recurring phenomenon—which is resolved by giving priority to social demands. Examples may be seen in the annulment of a woman's vows by her father or husband (Num 30:1-15)[22] and in the "exemption" of women from the requirement of the annual pilgrim feasts (Exod 23:17; 34:23; Deut 16:16). In both of these cases one may argue that responsibility to the family is the underlying principle and that it is understood as a religious, not merely a social, obligation; but a contrast remains between the understanding of a male and a female religious obligation.[23]

This explanation assumes a conflict of duty or interest (defined socially, not individually) as grounds for women's limited role in the Israelite

21. While the menstrual taboo is cultically defined and regulated, it is so universal a factor of human culture that it may be viewed as a general social concept apart from its specific interpretation and institutionalization in the Israelite cultus.

22. The divorced woman and the widow alone are free of overriding male authority.

23. The consequences and implications of this conflict in ordering, or contrast in defining, the religious priorities for women are far-reaching. In a society in which cultic service is accorded highest value, women are disadvantaged when they are excepted from that obligation. The various attempts within the Old Testament to extend to women obligations and options that were originally formulated with males in mind leave unaddressed the tension between the requirement and the ability to fulfill it.

cultus, but the limitation might also be explained by an understanding of the cultus as an originally, or essentially, male institution or association. The evidence suggests that there is truth in both views.

Wellhausen was surely right in recognizing behind the generic language of many texts and translations a cultus conceived and operated as a male association to which women were related, if at all, in a marginal and mediated way. Evidence for an understanding of the cultic community as fundamentally a body of males is substantial. While the best examples relate to the early period, they are not confined to it: for example, the prescription for the pilgrim feasts ("Three times in the year shall all you males appear before the Lord God," Exod 23:17; cf. Deut 16:16); the instructions to the "people" at the mountain of God ("Be ready by the third day; do not go near a woman," Exod 19:15); the tenth commandment ("You shall not covet your neighbor's wife," Exod 20:17); and other injunctions, exhortations, blessings, and so forth, that address the cultic community as male ("Blessed is everyone who fears the Lord. . . . Your wife will be like a fruitful vine," Ps 128:1-3; "Jeremiah said to all the people and all the women," Jer 44:24).

Further evidence may be seen in the Hebrew onomasticon, where theophoric names describing the individual as a worshiper or votary of the deity (names compounded with 'ebed/'ōbēd, i.e., "servant of") are reserved to males and have no female counterpart—in contrast to Akkadian and Phoenician practice.[24]

Objections to Wellhausen's view that seek to show broad participation of women in religious and cultic activities fail to challenge his basic argument, which is not that women were prohibited from participation, but rather that their participation was not essential and that it played a less central or less important role in women's lives than in men's. Wellhausen's insight was also sound in positing an "original" coincidence or congruence of military, legal, and cultic assemblies; the three represent the primary institutions of the public sphere, which is everywhere the sphere of male activity. His understanding of the correspondence of rights and duties in these overlapping realms can also be substantially affirmed, though areas of divergence require greater attention together with cases of status incongruity. A further modification is required by the extension of both the cultic and the legal spheres beyond the circle of males to encompass

---

24. Old Babylonian *amat*-DN names, i.e., "handmaid of [divine name]," exceed *warad*- ("servant-") names proportionally, even when the names of *naditu* women are excluded as cloister names. The data for these comparisons together with a full analysis of sexual distinction in naming are found in my unpublished study, "Sexual Distinction in Israelite Personal Names: A Socio-Religious Investigation."

the broader community.[25] As a consequence, women, who were excluded from the governing or representative institutions of both (namely, the priesthood and the cultic assembly, and the council of elders and the assembly of landholders), were nevertheless brought within their spheres of interest and authority.[26] Thus women possessed dual status in the legal and cultic realms, being members of the outer circle governed by the community's norms but restricted in varying degree from the inner circle where the norms were formulated, inculcated, and rationalized.

In the cultic realm, differentiation of roles is associated with a hierarchy of offices and prerogatives ordered according to a concept of graduated degrees of holiness (represented spatially, e.g., in the plan of the temple and its courts). At the center, which is also the apex of authority, stands the priest or high priest, surrounded by other members of the priesthood and/or other orders of cultic personnel (the local shrine represents the simplest form of cultic leadership, invested in a resident priest—and his family—while the temple cultus occupies the other end of the spectrum, with its elaborate, graded system of special orders and offices). Beyond the priesthood stand members of the community (more specifically, the free citizens), bound by duty of pilgrimage, addressed directly by the cultic proclamation and having limited rights of sacrifice (varying according to period). The outer circle is represented by women, dependents, and resident aliens. They are also addressed by the cultic proclamation, but usually indirectly; both their hearing and their response are commonly mediated by a male guardian.

While this scheme gives a general picture of the relationship of women to the Israelite cultus, it must be qualified in a number of ways, especially with regard to changes or variations in internal and external relationships

25. The cultic assembly is not, I believe, to be understood as a male sect or society (though the early cultus has many of the features of a men's religious organization) but rather as a male-constituted and -directed institution at the center of Israelite society, representing the community as a whole and directing and controlling its life. The way in which it related to the larger community and the understanding of its own constitution seem to have changed over time in the direction of greater openness and inclusiveness, in respect not only to women but also to slaves, dependents, and resident aliens (cf. Deut 16:10-11, 13-14). See Conclusion below.

26. Thus women shared many of the same rights and duties as men, made use of the same aid provided or mediated by the institutions, and, as men, were held accountable by them. Women, in common with men, prayed, consulted oracles, attended festivals, and sought justice in the courts, received theophanies and divine commissions, sought oracular judgments and legal redress for wrongs suffered and received punishment for wrongs committed. It appears that they were not as a rule prohibited from general religious practices but rather were hindered from fuller participation by competing interest or duty (see below) or attracted by their own particular circumstances to make use of some means of religious expression more than others.

over the Old Testament period, some of which appear to have significant consequence for the nature and extent of women's participation. Factors requiring consideration include the number of cultic centers, the types of activities associated with them, and the relationships among them; the status and affiliation of the cultic personnel, the degree of centralization, and the extent of professionalization or specialization of cultic maintenance roles; and the relationship of the central cultus to other institutions and spheres of life.

While this chapter does not permit detailed study of the complex assortment of data embedded in the Old Testament text, a summary review of the more prominent features of the major periods may help to provide a context for a series of concluding hypotheses concerning patterns of participation and changes in women's relationship to the cultus.

The fullest and richest evidence for women's religious activity is found in literature pertaining to the premonarchic period, which also provides the richest portrait of women in leadership roles. We see Miriam leading the Israelites in a song of victory at the sea (Exod 15:20-21), punished for claiming equality with Moses as one through whom the Lord had also spoken (Num 12:2), and ranked with Aaron and Moses as leaders of the people (Num 12:2-8; Mic 6:4);[27] women "ministering" at the tent of meeting (Exod 38:8; 1 Sam 2:22); Deborah honored as a "mother in Israel" (Judg 5:7), as a judge and a prophet summoning the forces of Israel to holy war at Yahweh's command and accompanying them into battle (Judg 4:4-10; 5:7, 12-15), and as a singer of Israel's victory through Yahweh (Judg 5:1); Jephthah's virgin daughter "initiating" an annual ritual of mourning by the daughters of Israel (Judg 11:34-40);[28] Micah's mother commissioning an image for the family shrine established by her son (Judg 17:1-13, esp. v. 4); women dancing at the yearly feast at Shiloh (Judg 21:19-21); Hannah and Peninnah accompanying their husband on his annual pilgrimage to Shiloh and sharing the portions of the sacrifice (1 Sam 1:1-4); and Hannah, weeping, praying, vowing at the sanctuary, and finally paying her vow with the dedication of the child (1 Sam 1:9-28). In these images we see most of the roles attested in the later period.

Sources pertaining to the period of the monarchy and to the postexilic period expand the references to heterodox practices and sharpen the distinction between legitimate and illegitimate roles and activities. Two

27. Miriam's historical role is impossible to reconstruct, but her ranking alongside Moses and Aaron suggests a position of considerable importance—and a cultic role. She is not identified by a husband but by her "brothers," the priest and the prophet. The roles of cultic singer and prophet are suggested.

28. The mythic and etiological character of the narrative does not limit its value as evidence for a women's ritual.

female prophets, Huldah (2 Kgs 22:14-20) and the unnamed *nĕbî'â* of Isa 8:3, are the only women portrayed in approved cultic roles.[29] The rest are viewed as illegitimate. These include references to *qĕdēšôt* (Hos 4:14; Deut 23:18);[30] to queens and queen mothers who introduced foreign cults and cult objects (Maacah—1 Kgs 15:13; Jezebel—1 Kgs 18:19 [cf. 16:31-32]; Athaliah—2 Kgs 11:18; cf. Solomon—1 Kgs 11:1-8); to women weaving vestments for Asherah (2 Kgs 23:7); and to women baking cakes/burning incense for the Queen of Heaven (Jer 7:17-18; 44:15-25), weeping for Tammuz (Ezek 8:14), and engaging in sorcery ("prophesying"—Ezek 13:17-23). Postexilic literature yields only a prophet who opposed Nehemiah (Noadiah—Neh 6:14), showing a continuation of women in the class of prophets.[31] The number and nature of references to women's religious roles and activities during the monarchy appear to reflect the consequences of the centralization of the cultus under royal control and a tendency, culminating in the Deuteronomic reform, to brand all worship at the local sanctuaries idolatrous/promiscuous.[32]

Evidence from the patriarchal traditions depicts a family-centered or clan type of cultus in which the patriarchs perform all of the roles of sacrifice and blessing and are portrayed as founders of various local shrines or cults (Gen 22:9-14; 26:23-25; 28:18-19; 35:6-7, 14-15).[33] Rachel's stealing of the teraphim (as cultic objects belonging to her father) is further witness to clan-based religious practice, but it tells us nothing about women's religious roles. Her audacious and amusing act of theft and cover-up in which she "protects" the sacred objects by professing defilement does not describe the institutionalization of an action. Rachel remains a dependent as she cleverly assists her husband in robbing her father.

---

29. The meaning of *nĕbî'â* in the latter case is disputed. It is clear, however, that the term in Isa 8:3 is used as a role designation ("*the* prophetess," not "my wife") whether or not it designates Isaiah's wife, and that it designates one who is to assist in the symbolic act that will complete Isaiah's sign.

30. The term used in Gen 38:21-22 is intended to describe a Canaanite practitioner in a Canaanite (and pre-Israelite) setting. Cf. n. 41 below.

31. Here opponents of Nehemiah. The Greek and Syriac apparently understood the name as masculine.

32. The narrowing of acceptable roles for women is correlated with a general narrowing of options in religious practice. The greater variety of roles and the fuller or more candid descriptions of practice in the premonarchic period in comparison with the later period raises the question whether the earlier practices disappeared or were simply reinterpreted (as heterodox) and/or suppressed. What is allowed to stand in the tradition of the earlier period was interpreted, in part at least, as evidence of the low moral state of the time—a judgment made explicit in the final editing of the book of Judges (19:1, 30; etc.).

33. Use of the patriarchal traditions as sources for social reconstruction requires particular caution; they depict individuals or families with little attention to social context and treat them as representative or symbolic figures.

Summary Generalizations

The following is an attempt to summarize the evidence in a series of preliminary generalizations.

Women in Cultic Service

1. Leadership of the cultus appears at all times to have been in the hands of males (though with differing patterns and sources of recruitment into the leadership group). Women, however, were not excluded absolutely from cultic service or sacred space, though increasing restriction is suggested, correlated with increasing centralization, specialization, and power (at least in Judah) under a royally sanctioned Zadokite priesthood. Persistence of women in cultic roles in the later period is identified in the canonical texts with heterodox practice.

2. The attested roles of men and women in the service of the cultus appear to exhibit a sexual division of labor corresponding closely to that discernible in the society as a whole.

a. Males occupy the positions of greatest authority, sanctity, and honor and perform tasks requiring technical skill and training. They preside over the presentation of sacrifices and offerings,[34] have charge of the sacred lots, interpret the sacred law and instruct the congregation, pronounce blessing and curse, declare absolution and pardon, and guard the purity of the sanctuary and the worshipers; that is, they perform the priestly service in both sacrificial and oracular functions. Priestly office in Israel, as in the rest of the ancient Near East, was reserved to males. Contrary to popular opinion, Israelite Yahwism was not distinguished from the surrounding religions by its rejection of women in priestly office, but con-

---

34. The one religious activity from which women appear to have been excluded by principle rather than circumstance was the offering of sacrifices, which eventually became the sole prerogative of the priest. The exclusion may ultimately be connected with the menstrual taboo, but it is not confined to periods of menstrual impurity. It appears, rather, to have been common practice elevated to a principle (cf. Winter, *Frau und Göttin*, 38–40) or to have been understood more in symbolic than in practical terms. Efforts to show that women offered sacrifices fail, I believe, in the case of biblical evidence. Presenting a sacrificial offering to the priest is not itself a sacrificial action (contra Peritz, "Women in the Ancient Hebrew Cult," 126–27) but an act of offering to which all are bound. In the case of the offering required for a woman's purification (Lev 12:6-7), a clear distinction is made between the woman's presentation of the animal to the priest ("she shall bring a lamb . . . to the priest," v. 6) and the offering made *by* the priest *for* the woman ("and he shall offer it . . . and make atonement for her," v. 7) (cf. Lev 15:19-33). Nor is the sharing of a sacrificial meal an act of sacrifice, though it is an important form of cultic participation, as Peritz insists ("Women in the Ancient Hebrew Cult," 123-25). Manoah prepares and offers the sacrifice on behalf of his nameless wife to whom the angel has appeared (Judg 13:19), and Elkanah sacrifices (*wayyizbaḥ*) at the shrine of Shiloh, distributing portions to his wives and children (1 Sam 1:4).

formed to common practice.[35] The Israelite cultus in its basic institutional forms appears to have shared the essential features of the cultus known in surrounding cultures.

b. Women's cultic service seems to have been confined largely to maintenance and support roles, essential to the operation of the cultus but not requiring clergy status—or prescription in texts concerned with the proper performance of the required rituals. Since these roles are poorly documented in the biblical sources, we can only speculate based on chance clues, parallels in domestic life, and the suggestions afforded by comparative studies of cultic organization and maintenance elsewhere in the ancient Near East. The following tasks appear likely (further suggestions

35. Johannes Renger's study of the Old Babylonian "priesthood" based on the *lú = amēlu* list shows only one among the nineteen classes identified as *Kultpriester* in which men and women are identified by a common term, namely, the *en*, the highest ranked and earliest attested office in the list ("Untersuchungen zum Priestertum in der altbabylonischen Zeit," *ZA* NF 24 [1967] 110–88, esp. 113). The sex of the *en* appears to have been complementary to that of the deity, suggesting that the *en* was understood to represent the divine spouse. The rest of the classes are distinguished by gender and nomenclature and grouped (with the exception of the *entum*, the later Akkadian designation of the female *en*) in the typical hierarchical order of male-female, strongly suggesting sexual division of labor within the cultus rather than shared roles. Despite Renger's use of the term *Priesterinnen* to describe the female classes, they do not appear to have performed activities that would properly be described as "priestly." Use of the term "priestess" to describe such women is misleading, since it suggests comparable, if not identical, roles and equal status with priests.

The third group in the *lú = amēlu* list, exorcists, consists of five classes, all male—as we might expect, since these represent offices requiring technical skills and mastery of a body of esoteric knowledge, like the *baru* diviners in the second group. It is only in the second group, comprising the oracular speakers, that we find professional classes with both male and female members, namely, the *šā'iltum/(šā'ilum)*, *maḫḫum/maḫḫūtum*, and *āpilum/āpiltum*. The pattern presented in the Old Babylonian sources corresponds exactly to that which the more meager, and less specialized, Old Testament data suggest: priestly roles involving technical expertise and leadership in the sacrificial cult or other cultic ritual were male, as well as other roles demanding specialized knowledge, while the more charismatic forms of divination, open to lay as well as professional practitioners, involved women as well as men, just as their Old Testament prophetic counterpart did. Cf. Rivkah Harris: "Except for the religious functions of royal women and dream interpretation and divination, women played a minor role in cultic life. Only in the lower echelons of the 'clergy' did female singers, dancers, and musicians participate in the cult" ("Woman in the Ancient Near East," *IDBSup*, 962).

Syrian and Canaanite sources are too meager to confirm a pattern. The Ugaritic texts contain no reference to any class of female cultic personnel as a recognizable group. Phoenician and Punic sources contain the only known ancient feminine form of *khn* ("priest"). In the Eshmunazar sarcophagus inscription (*KAI*, 14:15) it is applied to the queen of Sidon as royal patron, and hence chief official, of the city god Ashtart. I would interpret this as evidence of a royal cultus in which the king/queen, qua ruler, assumed the title and role of priest/presider in the official cultus, not as evidence for a class of female priests. The status and function of the women bearing this title in several Punic inscriptions (*KAI*, 70:1; 93:1; 145:45[?]; 140:2) cannot be determined. See now Jo Ann Hackett, *The Balaam Text from Deir 'Allā* (HSM 31; Chico, Calif.: Scholars Press, 1984) 25.

must await a fuller study of comparative materials): the weaving and sewing of vestments, hangings, and other textiles for cultic use;[36] the preparation of cultic meals or foods used in the ritual;[37] and the cleaning of cultic
vessels, furniture, and quarters.[38]

   c. Some references to women associated with the cultus point to more
public and representative or symbolic roles, suggesting a need to include

36. While the women weavers expelled from the temple by Josiah were associated with
the service of a "foreign" deity or cult object, the Yahweh cultus also had need of such service.
According to Exod 35:25-26, the material for the tabernacle hangings was spun by women.
The weaving of the hangings, however, was supervised by the master craftsman Bezalel or
his male assistant (Exod 35:35), an example of the male professionalization of female crafts
observed in cross-cultural studies of gender roles. It is not certain who actually did the work;
the *kol-ḥăkam-lēb bĕʿōśê hammĕlāʾkâ* ("everyone able to do the work," Exod 36:8) with its
masculine plural verb could be a generic use of the masculine to describe a group of workers
of mixed gender.

37. This is suggested on the analogy of work in the domestic sphere, though cultic specialization might well make cooking and baking male activities. Nevertheless it is worth
speculating who prepared the sacrificial victims for the communion meals eaten at the sanctuary and who baked the shewbread. In the report of the "priests' custom with the people"
in 1 Sam 2:13-17, it is clear that neither the priest nor the priest's servant is involved in boiling
the meat, since the priest's servant takes or demands the portion desired by the priest. The
man sacrificing is addressed in 1 Sam 2:15, but did he cook as well as slaughter the animal?
Might not his accompanying wife have performed her usual work for the family feast? Or
when the sacrifice later became a priestly prerogative, might women of priestly families have
performed this service?
   Ezekiel's provisions for the restored temple include designation of areas for cooking and
baking within the temple complex, carefully separating the place where the priests were to
boil the *ʾāšām* and the *ḥaṭṭāʾt* offerings and bake the *minḥâ*—which was to be within the
inner court (Ezek 46:20)—and the "kitchen" (*bēt hammĕbaššĕlîm*) where "those who min-
ister at the temple" (*mĕšārĕtê habbayit*) were to boil the "sacrifices of the people" (*zebah
hāʿām*)—which were located in the outer court (Ezek 46:21-24). This late scheme clearly
assigns all actions related to the sanctuary to priests, guarding this sphere from that in which
the preparation of meals for the people took place. Hearths are provided for the latter purpose and the activity was supervised by a lower class of temple personnel (not priests). This
stage of prescription for the cultus has professionalized actions earlier performed by the
worshiper, including the slaughter of the sacrificial victims, which is now assigned to the
Levites (Ezek 44:12; cf. Lev 2:4-7 and 3:1-17).
   The mention of women as cooks and bakers in the palace service (1 Sam 8:13) may also
provide a clue, at least for the earlier period, since the administration of the temple was
similar in many ways to the administration of the palace. A third type of female work mentioned in 1 Sam 8:13, that of "perfumers," has a counterpart in the cultus in the preparation
of the holy anointing oil, a special skill described by the use of the same verb (*raqqāḥôt;
rōqēaḥ*, Exod 30:25). However, the distinction in the use of the aromatic oils produced for
the cultus may make this a male specialty in the cultic setting.

38. The suggestion is again by analogy to the almost universal assignment of house-
cleaning to women—or slaves. In large public buildings, palaces, etc., such work is usually
done by slaves or low-caste groups, with tasks divided by sex, and that may have been the
case in the temple too. But at local shrines presided over by a single priest, the housekeeping
chores of the deity's house might well have fallen to the female members of the priest's
family.

within the cultus activities or attributes specifically identified with women, for example, as singers and dancers[39] or as attendants in the sanctuary. Both the *ṣōbĕʾōt* (Exod 38:8; 1 Sam 2:22)[40] and the *qĕdēšôt* (Gen 38:21-

39. Women are widely identified with singing and dancing as well as instrumental music making in both biblical and extrabiblical texts and in pictorial representations (see, e.g., *ANEP*, 63–66, 111, 346; Ilse Seibert, *Woman in Ancient Near East* [Erfuhrt: Fortschritt, 1974], pls. 10, 34, 99; Othmar Keel, *The Symbolism of the Biblical World* [trans. Timothy J. Hallett; New York: Seabury/Crossroad, 1978] 336–39). None of these activities was restricted to women (cf. *ANEP*, 63–66, David's reputation as a singer, and his dance before the ark, 2 Sam 6:14, 16), though some types of instruments and performance may have been regarded as peculiarly or typically female. The "timbrel" (*tōp*), e.g., appears to have been a preferred instrument of women (cf. Winter, *Frau und Göttin*, 33 n. 164; Eric Werner, "Musical Instruments," *IDB* 3:474); women musicians and dancers are widely attested as professional entertainers of men (cf. the Arabic *shayka*, the Japanese geisha, and the Old Testament image of the prostitute as a troubadour, singing to the tune of her harp [Isa 23:14-15]); and women typically formed a welcoming chorus line to greet warriors returning from battle (Exod 15:20; 1 Sam 18:6). The disputed question is whether women participated as musicians or dancers in cultic celebrations and whether they belonged to the personnel of the sanctuary.

The question is too complex for adequate treatment here. It may be that references to cultic dancing should be eliminated altogether, or at least those described by *māḥôl/mĕḥōlâ* and verbal forms of *ḤWL*, which appear always to designate actions of the congregation or groups of laywomen, not a professional activity, and may refer to antiphonal singing rather than dance (see Jack M. Sasson, "The Worship of the Golden Calf," in Harry A. Hoffner, ed., *Orient and Occident: Essays Presented to Cyrus H. Gordon* [AOAT 22; Kevelaeri: Butzon & Bercker; Neukirchen-Vluyn: Neukirchener Verlag, 1973] 157; cf. Winter, *Frau und Göttin*, 32–33). The function of the three daughters of Heman, mentioned in a parenthetical note in 1 Chr 25:5, is unclear, though the sons constituted a major Levitical guild of musicians in the Second Temple. The *mĕšōrĕrîm ûmĕšōrĕrôt* of Ezra 2:65 clearly represent a different class from the temple singers described by the same term (masculine plural) in Ezra 2:41; Neh 7:44. Their place in the list following male and female servants and preceding the horses suggests a menial class of entertainers.

It seems likely that the public, professional roles of musicians in the temple service were assigned to males, at least in the later period of the monarchy and the Second Temple period, while women's specialized musical activity was limited to secular entertainment and funeral dirges (a "home" ritual). The earlier period, however, suggests a different picture in the attribution of two important songs of praise to women, both called prophets (Exod 15:20-21; Judg 4:4; 5:1; cf. 1 Chr 25:1, which describes the function of the temple musicians as "prophesying" with lyres, harps, and cymbals). While the narrative contexts point to a traditional secular role of women in greeting returning warriors (cf. Winter, *Frau und Göttin*, 33), both texts may also be understood to describe cultic actions, whose setting is the celebration of Yahweh's victories, not simply as onetime historical acts, but as repeated cultic actions recalling the great victories (or does the shift in attribution of the Song at the Sea from Miriam to Moses reflect a cultic institutionalization of the victory song in which the secular/lay role of the woman leader is transformed into a cultic/professional male role?). Psalm 68:26 suggests that in the First Temple period at least women formed a recognized group among the temple musicians (*ʿălāmôt tôpēpôt*, mentioned between *šārîm* and *nōgĕnîm* in the procession to the sanctuary; cf. Winter, *Frau und Göttin*, 34–35).

40. The many questions about these women cannot be explored adequately here, much less resolved. For the most recent discussion and review of literature, see Winter, *Frau und Göttin*, 58–65. Both the Samuel and the Exodus passages suggest the persistence of the office or institution after the initiation of the Yahwistic cultus and its tent shrine in the desert.

22; Deut 23:17 [Heb. 18]; Hos 4:14)[41] are associated with the service of the sanctuary, though the exact nature and form of their respective service remains unclear. Both represent classes rejected or superseded by the normative cultus that preserved the record of their existence, suggesting that they played a larger role (for a longer period of time) than the meager references would at first intimate. The identifying symbol or implement of the former group (a mirror) and the innuendo in references to the latter suggest that in both cases female sexuality was a significant aspect of the role.

   d. If we posit any specialized service of women within the cultus, we must also consider the social organization that would enable permanent or continuous (short-term or long-term) cultic activity. Since women's place in society is determined by their place within the family, women are not normally free to operate for extended periods outside this sphere. The well-known exceptions are the widow, the prostitute, and the hierodule. Two possible arrangements may be suggested to account for women's service in the Israelite cultus. One would see the women as members of priestly families, hence resident at or near the sanctuary and sharing in some degree the special sanctity of the priest, which would give them access to the sacred space. The other would assume that they are women without families (whether widows, virgins, or women separated from

---

Winter has seen rightly, I believe, that the significant information in the archaic Exodus tradition is the reference to the mirrors (*Frau und Göttin*, 60). For a critique of his interpretation, which views the mirror as the symbol of a female deity associated with fertility and the women as *Hofdamen* visiting the sanctuary, rather than cultic personnel, see my forthcoming work. Cf. Julian Morgenstern, "The Ark, the Ephod, and the Tent," *HUCA* 17 (1942–43) 153–265, *HUCA* 18 (1943–44) 1–52, for an interpretation of the women as shrine attendants based on pre-Islamic Arabic parallels.

   41. This is not the place to review the evidence and arguments concerning the *qĕdēšâ*. The literature is far larger than that on the women at the entrance to the tent of meeting, and the presence of cognates and of presumed parallel institutions in other ancient Near Eastern cultures requires a more thorough investigation and report than the chapter in this present volume permits. Of the three Old Testament references, two suggest a foreign origin or, at least, a non-Yahwistic institution (Deut 23:17 and Gen 38:21-22), while all three parallel the term with *zônâ* ("prostitute"). The cultic nature of the office or role is clear from the etymology and from the one text that describes an activity (Hos 4:14): "[The men] sacrifice with *qĕdēšôt*." Since the term is paired in Deut 23:17 with the masculine *qādēš*—in the reverse of the normal male-female order—any judgment about the *qĕdēšâ* must involve consideration of the whole class of cognate terms. In overview, it appears that the Old Testament usage is so generalized and polemical that it may serve more as a cover term for proscribed cultic roles than as the precise designation of a particular office or function. Since all of the masculine references (all apparently collective, except Deut 23:17, and therefore conceivably inclusive) are in Deuteronom(ist)ic contexts, the possibility must be considered that the term was used in Deuteronomistic circles to describe roles or offices, such as that of the *ṣōbĕʾôt* of the tent of meeting, that were at one time considered a legitimate part of the Israelite cultus.

their families by a vow). In the latter case we may expect, as in the case of the various classes of Babylonian hierodules, that the cultus will assume the authority and control of father or husband and that restrictions, comparable to those applying within the family, will be placed on the woman's sexual activity for the duration of her service (whether as a prohibition of sexual activity or of having or keeping children).

e. Women might also on occasion play a role in the royal cultus through their roles in the ruling house. A queen, in the absence of a male ruler (or in the presence of a weak one), might assume the role of titular head and patron of the state cult. Since our best Old Testament example is provided by a foreign queen (Jezebel), presiding over a foreign cult, the cultic role of the king's wife or mother may not have been as fully developed in Israel as elsewhere—or it may have been rejected. This specialized cultic role is in any case dependent upon a secular role and the particular politicoreligious relationship of the royal cultus.

3. The most important and best-documented religious office occupied by women in ancient Israel, that of prophet, stands in an ambiguous relationship to the cultus. Whatever the role of the prophet within the cultus, it was clearly not a priestly office. Since recruitment was by divine designation (charismatic gift) and not dependent upon family or status, it was the one religious office with broad power that was not mediated or directly controlled by the cultic or civil hierarchy and the one religious office open to women. Because recruitment to and exercise of the role did not depend on socially or sexually defined status but on personal attributes, it was also the one role shared by men and women, a pattern attested in Mesopotamia and in cross-cultural studies.

The lack of formal restrictions to women's assumption of the office does not mean, however, that women were equally free to exercise it. Here, as in the case of other extrafamilial roles, women were confronted with a dual vocation, which was normally—and perhaps always—resolved in favor of the domestic obligation. Women prophets probably exercised their charismatic vocation alongside their family responsibilities or after their child-rearing duties were past. As a consequence of this complementary or sequential pattern of women's prophetic activity—and as a consequence of the normal patterns of social organization, which placed women as dependents in family-centered units—one would not expect to find women organized in prophetic guilds (the professional guild is a male form of organization). Nor would one expect to find women prophets as heads of schools or having the freedom of action and access to political and cultic power that is apparent in the case of their most prominent male counterparts. It is therefore not unexpected that no prophetic books carry the names of women, and it requires no explanation of prejudice or conspiratorial silence—but rather conflict of duty, which made every woman a mother before she could exercise another vocation.

4. Some forms of cultic service by women associated with the central Yahwistic cultus were judged heterodox or foreign by the canonical sources. In addition to these references the Old Testament contains frequent references to local cults of alien gods and to foreign cults brought into the central cultus. These references, which are always polemical and usually formulated in very general terms, do not supply us with adequate information about the related cultic personnel, but presumably some of these were women (e.g., *qĕdēšîm* in 1 Kgs 15:12; 2 Kgs 23:7 may be understood as an inclusive use of the generic plural).[42] It is impossible on the basis of our sources, however, to determine whether women played a larger role in the service of non-Yahwistic cults. Evidence for a female deity or female aspect of deity as a persistent and at times, perhaps, legitimate element of the Yahwistic cultus requires reassessment of the terms "foreign" and "syncretistic" as descriptions of discredited worship as well as a reassessment of the ritual and personnel of such cults. The sources suggest that disavowal, rather than discontinuance, of the practices and beliefs is what is indicated in the increasing and increasingly polemical attention to "foreign" cults and cultic practices in late sources.

Women as Worshipers

1. Since women rarely emerge in the text from behind the facade of generic male terminology, it is impossible to determine with certainty the extent of their participation in prescribed or reported activities. Isolated clues suggest, however, that women attended the major communal feasts and rituals, insofar as personal and domestic circumstances permitted, and presumably contributed to the preparation of meals and of food (especially grain) offerings. Animal slaughter and sacrifice, as an action of the worshiper, was reserved to males—as elsewhere generally—but this appears to have been the sole specific exclusion or reservation. In the major pilgrim feasts and other festivals at local shrines, as well as in family-based ritual meals, the woman participated as a member of a family unit. But she could also exercise her role in "the great congregation" and as "a daughter of Israel" bound by covenant law in individual acts of devotion and duty: in songs of praise (1 Sam 2:1-10) and prayers of petition (1 Sam 1:10-16), in the making and performing of vows (1 Sam 1:11, 24-28; Num

[42. I no longer believe that the term in these two verses may be taken as evidence for women in this class, although I believe that the Deuteronomistic editor intends it as inclusive. See now my article, "The End of the Male Cult Prostitute: A Literary-Historical and Sociological Analysis of Hebrew *qādēš-qĕdēšîm*," in John A. Emerton, ed., *Congress Volume: Cambridge, 1995* (VTSup; Leiden: Brill, forthcoming).]

30:3-15), in seeking oracles (2 Kgs 4:22-23; cf. 1 Kgs 14:2-5), in bringing offerings, and in performing the rituals prescribed for ritual cleansing, absolution, and so forth (Lev 12:1-8; 13:29-39; 15:19-29). The locus of these activities might be the central shrine (on occasions of pilgrimage) but was surely most commonly a local shrine or holy place or simply the place of daily activity. That women's communion with the Deity was common and that women were recipients of divine communications is indicated by a number of theophany traditions—though where the response to the appearing Deity takes cultic form, as in the case of Manoah's wife, the action shifts to the male (Manoah presents the offering and questions the angel; cf. Judg 13:2-7 and 8-20).

2. Of family-centered ritual we know even less, except in the case of the Passover. We may expect in this and in other cases that the normal male and female roles in the family will be reflected in the ritual, with food preparation belonging to the women and the presiding role, reading and recitation, assumed by males. The alternative practice of segregated dining and ritual, common in Islamic custom, was more likely the rule in cultic meals of larger groups or societies formed for such purposes.

3. Peculiarly or predominantly female forms of ritual and worship are suggested in the canonical sources only in reference to heterodox cults, the clearest examples of which are the women weeping for Tammuz (Ezek 8:14) and making offerings to the Queen of Heaven (Jer 7:17-18; 44:19). Though the whole population is explicitly implicated in the latter case, the women seem to have a special role. Prophetic use of the metaphor of the promiscuous bride to describe Israel's apostasy may reflect a special proclivity of Israelite women for "foreign" cults, but the sin that is condemned is the sin of the people, and this usage alone is insufficient to demonstrate a pattern. Of possibly greater significance for an undertsanding of women's religious participation and the total religious life of the community is the hidden realm of women's rituals and devotions that take place entirely within the domestic sphere and/or in the company of other women. Cross-cultural studies show that these often constitute the emotional center of women's religious life as well as the bulk of their religious activity, especially where their participation in the central cultus is limited. For such practices, however, we have little or no direct testimony, as this order of religious practice is generally seen as unworthy of note unless it challenges or undermines the central cultus. (Women's rites may even be unknown to men, who have no part in them.) Ceremonies and practices that belong to this category might include birth and mourning rites and other rituals of the life cycle performed in the home or the village, especially with a woman as ritual specialist; prayers; vows and their performance in such actions as holding a feast, endowing a shrine, or dedicat-

ing some prized possession; making pilgrimages; consulting mediums and seers; and participation in spirit-possession cults or rituals. The line between religion and magic or orthodox and heterodox is more difficult to draw in this realm of practice and belief since the controls of the central cultus, its priesthood and theology, are largely absent. Like folk religion everywhere, it is typically seen as debased or corrupted and often as syncretistic.

The freedom to engage in such actions may vary considerably, relating in part to the degree to which they may be seen as convergent with or contrary to cultically prescribed duties. For example, ritual prescriptions governing the state of impurity associated with childbirth draw the otherwise private birth event into the sphere of the central cultus in its attempt to maintain the purity of the people as a cultically defined community. But the satisfaction of the cultic requirement does not exhaust the ritual need associated with the birth, which may be supplied by a naming ceremony, circumcision feast, and/or special rituals to assist the mother in the birth—rituals in which a female specialist such as a midwife may play a role closely analogous to the role of a priest in other situations of crisis. Women's private rituals or actions favored by women may also be opposed by male authorities as frivolous, superstitious, costly, and unnecessary. But opposition does not always guarantee compliance. Women may take vows that are costly and undertake forbidden pilgrimages as actions of rebellion or flight from oppressive household responsibilities and restrictions. As religiously sanctioned actions they may offer limited relief to women whose options for action were often severely circumscribed.

4. On the boundary of the sacred sphere that is organized by the central cultus or claimed by rival cults, a sphere extended in the name of the principal deity, or deities, to the rituals of daily life, there exists a quasi-religious sphere of spirits, demons, and various malevolent or amoral forces that trouble people and over which they attempt to gain control by special knowledge and defensive action. Those skilled in discerning and controlling these forces, by sorcery, witchcraft, necromancy, medicine, or other means, may be acknowledged by the cultus as practitioners of valuable practical arts or proscribed as challenging the fundamental claims of the deity to embody or control all forms of superhuman power. While some religions might incorporate such beliefs and practices into their belief systems, Israelite Yahwism, from the time of Saul, proscribed the practices and banned the practitioners (1 Sam 23:3, 8). It has often been suggested that women had a special attraction to these quasi-religious practices, both as clients and as practitioners, and it makes sense that women should prefer to seek help for their problems from a local specialist than from a general practitioner or ritual specialist serving a remote

God. That women should also constitute a significant proportion of the mediums and other specialists in spirit manipulation is also understandable. However, the Old Testament evidence is insufficient to confirm such a pattern of preference and contains more references to male than to female classes of occult practitioners.

Conclusion

During the period reflected in the Old Testament sources there appear to have been a number of changes within the cultus and in its relationship to the population as a whole that had significance for women's participation. The progressive movement from multiple cultic centers to a central site that finally claimed sole legitimacy and control over certain ritual events necessarily restricted the participation of women in pilgrim feasts and limited opportunities for women to seek guidance, release, and consolation at local shrines, which were declared illegitimate or demolished. At the same time, increased specialization and hierarchical ordering of priestly/Levitical ranks within the royal/national cultus deprived males in general (as well as Levites) of earlier priestly prerogatives, increasing the distance or sharpening the boundary between the professional guardians of the cultus and the larger circle of male Israelites who comprised the religious assembly. Reorganization of the cultus under the monarchy and again in the postexilic period appears to have limited or eliminated roles earlier assigned to women. On the other hand, there appears to have been a move (most clearly evident in the Deuteronomic legislation) to bring women more fully and directly into the religious assembly, so that the congregation is redefined as a body of lay men and women. As the priesthood became more powerful and specialized, the primary cultic distinction or boundary within the community became that between priest and laity rather than between male and female.

5

ISRAELITE RELIGION
AND THE FAITH OF
ISRAEL'S DAUGHTERS:

Reflections on Gender and
Religious Definition

A S A CONTRIBUTION TO THE PROJECT OF APPLYING SOCIAL SCIEN-
tific perspectives and methods to the study of the Hebrew Bible, a
project deeply indebted to our honoree, I have attempted in various ways
over the past decade and a half to "place" women in the social world of
ancient Israel.[1] These efforts to reconstruct the lives of Israelite women

Originally published in David Jobling, Peggy L. Day, and Gerald T. Sheppard, eds., *The
Bible and the Politics of Exegesis: Essays in Honor of Norman K. Gottwald on His Sixty-Fifth
Birthday* (Cleveland: Pilgrim, 1991) 97–108, 311–17. Cross references to articles that are reprinted in this volume are indicated by an asterisk in square brackets following the original
page number.
   1. Two [unpublished] papers were presented in the SBL (-ASOR) "Social World" project:
"Sexual Distinction in Israelite Personal Names: A Socio-Religious Investigation" (SBL Seminar on the Social World of Ancient Israel, 1976), and "Women's Religious Participation in
the Monarchy" (SBL-ASOR Seminar on the Sociology of the Monarchy, 1986). Related work,
stimulated in large measure by the seminars, includes the following articles: "The Place of
Women in the Israelite Cultus," in Patrick D. Miller, Jr., Paul D. Hanson, and S. Dean
McBride, eds., *Ancient Israelite Religion: Essays in Honor of Frank Moore Cross* (Philadelphia:
Fortress Press, 1987) 397–419 [*81–102]; "The Harlot as Heroine: Narrative Art and Social
Presupposition in Three Old Testament Texts," in Miri Amihai, George W. Coats, and Anne
M. Solomon, eds., *Narrative Research on the Hebrew Bible* (*Semeia* 46; 1989) 119–39 [*197–
218]; "'To Play the Harlot': An Inquiry into an Old Testament Metaphor," in Peggy L. Day,
ed., *Gender and Difference in Ancient Israel*, (Minneapolis: Fortress Press, 1989) 75–94 [*219–
36]; "Women's Religion in Ancient Israel," in Barbara Lesko, ed., *Women's Earliest Records:
From Ancient Egypt and Western Asia* (BJS 166; Atlanta: Scholars Press, 1989) 283–98;

and locate them within the fabric of an ancient patriarchal society have confronted me increasingly with questions about the nature of the enterprise and its presuppositions.[2] I have been brought by my latest work to focus on questions of definition and boundaries, questions raised by attempting to view social institutions and relationships through women's eyes or with attention to women's participation and experience.

The question of definition is focused in this essay by the question of religion. In shifting attention from "the place of women in the Israelite cultus" to "the faith of Israel's daughters,"[3] I found myself asking repeatedly what I was looking for and how I would recognize it. I needed a theory of religion to guide my search and provide a grid that would help me locate women's religious practice. Standard works on ancient Israelite religion offered little help in their textually oriented and (evolutionary-) historical treatments, whose compilations of diverse data on ritual practices, cultic personnel, and theological concepts lacked clear articulation of a guiding concept or sense of a unified whole. They also gave little, or no, attention to women, either as participants in communal rituals or as engaged in distinctive religious practices.[4] Anthropological treatments of

---

"Women (OT)," *ABD* 6:951–57 [*52–66]. See also my earlier work, "Images of Women in the Old Testament," in Rosemary R. Ruether, ed., *Religion and Sexism: Images of Women in the Jewish and Christian Traditions* (New York: Simon and Schuster, 1974) 41–88; reprinted in Norman K. Gottwald, ed., *The Bible and Liberation: Political and Social Hermeneutics* (Maryknoll, N.Y.: Orbis, 1983) 252–88 [*13–51].

2. See Bird, "The Place of Women," 398–99 [*83–84], for an initial statement of aims in reconstruction. The problem that concerns me is the continued segregation of women in the social reconstruction of ancient Israel—both topically (as subjects of research) and in division of research labor. Can we continue to analyze and reconstruct the society (social order, institutions, worldview, etc.) by reference to men's activities and symbolic constructions and then try to insert women into the picture we have drawn? Have we not already prejudiced the categories and the terms of analysis? Recognition of this conceptual and procedural problem does not lead to ready solutions, but rather to awareness of deeper problems. If we attempt to include women at the "ground level" of our analysis, we are immediately confronted with the problem of how to represent them when our sources deny them voice. We lack direct access to women's perceptual world through written sources, and our limited artifactual evidence (which is of undetermined "authorship") is mute. The obstacles to social analysis that would treat women as subjects of social processes alongside—and in interaction with—men are formidable. They are also most acute in the realm of articulation of meanings—and hence the area of religion. I have argued elsewhere that the obstacles are not insurmountable and that we must at least make a deliberate and disciplined effort to imagine the missing partners in any attempt to describe "Israelite" society and religion (Bird, "The Place of Women," 399–400 [*84–86]; cf. idem, "Women's Religion," 284–88).

3. For the latter title, see n. 6 below; for the former, n. 2 above.

4. See, e.g., Georg Fohrer, *History of Israelite Religion* (trans. David E. Green; Nashville: Abingdon, 1972); Hans-Joachim Kraus, *Worship in Israel: A Cultic History of the Old Testament* (trans. Geoffrey Buswell; Richmond: John Knox, 1966); Helmer Ringgren, *Israelite Reli-*

THE FAITH OF ISRAEL'S DAUGHTERS   105

religion offered the kind of systemic analysis I sought, but they too lacked
awareness of women as religious subjects, employing categories that either
excluded or marginalized women's contributions and offering little help
in identifying and interpreting women's religious practice.[5] In my search
for society-encompassing constructs and in my attempts to interpret indi-

gion (trans. David E. Green; Philadelphia: Fortress Press, 1966); H. H. Rowley, *Worship in
Ancient Israel: Its Forms and Meaning* (Philadelphia: Fortress Press, 1967); Roland de Vaux,
Ancient Israel: Its Life and Institutions (New York: McGraw-Hill, 1961) part IV, "Religious
Institutions," 271–517. Although some treatments focus on cognitive-affective dimensions
(theology and worship) and others on institutions, all of necessity include attention to both.
The difficulties of integrating cognitive and institutional aspects in a single analytical system
are illustrated by the variety of approaches and organization represented in these volumes.
I have listed here only those works that focus on religion as an institution and/or system
of beliefs and practices, although conceptions of religion and analyses of religious institutions and ideas play a significant role in histories of Israel and introductions to the Old
Testament/Hebrew Bible. Unique among the available treatments is Gottwald's effort to integrate sociology and theology in his analysis of Israel's religion; see *The Tribes of Yahweh: A
Sociology of the Religion of Liberated Israel, 1250–1050 B.C.E.* (Maryknoll, N.Y.: Orbis, 1979);
and "The Theological Task after *The Tribes of Yahweh*," in Gottwald, *The Bible and Liberation*,
190–200. I find his insistence on the continuity of religion with other social and political
processes appealing even though I cannot fully accept his construct and would emphasize
the complexity of religious symbols (with Bynum, n. 5 below). Gottwald's attention to social
processes in the analysis of religion has allowed him to introduce women into the picture
more frequently than do other general studies, but women are still not fully represented as
subjects of the sociohistorical processes he describes.

5. For a helpful survey and analysis of anthropological approaches, see Brian Morris,
Anthropological Studies of Religion: An Introductory Text (Cambridge: Cambridge University
Press, 1987). See also Michael Banton, ed., *Anthropological Approaches to the Study of Religion*
(New York: Praeger, 1986); and Robert L. Moore and Frank E. Reynolds, eds., *Anthropology
and the Study of Religion* (Chicago: Center for the Scientific Study of Religion, 1984). For a
critique of one influential theory from the perspective of its ability to interpret women's
experience, see Caroline Walker Bynum, "Women's Stories, Women's Symbols: A Critique of
Victor Turner's Theory of Liminality," in Moore and Reynolds, *Anthropology and the Study
of Religion*, 105–25. Cf. Bynum, "Introduction: The Complexity of Symbols," in Caroline
Walker Bynum, Steven Harrell, and Paula Richman, eds., *Gender and Religion: On the Complexity of Symbols* (Boston: Beacon, 1986) 8–10, for a feminist analysis of the understanding
of religious symbol in the theories of Victor Turner and Clifford Geertz. One could argue
that Geertz's understanding of religion as a system of symbols ("Religion as a Cultural System," in Banton, *Anthropological Approaches to the Study of Religion*, 4, 8–9) prejudices the
analysis in favor of men's experience, since the construction of symbol systems is typically
associated with the sphere(s) of male activity and reflects male perceptions and experience.
Bynum focuses instead on Geertz's understanding of symbol, which she finds inadequate.
Insisting that "no theory of symbol can be adequate unless it incorporates women's experience and discourse as well as men's" ("The Complexity of Symbols," 15), Bynum suggests
that "women [may] have . . . certain modes of symbolic discourse different from those of
men" (16), arguing that "even where men and women have used the same symbols and
rituals, they may have invested them with different meanings and different ways of meaning."
These conclusions anticipate some of my own, formulated independently (see below). See
also n. 35 below.

vidual actions and beliefs I found repeatedly that women's practice either did not fit the conventional categories of analysis or transgressed the boundaries (spatial and conceptual). Asking the question of women's religious practice and belief entails a shift of perspective that affects both the contours and content of the phenomenon known as "Israelite religion." This essay is an attempt to identify some of the issues of definition that arise from this shift of perspective. It originated in an effort to present to a general audience some of the fruits of my current research on women's religious lives in ancient Israel.[6] It is not a presentation of results but of questions along the way, questions I shall introduce in the same manner that they presented themselves to me, namely, in consideration of particular examples.

In my attempts to reimage Israelite religion so as to bring women fully into focus, I have drawn largely upon anthropological studies of contemporary women's religious practice in which descriptions of actions are accompanied by the interpretations of actors and observers.[7] I begin with four examples that illustrate in different ways and in different contexts problems of defining or classifying religious activity involving women.

The first is an account of a funeral in an Iranian tribal village, which the anthropologist Erika Friedl characterizes as an "open-air religious ceremony:"

> During a funeral . . . women function as mourners, crying and singing around the body in the cemetery, while the men dig the grave. As soon as the body is buried and the prayers begin—in other words, as soon as the ceremony takes on a *distinctly religious* character—the women must leave.[8]

6. See Bird, "Gender and Religious Definition: The Case of Ancient Israel," *Harvard Divinity Bulletin* 20 (1990) 12–13, 19–20. This essay is adapted from the lecture, but retains much of its original character, attempting to speak broadly about issues I have addressed elsewhere in more narrowly focused and/or technical studies, to identify underlying problems and themes, and to link the analysis of women's religious lives in ancient Israel more explicitly with contemporary examples of women's piety and theoretical discussion in feminist anthropology and gender studies.

7. On the uses of anthropology for reconstructing women's roles and activities in ancient Israel, see Bird, "The Place of Women," 400–401 [*85–87] and "Women's Religion in Ancient Israel," 288–91. Carol Meyers (*Discovering Eve: Ancient Israelite Women in Context* [New York and Oxford: Oxford University Press, 1988]) also draws heavily on anthropological studies for her critique of common feminist misconstruals of Israelite patriarchy and for her reconstruction of gender relations in early Israel, though with conclusions and emphases that differ from my own at significant points.

8. Erika Friedl, "Islam and Tribal Women in a Village in Iran," in Nancy Auer Falk and Rita M. Gross, eds., *Unspoken Worlds: Women's Religious Lives* (Belmont, Calif.: Wadsworth, 1989) 127 (emphasis mine).

My next two examples come from a study of the religious lives of elderly Jewish women, mostly Kurdish immigrants from Iraq, who frequented a day center in Jerusalem in 1984–85. The author, Susan Starr Sered, characterizes the women as illiterate and uneducated, in a community where religion in its dominant, male expression is highly literate and book-oriented. According to Sered, women and men in the Sephardic village culture represented by these women occupy different religious worlds, "sometimes diametrically opposed, sometimes complementary, sometimes overlapping."[9]

The first example from Sered's study concerns the major holidays, in particular Passover, which Sered's informants considered the ultimate religious holiday. Their preparations began months in advance and centered on cleaning and food preparation, both rooted in biblical prescriptions but shaped by later custom. In their cleaning the women go far beyond the law that requires the removal of forbidden grain and other substances. "Investing weeks creating an immaculate house is one of the most important measures of a pious woman," according to Sered. "Even when the women moan and groan about the work," she says, "there is a definite element of pride in their ability and willingness to carry out a divine command in what they perceive to be the correct, female manner."[10]

Food preparation plays a central role in women's "celebration" of all major holidays, according to Sered. When asked what they or their ethnic group did on Passover, Purim, Hanukkah, and so forth, the women's answers always pertained to food or food preparation. "Food is the central symbol of each holiday for the women," Sered concludes, and "food preparation is the most important *ritual* activity . . . they perform."[11] One of the women's most difficult Passover tasks was cleaning the rice (eaten by Sephardic Jews during Passover, in contrast to Ashkenazic practice). The women sort through the rice grain by grain (sometimes as much as ten to fifteen kilos for a large extended family), repeating the process for a total of seven times. This "unnecessary" repetition, Sered argues, was understood as "a form of worship." "These women believed that sorting the rice pleases God in much the same way that it pleases God to hear prayers or Psalms of praise."[12]

A second example from Sered's study relates to tombs. "The old

9. "Women as Ritual Experts: The Religious Lives of Sephardi Jewish Women in Israel" (Ph.D. diss., Hebrew University, 1986) 2–3. [Subsequently published in revised form as *Women as Ritual Experts: The Religious Lives of Elderly Jewish Women in Jerusalem* (New York and Oxford: Oxford University Press, 1992).]

10. Ibid., 54–55.

11. Ibid., 55.

12. Ibid., 56.

women who frequent the Day Center" see themselves, Sered reports, "as the spiritual guardians of their extended families." "As young and middle-aged women they tended and cared for their families, and in old age this role has become spiritualized." "Seeing themselves as the link between the generations," she says, "old women are responsible for soliciting the help of ancestors whenever their descendants are faced with problems such as illness, infertility, war, or economic troubles." "Guarding over, petitioning, visiting and negotiating with ancestors [who may be biological ancestors, or 'mythical' ancestors such as saints and biblical figures] is an important part of their religious lives." The women "remember" their ancestors in a variety of rituals, including lighting candles on the Festival of the New Moon (a festival that is hardly acknowledged by the men but is celebrated by all of the women) and visiting cemeteries and holy tombs.[13] At the tombs, they typically kiss and caress the structure and cry—in a manner Sered describes as "ritualistic." In the old country the women would often stay all night, but are prevented from doing so now by the government, which supervises the tombs.[14]

My final example is an excerpt from an interview with a twenty-year-old maid in Salé, Morocco, recorded by the Moroccan sociologist Fatima Mernissi.[15] It concerns a visit to a *marabout,* a North African saint's shrine, often at the site of the saint's tomb.

Q: *Do you go to the Marabout often?*
A: Yes, quite often. For example, I prefer to go there on the days of Aïd [religious festivals]. When one has a family as desperate as mine, the shrine is a haven of peace and quiet. I like to go there. . . . I stay there hours, sometimes whole days.
Q: *The day of Aïd it must be full of people.*
A: Yes, there are people, but they are lost in their own problems. So they leave you alone. Mostly it's women who cry, without speaking, each in her own world.
Q: *Aren't there any men at the shrine?*
A: Yes, but men have their side, women theirs. Men come to visit the shrine and leave very quickly; the women, especially those with problems, stay much longer.
Q: *What do they do and what do they say?*
A: That depends. Some are happy just to cry. Others take hold of the saint's garments and say, "Give me this, oh saint, give me that."[16]

13. Ibid., 29, 34–36.
14. Ibid., 30, 141.
15. Fatima Mernissi, "Women, Saints, and Sanctuaries in Morocco," in Falk and Gross, *Unspoken Worlds,* 112–21.
16. Ibid., 112–13.

I have chosen this final example from contemporary sources because of similarities to the tomb visits of the Iraqi Jewish women, but also because of resemblances to the biblical story of Hannah at the sanctuary in Shiloh (1 Sam 1:1-28, esp. vv. 9-18), weeping in deep distress, without words, praying in her heart for a child, and making a vow (a typical form of women's devotion in Islam). While this example is not primarily concerned with religious boundaries and definitions, it illustrates the way in which women use general or male-dominated religious institutions and occasions for their own purposes to suit their own peculiar needs, investing them at times with their own rituals and meanings (as when the Jewish women light candles at the tombs or throw unlighted candles through the grating where they are prevented from direct access to the tomb).[17]

The *marabout,* or the local sanctuary in Israel, is a place where a woman can go according to her own needs and opportunities. Her visits may coincide with a communal festival, especially where a pilgrimage is involved (in which case we should probably speak of a regional, rather than a local, sanctuary). Her visits are not determined, however, by calendrical observances and prescriptions—that is, by feasts of the agricultural year, related primarily to men's cycle of labor—except in dependence on men's obligations. Within the total spectrum of religious observances, individual pilgrimages to shrines and visits to graves appear to play a more important role in women's religious lives than in men's. Thus a practice that may be secondary or peripheral for men may be central for women.

In the case of Hannah, the occasion for the visit to the sanctuary was the annual pilgrimage of her husband Elkanah. This pilgrimage is usually understood to have been one of the three mandated feasts when "every male" was to appear "before the Lord" (Exod 23:17), although it may have been a clan festival.[18] In either case it is the man's obligation that determines the visit, but it entails family participation of wives and children, all of whom share in the sacrificial meal. Hannah, however, uses this occasion to bring her desperate distress to the attention of the deity and to make her vow. She must certainly have prayed often and fervently for a child in her home, but she apparently regarded the sanctuary at Shiloh as an especially efficacious place for her petition—a place where the deity was felt to be present in a special way, just as the saint's spirit is understood to be present in the *marabout.*[19]

17. Sered, "Women as Ritual Experts," 75–77.

18. P. Kyle McCarter, Jr., *I Samuel: A New Translation with Introduction, Notes, and Commentary* (AB 8; Garden City, N.Y.: Doubleday, 1980) 58 n. 3, citing Menahem Haran, *VT* 19 (1969) 11–22.

19. Cf. Sered, "Women as Ritual Experts," 31, for the belief that the saint was physically present in his tomb.

Two of my examples concern ancestors, saints, and tombs, with which women appear to have a special affinity. The association of women and tombs is not limited to modern Judaism and Islam. Peter Brown notes the attraction of women to tombs in his book on the cult of the saints in Latin Christianity. He comments that throughout the Mediterranean world (of late antiquity) the cemetery was the only place where women could find respite and protection.[20] Ancient Israel, however, or at least the tradition canonized in the Hebrew Bible, had no place for the cemetery or for ancestors in its worship. Both ancient Israel and later Judaism attempted to draw a firm line between the world of the living and the world of the dead. The God of Israel was a God of the living, not of the dead (Ps 88:5-6; Isa 38:18-19; cf. Matt 22:32; Mark 12:27; Luke 20:38). Attempts to communicate with the dead were condemned and mediums banished (1 Sam 28:3, 7-19). Tombs are desacralized in the Hebrew Bible—but they persist in the landscape to emerge in etiological notices (Gen 35:8 [Deborah]; Judg 16:31 [Samson]; Josh 24:30 [Joshua]), incidental remarks ("you will meet two men by Rachel's tomb" [1 Sam 10:2]), and prophetic denunciations of practices that "provoke the Lord" ("sitting inside tombs" [Isa 65:4]).

Sered's report of the women's rituals relating to graves and her interpretation of their actions suggest a number of questions about the *religious* meaning of graves and ancestors in ancient Israel and the relationship of women to such actions and beliefs. I can only touch on these, noting first of all that the women's "devotion" to the ancestors reported by Sered finds no basis in ancient or modern (Israelite/Jewish) religious prescriptions; in fact it is discouraged. This should alert us to the possibility of ritual activities and religious beliefs that receive no mention in our texts but nevertheless play a significant role in the lives of ancient Israelite women—or men. Popular practice and belief that is not seen as directly threatening may go unreported—the more so, one may speculate, if identified with women.

The question of ancestral cults or a cult of the dead in ancient Israel needs to be raised again,[21] and more particularly the question of women's roles in such cults. Earlier reconstructions of Israelite religion that found its origins in a cult of the deified ancestor typically argued that women had little or no place in Israelite religion, because only a male heir could perform the essential duty of representing and propitiating the deceased ancestor.[22] Such reasoning appears sound insofar as continuity of "name"

20. Peter Brown, *The Cult of the Saints: Its Rise and Function in Latin Christianity* (Chicago: University of Chicago Press, 1981) 44.
21. The two should be distinguished, although they have much in common and may at times coincide. On cults of the dead, see now Theodore J. Lewis, *Cults of the Dead in Ancient Israel and Ugarit* (HSM 39; Atlanta: Scholars Press, 1989).
22. Bird, "The Place of Women," 397 n. 3.

or lineage is the primary concern of the cult; but Sered's report of the Iraqi women's understanding of themselves as the link between the generations, "mothers" of the deceased as well as the living, gives us reason to ask whether women, precisely in their role as mothers (the one role singled out for equal honor with men) might have had a role in an ancestral cult alongside the male head of the household or lineage.

The suggestion by Karel van der Toorn that the teraphim should be understood as ancestral images, in the sense of a deified ancestor, raises further interesting questions about women's role in such a family cult.[23] Although the account of Rachel's theft of the teraphim (Gen 31:19, 30-35) clearly identifies them/it[24] as belonging to her father, it is interesting to note that the only two narrative references to teraphim in the Hebrew Bible place them in women's hands (Michal in 1 Sam 19:13, 16).[25]

Attention to women's religious practice raises questions of religious definition and boundaries in relation to family or ancestral cults, regional and local cults, magic and mediation. In general, women appear to be identified primarily with local rather than national or centralized forms of religious expression, and with "folk" practice (often viewed as "superstition") rather than the learned tradition. For ancient Israel, we need to ask about the existence, form, and function of a family cult alongside the national or pan-tribal cult of Yahweh: How were family and national cult related?[26] What role did women play in family or household cults? Was the family cult necessarily an ancestral cult?

23. Karel van der Toorn, "The Nature of the Biblical Teraphim in the Light of the Cunei-form Evidence," *CBQ* 52 (1990) 215–16, 222.

24. Despite the plural form of the noun, it appears to describe a single object in 1 Samuel 19 (van der Toorn, "The Nature of the Biblical Teraphim," 206).

25. Van der Toorn notes that Wellhausen had "noticed the predilection of women for the cult of the teraphim." Observing that a number of texts show Israelite women engaged in ritual activities of their own, he asks whether we should add the involvement with the teraphim to this list. "Women certainly had access to the teraphim, and the story of Rachel's theft is suggestive of an emotional attachment to the images," he argues, although he finds evidence in Laban's indignant response that "the cult of the teraphim was by no means the exclusive business of women" ("The Nature of the Biblical Teraphim," 210). In both of these texts involving women the teraphim appear to belong to the sphere of "family devotion" or "domestic piety" (210). References to the teraphim in Judges 17–18 and Hos 3:4, however, in which the term is paired with "ephod," suggest to van der Toorn that they also had a place in the public cult (211–12), more particularly in divination (213, 215). Whatever role they may have played in later cultic practice—and/or cult polemic—the Genesis and Samuel texts point to a primary association with domestic religion.

26. This question has received considerable attention in Mesopotamian studies in rela-tion to personal names, which constitute an important source for understanding personal, and family, piety as distinct from the state cult. Attention has focused on the particu-lar deities mentioned in theophoric names, the content of the petitions and praise, and the interpretation of apparently generic references to "the god" or "my god" as evidence for a "personal god." See, e.g., Robert A. DeVito, "Studies in Third Millennium Sumerian Onomastics: The Designation and Conception of the Personal God" (Ph.D. diss., Harvard

The importance of regional sanctuaries has long been recognized, although the question of distinct regional cults has usually been relegated to the premonarchic period. The meaning of these sanctuaries, however, as well as the local shrines (*bāmôt:* "high places") denounced (in Deuteronomistic circles) as places of pagan worship, needs to be reexamined with reference to women's practice and women's religious needs. Mernissi's account, which can be paralleled elsewhere in the Muslim world, suggests that visits to local shrines, pilgrimages, and individual acts of petition and dedication related to particular needs were favored by women and better suited to the general rhythms and the exigencies of their lives than were the major communal rites and celebrations.

A variant of this shrine-oriented pattern of seeking supernatural aid might be seen in visits to mediums or seers. It is difficult to assess the evidence for gender-differentiated involvement in such practices, partly because the activity is generally discouraged or condemned by religious elites and partly because of inadequate sources and problems of terminology.[27] The predominance of women as mediums and clairvoyants has been noted in many cultures, as well as the prominence of women as participants in ecstatic cults.[28] Women are more commonly accused of sorcery and identified as witches;[29] they are also popularly viewed as more inclined

University, 1986). Although personal names have been seen as a source for understanding popular religion in Israel (Martin Noth, *Die israelitischen Personennamen* [Stuttgart: Kohlhammer, 1929], esp. 132–35), lack of dramatic disjunction between a state pantheon and the deities invoked in personal names has meant that little attention has been given to the relationship of personal or family piety to the state cult in Israel.

27. See Bird, "The Place of Women," 410–11 [*101–2]. The medium of Endor (1 Samuel 28) is a well-known example of a female practitioner of necromancy in the Old Testament, described in v. 7 by the expression *'ēšet ba'ălat 'ôb* ("woman possessing a familiar spirit/ghost"). Elsewhere the term *'ôb* is used alone to designate the medium, usually paired with the masculine term *yiddě'ōnî* (Deut 18:11 [sg.]; Lev 19:31; 20:6, 27; 2 Kgs 21:6; 23:24 [pl.]). A noteworthy feature of this pairing is the highly unusual feminine-masculine order (*'ōbôt-yiddě'ōnîm*), which appears to confirm the predominance of women among this class of specialists. In contrast, diviners, who used technical means of inquiry and in Assyria and elsewhere were organized in professional guilds and supported by the state, are designated in biblical sources only by masculine forms: *qōsēm, měnaḥēš, mě'ôněnîm* (the *qal* feminine participle in Isa 57:3 is not a professional designation, but a generalized term of slander).

28. See esp. I. M. Lewis, *Ecstatic Religion: An Anthropological Study of Spirit Possession and Shamanism* (New York: Penguin, 1971). See also the case studies in Falk and Gross, *Unspoken Worlds:* Martha B. Binford, "Julia: An East African Diviner" (3–14); Youngsook Kim Harvey, "Possession Sickness and Women Shamans in Korea" (37–44); and Ross S. Kraemer, "Ecstasy and Possession: Women of Ancient Greece and the Cult of Dionysus" (45–55). Cf. Anita Spring, "Epidemiology of Spirit Possession Among the Luvale of Zambia," in Judith Hoch-Smith and Anita Spring, eds., *Women in Ritual and Symbolic Roles* (New York: Plenum, 1978) 165–90.

29. For discussion of ancient Near Eastern evidence, see Sue Rollin, "Women and Witchcraft in Ancient Assyria (c. 900–600 BC)," in Averil Cameron and Amélie Kuhrt, eds., *Images*

to the use of magic. The issues involved in this assemblage of marginal or quasi-religious practices are too complex for discussion here. What requires note, however, is that the criteria that are often used to distinguish these types of activity from recognized and/or approved religious practice often coincide with common distinctions between male and female realms or patterns of action.

Women's practice cannot simply be identified with magic or mediums or local cults, because it transgresses these boundaries; but because it is so frequently characterized by practices that are normally located at or outside the limits of normative/male-defined religion, focusing on women draws attention to the problematic character of these limits. This may be illustrated by another class of evidence that refers to women's world, at least symbolically, but whose meaning remains uncertain precisely because it cannot be neatly located by conventional categories of classification. That is the small terra-cotta figurines of a naked female found throughout Iron Age Palestinian sites. Variously described as images of a goddess or of a pregnant/fertile woman, as objects of veneration, amulets, or toys, they have baffled interpreters because of their anomalous distribution. They are found both in domestic sites, occurring singly in private houses, *and* in collections associated with sanctuaries, especially of the extramural/peripheral type.[30] We are uncertain of their function or name,

---

of *Women in Antiquity* (Detroit: Wayne State University Press, 1983) 34–45. Cf. Stanley D. Walters, "The Sorceress and Her Apprentice: A Case Study of an Accusation," *JCS* 23 (1970) 27–38; and Tzvi Abusch, "The Demonic Image of the Witch in Standard Babylonian Literature: The Reworking of Popular Conceptions by Learned Exorcists," in Jacob Neusner, Ernest S. Frerichs, and Paul V. M. Flesher, eds., *Religion, Science, and Magic in Concert and in Conflict* (New York and Oxford: Oxford University Press, 1989) 27–58.

30. T. A. Holland, "A Study of Palestinian Iron Age Baked Clay Figurines with Special Reference to Jerusalem: Cave 1," *Levant* 9 (1977) 121–55; Mervyn D. Fowler, "Excavated Figurines: A Case for Identifying a Site as Sacred?" *ZAW* 97 (1985) 333–44; Urs Winter, *Frau und Göttin: Exegetische und ikonographische Studien zum weiblichen Gottesbild im Alten Israel und in dessen Umwelt* (Freiburg: Universitätsverlag; Göttingen: Vandenhoeck & Ruprecht, 1986) 128–29; John S. Holladay, "Religion in Israel and Judah under the Monarchy," in Miller, Hanson, and McBride, *Ancient Israelite Religion*, esp. 270–82 and 291 n. 109.

Holladay distinguishes two religious traditions according to archaeological evidence: (1) an officially sanctioned aniconic cult associated with sanctuaries in the capital and neighborhood shrines connected with the residences of important officials (apparently concerned largely with formal sacrificial ritual, including probably the eating of ritual meals) (280); and (2) a "totally different form of religious expression," witnessed in both north and south, by "small clusters of cultic artifacts, heavily biased toward the iconographic, discontinuously distributed (both spatially and temporally) throughout domestic quarters and by larger clusters centered on extramural locations near major cities," with "smaller Judean ('local' or 'neighborhood') cult areas, featuring modest supersets of the domestic clusters" attested near cave mouths (281). Holladay suggests that "the primary participants in this cultus were women" (294 n. 126), but does not elaborate on the basis for this identification.

What is of particular interest in the second type of cultic evidence is the distribution of

and we cannot connect them with certainty to anything in the biblical text. They challenge the conventional boundaries between sacred and secular, domestic and foreign cult, orthodox (Yahwistic) and idolatrous practice.

Another kind of question about definitions and boundaries is illustrated by my first example. Here we see a case in which women play an essential, and ritually elaborated, role as mourners in a communal ceremony; but only the prayers, recited by the men, are understood as religious. Nevertheless, Friedl characterizes the ceremony as a whole as "religious." On what basis is that assessment made? From whose point of view? Friedl describes the women of this village as holding essentially the same views as the men concerning the requirements of religion (in this case Islam). Because of their inability to fulfill the gender-blind demands in an optimal manner, the women generally considered themselves to be "bad Muslims" and even "heathens," concurring in the men's low assessment of their religious character.[31] A cycle of low expectations, lack of religious training, and obstacles to full participation in communal religious practices centered in the mosque worked to reinforce women's religious marginality. Unlike their urban counterparts, they had no religious rituals or activities of their own to complement men's rituals, from which they were almost completely excluded.[32] It appears likely then that both the women and the men viewed the prayers alone as religious.

One of the questions raised by this example concerns the extension of religion into the "secular" realm or the realm outside the sanctuary or recognized holy place.[33] Common means of extending the realm of the

---

the figurines in both domestic and cult sites. Whether or not this denotes a cultic activity in which women were the major participants, it does describe a pattern attested cross-culturally for women's religious activity. Women's rituals tend to be centered in the home, and their participation in public rituals typically links the domestic realm to the public religious realm.

31. Friedl, "Islam and Tribal Women," 169.

32. Ibid., 163; cf. Anne H. Betteridge, "The Controversial Vows of Urban Muslin Women in Iran," in Falk and Gross, *Unspoken Worlds*, 102–11.

33. I am struck (unexpectedly) by the power of sacred places—and to a lesser degree persons and objects—to define what is religious. Although the holy may be viewed as pervading all of life, it is hard to identify it, grasp it, or sense its presence when it is not embodied in some concrete form. It is concentrated at sanctuaries—where it is typically under male control. Men are its primary guardians, representatives, and interpreters. Where women have access to it, either as guardians or supplicants, it is normally in forms derived from their everyday roles and activities as mothers, daughters, and wives: baking cakes for the Queen of Heaven, weaving garments for the Asherah, weeping for Tammuz, bewailing the virginity of Jephthah's daughter, celebrating the victory of Yahweh's armies in song and dance, serving at the tent of meeting. Of these six examples, the first four describe religious expressions rejected by normative Yahwism—or by the tradition that received canonical status—while modern interpretations of the last two repeatedly question whether the acts are religious or secular, and in the last case, legitimate or illegitimate.

holy into the realm of the profane include prayers and blessings that invoke the deity, actions of sacred persons or religious experts, and use of sacred objects or texts. Do these special actions or symbols transform the entire event into a religious event, or does it become "religious" only at the point where explicitly religious language and symbols are introduced?[34]

There is a deeper question, I think, about the assessment of religious meaning in the gender-differentiated actions of the funeral ceremony that is not adequately answered by identifying the religious element with the prayers alone. It concerns the definition of "religion" and "religious," and the ability or right to define. The view that identifies the prayers as the religious element of the ceremony represents a narrow definition of religion identified with a set of formal practices or symbols. There is, however, a wider area of practice, feeling, and cognition characterized by understandings of social obligation and welfare, of duty to family, community, nation, or people, of "right" action or conduct pleasing to God, that might be subsumed under a broader definition of religion. Sered draws on such an understanding in interpreting the actions of her informants as "religious."[35] Following her lead, we might ask in a broader way how the women mourners understood their role: as a duty—or as a "natural" response, as something needed by the deceased? As required or desired by God? One might argue that the women's sense of the necessity and appropriateness of their culturally specified part in the funeral ceremony was functionally equivalent to that of the men in the performance of their culturally specified actions.[36]

34. Asymmetry of religious symbolism may be seen in other Muslim ceremonies, such as the wedding, in which the groom, with his male companions, proceeds to the mosque before entering the bridal chamber (as a sanctified warrior). The bride has no corresponding religious act (analysis based on the film *Some Women of Marrakech* [Granada]).

35. Sered, "Women as Ritual Experts," 12–13. Sered states that she could find no definition of religion particularly relevant to her study "since all accepted definitions of religion were composed by scholars who were considering primarily male religious experience" (13). She chose to use as a working definition a combination of Eliade's idea of the "sacred" (Mircea Eliade, *The Sacred and the Profane* [New York: Harper, 1961] 8–18) and the five-category model (religious experience, ideology, ritual, knowledge, and secular consequences) of Charles Glock and Rodney Stark (*Religion and Society in Tension* [New York: Rand McNally, 1965]). This allowed her to consider issues such as food preparation "that would not normally lie within the sphere of the study of religion" (13).

36. I recognize that the notion of equivalence is fraught with hazards, since it always involves comparison of phenomena that are commonly defined as dissimilar. I nevertheless believe that comparison aimed at identifying unobserved or discounted commonalities is essential and constitutes one of the contributions of the outside observer to an understanding of the way societies "work" (see below). A significant contribution to the notion of equivalence as it relates to women's religious activity is drawn from women's own self-understandings of the nature and worth of their distinct activities and duties. See Sered, "Women as Ritual Experts," 13.

Insofar as lamentation and prayers are both required rituals of the burial ceremony and recognized as such, the formal distinction between "religious" and "not religious" loses some of its force, although it does not disappear completely. If we were to ask further about the women's own understanding of their role, we might discover that while acknowledging the men's monopoly of the religious symbols, they themselves accord these symbols less weight than do the men. When the men complain that the women have little religious "sense" or sensibility, they may be confirming that in fact the women have less involvement, and/or investment, in the symbolic world controlled by the men. We must consider the possibility that the distinction between the sacred and the profane falls at a different place or carries different weight or implications for women than it does for men in the same society.

I realize that the question of who defines what is religious can be understood as meaningless or moot. The obvious answer is that the society defines, in the complex way that societies create culture and institutions, generate myths, values, and rules of conduct, and in general construct and maintain a worldview. To say that society defines, however, means in ancient Israel, and in modern Iran, that men define, because the means of creating and enforcing common cultural understandings lie in the sphere of male activity and male control. If the public sphere, the sphere of the society's overarching and integrating institutions, is not exclusively a sphere of male activity, it is still a sphere dominated by males and male interests; and if women play a significant role in transmitting and inculcating the society's perspectives and values and may thereby affect the shape of those cultural understandings, they still lack control of the means for developing a distinctive voice or vision of their own. A fundamental characteristic of patriarchal societies is asymmetry of gender-differentiated roles and institutions. The primary spheres of male and female activity are not strictly complementary; rather, the public sphere, dominated by males, encapsulates and penetrates the domestic sphere through its laws, religious values, and worldview.

I have already suggested one way in which this male power of definition may need to be qualified—not at the level of content, but in the degree of authority or ultimacy accorded to it and in the relative weight given to various constitutive elements. Although I would maintain that men and women in the same society do not hold different worldviews, women's perspective on, and investment in, that common worldview is conditioned by their different location within it and by the degree to which they possess freedom and power to manipulate its symbols.[37]

---

37. Cf. Hennrietta L. Moore, *Feminism and Anthropology* (Oxford: Polity, 1988) 3–5 and 199 n. 1.

The society defines what is religious and what is not, just as it determines the content of religious belief and the forms of religious practice; and it is the historian's or anthropologist's first duty to articulate the meaning of this institution or aspect of culture in a manner that would "make sense" to members of that society. But the effort of "making sense" is always a creative act, whether done from the inside or the outside. The outside observer invariably brings to the task views and understandings alien to the society being observed. There is a sense, then, in which any society or institution viewed from the outside is defined by the observer. "Religion" is a construct imposed on the ancient society by a modern observer who attempts to understand and delineate its referent by comparing it with similar phenomena in other societies. The historian or anthropologist has a unique freedom, as an outsider, to see what no member of the society can see, to achieve an overview, but also to discern tensions and cleavages that may not be recognized or articulated from within, that may be felt but never formulated.

The contribution of feminist criticism has been to identify gender as a critical factor in the social and symbolic construction of the world and to analyze its role in the distribution of power and honor. In the case of the funeral, the question of religious definition—the shape and boundaries of the sacred realm—leads to recognition of a fundamental asymmetry in the men's and women's roles, both of which are essential to the performance of the ceremony. The element of the ceremony or ritual process that makes it "religious" is reserved to males, but the ceremony requires the contributions of both men and women—both of which take ritual form. Funerals require mourners (perhaps even more than prayers)—and cross-culturally women play a prominent specialized role in mourning, which may acquire professional status and involve special training. This phenomenon is well attested in the Hebrew Bible (Jer 9:17 [Heb. 16], 20 [Heb. 19]; 2 Chr 35:25) and is illustrated by tomb paintings from Egypt and sculptured reliefs on a royal sarcophagus from Byblos.[38]

The role of women in relation to feasts (which generally have some religious occasion) may be seen as analogous to their role in funerals, except that it is more clearly confined to the preparatory stages, with spatial and temporal separation of the men's and women's actions—especially in those cases where the sacred meal is consumed only by men, or in which only the men's segregated eating is ritually elaborated.[39] It is not

38. See Edmond Jacob, "Mourning," *IDB* 3:452–54; and Bird, "Women's Religion in Ancient Israel," 295–96.
39. The example of meal preparation may be taken as representative of the various situations in which men's religious activity depends on support actions of women. In modern observance of kashrut, the woman's critical role is invested with religious significance, but this appears to be a special development reflecting the shift of religious focus in diaspora

clear what sort of ritual actions may have been performed at sacred meals in early Israel, if any (the symbolic actions may have related only to the sacrifice).

Both funerals and festival meals celebrated in the home represent a class of ceremonies located outside the sanctuary or cult site. In these celebrations the domestic and public realms meet and overlap (or interpenetrate). Men bring the prayers, blessings, and ritual actions of the sanctuary into the home or kinship gathering,[40] while women contribute actions that are elaborations or extensions of their normal roles and activities within the household. The professional mourner represents a specialization of the woman's "natural" role as grieving mother. These gender-differentiated actions also extend to actions related to the sanctuary. Elkanah sacrifices annually; Hannah dedicates her child and annually brings him a little robe that she has made for him (1 Sam 2:19): two forms of devotional action—or fulfillment of obligation. Are both religious? Of equal value?

Forms of religious observance that take place apart from sanctuaries and without a recognized religious specialist are difficult to assess. Here the line between religion and magic, sacred and profane is less sharply or clearly drawn. But it is precisely here that women are most involved.[41] Even more difficult to evaluate, however, are activities involving only women, or centered on women's experience and performed in women's space, such as rituals of birth and menarche. In Mesopotamia there is evidence for the Old Babylonian period of a class of priestesses associated with the midwife in a birth ritual, but this cultic association—or the religious function assumed by the midwife— seems to have been lost in the subsequent period.[42] In Israel the midwife has no religious function, though blessings associated with birth suggest a religious association.[43]

Judaism from temple to home as the primary place of ritual action. Here we need to ask how women are motivated to do their required part. Do they understand it as religious duty comparable to men's religious duties—or simply as their allotted work, or as an added burden?

Although pilgrim feasts may be understood as family meals, that pattern cannot be assumed for all cultic or communal meals. See Bird, "Women's Religion in Ancient Israel," 293–94.

40. The funeral may be understood as essentially a family affair, even when it involves the entire village.

41. Evidence for a primary identification of major (central) sanctuaries with male worshipers might be seen in Eli's misinterpretation of Hannah's behavior—behavior that is precisely *typical* of the women at the *marabout*!

42. See Joan Westenholz, "Tamar, Qĕdēšā, Qadištu, and Sacred Prostitution in Mesopotamia," *HTR* 82 (1989) 245–65; and my forthcoming monograph on the qĕdēšâ and qadištu.

43. Cf. Ruth 4:14, where blessing—and naming (!)—is performed by a group of women. While this is an anomalous text, it does point to otherwise unattested communal celebra-

I have only touched on the issues that are raised in trying to place women in religious systems defined by male participation and male constructions of meaning. The problems involve both placement and interpretation of women's roles and activities. The limited examples I have offered suggest that women may respond in quite different ways to their exclusion or marginalization in a male-defined system.[44]

For ancient Israel I believe it is essential to recognize gender-differentiated roles, activities, and experience as a fundamental characteristic of religious as well as social, political, and economic life, and to recognize asymmetry as a fundamental feature of these relations. Religion defined in male terms or according to male models has difficulty placing women and assessing their piety, whether it imitates men's, in which case it rarely achieves parity, or assumes distinctive female forms, which may either go unacknowledged or be identified with foreign or heterodox cults. The whole question of religious pluralism *within* a national Yahweh cult is just beginning to be explored in relation to evidence for Asherah as a symbol

---

tions and rituals of women. On rituals of menarche we have even less evidence, though the story of Jephthah's daughter (Judg 11:34-40) seems to presuppose some such ritual.

44. E.g., the Iranian village women understood religion as essentially a male affair in which they could not participate on equal terms. Prevented by menstruation and child-care responsibilities from regular attendance at the mosque and segregated to a place of marginal visibility and audibility when they did attend, they took little interest in the mosque and appear to have cultivated no alternative religious life. The women of the day center also recognized a realm of male religious activity (in this case the yeshiva) into which they could not enter, but in which they took high interest, blessing it and offering financial support, as essential to their own well-being. Unlike the universalizing demands of Islam, however, their religious tradition, or at least these women's interpretation of it, allowed for highly differentiated male and female expressions of religious obligation and fulfillment. As a consequence, the women invested their required tasks with religious meaning and ritual actions—of their own devising—insisting that they did not need to be instructed by the rabbi. At times, in fact, their religious practices clearly conflicted with the demands of the religious authorities.

In both of these cases, the women accepted the legitimacy of the male-dominated and -defined religion, but in the case of the Jewish women, they created a religion of their own, within the structures of the male-dominated religion and society. In their own differentiated practice—and in their support of the male activities—they affirm and elaborate their role as mothers and caretakers, which appears to be critical for their own self-understanding and for their standing/status within their social world.

An alternative response of women to male-dominated religion in a highly gender-segregated world may be illustrated by urban women in Teheran—sharing the same Shiite faith but living in a different social world (Betteridge, "The Controversial Vows," 102–11). Here we find women's religious rituals that parallel men's and that may even be led by women ritual specialists trained in the same textual and liturgical traditions as their male counterparts. I am inclined to see this development of parallel institutions as a modern one related to the modern education of women and their entry into professions shared by men, or parallel to men's professions. I doubt that such developments should be projected into the ancient world. What is interesting to note, however, is that even in the case of parallel institutions, the women's celebration takes a distinctly female form.

operating within Israelite Yahwism. Women's religion cannot be equated with goddess worship, but there is sufficient evidence to suggest that women's religion did represent a significantly differentiated form of religious expression within Yahwism, which must be studied along with other forms of pluralism in the religion of ancient Israel. To speak of the faith of Israel's daughters means at the very least to reexamine the boundaries of the religion we have reconstructed and to make room for more differentiated forms of piety than we have hitherto imagined—with attention to hierarchies of power in a gender-differentiated system of roles and offices.

III

GENESIS 1–3

_____

6

"MALE AND FEMALE HE CREATED THEM":

Genesis 1:27b in the Context of the Priestly Account of Creation[1]

I N THE HISTORY OF BIBLICAL INTERPRETATION AND DOGMATIC SPEC-ulation, Gen 1:26-28 has proved remarkably fecund as a source of exegetical and theological reflection. Literature on the passage is now boundless, but shows no sign of ceasing or abating, despite the appearance in recent decades of several exhaustive treatments of the text and the existence of substantial consensus among biblical scholars.[2] The reason for

Originally published in *HTR* 74 (1981) 129–59. Cross references to articles that are reprinted in this volume are indicated by an asterisk in square brackets following the original page number.

1. I would like to thank Frank M. Cross for his comments on the manuscript and William L. Moran for advice on the Akkadian transliterations and translations.

2. It is impossible to list even the major works on the passage. For the history of modern exegesis, however, two studies require special note: Paul Humbert, "L' '*imago Dei*' dans l'Ancien Testament," in *Études sur le récit du paradis et da la chute dans la Genèse* (Mémoires de l'université de Neuchâtel 14; Neuchâtel: Secrétariat de l'université, 1940) 153–75; and Ludwig Koehler, "Die Grundstelle der Imago-Dei-Lehre, Gen 1:26," *ThZ* 4 (1948) 16–22. Recent detailed exegetical treatments of the Priestly creation account as a whole, with compilations of the most important literature, are offered by Claus Westermann, *Genesis* (BKAT 1/3; Neukirchen-Vluyn: Neukirchener, 1968) 203–22, esp. 203–4; and Werner H. Schmidt, *Die Schöpfungsgeschichte der Priesterschrift* (3d ed.; WMANT 17; Neukirchen-Vluyn: Neukirchener Verlag, 1973). Subsequent specialized literature includes the following: Bernhard W. Anderson, "Human Dominion over Nature," in M. Ward, ed., *Biblical Studies in Contemporary Thought* (Somerville, Mass.: Greeno, Hadden, 1975) 27–45; James Barr, "The Image of God in the Book of Genesis—A Study in Terminology," *BJRL* 51 (1968) 11–26; idem, "The Image of God in Genesis—Some Linguistic and Historical Considerations," *Outestamentiese Werkgemeenskap van Suid-Afrika: Proceedings of the 10th Meeting, 1967* (1971) 5–13; idem, "Man and Nature—The Ecological Controversy and the Old Testament," *BJRL*

the perpetual fascination of the passage lies in the nature and limits of the text. The verses contain a fundamental, and unique, statement of biblical anthropology and theology—presented in a terse and enigmatic formulation. A rare attempt within the Old Testament literature to speak directly and definitively about the nature of humanity in relation to God and other creation, the statement is at once limited in its content, guarded in its expression, and complex in its structure. As a consequence, philologist and theologian are enticed and compelled in ever new contexts of questions and understandings to explore anew the meaning and implications of creation "in the divine image"—for it is this striking and unique expression, above all, that has dominated the discussion.

A legacy of the long and intense theological interest in the *imago Dei* has been an atomizing and reductionist approach to the passage, in which attention is focused on a single phrase or clause, severing it from its immediate context and from its context within the larger composition, a fixation and fragmentation which has affected exegetical as well as dogmatic discussion. A further legacy of this history of speculation has been the establishment of a tradition of theological inquiry and argument with a corresponding body of knowledge and norms separate from, and largely independent of, exegetical scholarship on the same passage.[3] The rise of a

---

55 (1972/73) 9–32; Gerhard Hasel, "The Meaning of 'Let us' in Gen 1:26," *AUSS* 13 (1975) 58–66; idem, "The Polemic Nature of the Genesis Cosmology," *EvQ* 46 (1974) 81–102; Norbert Lohfink, "'Seid fruchtbar und füllt die Erde an!' Zwingt die priesterschriftliche Schöpfungsdarstellung in Gen 1 die Christen zum Wachstumsmythos?" *BK* 3 (1975) 77–82; Oswald Loretz, *Die Gottebenbildlichkeit des Menschen: Mit einem Beitrag von Erik Hornung: Der Mensch als 'Bild Gottes' in Ägypten* (Munich: Kösel, 1967); Tryggve N. D. Mettinger, "Abbild oder Urbild? 'Imago Dei' in traditionsgeschichtliche Sicht," *ZAW* 86 (1974) 403–24; J. Maxwell Miller, "In the 'Image' and 'Likeness' of God," *JBL* 91 (1972) 289–304; John F. A. Sawyer, "The Meaning of *bĕṣelem ʾĕlōhîm* ('In the Image of God') in Genesis I–XI," *JTS* 25 (1974) 418–26; Norman Snaith, "The Image of God," *ExpTim* 86/1 (1974) 24; Phyllis Trible, *God and the Rhetoric of Sexuality* (OBT; Philadelphia: Fortress Press, 1978) 1–30.

A fuller listing of titles would reveal even more clearly how discussion of Gen 1:26-28 has concentrated on the *imago Dei* and the first person plurals of the divine address in v. 26. More limited interest has been shown in the imperatives of v. 28, esp. in recent literature concerned with the ethical issues of population, reproduction, and ecology. Relatively little attention has been given to the specification of male and female in v. 27b, with the exception of recent feminist literature or literature generated in response to feminist critique of the Old Testament's androcentric anthropology. Most of the latter is of a relatively popular nature and while of considerable importance for the question of hermeneutics, has contributed little in the way of new exegetical insight.

3. Cf. Karth Barth's criticism of the neglect of the text by theologians who regularly cited it, a practice which he traces back into the early church (*CD* 3/1 192–93). On the legacy of a problematic anthropology derived from Gen 1:27 in the earliest period and determinative for later discussion, see also Karl Ludwig Schmidt, "Homo imago Dei im Alten und Neuen Testament," in Leo Scheffczyk, ed., *Der Mensch als Bild Gottes* (Darmstadt: Wissenschaftliche Buchgesellschaft, 1969) 17–20.

biblical science distinct from dogmatic theology resulted in a dual history of scholarship on the passage with little significant dialogue between the respective specialists.[4] To the biblical exegete, the interpretation of the theologian appears frequently strained, sometimes false, and often simply unrecognizable as commentary upon the text.[5] While biblical scholars may feel compelled to challenge or accommodate dogmatic claims or assess current theological interpretation of the text, theologians appear for the most part content simply to "touch base" with the biblical passage, dismissing or ignoring the technical exegetical literature. There may be good reason to ignore or decry restrictive interpretations and proprietary claims of biblical specialists, but absence of dialogue can hardly be viewed as a healthy state for theology. How, in the present organization and functioning of the disciplines, such needed dialogue can take place is not clear, however, though ventures from both camps would seem to be essential.

An underlying concern of this essay, focused by examination of the literature on Gen 1:26-28, is the question of the relationship between text-critical or historical-exegetical interpretation and constructive interpretation in theology. I am convinced that collapse of the distinction between historical and constructive tasks is fatal, not only to the integrity of the scriptural witness, but also to the credibility of theology. The two tasks describe or relate to distinct modes or moments in the work of theology, however they may be united in the interpretive art of individual scholars. But isolation of the tasks and lack of a critical methodology for relating them appear to me equally disastrous for theology.

The problem may be illustrated by reference to Karl Barth's widely influential treatment of the *imago* passage.[6] His critique of a history of spec-

4. The origins of an Old Testament exegetical tradition distinct from the dominant philosophical and theological tradition and generally critical of it are usually traced to Theodor Nöldeke ("ṣlmwt und ṣlm," ZAW 17 [1897] 183–87) and Hermann Gunkel (*Genesis* [HKAT 1; Göttingen: Vandenhoeck & Ruprecht, 1901]). Their interpretation of the "image" as a physical resemblance, confirmed by the word studies of Humbert (*Études*) and Koehler ("Grundstelle"), became the basis of subsequent Old Testament discussion. Cf. Johann Jakob Stamm's review of the history of Old Testament scholarship in "Die Imago-Lehre von Karl Barth und die alttestamentliche Wissenschaft," in *Antwort*, Festschrift Karl Barth (Zollikon-Zurich: Evangelischer Verlag, 1956) 84–96. Old Testament treatments of the passage often take up the older theological and philosophical views as a part of the history of scholarship and/or to show their inadequacy (see, e.g., Westermann, *Genesis* 1/3, 205–6; and Loretz, *Gottebenbildlichkeit*, 9–41). Theologians, as heirs to the dominant tradition of speculation, more commonly confine their discussion within it, showing little recognition that an independent exegetical tradition has emerged alongside it. See, e.g., the articles collected under the heading, "Die systematische Durchdringung," in the volume edited by Scheffczyk (*Der Mensch als Bild Gottes*, 331–525).

5. See, e.g., Mettinger, "Abbild oder Urbild?" 410. Cf. Stamm, "Die Imago-Lehre von Karl Barth," 94.

6. *CD* 3/1, 183–206.

ulation divorced from exegesis—or of speculation construed as exegesis—
is apposite and appealing:

> We might easily discuss which of these and the many other similar
> explanations is the finest or deepest or most serious. What we cannot
> discuss is which of them is the true explanation of Gen 1:26f. For it
> is obvious that their authors merely found the concept [of the *imago*
> *Dei*] in the text and then proceeded to pure invention in accordance
> with the requirements of contemporary anthropology, so that it is
> only by the standard of *our own anthropology,* and not according to
> *its* anthropology and on exegetical grounds, that we can decide for
> or against them.[7]

Appealing too is Barth's conversance with contemporary Old Testament
scholarship and his attempt to incorporate that understanding in his
work. Yet his own interpretation of the passage is as problematic as any
that he criticizes—and for the same reason. Despite close reference to the
biblical text as his primary source, he has failed to discern *its* anthropology—and theology—and has advanced only a novel and arresting variation of the classical trinitarian interpretation, an interpretation characterized by the distinctly modern concept of an "I-Thou" relationship, which
is foreign to the ancient writer's thought and intention at all three points
of its application (God in the relationship within the Godhead, humanity
in the relationship between the sexes, and God and humanity in relationship to each other).[8] At its most fundamental level Barth's exegesis fails to
understand the grammar of the sentences he so ingeniously manipulates.

The most serious problem with Barth's impressive theological creation,
however, is not its provocative thesis, which must ultimately be judged on
internal grounds of adequacy and truth, nor his understanding of the key
texts, which can and must be challenged by biblical scholars. It is the fact
that his work is so widely accepted as definitive exegesis, obviating or
impeding independent access to the text. Approval of the theological
construction is taken as validation of the exegesis.[9] Barth's synthesis of

---

7. *CD* 3/1, 193.

8. Dietrich Bonhoeffer appears to have been the first to interpret the *imago Dei* in terms
of an *analogia relationis* in which the male-female duality is the defining human relationship
(*Schöpfung und Fall* [Munich: Kaiser, 1933] 29–30). It is Barth's development of the idea,
however, as a keystone of his anthropology (*CD* 3/1, 194–95), that has made it—and its faulty
exegesis—such a widely influential notion.

9. See, e.g., the argument of Clifford Green ("Liberation Theology? Karl Barth on
Women and Men," *USQR* 29 [1974] 221–31), who quotes with general approbation a critique
of Barth's exegesis in 3/1 (esp. 183ff., 289ff.) by Paul Lehmann ("Karl Barth and the Future of
Theology," *RelS* 6 [1970] 113): "[This] elaborate interpretation . . . offers an impressive correlation of ingeniousness and arbitrariness, which allows Barth to ascribe insights and affir-

exegetical and constructive tasks is attractive in demonstrating the rich possibilities of a theology in close conversation with the biblical text, but it is a dangerous synthesis insofar as it becomes a substitute, rather than a model, for continuing dialogue between theologian and biblical scholar.

I have cited Barth's treatment of Gen 1:26-28 because of the justice of his critique, because of his laudable effort to ground theology in exegesis informed by current biblical scholarship, because of the prominence and popularity of his interpretation (at least in secondary theological literature), and because of the unacceptability of his exposition to most Old Testament exegetes.[10] Barth's attractive, but mistaken, interpretation of the meaning of sexual distinction in Gen 1:27 has served as a catalyst for this reexamination of the neglected clause in the Priestly account of the creation of *adam* and has served to focus the question of the relationship between historical and constructive theology, both of which may claim the title "exegetical." But the question of meaning which impels the study has arisen elsewhere. It is feminist theology, or the feminist critique of traditional theology and exegesis, that has made necessary a new look at the passage and forged the encounter with Barth.[11]

For critics of a biblical and theological anthropology which ascribed to women an inferior or derived nature, Gen 1:27 has emerged as a text upon which a corrective anthropology of equality might be built. Barth's interpretation of the passage has had particular appeal because of his attempt to ground a relationship of mutuality between the sexes in a corresponding relationship within the Godhead itself. Feminist theology turned to

---

mations to ancient writers which, as historical human beings, they could not possibly have entertained." Green qualifies this assessment, however, with the following statement: "This criticism does not, in my view, apply to Barth's reading of the *imago Dei*, which is liberating for women and men alike" (225). Green's argument appears typical of much recent literature, which concerns itself with the consequences or implications of the idea (e.g., is it liberating or not?), but does not question or examine its exegetical base.

10. See, e.g., the critique of Stamm ("Die Imago-Lehre von Karl Barth," esp. 94). Cf., however, Friedrich Horst ("Face to Face: The Biblical Doctrine of the Image of God," *Int* 4 [1950] 259–70), who follows closely Barth's argument concerning the *analogia relationis* (266–67).

11. By "feminist" theology or critique I refer to that work which is characterized by an awareness that traditional theology and biblical interpretation have been dominated, in one way or another, by "patriarchal" or androcentric perspectives, values, and judgments. Awareness of this persistent bias has led to various attempts to expose, explain, and reinterpret texts that have traditionally carried the patriarchal message and to identify, where possible, sources which qualify or contradict it. These efforts differ considerably in methodology, attitude toward the tradition and its authority, and knowledge of the relevant disciplines and scholarly tools. Much is the work of amateurs, for the origins of the critique and new constructions were almost entirely "outside the camp"—precisely because those within the scholarly guilds lacked the necessary experiential base, or, for other reasons of restricted environment, failed to recognize the problem.

Barth, whether to embrace or attack his views, because his exegetical approach to theology required him to take account of the prominent attention given to sexual distinction in both of the biblical accounts of human creation.[12] But the search that led to Barth must return to the text. The rationale for our reexamination of the passage is this: a new sociotheological context, characterized by new questions, perceptions, and judgments, requires a new statement of the meaning of the passage in its primary Old Testament context—even if this be largely a restatement of older findings and arguments. The result, I believe, is more than a restatement, though few of the elements are entirely novel.

The argument of this essay may be summarized as follows. Gen 1:27 must be understood within the context of vv. 26-28, and this complex within the larger structure of the Priestly creation account. V. 27 may not be isolated, nor may it be interpreted in relation to v. 26 alone; vv. 27-28 form an expanded parallel to v. 26, in which 27b is a plus, dependent upon and preparatory to the following statement in v. 28 and dictated by the juxtaposition in vv. 27-28 of the themes of divine likeness and sexual reproduction. The specification of human sexual distinction and its position in the text are determined by the sequence of themes within the account and by the overall structure of announcement and execution report within the chapter. Our understanding of the place and function of this

12. The ambivalence of feminist response to Barth may be attributed to a number of factors, including selective reading of an extensive and complex treatment of the relationship of the sexes and dependence on an inadequate English translation. Most criticism has focused on his discussion of order in the male-female relationship, developed in relation to New Testament texts and Genesis 2 (CD 3/4). The notion of "ontological subordination" ascribed to Barth on the basis of this reading has become a commonplace, though Green ("Liberation Theology," 222–23 and 229) argues that the expression cannot be attributed to Barth and that it misconstrues his intention—and language. Cf. Mary Daly, *Beyond God the Father* (Boston: Beacon, 1973) 3, 22; Linda L. Barufaldi and Emily E. Culpepper, "Androgyny and the Myth of Masculine/Feminine," *Christianity and Crisis* 33/6 (16 April 1973) 69; and Sheila Collins, "Toward a Feminist Theology," *Christian Century* 89 (2 August 1972) 797–98.

A serious problem involves the key term *ungleich*. Barth characterizes the duality of I-and-Thou in Gen 1:26-27 as a "correspondence of the *unlike*" (CD 3/1, 196; = "Entsprechung des Ungleichen" [KD 3/1, 220]), but appears to spell this out in his discussion of Gen 2:18-25 as a relationship of inequality ("*unequal* duality" [CD 3/1, 288]) (Joan Arnold Romero, "The Protestant Principle: A Woman's-Eye View of Barth and Tillich," in Rosemary R. Ruether, ed., *Religion and Sexism: Images of Woman in the Jewish and Christian Traditions* (New York: Simon and Schuster, 1974] 324). However, the German adjective is identical in both passages ("ungleiche[n] Zweiheit" [KD 3/1, 329]) and means to negate the idea of "sameness," not "equality," in the pair (Green, "Liberation Theology?" 229 n. 14).

For feminists who have been able to read Barth's exposition of the *analogia relationis* in Gen 1:27 apart from—or over against—his treatment of the male-female relationship in other contexts, the possibilities it suggests for a new appreciation and evaluation of human sexual distinction have been attractive. See, e.g., Paul Jewett, *Man as Male and Female* (Grand Rapids: Eerdmans, 1975) esp. 33–48; and Emma Justes, "Theological Reflections on the Role of Women in Church and Society," *Journal of Pastoral Care* 32 (1978) 42–54.

specification in the account dissociates the word of sexual distinction, specifically sexuality, from the idea of the divine image and from the theme
of dominion, and associates it with a larger theme of sustainability or
fertility running throughout the narrative of creation. A general contribution of this investigation is a clearer articulation of the relationships
among the several statements about *adam* (image, dominion, sexuality,
blessing) and a clearer statement of the meaning and function of each
within the Priestly account of creation. The analysis concludes with an
attempt to spell out the consequences and implications of this understanding for the theology of P, for a comprehensive Old Testament anthropology, and for contemporary theological anthropology.

The Priestly Account of Creation: Overall Structure and Themes

The Priestly account of creation is an exceedingly compressed account,
marked by a repetitive structure of announcement and execution report
(*Wortbericht* and *Tatbericht*). But it is also comprehensive in its intention
and design, attempting to identify, locate, and describe in their essential
features all of the primary elements and orders of creation. The author
has chosen his terms with care, from names to descriptive statements.[13]

13. I assume for Gen 1:1—2:3 a unified work by a priestly editor/author active in and
during the Babylonian exile, who edited an already existing Israelite creation account (perhaps extant in multiple variants, or supplemented by material from other traditions) to form
the opening chapter of a great history of beginnings reaching from creation to the death of
Moses and climaxing in the revelation/legislation at Sinai. Whether the author/editor was a
single or corporate "individual" is irrelevant to the argument of this essay. The two essential
assumptions of my analysis are (1) that the present (final) edition of the material displays a
unified overall conception characterized by recognizable stylistic and theological features
and forms part of a larger whole displaying similar literary and theological characteristics;
and (2) that the present form of the composition in Genesis 1 is the result of a complex
history of growth, stages of which are apparent in the received text, but can no longer be
isolated or fully reconstructed.

I agree with Werner Schmidt (*Schöpfungsgeschichte*) that the framing structure of *wayyō-
'mer 'ĕlōhîm + wayěhî-kēn* and the *Wortberichte* as a whole belong to the final editor and
give evidence of selection, shaping, and expansion of older material. I am less certain about
the recovery of the underlying tradition or of the relationship of *Wortbericht*/announcement
to *Tatbericht*/execution report. I retain the terms to refer not to independent literary compositions, or traditions, but to literary features of the final composition. Bernard W. Anderson's
insistence on the stylistic unity of the Priestly creation account and his attention to the
controlling patterns of the final form of the text ("A Stylistic Study of the Priestly Creation
Story," in George W. Coats and Burke O. Long, eds., *Canon and Authority: Essays in Old
Testament Religion and Theology* [Philadelphia: Fortress Press, 1977] 148–62, esp. 151) represent a welcome shift from earlier dissecting approaches; however, I do not think that his
analysis invalidates much of Schmidt's observations and explanations of disparity between
Wort- and *Tatberichten.* I find it necessary, in any case, to posit a prehistory of Israelite usage;
Genesis 1 is in my view neither a "free" composition nor a direct response to any known

As Gerhard von Rad has rightly emphasized, only what is essential is here; nothing is accidental or included merely because it stood in the received tradition.[14] Though bound in significant measure to the items, order, and conception of process found in older creation accounts of the ancient Near East and circulating in Israelite tradition, the Priestly author has selected from the tradition and shaped it to carry his own message. And though the history of the Priestly composition is itself complex, the final design and wording is governed by a unified conception and purpose and the account set as the lead statement in a larger historico-theological work. Thus every assertion and every formulation in this highly compact and selective account warrants careful attention and questioning with regard to its origin and meaning. How does it function within the Priestly composition? Why was it included? Is it unique to P, a new idea, or a new formulation? Was it present in essentially the same form in older tradition or does it represent an alteration of the tradition, a substitution, or a reformulation?

Because descriptive statements are so limited in P's account, the two which amplify the report of *adam's* creation are immediately striking:

(27aβ)   *běṣelem ʾĕlōhîm bārāʾ ʾōtô*
(27b)   *zākār ûněqēbâ bārāʾ ʾōtām*
(27aβ)   in the image of God he created him;
(27b)   male and female he created them.

The parallel construction invites the question of how the two clauses are related. But other questions impose as well. Why does 27aβ repeat the content of 27aα? What is the relationship of v. 27 to vv. 26 and 28? And why of all that might be said about *adam* does the author choose to emphasize their bisexual nature, using language employed elsewhere by P to characterize the animal orders but omitted from their description in Genesis 1? The answer to all of these questions lies in an analysis of the structure of vv. 26-28 as a whole and of the place and function of these verses within the overall structure of Gen 1:1—2:3 and the larger Priestly work.[15]

Mesopotamian or Canaanite myth, despite clear evidence of polemical shaping (cf. Hasel, "The Polemic Nature of the Genesis Cosmology"; and Victor Maag, "Alttestamentliche Anthropogonie in ihrem Verhältnis zur altorientalischen Mythologie," *Asiatische Studien* 9 [1955] 15–44).

14. Gerhard von Rad, *Genesis: A Commentary* (trans. John H. Marks, OTL; Philadelphia: Westminster, 1961) 45.

15. Vv. 29-30 are an essential part of P's statement about the nature and role of *adam* within the created order and form a significant link with the later P complex, Gen 9:1-3, bringing to the received tradition a peculiar interest of the final Priestly writer (Schmidt, *Schöpfungsgeschichte*, 152–53; cf. Westermann, *Genesis*, 227–28; Sean E. McEvenue, *The Narrative Style of the Priestly Writer* [AnBib 50; Rome: Biblical Institute, 1971] 66–71; and Miller, "In the 'Image' and 'Likeness' of God," 299–304). We omit consideration of these verses here

The primary concerns of the Priestly creation account are two: (1) to emphasize the dependence of all of creation on God—made explicit in the framing structure that marks each stage of creation: "God said . . . and it was so,"[16] and (2) to describe the order established within creation—as an order determined by God, from the beginning.[17] Secondary or subordinate concerns are evident in emphasis on the permanence, or maintenance, of the created cosmos and its orders, and in anticipation of the history which will be played out within it, a history centering upon *adam* and initiated in the final, climactic word of creation and blessing.

(26) *wayyō'mer 'ĕlōhîm*
       na'ăśeh 'ādām bĕṣalmēnû kidmûtēnû
       wĕyirdû bidgat hayyām ûbĕ'ôp haššāmayim
       ûbabbĕhēmâ ûbĕkol-hā'āreṣ
       ûbĕkol-hāremeś hārōmēś 'al-hā'āreṣ
(27) *wayyibrā' 'ĕlōhîm 'et-hā'ādām bĕṣalmô*
       bĕṣelem 'ĕlōhîm bārā' 'ōtô
       zākār ûnĕqēbâ bārā' ōtām
(28) *wayĕbārek 'ōtām 'ĕlōhîm*
       wayyō'mer lāhem 'ĕlōhîm
       pĕrû ûrĕbû ûmil'û 'et-hā'āreṣ wĕkibšūhā
       ûrĕdû bidgat hayyām ûbĕ'ôp haššāmayim
       ûbĕkol-hayyâ hārōmeśet 'al-hā'āreṣ[18]
(26) And God said:
       "Let us make *adam* in our image, according to our
          likeness,
       and let them have dominion over the fish of the sea and
          the birds of the air,
       and the cattle and all the earth
       and everything that creeps upon the earth."
(27) And God created *adam* in his image,
       in the image of God he created him;
       male and female he created them.

---

because they constitute a distinct unit and lack any connection, direct or indirect, to v. 27b, which is the focus of this investigation.

16. The full series is found only in the LXX. Cf. Anderson, "A Stylistic Study," 152.

17. The theme of order and the specification of orders cannot be reduced to cultic interest, though elements of that are present. Nor can it be subsumed under the needs of *adam*, though the account is certainly anthropocentric. It is rather a broad and fundamental theological concern, which may properly be characterized as "scientific" in its interest and observations.

18. Textual variants are few and of minor significance for our analysis. LXX has a conjunction (*kai*) between *bĕṣalmēnû* and *kidmûtēnû* in v. 26 and reads only the second *bĕṣelem* in v. 27a (see discussion below), while individual manuscripts and versions assimilate the singular and plural object pronouns or eliminate *bārā' 'ōtô* in v. 27aα. LXX also renders more uniform parallel lists and formulas repeated with variation in MT (28b // 26b; 28a // 22a). See commentaries.

(28) And God blessed them,
      and God said to them:
         "Be fruitful and multiply and fill the earth and subdue it,
         and have dominion over the fish of the sea and the birds of
            the air
         and every living creature that creeps upon the earth."

Image and Dominion

The order described in Genesis 1 is progressive, structured as a twofold movement oriented toward the earth and culminating in *adam*.[19] The crowning species in this account is defined, uniquely, in terms of a dual relationship or identity, a relationship to God and to coinhabitants of the earth. Humanity, according to this statement, is created "like God"[20] and with dominion over other creatures. The two statements of v. 26 must be understood in conjunction; in P's construction they belong to a single thought complex. Nature or design in creation is related to function and status, or position: the firmament is to divide the waters, the luminaries are to give light (and in their specific identity as planets, to mark time and seasons, etc.), and humankind is to rule over the realm of creatures.[21] The presupposition and prerequisite for this rule is the divine stamp which sets this creature apart from all the rest, identifying *adam* as God's own special representative, not simply by designation (command), but by design (nature or constitution)—that is, as a representation of God.[22] The

19. Anderson, "A Stylistic Study," 154–59.

20. The basic meanings of the terms *ṣelem* and *dĕmût* are "representation" and "likeness" (see further below). The prepositions, which are used synonymously, create parallel and synonymous adverbial clauses which describe the manner and end of construction (*adam* is "modeled" on *'ĕlōhîm* and is consequently a model of *'ĕlōhîm*). The intention is to describe a resemblance of *adam* to God which distinguishes *adam* from all other creatures—and has consequence for *adam*'s relationship to them.

21. For the understanding of *wĕyirdû* . . . as a purpose or result clause, see, inter alios, Schmidt, *Schöpfungsgeschichte*, 127 ("damit sie herrschen"); NEB ("to rule"); Snaith, "The Image of God," 24; and Westermann, *Genesis*, 216. The function of *wĕyirdû* as specification of purpose or consequence has been understood in a number of different ways, often as a direct explication of the image, or of creation in the divine image (cf. von Rad, *Genesis*, 57; Snaith, "The Image of God," 24). Westermann observes that specification of purpose or goal is a characteristic feature of accounts of human creation (*Genesis*, 218).

22. Westermann has correctly emphasized the adverbial character of *bĕṣalmēnû kidmû-tēnû* (*Genesis*, 214), basing his analysis on the consensus of recent scholarship which rejects the *b-essentiae* interpretation and recognizes the essentially synonymous meaning of the two phrases, whose interchangeable prepositions must have the meaning "according to," "nach" (so LXX [*kata* for both] and Vg ["ad" for both]) (*Genesis*, 201; cf. Sawyer, "The Meaning of *bĕṣelem 'ĕlōhîm*," 421; Mettinger, "Abbild oder Urbild?" 406–7; Miller, "In the 'Image' and 'Likeness' of God," 295). This grammatical analysis leads Westermann to argue that the text "macht nicht eine Aussage über den Menschen, sondern über ein Tun Gottes" (*Genesis*, 214).

notion of the divine image serves here to validate and explain the special status and role of *adam* among the creatures.

The adverbial modifier *běṣelem-*, further qualfied by *kidmût-* in v. 26,[23] describes a correspondence of being, a resemblance—not a relationship or an identity, even partial identity. And it is a resemblance described in terms of form, not of character or substance.[24] *Ṣelem* as a metaphor for

---

But the alternatives are too exclusively drawn. What describes the act or mode of construction cannot be excluded from an understanding of the product; i.e., construction (as process and design) determines or affects construction (as product or result). Surely the Priestly writer intended to characterize *adam* by this formulation, to specify more closely the essential nature of humanity, while avoiding direct description. P intends a comparison between God and *adam*, but he intends it to be indirect. The prepositions guard against identity, even the identity of an image or icon. Strictly speaking, *adam* is not the image of God (so rightly Westermann) nor one possessing the divine image, but only one who is like God in the manner of an image or representation.

Since *běṣelem ʾĕlōhîm* describes, indirectly, the nature of *adam*, it characterizes all humankind in all time and not simply the original act, or specimen, of creation. The stamp of divine likeness must therefore be understood to be transmitted not through repeated acts of God but through the process by which the species is perpetuated in its original identity, viz., through procreation (Gen 5:3).

23. So correctly Koehler ("Grundstelle," 20–21), building on Humbert (*Études*, 163); the qualifying character of *kidmût* is suggested by its position as the second term (Sawyer, "The Meaning of *běṣelem ʾĕlōhîm*," 421) as well as by its common lexical meaning and use. As an abstract term, whose very meaning suggests approximation, it weakens or blurs the outline of the preceding concrete term. *Děmût* is used by P's contemporary, Ezekiel, in the same sense of qualified resemblance that it has in Genesis 1; and it is employed elsewhere by P, alone (in 5:1), where the specific content or connotation of *ṣelem* is not required or desired. *Ṣelem*, in contrast, is the specialized and unique term, "defined" by its use in Genesis 1.

Miller's argument for the priority of *děmût* ("In the 'Image' and 'Likeness' of God," 299–304) is not convincing. *Děmût* belongs to the final P edition of Genesis 1 and occurs alone in 5:1, which is a purely P construction, creating a bridge between the creation story (traditional material shaped by P) and the genealogical framework of the Primeval History. There, in 5:1-2, the essential content of 1:26-28 is recapitulated in P's own terms—with the addition of the naming motif that prepares for the transition from collective *adam* in Genesis 1 and 5:1-2 to the representative individual, Adam, who heads the genealogy of 5:3ff.

24. See Humbert (*Études*), Koehler ("Grundstelle"), and n. 34 below. *Ṣelem* in P's use is neither the crudely or naively literal image assumed by those who fail to recognize the determining metaphor, nor the description of a conversation partner or counterpart. Recognition that the term is basically concrete in its meaning has not stopped commentators from asking wherein the resemblance lies and from drawing on other Old Testament texts, as well as modern psychology, for their answers. Thus, e.g., Koehler sought the resemblance in *adam*'s "upright stature" ("Grundstelle," 20), while others endorse a more general physical resemblance, noting, however, that Hebrew thought treated the individual as a psychosomatic unity, thereby excluding the notion of merely external correspondence (so, e.g., Gunkel: "das Geistige [ist] dabei nicht ausgeschlossen" [*Genesis*, 99]; cf. von Rad [*Genesis*, 56] and Westermann [*Genesis*, 207–8]). For many interpreters influenced by Barth, the correspondence suggested by the metaphor is spelled out as a relational correspondence describing a capacity and need for relatedness, including communication. Thus Stamm sees the meaning of the *imago* as "Partnerschaft und Bündnisfähigkeit" (*Die Gottebenbildlichkeit des Menschen im Alten Testament* [Theologische Studien 54; Zollikon-Zurich: Evangelischer Verlag, 1959] 19), while Horst would

likeness is concrete, formal, holistic—and "empty," lacking specific content, and thus an ideal term for P, who employs it with changing connotations in changing contexts (cf. 5:1, 3 and 9:6). Here, in its primary and initial use, its content or implications must be spelled out, and that is the contribution of *wĕyirdû*. The *ṣelem 'ĕlōhîm* in Genesis 1 is, accordingly, a royal designation, the precondition or requisite for rule.

The interpretation of the expression as a royal motif is not simply dependent, however, on the context of its use in Gen 1:26. Though the term *ṣelem*, by itself, lacks specific content, the phrase *ṣelem 'ĕlōhîm* appears to derive its meaning from a special association with the royal ideology of the ancient Near East.[25] It is true that Old Testament uses of *ṣelem* do not point to such a thesis, nor does the Old Testament's ideology or lexicon of kingship.[26] If a royal image lies behind the use of *ṣelem* in Gen 1:26-27, it must rest on an idea or expression of kingship found outside preserved Israelite sources. That appears to be supplied by evidence from Egypt, where the idea of the king as "image" of the god is a common one, finding

---

have it describe a special capability of intercourse with God ("Face to Face," 267), making *adam* "the vis-à-vis (*Gegenüber*) of God in the same manner as the woman, in Gen 2:20, is a helpmeet 'as over against' (*im Gegenüber*) the man" (265). This argument is faulty on a number of grounds. There is no similarity in language or idea between the *kĕneged* of Gen 2:18, 20 and the *bĕṣelem-/kidmût-* of 1:26. And it is obvious from the (secondary) use of *ṣelem* in 5:3 and 7:6 that it does not describe a quality of relationship or even precondition of relationship. P is not concerned with communication between Adam and Seth, but with the preservation of an essential likeness of the species through successive generations. Cf. also the critique of Victor Maag ("Alttestamentliche Anthropogonie," 34).

In response to continuing attempts to spell out the content of the image, James Barr has recently argued that the term *ṣelem* was deliberately chosen for its opaque etymology and ambivalent connotations as the best term available in Hebrew to describe a likeness without giving it a particular content ("A Study in Terminology," 18, 20–21; cf. idem, "Some Linguistic and Historical Considerations," 12–13). Recent literature has also stressed the fact that the notion of humans as godlike creatures, created according to a divine model or prototype and standing in a special relationship to the gods, is not unique to Israel, but is a widely shared notion, though implications of this likeness may be spelled out in quite different ways. The concept, in this analysis, is an inherited one for P, whose problem was to fit it to Israelite theology and exclude as far as possible false understandings which may have accompanied it (Maag, "Sumerische und babylonische Mythen von der Erschaffung der Menschen," *Asiatische Studien* 8 [1954] 96–98; cf. idem, "Alttestamentliche Anthropogonie," 36–37; Westermann, *Genesis*, 212–13; and Loretz, *Gottebenbildlichkeit*, 63–64).

25. The first scholar to read the expression of Genesis 1 as the adaptation of a royal title or designation appears to have been Johannes Hehn in 1915 ("Zum Terminus 'Bild Gottes,'" in Gotthold Weil, ed., *Festschrift Eduard Sachau* [Berlin: Reimer] 36–52). Hehn's lead has been followed by von Rad (*Genesis*, 58); Hans Wildberger ("Das Abbild Gottes, Gen 1:26-30," *ThZ* 21 [1965] 245–59, 481–501); and Schmidt (*Schöpfungsgeschichte*, 137-48), inter alios.

26. It is often noted that *ṣelem* and *dĕmût* are not used in the Old Testament to speak of the king. Anderson stresses the contrast between Genesis 1 and Psalm 8 precisely in respect to royal language and theology ("Human Dominion," 39), though he allows that "vestigial remains" of a royal theology can be seen in Genesis 1, especially in "the motif of the image of God which entitles Man to have dominion over the earth" (36).

expression in a rich and diverse vocabulary of representation which describes the pharaoh as image, statue, likeness, picture, and so on of the deity (usually the chief, creator god).[27] However, the expression in Egyptian royal usage is closely linked to the idea of the pharaoh as the incarnation of the god, the deity's visible form on earth[28]—an idea foreign to Israelite thought. If an Egyptian root for the expression is to be sought, it is the wisdom tradition, with its reference to general humanity and its language of analogy rather than representation, that offers the closest parallels.[29]

Evidence from Mesopotamia is more limited, but appears closer to the Priestly usage in language, conception, and time. One text of Middle Assyrian provenance and three of Neo-Assyrian and Neo-Babylonian date employ the identical cognate expression, ṣalam-DN, as a designation of the king.[30]

    (1) (KN) šūma ṣalam Enlil dārû
        He (KN) is the eternal image of Enlil. [MA][31]
    (2) šarru bēl mātāti ṣalmu ša ᵈŠamaš šū

27. See esp. Hornung, "Der Mensch als 'Bild Gottes' in Ägypten," in Loretz, Die Gottebenbildlichkeit des Menschen, 123–56; and Eberhard Otto, "Der Mensch als Geschöpf und Bild Gottes in Ägypten," in H. W. Wolff, ed., Probleme biblischer Theologie, Festschrift Gerhard von Rad (Munich: Kaiser, 1971) 334–48. Schmidt and Wildberger both draw upon Egyptian texts to suggest parallels, and a source, for the expression in Gen 1:26, 27. Of particular interest to Schmidt is the "democratized" usage found in the wisdom literature, in which a title that originally designated, and distinguished, the king is "extended" to humanity as a whole, and associated more particularly with their creation (cf., e.g., "The Instruction of Merikare," Schöpfungsgeschichte, 139). This evidence, combined with a more limited occurrence of the same expression in Mesopotamian royal designations, suggested a common ancient Near Eastern royal ideology. That the expression of Gen 1:26-28 was anchored in this tradition was made virtually certain, Schmidt argued, by the explicit royal language used in Psalm 8, the only Old Testament parallel to the Genesis 1 account (140).

28. Otto, "Der Mensch als Geschöpf und Bild Gottes," 344–47; and Hornung, "Der Mensch als 'Bild Gottes' in Ägypten," 147–51. Otto distinguishes the royal usage sharply from the use of similar (in some cases identical) expressions to describe the relationship of non-royal figures to the god or gods. The royal usage implies—and depends upon—a notion of identity, he insists, while the nonroyal usage describes only a form of analogy. The distinction lies in the ancient and fundamental Egyptian distinction between royal theology and (general) anthropology (344).

29. So, apparently, Hornung ("Der Mensch als 'Bild Gottes' in Ägypten," 150), who notes that the expression appears in the wisdom tradition prior to and independent of the royal usage. Neither Otto nor Hornung recognizes a development within the complex Egyptian usage which could be described as the "democratizing" of an original royal concept and designation.

30. The following texts are cited in CAD (Ṣalmu: nos. 2–4) and AHW (Ṣalmu: all) under the heading of "transferred meanings," with the translation "likeness"/"Abbild."

31. From a fragment of the Tukulti-Ninurta Epic, probably composed not long after the defeat of Kashtiliash IV (1232–25) (W. G. Lambert, "Three Unpublished Fragments of the Tukulti-Ninurta Epic," AfO 18 [1957] 38–51; and William L. Moran, private communication).

The king, the lord of the lands, is the very image of Shamash.
[NA]

(3) *abūšu ša šarri bēlīya ṣalam Bēl-ma šū*
     u šarru bēlī ṣalam Bēl šū
     The father of the king, my lord, was the very image of Bel,
     and the king, my lord, is likewise the very image of Bel. [NA][32]

(4) *šar kiššati ṣalam Marduk attā*
     O King of the universe, you are the image of Marduk. [NB][33]

Akkadian *ṣalmu* exhibits the same range of meaning as its Hebrew cognate, designating in its basic use a statue (in the round), a likeness or representation, usually of a deity or king, especially as set up in a temple as a visible sign and manifestion of the living god or person. It may also describe a relief or drawing, again usually of a king or deity. In transferred uses the basic idea of a likeness is maintained, with emphasis on resemblance, correspondence, and representation.[34]

The statement occurs in a hymn of praise to the Assyrian king, which compares him to a god in his stature (1.16; Moran, citing *AHW* 374b; cf. Lambert, 51) and birth (1.17) and proclaims his exaltation to a position next to Ninurta himself (1.20):

(18) He is the eternal image of Enlil, who hears what the people say, the "Counsel" of the land.

. . . .

(20) Enlil, like a physical father (*kīma abi ālidi*) exalted him (*ušarbīšu*) second to (*arki*) his firstborn son [i.e., Ninurta] (Lambert, 50–51).

32. Nos. 2 and 3 are from petitions of the court astrologer Adad-šumu-uṣur to Esarhaddon and his son Ashurbanipal, respectively (Simo Parpola, *Letters from Assyrian Scholars to the Kings Esarhaddon and Assurbanipal,* Part 1 [= AOAT 5/1; Kevelaer: Butzon & Bercker; Neukirchen-Vluyn: Neukirchener Verlag, 1970] nos. 143 [= ABL 5] r 4ff. [112–13] and 125 [= ABL 6] 17f. [98–100]; cf. Leroy Waterman, *Royal Correspondence of the Assyrian Empire,* Parts 1 and 3 [Ann Arbor: University of Michigan Press, 1930–31]). In no. 2 the writer draws an analogy with the sun god (Shamash) who, he says, stays in the dark only half a day. The king, he urges, should not remain indoors for days on end, but like the sun, whose image he is, come out of the dark (Parpola, 113). No. 3 belongs to a profession of loyalty to the new king. Both texts are a courtier's words of adulation, but the terms of exaltation are hardly his invention.

33. From a Babylonian astrological report (= R. C. Thompson, *The Reports of the Magicians and Astrologers of Nineveh and Babylon in the British Museum* 2 [London: Luzac, 1900] no. 170 r 2). The text appears to liken the king to Marduk in his display of anger—and reconciliation—toward his servants (Moran, private communication; cf. Thompson, *Reports,* lxii; and Ernst Weidner, *OLZ* 15 [1912] 319).

34. *CAD/AHW: ṣalmu;* BDB: *ṣelem.* The notion of representation goes beyond that of a representative in suggesting a measure of identity, or an essential correspondence. Such identity, however, is not identity of substance or being, but of character or function (and power), for the image is always a copy, not a double or derivative; it is of different material or kind than the original. The image stands for the original, which it reproduces and shows forth. The term is basically concrete. It does not refer to an idea, nor does it describe a model, pattern, or prototype (contra Mettinger, "Abbild oder Urbild?" esp. 411). Since *ṣalmu/ṣelem* describes a formal resemblance and holistic representation, the particular attributes of the

The passages cited above use the expressions *ṣalam-DN* figuratively to designate one who, according to Mesopotamian royal ideology, is understood to be a special representative of the god or gods, possessing a divine mandate to rule, and hence divine power, but who is himself neither deity nor divine—except in the limited terms of election and exaltation.[35] In these texts the designation of the king as "image of the god" serves to emphasize the godlike nature of the king in his ruling function and power.[36] But this usage, despite close affinity to the Priestly formulation, is hardly its source. Though our primary clues to the meaning of the language and constructs of Genesis 1 must be sought in Akkadian and Egyptian texts, their origin is presumably in neither, but in a still unknown "Canaanite" tradition. That silent source must have incorporated and mediated both Mesopotamian and Egyptian influences, but it appears to have stood closer to the former in the basic language and thought. To the extent that the Genesis creation account may be viewed as an alternative, or counter-, myth, either in its original Yahwistic formulation or in its final Priestly edition, the elements with which it most clearly compares and contrasts are found in traditions known from Mesopotamia. Since the final editing of the work is also located there, a polemical reading of the

original which the *ṣelem* may be intended to manifest must be determined by contexts of use.

In Mesopotamia, the most common use of the term is to designate the statue of a god or king, while the largest class of metaphorical usage describes an individual as the "statue/image" of a god. In four of the five examples cited in *CAD* and *AHW*, the one designated "*ṣalmu* of the god" is a king. The fifth example describes a conjuror priest and belongs to a twofold identification, of word and person, which serves to emphasize the truth and efficacy of his conjuration: *šiptu šipat ᵈMarduk āšipu ṣa-lam ᵈMarduk*: "The conjuration (recited) is the conjuration of Marduk, the conjurer is the very image of Marduk" (*AfO* 14 150.225f. [*bīt mēsiri*]) (cited from *CAD*). In both royal and priestly designations the human representative is viewed above all as one possessing the power and authority of the god, whether for weal or woe. No "democratized" usage of the expression is attested in Akkadian sources; "likeness" to the god belongs only to the god's special representative(s).

35. Henri Frankfort, *Kingship and the Gods* (Chicago: University of Chicago Press, 1948) 215–61, 295–312, esp. 237, 307, 309.

36. Franz M. T. Böhl ("Das Zeitalter der Sargoniden," in *Opera Minora* [Groningen and Djakarta: Wolters, 1953] 403) found expression of the idea of the king as image of the god not only in the term *ṣalmu*, but also *ṣillu*, which he translated "Schattenbild" (403). The meaning of the term in his key text (ABL 652 = Parpola, *Letters*, no. 145) is disputed, however, as is the meaning of the proverb cited in the text (cf. Böhl, "Der babylonische Fürstenspiegel," *MAOG* 11, 3 [1939] 49; Frankfort, *Kingship*, 407 n. 35; and Parpola, *Letters*, 113). The final line appears, nevertheless, to contain a clear expression of the king's likeness to the god, in this case using the term *muššulu* (< *mašālu* "to be similar" [*CAD*]), a term corresponding to Hebrew *dĕmût* (cf. Wildberger, "Abbild," 254):

šarru šu [k]al! muššuli ša ili
The King is the perfect likeness of the god.

(Parpola, *Letters*, 113; cf. Böhl, "Fürstenspiegel," 49; and idem, "Zeitalter," 403)

account may be suggested, even if the terms of the polemic do not originate with the final composition.[37]

The genius of the formulation in Gen 1:26 may be seen in its use of a common expression and image of Mesopotamian (-Canaanite) royal theology to counter a common image of Mesopotamian (-Canaanite) anthropology, viz., the image of humanity as servant of the gods, the dominant image of Mesopotamian creation myths.[38] The language that describes the king as one who stands in a special relationship to the divine world is chosen by the author of Genesis 1 (perhaps under influence of Egyptian wisdom tradition) to describe humanity as a whole, *adam* qua *adam*, in its essential nature. The expression of Genesis 1 is unique in the Old Testament, determined, we would suggest, by the genre and context of composition. But the idea of the royal status of *adam* is not; it is prominent in Psalm 8, where the language of coronation is combined with the language of dominion to describe the distinctive status and role of humanity in creation. In our understanding, *şelem* and *RDH* belong to a single complex of ideas and describe a sequence of thought which parallels exactly the twofold statement of Psalm 8.

37. Polemical features of the account have been widely noted, often in relation to the dominant Mesopotamian creation myth, *Enuma Elish* (see, e.g., Maag, "Alttestamentliche Anthropogonie," 31–41, esp. 37; cf. Hasel, "The Polemic Nature of the Genesis Cosmology"). The Babylonian exile surely encouraged sharpening of the distinctive elements of Israelite theology, cosmology—and anthropology—in relation to the views of the surrounding culture. But Israel's dialogue with "foreign" culture did not begin there. Israel's theology was constructed from the beginning in dynamic critical appropriation of the religious heritage of Canaan and confrontation with the recurrent challenge of competing local and foreign cults and myths. The origins of the Priestly creation account and many of the features that characterize it as a countermyth must be placed during the monarchy rather than the exile.

The significance of the Akkadian cognate equivalents to the unique Old Testament expression, *şelem ʾĕlōhîm*, lies in their close association with the royal theology and their distribution in time; the usage spans the period from the origin of the Israelite monarchy and its temple cult to the seventh and sixth centuries, when the temple traditions received their final form. Past emphasis on the latter period as the significant period of cultural interchange, and polemic, may be attributed to the date of P—and to the dates of the extant parallels. The only early example among our citations, and the one in which the expression is most clearly part of a consciously articulated royal theology, was not published until 1957. Thus Böhl could argue in 1953 ("Zeitalter der Sargoniden," 403) that the idea of the king as image of the god was a new and distinctive feature of the Neo-Assyrian royal theology.

38. See, esp., *Enuma Elish* 6.34–35. The tradition that humankind was created to serve the gods, and thus free them from their onerous labor, is much older, however, as may be seen from *Atraḥasis* 1.194–97:

> (194) You are the birth-goddess, creatress of mankind
> (195) Create *Lullu* that he may bear the yoke,
> (196) Let him bear the yoke assigned by Enlil,
> (197) Let man carry the toil of the gods!

(W. G. Lambert and A. R. Millard, *Atra-ḥasis* [Oxford: Clarendon, 1969] 56–57.)

The Unique Creature

The special interest of God in this culminating act of creation and ordering is registered at a grammatical and lexical level by a shift in the word of announcement from intransitive verbal forms or verbs of generation to an active-transitive verb, and from third person to first person speech. The verb ʿāśâ, which has heretofore been used only in the execution reports, to emphasize the divine activity, is now taken up into the announcement itself. The becoming of adam is inconceivable apart from God's own direct action and involvement; the willing of this creation requires divine commitment.

The structure of the final word also differs from that of the words that describe the other orders of living things. For them no purpose or function is announced or reported.[39] And each order is referred to an already existing element of earth (land and water) as its locus and proximate source. In contrast, adam is assigned a function or task by the very word of announcement, a task defined in relation to the other creatures and to the earth, which is its habitat but not its source.[40] Humanity is also distinguished from other orders of life by its direct and unmediated dependence upon God. For adam, habitat is neither source of life nor source of identity.[41]

The Wortbericht emphasizes the exalted, isolated position of adam within the created order, as one uniquely identified with God and charged by God with dominion over the creatures. Yet the full account insists that adam is also creature, sharing both habitat and constitution with the other orders of animal life. The creation of humankind stands in the overall structure of the Priestly creation account as an amplification and specification of the creation of the land animals, and the two acts of creation together comprise a single day's work. This classification of adam with the other creatures of earth has required an adjustment in the account of the

39. The designation of the plants as food in vv. 29-30 is a secondary and subordinate theme and differs in structure from the purpose clauses or compound sentences of vv. 6, 9, 14-15, and 26. The specifications, "bearing seed" and "producing fruit," in v. 11 do not describe a purpose or function, but introduce the theme of fertility as a subtheme of the word about nature (see below).

40. The notion of task or function is suggested by the verbal form of the clause; the meaning of the verb itself, however, points to an emphasis on status and power as its primary message rather than exercise of a responsibility or function (see below).

41. P avoids, or counters, by this formulation not only the primitive notion of humankind "sprouting" from the ground (cf., e.g., "The Myth of the Pickax" and "The Myth of Enki and E-engurra"), but also the more elevated, but likewise unacceptable, notion of humanity as a mixture of earthly and divine substance (clay and blood [or breath?]; cf. Atraḫasis, Enuma Elish [and Genesis 2]). Nor is adam conceived in this formulation as a fallen god, but rather by original design as the "God–like" one among the creatures.

sixth day's work, for the formula of blessing which speaks of the filling of earth (parallel to the filling of the seas in v. 22) cannot be addressed to two orders occupying the same space. The expected blessing of the land animals has accordingly given way to the blessing of *adam*, the supreme land creature.[42]

The combination of events on the sixth day suggests that *adam* is to be understood as a special type or species of earth creature. In contrast to *adam*, all other life is described in broad classes, with subclasses or species (*mîn*) recognized but not named.[43] Thus grasses and fruiting plants represent the primary classes of vegetation, each with its myriad individual species, while "fish," fowl, cattle, and creepers describe comparable classes of animal life. *Adam*, however, is an individual, at once species and order, a creature among creatures yet apart from them and above them.

Sexual Distinction and Blessing

The word that most clearly locates *adam* among the creatures is the blessing of v. 28 and the specification which immediately precedes and prepares for it: *zākār ûněqēbâ bārā' 'ōtām*. But the theme articulated in these coordinated clauses reaches beyond the world of creatures addressed by the word of blessing to include all life. For P, there is a corollary to the idea that all of creation is derived from God and dependent upon God. It is the idea of the permanence and immutability of the created orders. For living things, with their observable cycles of life, permanence must be conceived in dynamic terms, as a process of replenishment or reproduction. Thus for each order of living thing explicit attention is given to the means by which it shall be perpetuated. That is the meaning of the cumbersome and seemingly unnecessary specification that both classes of vegetation were created bearing seeds—that is, equipped to reproduce their

---

42. Schmidt, *Schöpfungsgeschichte*, 147. Cf. Westermann, *Genesis*, 196. That the blessing of the land animals is to be understood as included in the blessing given to *adam* seems unlikely in view of the expansion of the latter blessing to include the subjugation of the earth (*wĕkibšūhā*). Equally unlikely is the notion that the land creatures receive their blessing through *adam*, or that they receive no blessing, since the "renewal" of the blessing after the flood addresses both classes—separately: Noah and sons in 9:1 and the animals in 8:17 (including birds as land-based creatures—a combination of classes treated as distinct in Genesis 1) (196). What this shows is a selective and flexible employment of categories and formulas, varied according to changing situations and need (e.g., omitting the sea creatures in 8:17).

43. Eduard König, "Die Bedeutung des hebräischen *mîn*," *ZAW* 31 (1911) 133–46. Cf. Schmidt, *Schöpfungsgeschichte*, 106–7, 123; Westermann, *Genesis*, 174–75. The differentiation of plant and animal life into species or types does not find a correspondence in the sexual differentiation of humankind, described in v. 27 (contra Schmidt, *Schöpfungsgeschichte*, 107 n. 1). See below.

kind.[44] And that is the meaning of the blessing that imparts to all creatures the power of reproduction: "Be fruitful and multiply and fill the earth/ waters."

While the immediate intention of this word in its expanded form (including *mil'û*) is surely to describe the filling of an empty earth through the multiplication of original specimen pairs,[45] there may be another intention as well, a polemical one. For P, the power of created life to replenish itself is a power given to each species at its creation and therefore not dependent upon subsequent rites or petitions for its effect.[46] The emphatic and repeated word which endows life with the means and the power of propagation undercuts the rationale of the fertility cult—and in yet another manner deposes and annihilates the gods; for the power to create life and to sustain it belongs to God alone, who incorporates the means of perpetuity into the very design and constitution of the universe,[47] and the power to rule earth and its creatures is delegated to *adam*. Thus the gods are denied all power, place, and function by this account, whether to create, renew, or rule.

Adam is creature, who with all other created life is given the power of reproduction through the word-act of creation, receiving it in the identical words of blessing addressed first to the creatures of sea and sky (v. 22). It is in relation to this statement that the specification, "male and female

44. Cf. Maag, "Alttestamentliche Anthropogonie," 39.

45. The terms used to describe each order and class are all singular collectives ([*deše'*], *'ēśeb*, *'ēṣ*, [*šereṣ*], *nepeš ḥayyâ*, *'ôp*, *bĕhēmâ*, *remeś*, *hayĕtô-'ereṣ*, *'ādām*) with the exception of *tannînîm*, a plural used to create a comparable class designation for the creatures of the sea. Each class is understood as an aggregate of species (*mîn*), which could conceivably be represented by individuals of each type (cf., e.g., Gen 2:19, where *adam* is a single individual—and also representative of the species). But the theme of reproductive endowment enunciated in the blessing assumes sexual differentiation and hence pairs as the minimal representation of each species. In fact, the image of a pair as the model of a species is so common that it needs no special articulation, especially in such a terse account. It is only where a particular need for clarification or emphasis arises that the assumption must be made explicit—as in 1:27, and 7:9 and 16. See below.

46. Maag's recognition of the polemical function of the repeated statement concerning the seed and his linking of this to the blessing of the creatures ("Alttestamentliche Anthropogonie," 39) seems to have been lost in the subsequent literature. I discovered it only after arriving at a similar understanding. My characterization of the polemic (below) is admittedly overstated. I mean thereby to suggest implications, and possible ancient readings of the text, which lie below the surface message and may escape the modern reader.

47. The blessing of fertility, as Westermann correctly notes, is not a separate or supplemental act, but one which completes the act of creation for the living creatures (*Genesis*, 192). The reason that the power of reproduction is conveyed in a blessing and not simply described as a feature of their constitution, as in the case of the plants, may lie in a recognition that unlike the "automatic" reproduction of plants, animal reproduction is a matter not simply of design, but also of will or of power to realize its end. The blessing activates the latent capacity and directs it toward its goal.

he created them," must be understood. The word of sexual differentiation anticipates the blessing and prepares for it. And it is an essential word, not because of any prehistory which related a separate creation of man and woman,[48] but because of the structure of the Priestly account and the order of its essential themes. Sexual constitution is the presupposition of the blessing of increase, which in the case of other creatures is simply assumed. In the case of *adam*, however, it cannot be assumed, but must be specially articulated because of the statement that immediately precedes it.

The word about *adam* is twofold in both *Wortbericht* and *Tatbericht*; it identifies humanity by nature or constitution and by position or function. And the primary word about the nature of *adam*, and the sole word of the *Wortbericht*, is that this one is like God, created in resemblance to God as an image or representation. This audacious statement of identification and correspondence, however qualified by terms of approximation, offers no ground for assuming sexual distinction as a characteristic of *adam*, but appears rather to exclude it, for God (*'ĕlōhîm*) is the defining term in the statement. The idea that God might possess any form of sexuality, or any differentiation analogous to it, would have been for P an utterly foreign and repugnant notion. For this author/editor, above all others in the Pentateuch, guards the distance between God and humanity, avoiding anthropomorphic description and employing specialized terminology (e.g., *bārā'*) to distinguish divine activity from analogous human action.[49] Consequently, the word that identifies *adam* by reference to divine likeness must be supplemented or qualified before the blessing of fertility can be pronounced; for the word of blessing assumes, but does not bestow, the means of reproduction.

The required word of qualification and specification is introduced in v. 27b. *Unlike* God, but *like* the other creatures, *adam* is characterized by

---

48. So Westermann, *Genesis*, 220–21.

49. The *naʿăśeh* of v. 26 has long troubled commentators mindful of the deliberateness and precision of P's language, especially in referring to the Deity. In view of the control exercised by P over the final composition and especially evident in the *Wortbericht*, the plural formulation cannot be regarded as a "slip" or as an undigested remnant of tradition. For though the expression depends ultimately upon the tradition of the divine council, in its Yahwistic and monotheistic adaptation, it appears also to have been *selected* by P as a means of breaking the direct identification between *adam* and God suggested by the metaphor of image, a way of blurring or obscuring the referent of the *ṣelem*. Cf. the *ṣelem 'ĕlōhîm* of v. 27aβ, which has a similar function in respect to the preceding *ṣalmô* (see below). The plural *'ĕlōhîm* has a useful ambiguity here (v. 27). It is not, however, to be viewed as suggesting a collectivity of male and female deities to which the male-and-female *adam* would correspond (contra Loretz, *Gottebenbildlichkeit*, 68).

sexual differentiation.[50] The parallel clauses of v. 27aβb form a bridging couplet between the primary and emphasized statement concerning the divine likeness, introduced in the *Wortbericht* (v. 26) and repeated as the lead sentence of the *Tatbericht* (v. 27aα), and the pronouncement of the blessing of fertility (v. 28)—a new theme found only in the *Tatbericht*. It recapitulates the word about the image, in an emphatic yet qualifying manner, and adds to it the word of sexual distinction:

> *bĕṣelem ʾĕlōhîm bārāʾ ʾōtô*
> *zākār ûnĕqēbâ bārāʾ ʾōtām*[51]

50. The specifying clause, "male and female he created them," must not be understood as distinguishing humans from other creatures or as giving to human sexual distinction a special meaning. In the economy of the Priestly writer's account it is mentioned here only out of necessity (see below). The same specification, in the same terms *zākār ûnĕqēbâ*, is made elsewhere with reference to the animals—and for a similar reason of clarification and emphasis. In the Priestly account of the flood story, the author wishes to make clear that the "two of every sort" of animals that are to be brought into the ark constitute a minimal pair, capable of reproduction, and thus he specifies, *zākār ûnĕqēbâ yihyû* ("they shall be male and female" [Gen 6:19]; cf. 7:9). The Priestly writer has chosen his terms, as well as their placement, with care. *Zākār* and *nĕqēbâ* are biological terms, not social terms—as *ʾîš* and *ʾiššâ* are in 2:22-24. Harmonizing of the creation accounts of Genesis 1 and 2 has affected the translation as well as the interpretation of the terms of 1:27, especially in the German tradition, where the rendering "Mann und Frau" (Westermann, *Genesis*, 108; Schmidt, *Schöpfungsgeschichte*, 127; inter alios) or "Mann und Weib" (Gunkel, *Genesis*, 103; Zurich Bible, 1942; "Luther Bible," rev. ed., 1964; inter alios) is common. Westermann seems to have fallen prey to the subtle persuasion of this traditional rendering, for despite his caution against overloading the interpretation of the clause, he avers: "Wohl aber ist hier ausgesagt, dass der zu zweit geschaffene Mensch sowohl im Verstehen menschlicher Existenz wie auch in den Ordnungen und den Institutionen des menschlichen Daseins als ein *zur Gemeinschaft bestimmter* gesehen werden muss" (*Genesis*, 221; emphasis added).

51. Most recent analyses of vv. 26-28 recognize a complex history of growth resulting in repetitions, expansions, and substitutions in the present text. There is little consensus, however, about primary and secondary elements or stages of growth or editing. Consequently, understandings of how the component parts fit together to make their statement differ considerably. E.g., Schmidt concludes that pre-P tradition is found only in vv. 26-27a—and no longer in pristine form. Within this material he finds that v. 27a gives the impression of particular antiquity (*Schöpfungsgeschichte*, 148–49). Westermann sees the present text as overloaded with "repetitions" (including vv. 26b and 27aβ as well as *bĕṣalmô* in v. 27aα), which he eliminates from his reconstructed text (*Genesis*, 198–99). The text which he creates by this surgery ("Lasst uns Menschen machen,/ nach unserem Bild, uns ähnlich: //Und Gott schuf die Menschen,/ er schuf sie als Mann und Frau," 198–99) is the text which Barth's exegesis requires, but which the MT with its deliberate qualifications does not allow.

I recognize, with most commentators, a history of growth in the tradition behind the present text, but I do not think the stages can be identified or isolated with any precision. I would regard the couplet in v. 27a as the work of a single author, more specifically, the final editor, and view the seemingly awkward or redundant *bĕṣelem ʾĕlōhîm* as a deliberate qualification of the preceding *bĕṣalmô*, perhaps employing a phrase from an earlier stage of

The two parallel cola contain two essential and distinct statements about the nature of humanity: *adam* is created *like* (i.e., resembling) God, but *as* creature, and hence male and female.[52] The parallelism of the two cola is progressive, not synonymous. The second statement adds to the first; it does not explicate it.[53]

Expansion and Conflation in the *Tatbericht*

The position of the specification of humanity's bisexual nature is dictated by the larger narrative structure of the chapter and by the themes it must incorporate. Here, following the pattern of the preceding acts or episodes, the *Wortbericht* conveys the essential content of the word about the order (viz., created according to divine likeness and given dominion), and the *Tatbericht* repeats it. And here, as in the parallel account of the sixth act of creation, the *Tatbericht* is expanded by a word of blessing, introducing the subtheme of sustainability alongside the primary theme of order. But in vv. 27-28 the introduction of the word of blessing, with its clarifying prefatory note, has broken the connection between image and dominion articulated in v. 26. In the expanded execution report, the word which conveys dominion is joined directly to the preceding words of blessing, creating an extended series of imperatives, all apparently governed by the rubric of blessing (*wayĕbārek 'ōtām* [v. 28])—and all apparently con-

---

the tradition. The repetition of *bĕṣelem* with its significant variation in v. 27aα and β has an important theological purpose. The reflexive singular suffix of v. 27aα requires that the image be referred directly to God, the sole and single actor, and not to a lower order of divine beings (contra Gunkel [*Genesis*, 98], inter alios). It thus "corrects" the impression of a plurality of deities which might be suggested by the plurals of v. 26. But *bĕṣelem 'ĕlōhîm* qualifies the masculine singular antecedent by repetition of the name, which in its third person formulation gives both precision and distance to the self-reference. With its ambiguous plural form and its class connotation, *'ĕlōhîm* serves, as do the plurals of v. 26, to blur the profile of the referent.

52. The shift from the collective singular (*'ōtô* ["him"]) in the first colon to (collective) plural (*'ōtām* ["them"]) in the second is significant. The author relates the notion of the divine image only to an undifferentiated humanity as species or order and thus takes pains to use the singular pronoun in both clauses of v. 27 employing *ṣelem*, despite the fact that the plural has already been introduced in the verb (*wĕyirdû*) of the preceding verse.

53. Contra Barth, who sees v. 27b as a "geradezu definitions-mässige Erklärung der Gottes-ebenbildlichkeit" (*KD* 3/1, 219). Cf. Trible (*God and the Rhetoric of Sexuality*, 16–21), who finds in the parallelism of v. 27 a metaphor in which "the image of God" is the tenor and "male and female" the vehicle (17). This interpretation rests on a faulty syntatical analysis which isolates v. 27 as a unit of speech/thought. The metaphor is the creation of the interpreter. Schmidt, who judged v. 27b a secondary addition on grounds of vocabulary, style, and meter, noted that apart from Gen 1:27 and 5:1-2 the themes of divine image and sexuality are associated nowhere else, either in the Old Testament or in the ancient Near East (*Schöpfungsgeschichte*, 146–47). He failed to recognize, however, why the two are juxtaposed here.

ditioned by the dual qualification of bisexual nature and divine resemblance. Such a reading of vv. 27-28, however, which treats the series of words addressed to *adam* as homogeneous and relates both statements of nature (Godlike and bisexual) to the whole series without discrimination, ignores the interpretive clues contained in the *Wortbericht* and in the parallel construction of v. 22. Fertility and dominion belong to two separate themes or concerns: one, the theme of nature with its subtheme of sustainability (fertility); the other, the theme of order with its interest in position and function. The word of sexual distinction pertains only to the first, and has relevance or consequence in P's theology only for the first.

There is no message of shared dominion here,[54] no word about the distribution of roles, responsibility, and authority between the sexes, no word of sexual equality. What is described is a task for the species (*kibšūhā*) and the position of the species in relation to the other orders of creatures (*rĕdû*). The social metaphors to which the key verbs point are male, derived from male experience and models, the dominant social models of patriarchal society. For P, as for J, the representative and determining image of the species was certainly male, as 5:1-3, 9:1, and the genealogies which structure the continuing account make clear.[55] Though the Priestly writer speaks of the species, he thinks of the male, just as the author of Psalm 8 does. But maleness is not an essential or defining characteristic. Against such reduction or confusion of attributes the word

54. Contra Anderson ("Human Dominion," 43) and Trible (*God and the Rhetoric of Sexuality,* 19), inter alios. Anderson rightly argues that "dominion is given to mankind as a whole," finding in this collective understanding a clear expression of the "democratization" of the royal motif (42). But then he explicates "mankind as a whole" to mean "man and woman." "Here," he notes, "the priestly view departs from royal theology in Egypt, for it is not said that Pharaoh *and* his wife represent together the image of God." Psalm 8 stands much closer to the royal theology, he argues, in that "'man' is spoken of in the singular and no reference is made to male and female" (43). Both contrasts are false, however, since the specification of male and female relates neither to dominion nor to the image. The "Egyptian pattern" of male representation is continued unqualified in the biblical tradition of Genesis as well as Psalm 8. See below.

55. When P moves from protohistory (creation) to "history" his view of humankind is limited to the male actor or subject. Thus *adam* becomes Adam and is renewed in Noah and his sons, not Noah and his wife. The blessing of fertility is addressed in 9:1 to the men alone, with no mention of the wives, who as necessary helpers in the task of maintaining the species are explicitly noted in the enumeration of those entering the ark. The pointed reference to the unnamed wives of Noah and of his three sons in 7:7 and 7:13 has the same function as the specification of "male and female" in 1:27. This theme of reproductive capability also finds expression in the phrase "other sons *and daughters,*" incorporated into the summarizing statement of each generation of P's otherwise all-male genealogical tables (5:4, 7, 10, 13, 16, 19, 22, 26, 30; 12:11, 13, 15, 17, 19, 21, 23, 25). The history in which P's theological interest lies is a history carried by males and embodied in males. Females come into view only where the issue of biological continuity or reproduction is raised.

of bisexual creation stands as guard, even if it provides only a minimal base for an anthropology of equality. The theme of sexuality (reproduction) has a limited function in this account. And the words which introduce it are bracketed within the *Tatbericht*. The divine address, initiated in the blessing of fertility, moves beyond the idea of increase to climax in the independent theme of dominion, resuming the thought and expression of the announcement in v. 26.[56] But the resumption in v. 28 appears to contain an expansion, extending *adam*'s dominion from rule over the realm of creatures to subjugation of the earth. The expression *wĕkibšūhā* forms a bridge in the present text between the word of increase and the word of sovereignty. In subject matter it appears linked to the latter, suggesting that *RDH* might be understood as an elaboration or specification of *KBŠ*.[57] Grammatically, however, it is an extension of the blessing, with an object and function distinct from that of the following verb, and must consequently be distinguished from the theme of dominion articulated by *RDH*.

The theme of divine blessing, specifically blessing of increase, is a key interpretive element within the larger Priestly work, located at strategic points in the account and formulated according to the particular demands of each situation. The vocabulary is neither fixed nor unique to P, though the root pair *PRH* + *RBH* forms a constant core of his usage and may be seen as a signature of his work.[58] Outside P, or dependent usage,[59] the closest parallels are found in exilic prophecies of restoration (Jer 3:16; 23:3; Ezek 36:11). In all usage, the word of blessing, whether direct or indirect, past or future, has a particular end or goal related to a particular situation of need; and in the majority of cases it is a territorial goal.[60]

---

56. The expansion of the introduction in v. 28 over the parallel in v. 22 may be related to the expanded statement which it introduces. The repetitive *wayyōʾmer lāhem ʾĕlōhîm* following *wayĕbārek ʾōtām ʾĕlōhîm*, in place of the simple *lēʾmōr* of v. 22, is usually explained in terms of emphasis and differentiation: in the case of *adam*, unlike the lower creatures, the divine word has become a word of address, an act of communication. But the twofold introduction may indicate an awareness that what follows is not simply blessing, but rather blessing together with a word conveying authority (Schmidt, *Schöpfungsgeschichte*, 148–49).

57. Cf. Schmidt, *Schöpfungsgeschichte*, 147; and Westermann, *Genesis*, 222.

58. Cf. Westermann, *Genesis*, 192–95; Schmidt, *Schöpfungsgeschichte*, 147–48.

59. P: Gen 1:22; 1:28; 8:17; 9:1; 9:7; [17:6 *PRH* alone (*hiphil*)]; 17:20 (*hiphil*); 28:3 (*hiphil*; Isaac as subject); 35:11; 47:27; 48:4 (*hiphil*); Exod 1:7. Dependent on P: Ps 105:24 (*PRH hiphil* + *ʿŚM hiphil*, reflecting Exod 1:7); Lev 26:9 (*PRH hiphil*); Exod 23:30 (*PRH qal*).

60. In extra-P usage, *PRH*, as a term for human and animal increase, is typically related to possession of (the) land and/or security against foes, with increase understood as the necessary condition or presupposition. Jer 3:16, 23:3, and Ezek 36:11 envision the increase of a remnant which shall again "fill" the land, while Exod 23:30 speaks of Israel's original possession of the land. All of the "historical" uses of *PRH* point to a future or restored Israel, closely associating the ideas of territorial possession and nationhood.

This is explicit in the Patriarchal History, where the language of blessing has been assimilated by P to the older tradition and form of the promise. Here the goal, given by the promise tradition, is possession of the land—a historical as well as a territorial goal.[61] In P's edition of the Primeval History, the language of increase has been adapted to the situation of prehistory and the emptiness of newly created earth in a three-part formula of blessing, repeated in Gen 1:22, 28, and 9:1: *pĕrû ûrĕbû ûmil' û* . . . ("be fruitful and multiply and fill . . ."). The orientation of the words of increase toward particular time and space is clear from the final term of the formula, *ûmil' û*, and from the placement of the blessing, addressing creatures classified by habitat (land and nonland creatures) and by "historical" circumstances (Noah and sons after the flood).[62]

The blessing of 1:28, directed to the first, representative specimens of humanity, adds an element lacking in the parallels of 1:22 and 9:1, one which establishes the conditions essential, and unique, to this species for continuing life and for history. The newly formed earth must not only be filled, but also tamed or "harnessed."[63] The author knows that earth will support human life only when it is brought under control—a condition distinguishing *adam* from the birds and sea creatures, who appear to be sustained by their environment rather than having to win life from it. The agrarian perspective is obvious and is shared with the Mesopotamian author of *Atraḫasis*, who views the task as drudgery, however, not as an act of mastery, a burden imposed upon humanity, not a blessing. It is also shared by the Yahwist, who distinguishes an "original" relationship to

61. That the historical goal may be future as well as past (assuming a programmatic or eschatological dimension to the Priestly Work) does not change this assertion. The promise of P is not open-ended. It envisions historical fulfillment.

62. The periodization of the Primeval History is overlooked by Lohfink, when he suggests that the blessing of 1:28 looks to the rise of the various nations and the settlement of their lands ("Seid fruchtbar," 82). He is right, however, in stressing that the imperative of Gen 1:28 is not a general word for all time, but a word that belongs to the situation of origins (80). Thus neither the historic problems of underpopulation or overpopulation are relevant to the interpretation of this word.

The repetition of the blessing in 9:1 focuses on the human species alone, whose history now becomes the subject of the continuing account. This renewed blessing sets in motion the growth which leads to the rise of nations, in which the history of Israel is hidden.

63. The basic sense of the root *KBŠ* is "subdue, bring into bondage" (BDB; preferable to KB: "treten, niedertreten, drücken"). All uses of the *qal*, *niphal*, and *hiphil* are exilic. The oldest usage is in 2 Sam 8:11, a *piel*, with King David as subject and *haggôyīm* ("the nations") as object. While the image is forceful, attention is directed to the resultant state, as subdued, deprived of (threatening) power, hence "pacified," controlled. Cf. George W. Coats, "The God of Death: Power and Obedience in the Primeval History," *Int* 29 (1975) 227–39, esp. 229 ("render productive"); and Barr, "Man and Nature," 63–64 ("work or till"). Most discussions of v. 28 treat this clause under the heading of "dominion" and do not distinguish between *KBŠ* and *RDH*.

earth from the historical one and thus accommodates, in sequential arrangement, both the sense of mastery and the experience of drudgery or
servitude. For P, who adapts the views of his cultural ancestors, the presupposition of history and culture is the subjugation of earth, rendering
it productive and responsive to a master, *adam*. Because this subjugation
is essential to the sustaining of human life it is included in the original
blessing.[64]

The theme announced by the final imperative, *ûrĕdû*, is distinct from
that of the preceding "commands," despite the similarity in meaning of
the verbs *RDH* and *KBŠ*. This theme describes the relationship of *adam*
to the other creatures who share the earth. Its concern is order and status,
rather than life and growth. Its message of human superiority and sovereignty over the creatures appears independently in the creation hymn,
Psalm 8, associated there as here with the idea of humanity's proximity to
the divine world, but there without any hint of the theme of increase and
subjugation of the earth.[65]

RDH in Old Testament usage describes the exercise of dominion, authority, or power over an individual, group, or territory (nation), often in
contexts that specify harsh or illegitimate rule.[66] The term cannot simply
be equated with the idea of governing, ruling, or managing, with or without emphasis on a caretaker function or maintenance of harmony and
order.[67] And, as is often noted, it is not exclusively, or even predominantly,
royal language, though, I have argued, it does describe a royal function or
prerogative in Genesis 1. When used of kings, it is usually to describe their
subjugation of other nations or peoples,[68] or rule over their own people
as though they were foreigners.[69] The term emphasizes superior position
and power rather than any particular activity, purpose, or quality of rule.[70]

64. It is not repeated with the blessing to Noah after the flood, since the blessing there
has a new and more limited function. The issue is no longer the preconditions of human
life and culture but the history of the nations. See above.

65. Anderson sees this absence of the increase-subjugation motif as the clearest evidence
for the independence of Psalm 8, but mistakenly links the theme of dominion to the blessing
in Genesis 1 ("Human Dominion," 36).

66. BDB gives as the basic meaning: "have dominion, rule [over . . .]." Cognate usage
suggests a prevailing negative connotation: Aramaic, Syriac: "chastise"; Arabic: "tread,
trample." In Old Testament usage the verb is often accompanied by qualifying expressions
such as *bĕperek* or *bĕhozqâ* (Lev 25:43, 46, 53; Ezek 34:4), *bāʾap* (Isa 14:6), or by parallel verbs
such as *NKH* (*hiphil;* Isa 14:6), *NŚʾ* (*hithpael;* Ezek 29:15), *NGP* (Lev 26:17), *ʿBD* (Lev 25:46).

67. *MŠL* is not chosen here, though it is used to describe the function of the sun and
moon in v. 16.

68. 1 Kgs 5:4; Pss 110:2; 72:8; Isa 14:6; 41:2.

69. Ezek 34:4; Lev 25:43, 46, 53.

70. I do not think that Lohfink's interpretation of *RDH* in Gen 1:26, 28 as "domestication"
of the animals (including fish and birds!) can be defended, though it rightly grasps the
elements of superiority and constraint which color the biblical use of the term ("Seid fruchtbar," 82). *RDH* is appropriate in this context to describe rule over those who are not of the

The sentiment expressed by the verb *RDH* in Gen 1:26, 28 is, in fact, very close to that expressed by the distinctively royal and hymnic language of Psalm 8, where the idea of dominion is spelled out as subordination/subjugation ("put all things under his feet," v. 7) and linked to the idea of exaltation. Human superiority over other creation is stressed in both accounts. The primary function of *RDH* in Genesis 1 is to describe *adam*'s place in creation. If there is also a message of responsibility here, it is not dependent on the content of the verb but on the action of God in setting *adam* over the creatures in an ordered and sustaining world.

Summary and Conclusions

If the foregoing analysis is correct, the meaning and function of the statement, "male and female he created them," is considerably more limited than is commonly assumed. It says nothing about the image which relates *adam* to God nor about God as the referent of the image. Nor does it qualify *adam*'s dominion over the creatures or subjugation of the earth. It relates only to the blessing of fertility, making explicit its necessary presupposition. It is not concerned with sexual roles, the status or relationship of the sexes to one another, or marriage. It describes the biological pair, not a social partnership; male and female, not man and wife. The specification is not dictated by any prehistory that told of a separate creation of man and woman. Rather, it is P's own formulation, dependent upon his overarching theme of the sustainability (fertility) of the created order. It may also serve, secondarily, to link the creation narrative to the genealogically structured history which follows.

These conclusions may disappoint in their largely negative formulation, but they have positive consequence as well. The Priestly writer appears in our analysis as a more consistent and intentional theologian in his treatment of the sexes. And the contemporary theologian-exegete is reminded that the Bible is often quite uninterested in, or unable to comprehend, the questions pressed upon the text from modern perspectives and experiences. To describe and to emphasize the limits of a biblical text is not to dishonor it or depreciate its message, but to give integrity and authority to its voice where it does have a word to speak. Sharpening the contours of a given text or profile of an author brings into our range of hearing a greater variety of voices and enables us to discern more clearly common themes and motifs, as well as dissonances. Questions of context (literary, historical, and theological) acquire greater prominence, prohibiting simple transfer of words from the past into modern contexts. The

---

same kind or order and who may be viewed in their created state as potentially hostile. This is not the rule of a "brother" but of a stranger. Cf. Westermann, *Genesis,* 219–20.

ancient text in historical analysis presents to the contemporary theologian not simply a vocabulary, a treasury of images and concepts, but also a grammar, or grammars, which are fully as essential to the message as the individual terms.

Emphasizing the literary and historical integrity of the ancient text draws more sharply the line between historical and constructive theology, but it may also enable recognition of affinity between the two disciplines, namely, in attention to process in interpretation. Both biblical and contemporary theology may be seen as creative responses to ever-changing contexts; ancient and modern word share a common dynamism which finds expression in changing forms and images, or in changing content of inherited forms and images. Past answers need not be forced to fit contemporary questions.

The task of the biblical exegete in enabling meaningful conversation with an ancient text is first of all to articulate as clearly and carefully as possible the message/intentions of the ancient author or authors at every stage or level of the tradition at which they are exposed within the relevant literary unit. The second task is to ask where they lead (i.e., what may be implied in them but not fully recognized or elaborated) and how they have been amplified, challenged, or corrected by subsequent or alternative understandings arising within the canon and without. The answers to these latter questions move beyond the primary competence of the biblical scholar, but are essential to the task of appropriating the biblical message. The final task of interpretation for the believer is the task of the theologian (which includes the exegete as theologian), viz., assessment of the truth of the message in the light of all available sources of knowledge and rejection or reformulation of the message in contemporary terms and in relation to contemporary questions and experience. The following is an attempt to take the first steps of generalization, comparison, and appraisal of our text within the larger Old Testament context. It does not aim to be comprehensive, but only to suggest some leadings.

In the case of Gen 1:26-28, it seems possible to say the following concerning the consequences or implications of our reading for an understanding of P's anthropology and its place in and contribution to the larger biblical anthropology. (1) The incongruous portrait of P as an equal-rights theologian is removed and Genesis 1 can be read in harmony with the rest of the Priestly work—in which the genealogies that form the essential link between creation and the establishment of the cult know only male names (unlike the older "family" stories incorporated into this lineal framework); in which the cult which represents the culminating word or work of God has no place for women in its service; and in which circumcision is the essential sign of identity for members of the covenant people. Gen 1:27 does not contradict this Priestly view of a special male role in history. (2) Our analysis also removes from P the equally incongruous notion of a correspondence between relationship of the sexes and relationship within the Godhead. For the Priestly theologian who so carefully guards the mystery, singularity, and distance of God from creatures, the thought of such a correspondence, albeit analogical, is neither tolerable nor conceivable. (3) The word of sexual distinction in Genesis 1 refers only to the reproductive task and capacity of the species; its consequences for social status and roles are left unspecified. Furthermore, all words of task or position address the species collectively. For the Priestly author of Genesis 1 the division of labor, honor, and responsibility within the human species is not a matter of creation; it belongs rather to history.

Thus the Priestly account of creation contains no doctrine of the equality—or inequality—of the sexes, either explicit or implied. It is, however, an indispensable text for any theology of sexuality, significant for its silence as well as its affirmation. The voice of P is not alone in the biblical story of creation, but must be heard alongside that of J, with attention to their juxtaposition within the canonical context. And though the creation accounts have special importance for theological anthropology as a unique locus of reflection on the essential nature of humanity, their word must be supplemented by the less direct, less conscious, and less comprehensive statements and images found in the historical, narrative, prescriptive, and prophetic literature. A full statement of the biblical understanding of human sexuality or sexual distinction must draw on a wider range of literature and relate the Genesis texts to it.[71]

Within that larger assemblage of texts Gen 1:27 contributes the notion, rightly understood if wrongly isolated and absolutized in traditional interpretation, that sex, as differentiation and union, is intended for procreation—a divinely given capacity and power conceived both in terms of blessing and command. But the word that activates the endowment addresses the species, not the individual, and is limited in its application by the setting in which it is spoken, a limitation made explicit in the qualifying amplification, "and fill the earth." It is a word for beginnings, not for all time; and wherever it is repeated it is with a definite, proximate goal in mind. The "command" is neither absolute nor universal.[72] It must be re-

---

71. See my limited attempt to do that in "Images of Women in the Old Testament," in Ruether, *Religion and Sexism*, 41–88 [*13–51].

72. If the word "command" is too strong, it nevertheless correctly insists that the word is not simply permissive or optative. The questions which then arise are: Whom is addressed and under what circumstances? Does it bind each individual? or pair? for all time? a reproductive lifetime? etc. Such questions make clear that this statement is insufficient as a guide to practice—if it is properly oriented to the historical situation at all.

peated and reinterpreted in changing historical/ecological situations. Yet its basic presupposition—the association of sexuality with procreation—is not repeated and thus stands as a generally relevant word concerning the nature of the species.

P's understanding of sexual reproduction as blessing, in humans as well as animals, is an important contribution to a theology of sexuality. Sex at its most fundamental, biological level is not to be despised or deprecated. It is God's gift and it serves God's purpose in creation by giving to humans the power and the responsibility to participate in the process of continuing creation by which the species is perpetuated. But P's statement is insufficient to guide the process, to give essential directives concerning the circumstances of its use. The concerns of creation, as concerns of nature, must be supplemented by the concerns of ethics to produce an adequate anthropology; and for the latter one must look beyond Genesis 1. For the Priestly account of origins ignores completely the question of the social structuring of roles and of individual and collective responsibility in carrying out the charge addressed to the species. The author may simply have assumed the roles and norms of his day, but he offers no theological rationale for them. P's silence at this point enables the interpreter to move readily into areas where that author had no answers or perceived no questions. In this movement into the areas of P's silence, texts such as Genesis 2–3, which offer differing or supplementary statements and perspectives, must be taken into account, with the possibility that they may ultimately challenge or qualify the thesis of the initial text.

That is the case with the Yahwistic account of creation, in which the primary meaning of sexuality is seen in psychosocial, rather than biological, terms. Companionship, the sharing of work, mutual attraction and commitment in a bond superseding all other human bonds and attractions—these are the ends for which *adam* was created male and female and these are the signs of the intended partnership. This is not to deny that the help which the woman was intended to give to the man was the help of childbearing (implied in Gen 3:16), but that does not express the full intention of the writer of Genesis 2–3, whose interest also includes the sociosexual bond. And because the social relationship of the sexes is addressed in this account, the question of equality or status is also addressed, though indirectly. The intended partnership implies a partnership of equals, characterized by mutuality of attraction, support, and commitment. That the story is *told* from the point of view of the man and is thus clearly androcentric in construction does not alter this basic tone of the account as a tone of mutuality and equality. But the most explicit statement of the intended equality of man and woman is found in the account of the "fall," J's picture of creation in its historical manifestation.

Here the consequences of sin, the disturbance of the original (i.e., intended) relationship between God and creation, is portrayed as the disturbance of the original/intended relationship between the man and the woman. And the sign of this disturbed relationship is this, that while the woman's relationship to the man is characterized by desire, the man's relationship to the woman is characterized by rule. The companion of chapter 2 has become a master. The historical subordination of woman to man is inaugurated—and identified as the paradigm expression of sin and alienation in creation. Thus Genesis 2–3 supplements the anthropology of Genesis 1, but also "corrects" or challenges it by maintaining that the meaning of human sexual distinction cannot be limited to a biological definition of origin or function. Sexuality is a social endowment essential to community and to personal fulfillment, but as such it is also subject to perversion and abuse. Genesis 2–3 opens the way for a consideration of sex and sexuality in history.

There remains a word about the image of Gen 1:26-27. Though the note of sexual distinction does not qualify or explain it, the juxtaposition of the two statements does have consequence for theological anthropology and specifically for a theology of sexuality. Sexuality and image of God both characterize the species as a whole and both refer to *adam*'s fundamental nature; but they do so in different ways. While the image is referred always and only to the species as a whole (*adam/'ōtô*—singular, undifferentiated collectivity), sexuality is referred to individuals of the species (*'ōtām*—plural, differentiated collectivity). Thus the grammar of the parallel clauses in v. 27 prevents identification or interchange of the defining terms. While P's own image of *adam* as the image of God was surely male, as the terms for task and position (*KBŠ* and *RDH*) as well as the note of 5:3 suggest, the carefully guarded language of 1:26-27 does not allow this masculine identification to define the image.

But if the divine image characterizes and defines the species as a whole, it cannot be denied to any individual of the species. To be human is to be made in the image of God. And if to be human means also to be male *or* female (the plural of v. 27 also works against any notion of androgyny), then *both* male and female must be characterized equally by the image. No basis for diminution or differentiation of the image is given in nature. Thus it cannot be altered or denied by history. What belongs to the order by constitution (creation) is immutable and ineradicable. It is essential to human identity. Distinctions of roles, responsibilities, or social status on the basis of sex—or other characteristics—are not excluded by this statement. But where such distinctions have the effect of denying to an individual or group the full and essential status of humanity in the image of God, they contradict the word of creation. Contemporary insistence that woman images the divine as fully as man and that she is consequently as essential as he to an understanding of humanity as God's special sign or representative in the world is exegetically sound even if it exceeds what the Priestly writer intended to say or was able to conceive. Like Paul's affirmation that in Christ there is no more "male and female" (Gal 3:28), the full content and implications of the Priestly statement lie beyond the author's ability to comprehend.

7

GENESIS 1–3 AS
A SOURCE FOR
A CONTEMPORARY
THEOLOGY OF SEXUALITY

I SHOULD LIKE TO BEGIN WITH A WORD OF APPRECIATION FOR THE contribution of the Frederick Neumann Symposium in fostering inter-disciplinary dialogue in the theological interpretation of Scripture. As the Bible belongs to the whole church, occasions and means must be sought to engage the various theological disciplines in conversation about its meaning, conversation made more difficult, and more essential, by the increasing specialization and compartmentalization of our knowledge. For the impetus given by this symposium to the recovery of a more inclusive and theologically oriented discourse about the Bible I am grateful.

I am also grateful for the selection of a topic that I view as critically important in our time, namely, creation, and for an approach to that topic that understands it as a Scripture-encompassing theme, not limited to the opening chapters of Genesis. While my own contribution is anchored in Genesis 1–3 (and confined to a single question within this corpus), my ultimate aim is to link these foundational texts with other canonical witnesses in a conversation shaped by contemporary questions, but attentive to ancient meanings. More specifically, I shall attempt to show how Genesis 1–3 may contribute to a constructive theological anthropology, with

Paper originally read at the Second Annual Frederick Neumann Symposium on Theological Interpretation of Scripture (theme: "Creation"), Princeton Theological Seminary, October 16–19, 1987; subsequently published in *Ex Auditu* 3 (1987) 31–44. Cross-references to articles reprinted in this volume are indicated by an asterisk in square brackets following the original page number.

particular attention to human sexuality—and how it may not. I am concerned to show the limits as well as the contributions of these overexploited texts. While the topic of sexuality represents an exceedingly narrow focus within the universe-encompassing question of creation, it is given disproportionate attention in the primary Old Testament texts. By reason of this placement and prominence, the biblical interpreter is directed to consider the meaning and end of human sexuality in the context of theological reflection on creation.

A word about nomenclature: I have used the term "sexuality" as a term encompassing both the idea of gender differentiation (or gender dimorphism) and sexual endowment—in all its biological, psychological, and social dimensions.[1] My intention in this usage is to employ a term that can comprehend the distinct interests and emphases of the two creation texts and at the same time allow formulation of questions based on contemporary understanding.

Genesis 1 and 2 are not the only Old Testament texts that speak of creation, but they are unique in that corpus in giving explicit attention to gender, or sexuality, as an essential and constitutive element of human creation.[2] Why does the author of Genesis 1 pause in his spare, cadenced account of the successive orders of creation to mark this order of creatures as bisexual? And why does the author of Genesis 2–3 break into the story of *adam* and the *adamah* ("earthling" [human] and the "earth") to recount the creation of another who is both derived from *adam* and stands over against him? What do these pointed expansions mean—for their ancient authors, and for modern theologians?

Traditional interpretation of Genesis 1–3 combined elements of two creation accounts (Gen 1:1—2:4a and 2:4b—3:24) to articulate a view of human origins, human nature, and the relationship of the sexes that continues to exercise a powerful influence on contemporary theological thought.[3] However, the conflate reading on which this understanding was based ignored the distinct language, dynamics, and intentions of the two

1. *Webster's Third New International Dictionary of the English Language,* ed. Philip Babcock Grove, (Springfield, Mass.: G. & C. Merriam, 1961). Cf. James B. Nelson, *Embodiment: An Approach to Sexuality and Christian Theology* (Minneapolis: Augsburg, 1978) 17–18.

2. I use the designations "Genesis 1" and "Genesis 2" as shorthand references for the two accounts contained respectively in Gen 1:1—2:4a and Gen 2:4b—25.

3. The analysis presented in this paper is based on a recently completed article, "Sexual Differentiation and Divine Image in the Genesis Creation Texts" (originally published in Kari E. Børresen, ed., *Image of God and Gender Models* [Oslo: Solum Forlag, 1991] 11–34 [1995: 5–28]), and an earlier, detailed study of the Priestly account alone, "'Male and Female He Created Them': Gen 1:27b in the Context of the Priestly Account of Creation," *HTR* 74 (1981) 129–59 [*123–54]. The latter article should be consulted for full argumentation and documentation of the lexical and syntactic issues discussed in relation to Genesis 1.

passages. One of the contributions of modern biblical scholarship has been to reexpose, and sharpen, the long-observed tension between the two accounts and to link each to a larger literary complex within the Pentateuch. By giving attention to stylistic and theological differences between the two accounts and identifying them with different historico-religious settings and purposes, modern critical scholarship has opened the way for a re-union of the texts in a reading that is attentive to their distinctive voices while honoring and preserving their peculiar contributions.[4]

I shall begin my treatment of the texts with a separate analysis of each literary unit, attempting to allow it to speak on its own terms. I shall then consider how the two may be heard together in a larger canonical and postcanonical context. Although my analysis of the primary texts must be abbreviated, I shall still give attention to the larger literary structure of each passage, which is critical to the interpretation of the key verses.

The Priestly (P) Account (Gen 1:1—2:4a)

In the creation account of Gen 1:1—2:4a (which I shall refer to by the conventional designation of "P" or "Priestly account") two distinct and unrelated statements about the creation, and therefore the nature, of humankind have been juxtaposed in 1:26-27. The first is concerned with the status and function of the human order in relation to the other orders of created life; it uses the language of divine image, or likeness, and of dominion, or rule—linked concepts in the tradition complex from which this language is drawn:

> Let us make humankind (*adam*) in our image,
>   according to our likeness,
> And let them have dominion over the fish of the sea and the birds
>   of the air,
>   and the cattle and all the earth
>   and everything that creeps upon the earth.
> (1:26)

This statement emphasizes human superiority over the other creatures, and responsibility for them, a superiority and a duty which it authorizes

4. While the present state of pentateuchal studies is characterized by wide-scale erosion of the consensus that dominated critical scholarship for most of this century, I still find it necessary to employ a form of the traditional "documentary" analysis in my treatment of the two accounts united in Genesis 1–3. Cf. Bird, "Male and Female," 135 [*129–30] n. 13. For a recent summary and assessment of modern pentateuchal criticism see R. N. Whybray, *The Making of the Pentateuch: A Methodological Study* (JSOTSup 53; Sheffield: JSOT Press, 1987).

by the notion of divine likeness in the manner of an image (more specifically, a representation and representative of the Deity).[5]

The second statement is concerned with fertility or reproduction, an expression of a more general theme that runs throughout the chapter, namely, concern for the sustainability of created life. That concern is addressed in the case of humankind by the blessing of fertility (shared with the other orders of living creatures, 1:22)[6] and by the specification of sexual constitution, which is its precondition:

> Male and female he created them.
> And God blessed them,
> and God said to them:
>   "Be fruitful and multiply. . . ."
> (1:27b-28)

The two themes, of dominion and fertility, are distinct. The one is not a function of the other. Humankind is an order bearing a special relationship to God and to other creatures, but belonging to the world of creatures and having like them the capacity and duty of sexual reproduction. Gender for the Priestly writer is not a sign of divine nature, whether by reflection or analogy; "male and female" does not explicate or interpret the divine image. Rather, it *adds* to the statement of Godlikeness the further specification of sexual constitution, which is indispensable for procreation. The parallel statements of v. 27 must be understood as sequential, not synonymous;

> God created humankind (*adam*) in his image,
>   in the image of God he created him;
> male and female he created them.

I cannot spell out here the full technical arguments for this simple and straightforward reading, which are laid out in an earlier article.[7] However, some further defense or explication of this interpretation may be called for in view of the popularity of Karl Barth's ingenious combination of Genesis 1 and 2 to find an "analogy of relationship" in the juxtaposed notions of image and sexual differentiation[8] and in view of Phyllis Trible's

---

5. Bird, "Male and Female," 136–46 [*130–40].
6. Here sea creatures; on the omission of the blessing for the land creatures, see ibid., 145 [*139–40].
7. Bird, "Male and Female."
8. Karl Barth, *CD* 3/1, 183–206, esp. 194–95. Cf. Bird, "Male and Female," 131–32 [*125–26].

similar reading, based on a rhetorical analysis.[9] Two points require particular attention: (1) the meaning of the Hebrew expression *zākār ûněqēbâ* ("male and female"); and (2) the order of the statements within the account of human creation.

The Hebrew terms *zākār* ("male") and *něqēbâ* ("female") are biological, not sociological, terms.[10] They are the same terms used elsewhere in the Primeval History by the same author to describe the pairs of animals Noah is instructed to bring into the ark:

> Of every living thing of all flesh, you shall bring two of every sort into the ark, to keep them alive with you; they shall be male and female (*zākār ûněqēbâ*). (6:19; cf. 7:9)

Here the writer makes his intention clear by this added specification: the two of every sort must be a reproductive pair in order to assure the survival of the species. It is the same language used in Genesis 1, and it expresses the same concern. Here, as elsewhere, the Priestly writer exhibits a "scientific" bent in his interest in classification, order, and process and in his precision of language, which results in monotonous repetition of technical terms to give exactness to his description.

The Priestly account of creation in its present form is concerned not only with the sequence of the orders of creation but with the means by which the orders of life will fill the newly created world and perpetuate themselves in it. Whether one sees this interest as related only to the time of beginnings (and new beginnings after the deluge, Gen 8:17) or as a broader interest in the capacity of created life to sustain itself, it has left a significant mark on the present shape of the text.[11] Not only is there added to the report of the first and last acts of the creation of living creatures (vv. 20-21 and 26-27) a word of blessing in direct speech enjoining the species to propagate, there is also added to the description of each class of plant life an explicit word concerning its means of propagation:

---

9. Phyllis Trible, *God and the Rhetoric of Sexuality* (OBT; Philadelphia: Fortress Press, 1978) 1–30. Trible's literary approach is distinguished from my own in that she is not interested in the intentionality of the author, while my concern is precisely to recover the author's intention, to whatever extent this is possible using literary-historical methods.

10. The clear distinction between the biological word pair *zākār* (male) and *něqēbâ* (female), used in Genesis 1, and the sociological terms *ʾîš* (man) and *ʾiššâ* (woman), used in Genesis 2, is obscured by harmonizing of the two accounts. Such harmonistic reading has affected German translations in particular, where the terms in Gen 1:27 are rendered "Mann und Frau" or "Mann und Weib" in several recent commentaries and Bible versions (see Bird, "Male and Female," 148–49 n. 50) [*143].

11. Fuller discussion in ibid., 146–47, 152 [*140–41, 146–47].

> And God said, "Let the earth put forth vegetation, plants *yielding seed,* and fruit trees bearing fruit *in which is their seed,* each according to its kind [or "by species"]. (1:11)

This added specification, which is cumbersome in Hebrew as well as English and stands out in this otherwise streamlined account, is unnecessary to a simple classification of plant life, even one oriented toward consumption. It is dictated by concern for the perpetuation of the species, the same concern behind the blessings. But whereas reproduction by seeds appears to be automatic, requiring only the proper organs, sexual reproduction (at least as understood by ancient observation) requires a union of individuals in a "willed" act of cooperation. So the capacity given in design must be activated by a command, formulated as a blessing.

But why, one may ask, does the author fail to include the word of sexual differentiation in his description of the nonhuman orders of animal life that he applies to them in the flood story? The reason, I think, is that in the economy of description in Genesis 1 it is not necessary; it is assumed by the blessing. It is necessary in 6:19 and 7:9, however, where exemplars of the species are explicitly reduced to two and where there is no command to multiply (the word that activates the pairs is not given until they are sent forth from the ark in 8:17, where the command is formulated indirectly and without the word of blessing).

It is also necessary in the case of humankind in Genesis 1, but for a different reason. Sexuality cannot be assumed for humankind at the point where the blessing must be spoken, because the single identifying mark of this order of creation that has been mentioned thus far is its resemblance to God, an identification introduced in the divine decree that initiates the act of creation ("Let us make humankind in our image, according to our likeness," v. 26) and repeated in the report of the divine action ("And God created humankind in his image," v. 27). For the Priestly writer the idea that God might possess any form of sexuality, or any differentiation analogous to it, must be viewed, I believe, as an alien and repugnant notion.[12] Something more had to be said about this creature before the blessing of fertility could be pronounced. That additional word is the word of sexual differentiation which expands the statement about the nature of humankind in preparation for the blessing. Unlike God, but like the other creatures, humanity is characterized by sexuality. This unique and exalted creature, whose special identity and vocation is determined by relation-

12. Cf. ibid., 148 [*142].

ship to God, is still creature, by nature and design, including sexual consti-tution.[13]

Before I proceed to the Yahwist's narrative, a word is in order about P's use of the term *adam*, which I have variously rendered "humans" or "humankind." In Genesis 1, in keeping with P's normative usage elsewhere and with the general usage of the Hebrew Bible, *adam* is a collective term requiring the translation "humankind" or an equivalent expression.[14] Its collective nature is particularly clear in this chapter because of the marked parallelism in the construction of the account in which successive new forms of life are introduced. In Hebrew all of the terms used to describe these orders of life are singular collective nouns,[15] like *adam*, and all are translated in English by collectives or plurals: *deše*ʾ, "vegetation," ʿ*ēśeb*, "plants," ʿ*ēṣ*, "trees," *šereṣ*, "swarms," *nepeš ḥayyâ*, "living creatures," ʿ*ôp*, "birds," *běhēmâ*, "beasts," and so on. What is designated by each is a broad class or order of life, with its subdivisions into species indicated by the repeated expression "according to its kind" (*lěmînô*, more accurately ren-dered "by species").[16] Only *adam* has no subdivision; humankind for the Priestly writer is both species and order.

This collective understanding of *adam* in Genesis 1 needs to be kept clearly in mind when one moves to the story of the first couple in Genesis 2–3 or to P's personification of the species in Gen 5:1 in a genealogical construction. In Genesis 1 all statements relating to human creation per-tain to the species as a whole. No basis is given in the parallelism of state-ments within the passage for associating sexual distinction with either sta-tus or function. The statement of sexual differentiation is structurally isolated in the verses devoted to human creation and is restricted in its intention to a biological concern. Precisely because P's terms of sexual distinction lack social definition or connection, however, the balanced symmetry of the language cannot be translated directly into a notion of sexual equality. Although Genesis 1 requires the inference of ontological equality of the sexes, it offers no help concerning the move from ontology to ethics, from the question of sexuality viewed in the context of nature to the question of sexuality viewed in the context of history and culture, a move that is essential to a full theological anthropology.[17] The Priestly account leaves the theologian with the problem of how to relate equality of

13. Ibid., 148–52 [*142–46].
14. *HALAT*, 1:14.
15. With the exception of the plural *tannînîm*, "sea monsters" in 1:21; see Bird, "Male and Female," 146 [*141] n. 45.
16. Ibid., 146 [*140].
17. See ibid., 155–58 [*149–53].

created nature to sexually differentiated roles, responsibilities, and values.

To summarize my analysis thus far: The meaning and function of the statement of sexual differentiation in the Priestly account of creation is considerably more limited than is commonly assumed. It says nothing about the image that relates humankind to God, nor about God as the referent of the image. Neither does it qualify the notion of human dominion over the creatures (or of subjugating the earth, v. 28). It relates only to the blessing of fertility, making explicit its necessary presupposition. It is not concerned with sexual roles, the status or relationship of the sexes to one another, or marriage. It describes the biological pair, not the psychosocial pair; male and female, not man and woman or husband and wife. It does not presuppose an original androgyne (the progressive specification of attributes is logical, not temporal), but a bisexual (gender dimorphic) order of creatures as the crown of creation. And it is to this order that all statements of task and position refer.

One final word must be added to this statement concerning the meaning of sexuality in the Priestly account of creation. In my analysis thus far I have attempted to clarify the message of the text at the level of its grammar and to limit my interpretation to the intentionality inferred from that grammar. But I must note that there is another message in the text, which stands in tension with the message recorded at the grammatical level. While the author of Genesis 1 intends to speak about nature, not culture, and about order as a corollary of nature, the language he uses to describe the relationship of humankind to the other orders of creation employs social metaphors based on male experience and male roles ("ruling," vv. 26, 28; and "subjugating," v. 28).[18] In this usage he exhibits the patriarchal assumptions attested elsewhere in his work (e.g., Gen 5:1-3; 9:1; and the male lineages that structure his history).[19] While the Priestly writer speaks of the species, he thinks of the male. He is, in short, no feminist, as some would have him be. But that does not mean that he cannot contribute to a feminist anthropology. The constraint of his language with respect to sexual distinction and the openness of his concept of image to new meanings invite theological speculation that moves beyond anything the Priestly writer intended or could conceive.

The Priestly author, I have argued, is concerned with the order of nature, not culture, and offers no theological reflection on the social consequences or correlates of human sexual differentiation. In contrast, the

---

18. I am not arguing that these roles or actions are by definition or necessity male. I am simply arguing that in Israelite society, as in most comparable societies, such roles and activities were normally identified with males.

19. Bird, "Male and Female," 151 [*145], esp. n. 55.

Yahwist focuses the attention of his two-part narrative on the tension between nature and culture, or the disparity between the created (intended) order and the historically experienced order—a tension exemplified in the relationship of the sexes.

The Yahwistic (J) Account (2:4b—3:24)

The Yahwistic account of creation differs from the Priestly account to which it is joined, in language, structure, theology, and temper. While it shows many signs of composite origin, its present literary form presents a two-part drama of interlocking episodes and ring construction that must be treated as a unit.[20] In the Yahwist's account, creation and "fall"[21] together tell the story of the conditions under which human life is lived. And although history begins outside the garden, the garden is the site of the estrangement that manifests itself in history. The seeds of destruction have already been sown when the journey of our ancestors begins.

This paper does not permit full consideration of the dynamics and intention of the Yahwist's account of origins, which is complex and shows signs of incorporating prior traditions. Nor does it permit an account of the place of Genesis 2–3 within the larger "historical" work. Consequently, I must limit my attention to those features of the composition that have particular significance for understanding the meaning of sexual differentiation in the account.

Of fundamental importance for an understanding of the author's statements about sexuality is the literary form and structure of the narrative. In the Yahwist's account, story and the storyteller's art replace the liturgical cadences and technical terminology of priestly declaration. Circular movement marks the narrative structure, in contrast to the linear progression of Genesis 1, and dramatic action is employed to describe states and relationships. Time has no meaning here and sequence of action no ontological significance. The first and final acts of creation together describe a single action; the creation of humankind is not complete until the woman stands beside the man, manifesting that essential aspect of humanity hidden or latent in the first exemplar. Only when the pair appear together on the stage do the divine-human interaction and the consequential action of the story begin. Similarly, in the account of the "fall," neither sequence

---

20. For fuller treatment and citation of literature see Bird, "Sexual Differentiation" (n. 3 above), sections of which are reproduced in the following exposition of the Yahwist's narrative.

21. The term "fall," as well as the concept, is alien to the text. I employ it only as a conventional designation. See Bird, "Sexual Differentiation," 30 n. 26 [1995: 24–25 n. 26].

of actions nor proffered motives is of consequence. The woman is not judged until the man has also eaten; and both are understood to have acted in full knowledge of the prohibition and its consequences.[22] Thus "order of creation" and "order of the fall" are notions foreign to the Yahwist's conception and composition.

How then does the Yahwist understand the relationship of the sexes and what is the meaning of his uniquely bifurcated account of human creation?[23] The essential plot of the Yahwist's narrative may be summarized as follows. Yahweh God forms "the human" (*hā'ādām*) as the first of the creatures, earth creature par excellence, by origin and vocation.[24] Presented as an individual (*hā'ādām,* with the article, in contrast to P's collective *'ādām,* without the article)[25] and envisioned as a male (specifically, a peasant farmer), the name by which he is designated betrays his true identity—and the problem of his singularity. For although he bears the appellation of the species, he does not fully represent it. The personification is defective in its limitation to the male alone. The remainder of the chapter describes in dramatic action the overcoming of that defect and the resolution of the tension latent in the initial presentation.[26]

22. Although Trible's contrasting of the woman's reflective act with the man's "belly-oriented" acquiescence is an effective counter to traditional interpretations of the woman's role in the fall (*God,* 113), I doubt that the author intended to differentiate the responses so sharply, if at all. I would refer the narrative depiction of the man's and the woman's actions to customary male and female roles in food preparation and consumption, though a more specific mythic or etiological tradition may underlie the representation. I take the woman's reasoning as describing the general human response with its attempt to justify disobedience. The storyteller allows the man and the woman in succession to represent thoughts and actions of the species: the man in naming the animals, the woman in rationalizing the desire for forbidden fruit.

23. While the separate creation of man and woman is known elsewhere (though not from the ancient Near East), the Yahwist's account is unique in its theme of the man's need for companionship (possibly an expression of the motif articulated elsewhere in the myth of the androgyne). It is also unique in encompassing the account of animal creation within the account of human creation, subordinating the animal orders to the human order by means of a circular structure comparable in effect to the linear structure of Genesis 1.

24. Formed from the earth (*'ādāmâ*) to till the earth (2:5, 7; 3:23). Cf. Bruce D. Naidoff, "A Man to Work the Soil: A New Interpretation of Genesis 2–3," *JSOT* 5 (1978) 2–14.

25. Cf. Ernest Lussier, "*ADAM* in Genesis 1,1—4,24," *CBQ* 18 (1956) 137–39; and D. Barthélemy, "'Pour un homme,' 'Pour l'homme' ou 'Pour Adam'? (Gen 2, 20)," in Maurice Carrez, Joseph Doré, and Pierre Grelot, eds., *De la Tôrah au Messie: Études d'exégèse et d'herménutique bibliques offertes à Henri Cazelles* (Paris: Desclée, 1981) 47–53.

26. This summary traces one line through the narrative. However, the multilayered nature of the account requires a multileveled interpretation. At one level, the name and the characterization of the first human must be seen as determined by the tale of the man and the garden with its *'ādām/'ădāmâ* (earthling/earth) etiology, the tale that provides the framing *inclusio* for the two chapters. At another level, the name and the depiction of its bearer are to be understood in terms of the class designation *adam* and its incomplete realization or representation in the single specimen. Linked to an etiology of sexual attraction, this understanding presents the species as essentially embodied in (a) man and (a) woman and

The narrative is androcentric in form and perspective. It is told from the man's point of view and describes the man's need for a companion and helper. The resolution of the problem is accordingly signaled by the man's response, in his recognition that the one who confronts him is truly like him, not merely in appearance, but in substance—"of the same bone and flesh" (2:33). This climactic word of recognition, emphasizing the identity and equality of the two (now designated by the alliterative social terms, ʾîš, "man," and ʾiššâ, "woman"), gains significance and impact from the tension-heightening action that precedes it. There Yahweh forms from the earth all of the animal species in a trial-and-error attempt to produce a suitable companion for the man. It is only with the woman, however, that the man's need is finally met, for unlike the animals, the woman is not a separate order of creation, but shares fully the nature of *adam*. The dramatic requirement of creating two from one, which arises from the initial presentation of a single representative of the species, leads to the ingenious solution of extracting a rib from the human-presented-as-a-man and "building" a woman—a solution that recognizes the woman as one substance with the man, and hence one nature, yet unique.

The Yahwist's account gives special emphasis to the bisexual nature of the human species in order to stress the relationship between the sexes, here presented in psychosocial rather than biological terms. And although the help which the woman is meant to give to the man is undoubtedly help in procreation, the account in Genesis 2 subordinates function to passion. The attraction of the sexes is the author's primary interest, the sexual drive whose consummation is conceived as a re-union.

Genesis 2, like Genesis 1, contains no statement of dominance or subordination in the relationship of the sexes, but its narratively constructed emphasis on the equality of the two is the foundation and prelude to its negation in Genesis 3. There we encounter an explicit statement of the woman's subordination to the man—not, however, as representing the order of creation but rather as a sign of its sinful perversion. The Yahwist sees the disobedience of the man and woman to the divine command as the root sin that disturbs the original harmony of creation, and he sees the consequences of that sin in the painful and alienated existence which he knew to be the human lot. The estrangement introduced into the divine-human relationship works itself out in every other relationship.[27] Estrangement from God manifests itself for the man in estrangement

views wholeness in terms of differentiation and union rather than identity or absorption. In the present form of the text, the latter interest dominates the chapter. However, I do not think one can eradicate the male image of *hāʾādām* from this passage as Trible attempts to do in *God*, 80 and 140 n. 8.

27. Gerhard von Rad, *Genesis: A Commentary* (trans. John H. Marks; OTL; Philadelphia: Westminster, 1961) 148–49.

from the earth, out of which he was created and on which he depends for his work, estrangement experienced as pain in his labor; and the estrangement from God manifests itself for the woman in estrangement from the man, from whom she was created and on whom she depends for her work, estrangement experienced in the pain of her labor, childbirth.[28]

But there is a further dimension of this pain of estrangement, which breaks the symmetry of suffering, and that is the destruction of companionship between the man and the woman. For the relationship of companionship, established in the creation and exhibited in the mutual drive of the sexes toward each other (*he* will leave father and mother, his own flesh and bone, to cleave to her [2:24], and *her* desire will be for him [3:16]), is broken by the added word of judgment: "he shall rule over her" (3:16). The companion of chapter 2 has become a master. The historical subordination of woman to man is inaugurated—and identified as the paradigm expression of sin and alienation in creation.[29]

Reuniting the Texts: Interpretive Conclusions and Inferences

The union of the Priestly and Yahwistic accounts of creation as successive episodes in a comprehensive statement of origins requires the canonical interpreter to observe both the order of the component accounts and the tension between them. It also requires attention to new meanings that

28. Reading ʾiṣṣĕbônēk wĕhērōnēk (3:16) as hendiadys with Claus Westermann (*Genesis* [BKAT 1; Neukirchen-Vluyn: Neukirchener Verlag, 1974] 356) and most commentators. I cannot accept Carol Meyers's view that the verse speaks of multiplying the woman's work *and* pregnancies or Meyers's elimination of the sense of painful labor from the parallel clause, bĕʿeṣeb tēlĕdî bānîm, though her article makes a valuable contribution to the study of women's roles in ancient Israel (Carol L. Meyers, "Gender Roles and Genesis 3:16 Revisited," in Carol L. Meyers and M. O'Connor, eds., *The Word of the Lord Shall Go Forth: Essays in Honor of David Noel Freedman* [Winona Lake, Ind.: Eisenbrauns, 1983] 334–46). For recognition of the parallelism between the man's and the woman's punishment, cf. Patrick D. Miller, Jr., *Genesis 1–11: Studies in Structure and Theme* (JSOTSup 8; Sheffield: University of Sheffield Press, 1978) 48 n. 49.

29. The divine word spoken in judgment is neither a curse nor an eternal decree determining the fate of all future generations, but rather the dramatic representation of the consequences of sin as experienced in the generations known to the author. An etiological tale of the painful conditions of life is joined by profound theological reflection on the root cause. That the examples chosen (field labor and childbirth) no longer represent the chief sources of pain in the lives of most Westerners today demonstrates their etiological and historically conditioned character. They must not be absolutized but read as signs of an underlying disorder, whose clearest persisting sign is the continuing alienation of male and female perpetuated by patriarchy. See, inter alia, Westermann, *Genesis*, 355–63; and Trible, *God*, 152–53 and 157.

move beyond the original terms and intentions of the individual accounts as they are brought within a new and larger context of interpretation. That interpretive context must finally include the canon as a whole, in interaction with the multiple and changing contexts of the interpreter. It requires, I believe, multivalent and multidimensional reading. What I shall offer is one interpretation, or rather one set of interpretive comments and questions formulated in the context of reflection on the meaning of sexuality, informed by women's experience and feminist critique of patriarchy and its theological legacy.

Theological anthropology has been dominated by the concept of the divine image as determinative for an understanding of humanity in its created nature, and rightly so, since this stands as the lead and controlling statement of the combined creation accounts, giving to the human species a unique identity and dignity, grounded in a special relationship to God. It is therefore the foundational concept for all canonical reflection on the nature of humankind—and its place within the created order—for the relationship to God, according to the Priestly formulation, determines the relation to other orders of creation. Thus the concept of the divine image is essentially a statement about relationships in a "vertical" plane, relating humanity to orders "above" and "below."

In contrast to this lead statement which defines and locates humanity in creation and in relationship to the Creator, the statement attributing sexuality to humankind is clearly a second-order statement. But it is no less essential (or consequential) for an understanding of the species and its individual members. As articulated in the twofold formulation of Priestly declaration and Yahwistic narrative, it is foundational for all relationships within the human order, social as well as biological. Thus it may be seen as the primary statement and root metaphor for relationships on the "horizontal" plane.

Traditional interpretation of Genesis 1–2 has commonly imposed the vertical concept of the image on the horizontal concept of sexual differentiation, transforming the hierarchy of orders into a hierarchy of the sexes. In the Priestly formulation, however, the two statements defining human creation are not connected, but presented as parallel and simultaneously valid declarations. How may they properly be related? Or can they be related at all? The silence of the text leaves to the interpreter the task of spelling out the implications of each of the juxtaposed statements for the other. However that is done, the integrity of each as an independent statement must be maintained.

My reflections and arguments in the remainder of this paper focus on these two primary statements of the Priestly writer, augmented or modified by the Yahwist, as I attempt to spell out their implications for a theol-

ogy of sexuality. The attempt has made me painfully aware that I am step-
ping at this point into an area (or areas) of specialization for which I lack
many of the essential tools. I grope with imprecise language and inadequate knowledge of the basic literature and categories of analysis (specifically in the fields of systematic theology and the study of human sexuality in its physical and psychological dimensions).[30] Often, I discover, I am
unable to do more than identify a problem, and must rest my analysis
with a question rather than a proposal.

1. The parallel statements about human nature in the Priestly creation
account are alike in referring to the species as a whole, but they differ in
two important ways: (a) while the divine likeness distinguishes the species
from other orders of creation, sexuality does not; and (b) while the concept of the image admits of no differentiation within the species, sexuality
is expressed only in differentiation.

2. In P's initial and determinative usage, the divine image characterizes
humanity as a whole. It must therefore characterize each individual of the
species and cannot be limited to any subgroup. Whatever gender distinction means, it cannot involve denial or diminution of the Godlike nature
that characterizes the species. To be human is to be created in the image
of God.

a. This understanding of the image as defining the species is not qualified by P's subsequent personification of the species in an individual
named Adam, who perpetuates the essential created nature of the species
by fathering offspring in his image. Adam is presented in Gen 5:1a, 3 as an
individual exemplifying the species. That the species *adam* is still understood as collective/plural and bisexual (i.e., sexually dimorphic) is evident
in P's recapitulation of 1:27 in 5:2 and in his explicit referral of the name/
common noun to the plural object: "Male and female he created them;
and he blessed them and named *them adam*" (5:2). The Priestly writer's
narrowed attention to the male line in history does not thereby limit humanity or the image to the male of the species, though it does betray the
author's cultural presuppositions. The tension that remains in the text
between *adam* as male and female and the male Adam who heads the
Priestly genealogy is an essential clue to the canonical interpreter.

b. The Yahwist's individualizing of *adam* in his story of the first human
pair also gives no support for collapsing the collective into a singular and
claiming for the one in his gendered particularity what belongs to the

---

30. The two books that I have found most helpful in treating sexuality in the context of
Christian theology are James B. Nelson, *Embodiment,* and Lisa Sowle Cahill, *Between the
Sexes: Foundations for a Christian Ethics of Sexuality* (Philadelphia: Fortress Press, 1985), both
discovered after I had completed the draft of this paper.

species as a whole. A consistent grammatical distinction is maintained between the anarthrous noun of Genesis 1 ('ādām, "humankind") and the noun with the article used in Genesis 2 (hā'ādām, "the human one"). (Thus a similar tension appears in the sequential reading of Genesis 1 and 2 to that observed in the relationship of chaps. 1 and 5.) And the Yahwist signals by narrative plot as well as grammar that "the human" and humankind are not fully coterminus in the first specimen of the species: There is something defective about the one standing alone.

    c. The notion of the divine image in Genesis 1 does not describe a possession which can be quantified or lost. It is not variable in degree within the species in relation either to gender or to character. Therefore the notion of equality, or inequality, is inappropriate as a qualifier. And it is not lost or effaced by the disobedience of the pair or the consequent divine judgment.[31]

    3. The concept of the divine image, though associated in the author's cultural milieu with the idea of ruling or governing, is essentially "empty" of content, describing a correspondence conceived in terms of form rather than substance: humankind is God's representation and representative within creation.[32] As an expression of a relationship to God employed to express a relationship to other creatures, the concept of the divine image invites ever new reflection on the content and character of both of these relationships in changing times and circumstances.[33] And as an expression that describes and defines the species as a whole, its content must be drawn out of the experience of the species as a whole, female as well as male. Where the interpretive content has been derived exclusively or disproportionately from male models it must be considered defective. How might the relationship between human and nonhuman creation be conceived if it were understood in terms of female models of relationship rather than the male models of dominion and subjugation?[34]

    4. Sexuality does not distinguish humankind from other orders of creatures, at least as P understands it; rather it is an aspect of human nature

31. See Bird, "Male and Female," 138 [*132–33] n. 22.

32. Ṣelem, "image," as a metaphor for likeness is concrete, formal, holistic, and lacking in specific content—which makes it an ideal term for P, who employs it with changing connotations in changing contexts (cf. 5:1, 3 and 9:6). See ibid., 138–39 [*132–33]. For its use as a royal motif in 1:26–28, see 140–44 [*134–40].

33. Ṣelem, which is employed in Genesis 1 only in an adverbial expression modifying the verb of creation, does not describe a relationship in the sense of a means or mode of relating (ibid., 139 [*133]). I use "relationship" here as a formal term.

34. Patrick Miller has suggested (in the discussion following the presentation) that the concept of nurture might provide a more adequate metaphor for the content of the relationship. A wealth of possibilities are suggested by roles of the mother as manager of the household, provider, trainer, teacher, mourner, etc.

shared with other forms of life. Consequently, a biblically informed theology of sexuality must address itself both to the nature and function of the reproductive capacity and to the meaning of its transhuman character. I shall limit my comments to the first question, leaving the second for further reflection.

a. P's statement concerning human sexuality, contained in the words of sexual differentiation and of blessing, focuses solely on its biological nature. It declares that sex, as differentiation and union, is intended for procreation and is to be understood as a divinely given capacity and power governed by blessing and command.

b. The word that activates the endowment, however, addresses the species, not the individual, and is limited in its application by the setting in which it is spoken, a limitation made explicit in the qualifying amplification, "and fill the earth."[35] It is a word for beginnings as it appears in Genesis 1, not for all time; the "command" to "be fruitful and multiply" is neither absolute nor universal. It must be repeated and reinterpreted in changing historical/ecological situations.[36]

c. Thus sexuality as reproductive capacity is an endowment of the species as such, but its employment is goal-oriented and historically conditioned. This conditioning of the capacity opens the way to ethical deliberation concerning the circumstances of its actualization.

5. Sexuality is expressed in differentiation—and union. It divides in order to unite. It creates both the need and the means to overcome the separation that it symbolizes. Sexuality is the primary means of self-transcendence on which all community depends. This dual aspect of sexuality as differentiation and union is masterfully portrayed by the Yahwist in his account of the oneness and otherness of the first representatives of the species.

a. J's account provides an essential complement to P by focusing on the psychosocial meaning of sexuality and its historical manifestations. Companionship, the sharing of work, mutual attraction and commitment in a bond superseding all other human bonds and attractions—these are the ends for which *adam* was created male and female and these are the

35. See Bird, "Male and Female," 152 [*146].

36. It is repeated in P in the following passages: (italicized citations are imperative [blessing form], others indicative): 9:1, 7 (Noah); 17:6 (causative with God as subject; Isaac as object); 17:20 (causative; Ishmael); 28:3 (causative; Isaac); 35:11 (Jacob); 47:27 (Jacob); 48:4 (causative; Jacob); Exod 1:7 (descendants of Israel). Dependent on P: Exod 23:30 (Israelites in Canaan); Lev 26:9 (Israel). In extra-P usage the root *PRH* ("to be fruitful"), as a term for human and animal increase, is typically related to possession of land and/or security against foes (usually in reference to a future or restored Israel). In all usage, the word of blessing, whether direct or indirect, future or past, has a particular end or goal related to a particular situation of need. See ibid., 152 [*146–47], esp. nn. 60, 61.

signs of intended partnership. For J, sexual differentiation is the ground and precondition of community, which requires the individual to reach beyond the self for fulfillment of basic needs.

b. But the requirement of an "other" to satisfy the individual's needs opens the way to exploitation, whose tragic consequences J so clearly depicts in the historical relationship of (the) man to (the) woman.

c. The Yahwist's attention to the social and historical dimensions of sexuality requires the canonical interpreter to consider the sociohistorical conditions under which the relationship of the sexes takes place. And the ethical judgment implicit in his account requires corresponding ethical reflection and judgment by the contemporary theologian. Biblical anthropology, as exemplified in the combined P-J creation account, joins to the question of nature or ontology the question of history and ethics. The movement from ontological speculation to ethical reflection and judgment, exhibited in the present order of the combined texts, thrusts the interpreter forward into the full canon of Scriptures as the arena in which the meaning of human existence as male and female must finally be understood—and prepares the reader to discover that meaning in negative as well as positive experience. The creation texts alone cannot adequately instruct us on what it means to be human and to be male and female.

6. Sexual differentiation as a mark of the species means that no individual—and no class composed of a single gender—can fully represent the species, an understanding reflected in the J narrative and the well-known German saying, "ein Mensch ist kein Mensch." Does this mean that the couple must be understood as the primary unit of the species, rather than the individual? And does this not imply that the divine image is not fully present in the individual, thereby qualifying my earlier statement that it applies to every individual of the species without qualification or quantification? My tentative answers to these questions are as follows:

While male and female together describe the species, which cannot be fully known without both, and while sexual union is the primary purpose of gender differentiation, the human couple cannot be viewed as the basic unit of the species, since it is neither a universal nor a naturally occurring phenomenon. It is rather a biosocial construction, a highly variable and achieved union of sexually mature individuals chosen from a range of possible partners. The multiple variables of age, physical capacity, inclination, number and duration of partners, and so on all militate against construing the socially and/or sexually united couple as the basic human unit. Consequently we must maintain that the individual, which is to say every individual, in his or her sexually defined particularity is "the" representative human being, fully human and in no way defective as a representative.

This means that the definition of the species and the definition of the individual are not fully coterminous, since the species has a communal nature which rests on individual differentiation. While the species is defined as male-and-female, the individual of the species is defined as male-or-female. The species is then both an aggregate, defined by its members (male and female), and an identity-giving entity (whether understood in terms of an abstraction or of shared "substance"), defining its members (divine image).

7. Do these observations mean anything more than that the species is made up of all of its members, young and old, black and white, left-handed and right-handed, and so on, and that in terms of species identification, all such variables are incidental? And may not the same be said of other species? More pointedly we may ask whether gender is a theologically significant variable in a way in which size, pigmentation, or cranial proportions are not. Is the isolation of sexuality as the single significant attribute of differentiation in the biblical creation accounts perhaps to be understood as the reflection of a set of economic and cultural needs or interests that no longer exist or no longer warrant the priority given to them by these accounts? Is it appropriate for contemporary theology to give so prominent a place to sexuality as a defining attribute of humankind? And to what extent must the biblical view of sexuality be modified by modern understanding of sexuality as a far more complex phenomenon than previously assumed? Again I venture tentative answers.

a. With respect to the prominence and isolation of sexuality from other observed variables of human constitution, I would argue that it deserves primary attention and theological reflection not simply because of its place in biblical tradition, which must be assessed and reappropriated, but also because it is essential to the survival of the species (biblically interpreted as the divinely ordained means of assuring the continuity of a "good" creation) and is universally recognized and universally invested with cultural (including religious) meaning. Perhaps one may say that it is of all attributes of the species the most extensively invested with symbolic meanings. It is an essential component of individual self-definition and of social location and assessment. For these reasons, I would argue, it must have a prominent place in any theological anthropology.

b. A final word concerning individual variation and the question of "arbitrary" definition: Gender as a dimorphic classification is based on observed genital differentiation (now known to be genetically determined), but sexuality as its expression is exhibited in a wide range of physical and psychological forms and an even wider range of behavioral and attitudinal variables. What is the significance of this variability for an understanding of gender? Does variation in sexual performance, size of physical organs, and so on mean that the individual is more or less male, or female? Here I think the answer must be the same as in the case of the question concerning the divine image. Gender is not quantifiable, nor is it properly subject to qualitative analysis. It is a given, a defining attribute of each individual. But as an attribute that is essentially social in its expression, it can and must be evaluated and regulated. It is the Yahwist's contribution to remind us that the good gift of sexuality may become the means and the sign of alienation within the species, that what was intended for fulfillment and self-transcendence may become the occasion and instrument of deprivation and oppression.

8

GENESIS 3 IN MODERN BIBLICAL SCHOLARSHIP[1]

GENESIS 3 HAS PLAYED A CRITICAL ROLE IN THE HISTORY OF Christian theological reflection on the nature of sin, sex, and gender relations. As the locus classicus for the doctrine of original sin, it introduced gender into the formulation of the doctrine through the terms of its narrative construction.[2] Thus the question of sin in Western thought has been intimately linked with questions of sex and gender, while traditional views of gender, and particularly of female gender, have been marked by associations with the origins of sin and death.

The Old Testament itself, in the shorter Jewish/Protestant canon, contains no further reference or allusion to the account. It is early Jewish and gnostic speculation that first directs attention to this text, focus-

This article was written for a volume of the *Jahrbuch für biblische Theologie* on the theme "Sünde und Gericht." It appeared in German translation as "Genesis 3 in der gegenwärtigen biblischen Forschung," *JBTh* 9 (1994) 3–24. It is published here in English for the first time. Cross-references to articles that are reprinted in this volume are indicated by an asterisk in square brackets following the original page number.

1. This essay represents a highly selective account of scholarship on a text which one author has characterized as having had a "greater impact upon the theology of the Christian Church and the art and literature of Western civilization" than any other story from the Old Testament (R. W. L. Moberly, "Did the Serpent Get It Right?" *JTS* 39 [1988] 1). Of the boundless literature, I have noted only recent or distinctly profiled examples, using Claus Westermann, *Genesis 1–11: A Commentary* (trans. John J. Scullion; Continental Commentary; Minneapolis: Augsburg, 1984), as representative of modern critical scholarship. Requirements of brevity have made it impossible to engage alternate or competing views in any detail.

2. The doctrine as formulated by Augustine drew heavily on Rom 5:12-21, an Adam-Christ typology in which Eve/woman plays no role. It nevertheless remains rooted in the Genesis text, interpreted with emphasis on the woman's agency in introducing sin into the world (see, e.g., *De civ.* 13.14; cited in Elaine Pagels, "The Politics of Paradise: Augustine's Exegesis of Genesis 1–3 versus that of John Chrysostom," *HTR* 78 [1985] 80).

ing specifically on the woman's role in introducing sin into the world.[3] This exegetical tradition, which often combined the creation accounts with other biblical and extrabiblical texts, finds its earliest attestation (ca. 180 B.C.E.) in Sir 25:24, "From a woman sin had its beginning, and because of her we all die." It stands behind the allusions to Genesis 3 in 1 Cor 11:2-12 and 1 Tim 2:11-15[4] and plays a significant role in developing Christian doctrine and doctrinal/ecclesiological disputes.[5] Misogynist readings combined with an Augustinian doctrine of original sin provided the lenses through which Genesis 3 was interpreted prior to the rise of modern biblical scholarship.[6]

A tradition of interpretation was established that made this text foundational for pronouncements concerning woman's physical and moral nature, prescribed role(s), and relationships to civil and religious authority. Enshrined in canon law and imbedded in the social and legal prescriptions of Western culture, traditional interpretations of Genesis 3 have left a painful and debilitating legacy in church, society, and psyche. Debates over consequences and correctives touch the deepest nerves of social and

3. This literature typically combines elements from the first three chapters of Genesis in a manner that identifies the divine image (Gen 1:26-27) exclusively or definitively with the male ("Adam") of Genesis 2–3 and makes woman a secondary and inferior creation, responsible for bringing sin and death into the world and depriving Adam of his original Godlikeness (e.g., *Sib. Or.* 1.5-37; *2 Enoch* 30.8-18, esp. 17; *Adam and Eve* 33, 35; Philo, *De opif. mundi* 136–44, 151, 153–65). See Bernard P. Prusak, "Woman: Seductive Siren and Source of Sin? Pseudepigraphical Myth and Christian Origins," in Rosemary R. Ruether, ed., *Religion and Sexism: Images of Woman in the Jewish and Christian Traditions* (New York: Simon and Schuster, 1974) 89-116; Anders Hultgård, "God and Image of Woman in Early Jewish Religion," in Kari E. Børresen ed., *Image of God and Gender Models in Judeo-Christian Tradition* (Oslo: Solum, 1991) 35–55 [1995: 29–49]; and Philip S. Alexander, "The Fall into Knowledge: The Garden of Eden/Paradise in Gnostic Literature," in Paul Morris and Deborah Sawyer, eds., *A Walk in the Garden: Biblical, Iconographical, and Literary Images of Eden* (JSOTSup 136; Sheffield: JSOT Press, 1992) 91–104.

4. See Lone Fatum, "Image of God and Glory of Man: Woman in the Pauline Congregations," in Børresen, *Image,* 110 [1995: 105] n. 73; and Prusak, "Woman: Seductive Siren?" 104, 106.

5. For attempts to set arguments about women's nature and religious roles in the context of theological and political struggles in the early church, see Jouette Bassler, "Adam, Eve, and the Pastor: The Use of Genesis 2–3 in the Pastoral Epistles," in Gregory A. Robbins, ed., *Genesis 1–3 in the History of Exegesis: Intrigue in the Garden* (Lewiston and Queenston: Mellen, 1988); Elaine Pagels, "Politics"; idem, *Adam, Eve, and the Serpent* (New York: Random House, 1988); Elizabeth A. Clark, "Heresy, Asceticism, Adam, and Eve: Interpretations of Genesis 1–3 in the Later Latin Fathers," in Robbins, *Genesis 1–3,* 99–133; and Susan E. Schreiner, "Eve, the Mother of History: Reaching for the Reality of History in Augustine's Later Exegesis of Genesis," in ibid., 135–86.

6. For efforts to trace this history of interpretation, focusing on the image of God in Gen 1:26-27, see Børresen, *Image*; for Genesis 1–3 as a whole, see Robbins, *Genesis 1–3;* and Morris and Sawyer, *A Walk in the Garden.*

religious identity and have given Genesis 2–3 a prominence in feminist theology unmatched by any other Old Testament text.[7]

While feminist interpretation has been preoccupied with the *Nachgeschichte* of Genesis 3, modern biblical scholarship directed primary attention to the history behind the text. Efforts were devoted to uncovering its long and complex prehistory, tracing its multiple connections to a variety of ancient Near Eastern sources, and describing its place and purpose within the evolving Pentateuch. Recognition of two distinct sources (J and P) in the creation account of Genesis 1–3 profoundly affected interpretation, challenging long-established views based on precritical exegesis.[8] The general result of modern critical study was to remove or undermine the foundations of the traditional doctrines of "original sin" and the "fall," and to raise the more general question of how exegesis can and should relate to dogmatic theology.[9]

I shall not attempt to bridge that gap in this essay, but only lay the foundations for a new conversation by summarizing the results of modern historical criticism. I approach the text from a feminist perspective[10] em-

---

7. For feminist theologians' interpretations of the creation texts, see Uwe Gerber, *Die feministische Eroberung der Theologie* (Munich: Beck, 1987) 58–76. See also Deborah F. Sawyer, "Resurrecting Eve? Feminist Critique of the Garden of Eden," in Morris and Sawyer, *A Walk in the Garden*, 273–89. The text also occupies a central place in the whole corpus of contemporary women's writing (Paul Morris, "A Walk in the Garden: Images of Eden," ibid., 21–22 and 33 nn. 3–6). On the text in debates concerning the role and status of Jewish women, see Paul Morris, "Exile from Eden: Jewish Interpretations of Genesis," ibid., 117–66.

8. Westermann, *Genesis*, 186. For various ways in which the two accounts were related in precritical exegesis, see Hultgård, "God and Image of Woman"; and Morris, "Exile From Eden." Much speculation concerned the question of whether the divine image in Genesis 1 described the woman as well as the man (*hā'ādām*) and how it was affected by the fall (see Børresen, *Image*).

9. Most biblical scholars find no such concepts here. Some take pains to deny traditional dogmatic constructions (e.g., Herbert Haag, "Die Themata der Sündenfall-Geschichte," in idem, *Das Buch des Bundes* [Düsseldorf: Patmos, 1980] 79–87; Westermann, *Genesis*, 275–78; Calum M. Carmichael, "The Paradise Myth: Interpreting without Jewish and Christian Spectacles," in Morris and Sawyer, *A Walk in the Garden*, 47); but many (perhaps most) do not bother to engage such interpretations at all, treating the text either as an ancient historical document, without consideration of modern meaning, or addressing it with a wide variety of new questions shaped by modern literary, sociological, psychological, and ideological interests. For the current state of renewed interest in the question of original sin on the part of systematic theologians and biblical scholars, see Christoph Dohmen, *Schöpfung und Tod: Die Entfaltung theologischer und anthropologischer Konzeptionen in Gen 2/3* (SBB 17; Stuttgart: Katholisches Bibelwerk, 1988) 281–93.

10. There are many feminisms, and feminist approaches to this text (e.g., Phyllis Trible, *God and the Rhetoric of Sexuality* [OBT; Philadelphia: Fortress Press, 1978] 72–143; Mieke Bal, "Sexuality, Sin and Sorrow: The Emergence of the Female Character [a Reading of Genesis 1–3]," *Poetics Today* 6 [1985] 21–42; Carol Meyers, *Discovering Eve: Ancient Israelite Woman in Context* [New York and Oxford: Oxford University Press, 1988] 72–121; Sawyer, "Resurrecting Eve?"), as well as feminist attitudes to the Bible in general. See Katharine Doob Sakenfeld,

ploying the methodology of literary-historical criticism, which has dominated Old Testament scholarship on the passage for the past century. Alternative approaches have gained recent popularity, especially among feminist interpreters, who have sought to deconstruct the misogynist readings of the past by constructing feminist counterreadings.[11] My choice of a historical-critical approach is not a rejection of other methods. This text, in particular, invites multiple readings, because it treats primordial events, and hence universal themes, employing language and symbols that have broad resonances in world literature, folklore, psychology, and art. Thus what is offered here is *one* reading, but one that represents the main lines of Old Testament scholarship over the past century.

Genesis 3 in Context

Genesis 3 forms part of a larger narrative unit comprising Gen 2:4b—3:24, a two-act drama which recounts the creation and "fall" of the first man and woman. The burden of chapter 3 in this larger unit is to account for a change in the terms of human existence between creation and life "outside the garden." The term "fall" does not appear in the text and is overloaded with connotations foreign to the story. It is, however, a convenient

---

"Feminist Biblical Interpretation," *TToday* 46 (1989) 154–68, for differing North American feminist views and approaches. Cf. Gerber, *Feministische Eroberung,* for European feminism, and the new Yearbook of the European Society of Women in Theological Research: 1 (1993) = *Feminist Theology in a European Context* (Annette Esser and Luise Schottroff, eds.).

Although I approach the text with a feminist consciousness and commitment, I do not offer a "feminist reading" in the sense of a reading that attempts to inscribe a feminist viewpoint in the text. For me, feminist interpretation emerges as a response to the text heard on its own terms, as the product of voices and visions from another world. The constructive task of theology (feminist or other) begins in this cross-cultural conversation, as new questions are addressed to the ancient texts from new contexts. The biblical scholar's contribution is to give fresh hearing to ancient voices drowned out by later interpreters. Such interpretation is never free, however, from its own distortions. On methodology in feminist biblical scholarship, see Adela Yarbro Collins, ed., *Feminist Perspectives on Biblical Scholarship* (Chico, Calif.: Scholars Press, 1985).

11. I include in the category of alternative methodologies a broad range of approaches: rhetorical, structuralist, canonical, and reader-response criticism. See, e.g., Morris and Sawyer, *A Walk in the Garden;* Daniel Patte, ed., *Genesis 2–3: Kaleidoscopic Structural Readings* (*Semeia* 18; Chico, Calif.: Scholars Press, 1980); Jerome T. Walsh, "Genesis 2:4b—3:24: A Synchronic Approach," *JBL* 96 (1977) 161–77; Joel W. Rosenberg, "The Garden Story Forward and Backward: The Non-Narrative Dimension of Gen 2–3," *Prooftexts* 1 (1981) 1–27; Francis Landy, *Paradoxes of Paradise: Identity and Difference in the Song of Songs* (Sheffield: Almond, 1983) 183–265; Richard H. Moye, "In the Beginning: Myth and History in Genesis and Exodus," *JBL* 109 (1990) 577–98; and Bal, "Sexuality."

178 MISSING PERSONS AND MISTAKEN IDENTITIES

metaphor to summarize the force of the chapter, conveying something of the sense of loss that is fundamental to the account.[12]

The story of the "fall" is an etiological tale describing the fundamental conditions of life as experienced by an ancient Israelite author, life characterized by painful toil, struggle with a hostile environment, estrangement in relationships human and divine, shame in self-consciousness, and death. Its starting point is its conclusion: life, as we know it, is a life of hardship, alienation, and limits. But this is not the way it was meant to be, the author insists, nor was it always so. Before this "state" was another, which is critical for understanding life today. Genesis 2–3 comprises an account of that prior state, the world of origins, and of its transformation into the world of reality or "history."[13]

The two chapters form the introduction to the "Primeval History," an account of origins based on a series of etiological narratives describing primary cultural distinctions and achievements.[14] It is also an account of divine-human interaction, which begins with a challenge to divine prerogative by the primal pair, resulting in alienation and expulsion from the divine presence, and ends with a challenge by united humanity, resulting in division and dispersion of all the peoples of the earth. Within this frame it depicts a widening of the sphere of sin/alienation to include all peoples and all relationships (between man and woman, brothers, father and son, ways of life, ethnic and linguistic groups, and nations), tracing broken relationships in the human community to a broken relationship between humans and God, beginning in the garden. Genesis 3 functions in this account as the interpretive clue to the whole history; everything that follows is to be read in its light.

Whether the primal act of disobedience is to be understood as "sin," and whether the concept of "original sin" expresses the intention of the narrative, depends in part on how the paradise story is read within the larger interpretive context constructed by the Yahwist, and reconstructed by the Priestly writer.[15] It also depends on the theological stance of the

12. There is also gain, which the metaphor obscures. See below. Cf. Westermann, *Genesis*, 275–76; and James Barr, *The Garden of Eden and the Hope of Immortality* (Minneapolis: Fortress Press, 1993) 11, who finds no atmosphere of guilt and tragedy and argues that there is no breakdown of relationship between God and the man and woman. Carmichael ("Paradise Myth," 48–49) characterizes the initial state of Adam and Eve in the garden as an undifferentiated one, an "untrue-to-life" state, rather than an ideal state.

13. See Susan Niditch, *Chaos to Cosmos: Studies in Biblical Patterns of Creation* (Chico, Calif.: Scholars Press, 1985) 25–43. Cf. Westermann, *Genesis*, 4–6, 19–22.

14. See Gerhard von Rad, *Genesis* (trans. John H. Marks; OTL; Philadelphia: Westminster, 1961) 73, 148–50; Westermann, *Genesis*, 1–73; and John Van Seters, *Prologue to History: The Yahwist as Historian in Genesis* (Louisville: Westminster/John Knox, 1992) 190–93.

15. Whatever the age and origins of the J and P "sources," P has become the interpreter of J in the present account. But the distinct voice of J has been preserved, resulting in a composition in which two differing views of the nature of sin, its consequences, and reme-

exegete and the community in which the text is read. Thus Jewish and Christian traditions have developed different language and conceptions for the origin of sin, or the primary impulse to wrongdoing, with different textual bases.[16] Our answer must await the literary-historical analysis.

The Yahwist's Account

The paradise story forms the second act of the Yahwist's account of origins, introducing the crime-and-punishment scheme used to structure each of the major episodes of the Primeval History (4:1-6; 6:1-4; 11:1-10).[17] Despite this structural link to the following narrative, the chapter exhibits multiple signs of independent origin, especially in its opening scene. At the same time it is so closely knit together with the material of Genesis 2 that it is difficult to separate independent sources or reconstruct stages of composition, although such efforts have dominated scholarly discussion of the passage.[18] What is clear from a surface reading of Genesis 2–3 is that a story about a snake, a woman, and a man has been introduced into a story about a solitary human (hā'ādām), who appears alone at the beginning (2:7) and the end (3:22-24) of the larger account. This frame story has now left its marks on the incorporated traditions ("the human" is the sole addressee and respondent in 3:9-11), which have in turn shaped the presentation and development of the opening scenes (2:15-18).

The frame story tells of the creation of humankind ('ādām) from the ground ('ădāmâ) in the form of a single representative of the species

---

dies may be discerned. Limited space in this essay allows us to consider only the Yahwist's view.

16. Postbiblical Jewish understandings of sin and its origins took a different route from that of Paul and did not focus on Genesis 3. For comparison of Jewish and early Christian views, see Stanley E. Porter, "The Pauline Concept of Original Sin, in Light of Rabbinic Background," *Tyndale Bulletin* 41 (1990) 3–30. Cf. Morris, "Exile"; Kevin Condon, "The Biblical Doctrine of Original Sin," *Irish Theological Quarterly* 34 (1967) 27–30; and Pagels, *Adam, Eve, and the Serpent*, xxi.

17. Westermann, *Genesis*, 193 and 53–54; cf. Norbert Lohfink, "Das vorpersonale Böse: Das Alte Testament und der Begriff der Erbsünde," in idem, *Das Jüdische am Christentum: Die Verlorene Dimension* (Freiburg: Herder, 1989) 190.

18. For the history of interpretation, see Westermann, *Genesis*, 186–90; cf. 190–97, and detailed commentary, 197–278. Newer attempts to define sources and stages of composition include Odil H. Steck, *Die Paradieserzählung* (Neukirchen: Kaiser, 1970); Ernst Kutsch, "Die Paradieserzählung Genesis 2–3 und ihr Verfasser," in Georg Braulik, ed., *Studien zum Pentateuch* (Vienna: Herder, 1977) 9–24; Howard N. Wallace, *The Eden Narrative* (HSM 32; Atlanta: Scholars Press, 1985); and Dohmen, *Schöpfung*. Van Seters (*Prologue to History*) argues against notions of a long prehistory, viewing the Yahwist's work as a whole as a late exilic composition (125) of antiquarian history by an author who drew on a wide variety of "traditional" materials (*"Wissensstoff,"* 128) from both eastern and western traditions to create a "vulgate tradition" (6) of Israel's prehistory. See esp. 1–23 and 107–34.

(*hā'ādām,* "the human").[19] Placed in a garden to till and watch over it
(2:8, 15), he is driven from it in the final scene (3:23-24), to till the ground
from which he was taken (3:23). This "ground" theme also finds expression in the etiology of *'ādām*'s return to the *'ădāmâ,* incorporated into
the man's "sentence" in 3:19. But what has occasioned the expulsion? According to 2:9, 16-17 and 3:22-23 it concerns a forbidden tree, or trees; but
here the story line becomes muddied, for the reported action does not
match the recorded threat, and the account of eating the forbidden fruit
involves a new cast of characters. A talking snake has the opening lines in
chapter 3, and they are addressed to a woman, not *hā'ādām.*

The tale of temptation in the garden, or at least its primary elements
(snake, woman, forbidden tree, garden of God), with their ties to well-
known ancient Near Eastern myths and motifs, clearly suggests a prehistory prior to its incorporation into the Yahwist's account. But it has just
as clearly been adapted to the Yahwist's purposes, and no earlier form of
the story is attested in ancient Near Eastern sources. The Yahwist has not
only shaped traditional themes to his own purposes in the temptation
account, he has incorporated it into the frame story in a way that transformed an etiological tale of *'ādām* into an account of the creation of man
and woman unique among myths of origin.

The author begins the integration by "planting" the forbidden tree,
along with the tree of life, in the garden which YHWH God created for
the human, thereby transforming the garden of the human's work (*'BD,*
2:15) into the paradisical garden of God, a garden filled with trees that
yield fruits of every sort, free for the taking (2:9, 16), a garden where
YHWH strolls in the cool of the day (3:8). The prohibition of the one tree
which may not be eaten is spoken in the context of an invitation to eat
freely of all the others. The context stresses divine magnanimity rather
than limits; only one tree is reserved for the divine landlord, the tree of
knowledge—but for eating of that tree the penalty is death. The stage is
now set for the test that such a restrictive edict anticipates,[20] but it does
not follow. Instead YHWH speaks again, changing the subject.

The test cannot follow, because the cast of characters required by the
temptation scene is not complete. The bridge to that scene is a folktale-
like composition (2:15-24) which completes and climaxes the creation
account of 2:7. It represents an ingenious solution to the problem of mov-

19. Westermann, *Genesis,* 201–2. Cf. Richard S. Hess, "Splitting the Adam: The Usage of
'ādām in Genesis I–V," in John A. Emerton, ed., *Studies in the Pentateuch* (VTSup 41; Leiden:
Brill, 1990) 2–5.

20. A prohibition in a story anticipates its violation and consequently directs attention
to the circumstances of the violation and the terms of the prohibition, inviting reflection on
its reasonableness, justice, motive, etc.

ing from a single representative of the species to the pair required by the following episode, and serves to introduce the animals, who play an essential supporting role.[21] The account emphasizes the need of the man and woman for each other, described in economic, social, and affective terms, as creatures of distinct identity yet single nature.[22] And in that emphasis on union and mutual dependence or need (portrayed from the man's point of view), the stage is set for the breaking of that relationship and redefining of the bond in the temptation and judgment scenes of chapter 3.

The starting point for the Yahwist's creation account is an etiological tale of the "earthling," which requires personification of the collective 'ādām, not only as an individual, but as a male—for his work as well as his destiny is determined by his relationship to the earth. The inadequacy of this representation is signaled by a divine judgment: "It is not good that the human should be alone; I will make him a helper as his partner" (2:18, NRSV). Two themes are sounded in this judgment: (1) Human life is life in community; it has an essential social dimension that cannot be represented by a lone individual.[23] And (2) the one alone is not only lonely, but needy/weak; alone he can neither survive nor perpetuate his kind. The story presupposes the fundamental sexual division of labor and the form it took in ancient Israel, male agricultural labor and female reproductive labor—the foundations for survival in the present and future.

The specification that the helper must be a creature "corresponding to" the human/man (kĕnegdô = "like his vis-à-vis/counterpart") serves to account both for the animals and their inferior nature and for the woman's unique correspondence to the man. A condition is established that must exclude every other order of creation, for woman is also 'ādām and not a distinct species. She cannot be formed from the ground, as the first human and animal species, but must be extracted from the already formed representative of the species. Not born (for birthing is the woman's exclusive prerogative) and not molded as a distinct type of creature, she is constructed (bānâ, "to build," v. 22) using a basic structural element

---

21. In contrast to 3:1-7, this account lacks verbal and thematic connections with ancient Near Eastern traditions. I view the account, with Van Seters (*Prologue to History*, 128–29), as the Yahwist's own creation, working with general themes of creation and "local" (Hebrew or West Semitic) etiologies. Cf. Westermann, *Genesis*, 192.

22. Phyllis A. Bird, "Sexual Differentiation and Divine Image in the Genesis Creation Texts," in Børresen, *Image*, 11–34 [1995: 5–28]; and Bird, "Genesis 1–3 as a Source for a Contemporary Theology of Sexuality," *Ex Auditu* 3 (1987) 31–44 [*155–73].

23. See Bird, "Genesis 1–3," 38 [*164–65]; idem, "Bone of My Bone and Flesh of My Flesh," *TToday* 50 (1994) 521–34; and Westermann, *Genesis*, 192, 196–97.

taken from the first specimen. YHWH's success in this constructive surgery is confirmed when the man recognizes the new creature as being of his very bone and flesh—and names her accordingly.

The two-stage creation of man and woman is dictated by the combination of themes in the larger narrative and has no ontological significance. The separate account of the woman's creation serves to emphasize the incompleteness of the first act of creation and the overcoming of this defect with the woman's appearance. It also shifts attention to the female of the species in preparation for chapter 3. "The human" in the Yahwist's depiction is not an androgynous being,[24] and the language and perspective of the account is thoroughly androcentric, exhibited, for example, in the continuing use of the species designation for the man. But the message communicated through this drama of progressive actions is the same as that proclaimed by Gen 1:27 in its statement of simultaneous creation: "male and female [God] created them."[25] There is no time in this account; and no action affecting the species—or the man and woman individually—takes place until the two stand together. Only then can the main action, suspended in v. 17, move forward; and in the first act of consequence it is the woman who acts as representative of the species.[26]

Chapter 3 opens with the introduction of a new character, the snake (nāḥāš, or serpent), who dominates the opening scene (3:1-7). The speaking parts are limited here to the snake and the woman, with the man appearing only in v. 6.[27] He is nevertheless understood to be present throughout, since he is said to be "with her," and the snake uses plural verb forms in addressing the woman (vv. 1, 4, 5). The woman likewise responds in the plural ("we may eat," v. 2)—even in citing the divine prohibition (v. 3), addressed in 2:7 to "the human" alone, before the woman's

---

24. Trible, *God*, 98 and 141 n. 17 (substituting "sexually undifferentiated" for her earlier characterization of *hā'ādām* in 2:7 as "androgynous"). Cf. Haag, "Themata," 86; and David J. A. Clines, "What Does Eve Do to Help? and Other Irredeemably Androcentric Orientations in Genesis 1–3," in idem, *What Does Eve Do to Help? and Other Readerly Questions to the Old Testament* (JSOTSup 94; Sheffield: JSOT Press, 1990) 40–41.

25. The meaning of this gender-differentiated creation differs markedly, however, in the two accounts. See Bird, "'Male and Female He Created Them': Genesis 1:27b in the Context of the Priestly Account of Creation," *HTR* 74 (1981) 129–59 [*123–54]; and idem, "Genesis 1–3," 36–39 [*163–66].

26. A transition is provided in 2:25 that points forward to the couple's state following their disobedience (awareness of nakedness as shameful, 3:7, 10) and to the agent of that transformation, whose "craftiness" (*'ārûm*, 3:1) plays on the couple's "nakedness" (*'ērôm*, 3:10; cf. 2:25; 3:7; 3:11).

27. Identified here simply as the woman's husband (*'îšāh*, lit. "her man"), not as *hā'ādām*.

creation.[28] The final verse (3:7) knows no distinction of actors or roles; the pair, having partaken of the forbidden fruit, are united in experiencing its consequences and in attempting to cover themselves.[29] The story clearly means to indict the man and the woman alike. Thus no consequences are reported until both have eaten—and neither the reported reasons (3:6) nor the recorded excuses (3:12-13) affect the judgment that will be passed on both.

The Woman First

But if the two are alike in their transgression and the judgment pertains to both, why does attention shift to the woman in detailing the act of disobedience? This question belongs to the oldest exegetical traditions concerning the passage. But the answers traditionally given, which saw the woman as the morally weaker of the sexes and susceptible to malevolent influences, must be revised in light of our current knowledge of the Yahwist's sources and constraints. Here he is not working freehandedly, but is shaping materials that are heavily freighted with cultural, and cultic, meanings. Space does not permit us to trace the complex lines of tradition that converge in this narrative, but some key elements require note in order to appreciate the Yahwist's art and message.

It has long been recognized that a particular tradition, or traditions, involving a woman and a snake must lie behind this account, although no known text offers a direct antecedent. In fact, the multiple links with tradition point in different directions, and scholars differ in the associations they choose to emphasize. The snake is the key figure in this linkage. He is clearly not the śāṭān of later Hebrew and Christian tradition, although his role makes him appear as an adversary of God (or simply a "wise guy" troublemaker?). He is not divine, or even semidivine, though he appears to possess a kind of divine knowledge; and he is not an embodiment of evil. He is, however, a figure with numerous and diverse ties to the mythic world of Israel's origins.[30]

28. Here she follows the snake's lead in 3:1. I do not think the discrepancy in number implies an original duality in the initial specimen, but it does recognize the representative character of that first creation. The prohibition concerns the species, whose duality is now fully manifest. With the woman speaking for the pair, the prohibition is naturally recast in an inclusive plural.

29. Here not even the normally gender-specific act of sewing is allowed to break the solidarity of the guilty pair.

30. See Karen R. Joines, "The Serpent in Gen 3," *ZAW* 87 (1975) 1–11; idem, *Serpent Symbolism in the Old Testament: A Linguistic, Archaeological, and Literary Study* (Haddonfield, N.J.: Haddonfield House, 1974); and Westermann, *Genesis*, 237–39. Cf. J. Alberto Soggin,

The snake in ancient Near Eastern literature and iconography, as well as other Old Testament passages, is associated with magic, wisdom, and life and death/immortality. A curious creature that seems to transgress the primary categories of existence, it navigates on land as a creature of the sea, bringing death with its venomous bite, but rejuvenating itself by discarding old skin for new. The Yahwist draws on the snake's liminal character of embodying opposites and transgressing boundaries in making him the agent of the couple's transgressing the boundary set between humans and God.[31]

The snake also has close ties with a goddess in Canaanite and Mediterranean/Egyptian sources, which depict a female figure, or associated cult object, holding snakes or entwined by a snake.[32] While the particular deity is not always certain, and need not be the same in each case, fertility connotations are apparent, linking these representations thematically to the tree of life.[33] Thus a "natural alliance" of snake and woman (as life bearer) may be assumed as a background to the tale—a connection reinforced by the etiology in 3:20 that interprets the woman's name (ḥawwâ, "Eve") as meaning "mother of all living."[34] It must be noted, however, that the associations of snake and woman were manifold and complex and included traditions of enmity (Gen 3:15) as well as affinity.

Woman and snake also figure in Mesopotamian tradition with close connections to the actors and themes of the paradise story. In the Gilgamesh Epic a woman (here a harlot, not a goddess) plays a key role in transforming a wild man from an animal-like state of ignorance/in-

---

"The Fall of Man in the Third Chapter of Genesis," in *Old Testament and Oriental Studies* (BibOr 29; Rome: Biblical Institute Press, 1975) 88–111, esp. 94–100.

31. Joines, *Serpent Symbolism*, 16–41; Westermann, *Genesis*, 238; Niditch, *Chaos to Cosmos*, 130–37.

32. Wallace, *The Eden Narrative*, 156–57. The best-known examples are the *Qudšu* reliefs from Egypt and the Taanak incense stand. A title *dt btn* "Lady of the snake" is also known from Proto-Sinaitic inscriptions. Frank M. Cross (*Canaanite Myth and Hebrew Epic: Essays in the History of the Religion of Israel* [Cambridge: Harvard University Press, 1973] 31–34) identifies the "snake goddess" with Asherah, suggesting a connection with *tnt* ("Tan[n]it") as well.

33. Joines, *Serpent Symbolism*, 110–13, 119–21. The biblical associations of Asherah with a tree, and Egyptian depictions of a tree as a (nurturing) goddess, provide another form of linkage among the primary figures of our story. See Othmar Keel, *The Symbolism of the Biblical World: Ancient Near Eastern Iconography and the Book of Psalms* (trans. Timothy J. Hallett; New York: Seabury/Crossroad, 1978) 186–87; and Wallace, *The Eden Narrative*, 106–7, 111–14. A Sumerian seal appears to depict a tree of life with a snake between two seated figures (ibid., 106–7).

34. The title is more appropriate for a goddess. See Wallace, *The Eden Narrative*, 157–59. On the etymology, which some link to the Aramaic word for snake, see Westermann, *Genesis*, 268–69; and Barr, *Garden*, 65.

nocence into a human/"civilized" state characterized by knowledge.[35] No snake appears in this scene of passage from prehuman to human (or nature to culture), achieved through sexual intercourse; but a snake figures elsewhere in the epic, as a symbol of the immortality sought, and lost, by the hero. In his quest for eternal life, Gilgamesh succeeds in obtaining a plant that will renew his youth, only to lose it in an unguarded moment to a snake, who eats it and thereby acquires its ability to rejuvenate itself.[36]

The Prohibition

The players and props of the Yahwist's story are given, and so are elements of the plot, but they have been recast to create a new composition. The key to the temptation scene is the divine prohibition introduced in the preceding chapter, the first word of limits addressed to the newly created human. Interpretation has focused on the nature and terms of the limit, but the present form of the text emphasizes the divine command over the content of the prohibition.[37] In the Yahwist's narrative, transgression of the divine command is the first and fundamental sin, not desire to become like God/gods. And although the initial statement of the prohibition (2:17) highlighted the property of knowledge, subsequent references to the tree by the woman (3:3) and God (3:17) eliminate this identification and emphasize the command. Yet the structurally subordinated themes continue to dominate the narrative, requiring attention to the particular content and context of the prohibition. As a consequence, no single message can be abstracted from the chapter without engaging the other voices that resound in the text.[38]

The question behind the prohibition is the question of human nature

35. Tablet I, iv.15–34 (*ANET,* 75). See John A. Bailey, "Initiation and the Primal Woman in Gilgamesh and Genesis 2–3," *JBL* 89 (1970) 137–50, esp. 138–42. Cf. Westermann, *Genesis,* 247, 226. The woman is not a "cult prostitute" (so Westermann, 247), but an ordinary prostitute (*ḥarimtu*), also called *šamḥatu* "pleasure girl," and has no cultic associations. She is the professional in matters of sex, brought from the city to initiate Enkidu into the ways of civilization/city life.

36. Tablet XI, 265–89 (*ANET,* 96); Westermann, *Genesis,* 213–14.

37. Cf. Westermann, *Genesis,* 192–93. Traditional theology likewise emphasized the divine command. Van Seters (*Prologue to History,* 126) sees here the Deuteronomic theology of obedience to the commandments, in a work created as a prologue to the Deuteronomistic History.

38. Thus there is justification for interpreting the "original" sin as hubris, desire for autonomy, self-interest, or lack of trust, but none of these views is fully adequate. The present form of the text requires attention to both formal and substantive elements and recognition of tensions or ambiguities in their combination. For the history of interpretation, see Westermann, *Genesis,* 222–24.

and the boundary between the human and the divine. Two distinctions mark this boundary, each represented by a tree: the tree of life (2:9; 3:22) and the tree of knowledge (2:9, 17; cf. 3:5, 11). Both figure in the final form of the Yahwist's narrative, but only one in the temptation scene. Both derive from ancient Near Eastern tradition, which associated superior wisdom and immortality with the gods. In contrast to the Gilgamesh Epic and other ancient Near Eastern myths,[39] however, the Yahwist's primary concern is with knowledge, not immortality. The latter theme is relegated to the margins in Genesis 2–3 and remains closer to the mythic level of its origins, as a prerogative maintained by God/the gods (3:22, pl.), who guards its source from human grasp by expelling "the human" (sg.) from the garden (3:23-24).

The two trees of Genesis 2–3 appear to derive from alternative representations of a single tree, but each plays a distinct and essential role in the final composition. The tree of knowledge is the focus of attention and is unique to this account, the Yahwist's own creation, a transformation of the common tree of life. The prohibition is also unique. What humans want and need, at least in the life we know, is placed before them—with a "hands off" sign, reinforced by a penalty of death. Moreover, the prohibition invites reflection, ironically calling forth the very quality it intends to withhold, reason or discernment, the weighing of good and bad—or so it seems. The problem of defining this knowledge is compounded by the snake, who though a subhuman creature of the field, appears to have knowledge of the divine world denied to the humans.

What is the knowledge represented by this tree, and why does God withhold it? There are no simple answers to the tensions and gaps in the narrative which invite readers to question the motive and morality of the prohibition. The basic meaning of the prohibition is simple, however; it represents a given of the primordial order as understood by the ancient author, the marker of a boundary—which will be breached. It is thus a requirement of the plot. Knowledge marked the boundary between gods and humans in the common tradition of the ancient Near East, but that boundary was not absolute; in fact the line was drawn more sharply between the human and the animal world than between the human and the divine. That humans are distinguished from animals by Godlike wisdom is stated explicitly in the Gilgamesh Epic, where the harlot, seeking to

39. Cf. the Adapa myth, in which Adapa is endowed with wisdom by Ea, but loses the chance of obtaining eternal life, when, on Ea's instructions, he refuses food of life offered to him by Anu, believing it to be food of death (*ANET*, 101–3). Cf. Westermann, *Genesis*, 246; Wallace, *The Eden Narrative*, 104; and Arvid S. Kapelrud, "You Shall Not Die," in André Lemaire and Benedikt Otzen, eds., *History and Traditions of Early Israel: Studies Presented to Eduard Nielsen* (VTSup 50; Leiden: Brill, 1993) 50–61, esp. 54–55.

console Enkidu for the loss of his animal strength and fleetness, says to him: "Thou art wise, Enkidu, art become like a god!"[40] The same acknowledgment is made in Gen 3:22, where God says: "See, the human has become like one of us, knowing good and evil."

In the Genesis account the distinguishing character of this Godlike knowledge is expressed by the paired terms, ṭôb wārāʿ, generally translated "good and evil," but including aesthetic as well as moral qualities. The syntax here is unusual and the meaning disputed.[41] In light of the commentary in 3:5, 22 and the tradition associating comprehensive knowledge with divinity, the paired terms must surely be understood as a *merismus* describing the range of knowledge;[42] but the use of evaluative terms to describe this range suggests an element of discrimination. In either case, the knowledge symbolized by the tree is not needed by the couple in the garden, where everything has been provided for them in abundance. It is needed, however, for survival in the "real" world, outside the garden.

This story is a story of passage from the world of origins to the world as we know it, and like Genesis 1 it portrays humans in their present state as possessing a Godlike quality. But what is given in Genesis 1 by divine design is grasped in defiance in Genesis 3, and accompanied by a sense of loss as well as gain. Knowledge in this account is a mixed "blessing"; it brings pain as well as pleasure, awareness of evil as well as good. It is accompanied by estrangement—estrangement from God and estrangement between man and woman. It also brings estrangement from the environment. The sense of loss and alienation finds its first expressions in shame and fear (3:10; cf. 2:25; 3:7-8). The nakedness of the couple in their natural state now carries a sense of exposure and vulnerability.[43] The first

40. Tablet I, iv.26–34 (*ANET*, 75).
41. On the syntax, see Wallace, *The Eden Narrative*, 115–16; cf. Westermann, *Genesis*, 213. On the history of interpretation, see Westermann, *Genesis*, 240–48. Westermann (247–48) follows Wellhausen and von Rad in viewing the phrase as an expression for broad or comprehensive knowledge, emphasizing mastery of one's own existence, while Barr (*Garden*, 62) favors power of discrimination, though he recognizes the comprehensive force. The present narrative offers two forms of commentary on this quality of the fruit: (1) it is desirable for "making wise" (*haśkîl*, 3:6, a term for practical wisdom and discernment with connotations of success and prosperity); and (2) the result of eating is described as an "opening of the eyes" (3:7), suggesting that previously the pair could not see clearly. The prior state may be assessed positively or negatively, as ideal or unreal. In that ideal/unreal world the woman perceives knowledge only as power and pleasure/delight; in possession of it, she finds that it has destroyed the veil of "innocence."
42. Wallace, *The Eden Narrative*, 121–29.
43. It is often suggested that the knowledge represented by the forbidden tree is sexual knowledge (see Westermann, *Genesis*, 243, for summary of views; cf. Soggin, "Fall," 108; and Wallace, *The Eden Narrative*, 143–47). Sexual allusions abound in the narrative (but see critique below): "nakedness" has an unmistakable sexual nuance and is employed elsewhere in the Old Testament as a term for sexual relations; "knowledge" in Hebrew includes carnal

form of the new knowledge they have received is awareness of themselves as vulnerable, awareness that results in attempts to protect themselves. In their ensuing efforts of self-preservation and self-justification the harmony of the original union is broken.

The players in this drama have antecedents or parallels in the traditions of Israel's ancestors and neighbors, and this explains in part the roles that they assume in the Yahwist's narrative. But they appear here in a new constellation with a new purpose, seen first of all in the etiologies of 3:14-19. The temptation scene provides the necessary first act of a crime-and-punishment story that accounts for the hardships of life. But it also serves a larger theological purpose in the Yahwist's history, for it concerns the fundamental terms and conditions of the divine-human relationship, focused on the place of human reason and divine command in that ongoing relationship. The story of the temptation exposes the problematic in the prohibition and invites reflection on the nature and role of knowledge in a world created by God for humans to govern in a way that challenges traditional interpretations of sin and "fall."[44]

Why is this tree off-limits, and why is the threat so dire? The question of every reader is the woman's question, but the inner debate that precedes conscious violation of a command is externalized here in a dialogue between woman and snake. And the initiative is given to the snake. In this move the Yahwist has attempted to answer a profound, and ultimately

---

knowledge in its range of meanings; and the snake is closely associated with fertility themes. What is striking, however, is that the sexual connotations are so restrained, and they do not lead in the direction we anticipate. The couple's sin is not sexual activity, which is assumed in Genesis 2—and assumed as good. And it is difficult to recognize any critique of a Canaanite fertility cult (pace Soggin, "Fall," 108–9) in the present narrative, which is marked more by a tone of tragedy or ambivalence than polemic. Cf. Westermann, *Genesis*, 244. A sexual reading may also obscure, or misinterpret, the primary sense of the key terms. Jonathan Magonet ("The Theme of Genesis 2–3," in Wallace and Sawyer, *A Walk in the Garden*, 39–46) argues that the primary significance of 'ārûm is not sexuality at all, but "a state of defenselessness and helplessness, without possessions or power," expressed here in the couple's fear and seeking shelter (43–44). Barr (*Garden*, 63) qualifies the notion of shame, arguing that htbšš means to "be embarrassed" or "shy," a matter of propriety, not wrongdoing.

44. This passage does not permit a simple opposition of reason and obedience or a view of the garden as an ideal state, which might be regained. The "fall" into reality is an irreversible journey, and like the loss of childhood is accompanied by gain. Reason is not condemned in this account; rather creaturely wisdom is shown to be deficient or subject to distortion by self-interest. The woman rightly saw the "good" of the tree, but failed to see the "evil" consequences of eating. The knowledge she gained included knowledge of "evil"—as personal experience and anticipated consequence. A foundation is laid for the Deuteronomic exhortations to obey the commandments, which are grounded in appeals to reason—to choose the good and reject the evil (Deut 30:15-20) by actively contemplating the conditions and consequences of the commands. To "know" God is to love and serve God with the whole heart/mind.

unanswerable, question about the origins of evil in a world created and ruled by a good God. He has not answered it, but displaced it; in so doing, however, he has removed some of the burden of guilt from the human transgressors. The impulse to disobedience comes from outside, and raises immediate defenses as the woman attempts to protect her will against the newly awakened desire by overstating the prohibition (3:13). The snake voices the woman's doubt, and her attempt to discern the rationale for the prohibition (3:4); God is keeping the best for himself, he argues, and is using a death threat as a scare tactic.[45] So now actively contemplating the forbidden tree, the woman sees that it is good for food and a delight to the eyes and desired to make one wise—and perceiving it thus, she takes of its fruit and shares it with her husband.

Does the snake speak the truth, and whence comes his knowledge? Does he know God's motive and response, or is he simply bluffing? And what of God, whose death threat fails to materialize? Part of the success of this story, and reason for its continuing debate, is that it permits no easy answer. The reader, like the woman, must weigh conflicting voices, each representing the tree and the prohibition in a different light. The snake appears to be right; the couple's eyes are opened, and they do not die.[46] But what they see is themselves—not as gods, but as weak, exposed, and vulnerable. Godlike knowledge does not make them divine; rather it increases their awareness of the boundary between themselves and God. Divine knowledge under human conditions brings pain as well as power. And limits remain, only they are redefined. Henceforth humans must live outside the garden, but they leave equipped with a Godlike power to order life that is no longer ordered for them.

The consequences of eating the forbidden fruit are threefold in the present narrative. The first is acquisition of knowledge, evidenced in new awareness of self and surroundings. The gain is underscored by the fact that they do not die. Instead, as a second consequence, a trial is held and

45. The snake's main function in the account is to initiate the process of reflection on the motives and consequences of the prohibition that will lead to its transgression. If the snake is viewed as an independent center of knowledge and action within the account, the woman is placed between two opposing forces, each apparently possessing superhuman powers (knowledge). Although there are lingering signs of the snake as an opposing deity or demon, who has "tricked" the woman (3:13), as Ea tricked Adapa, the narrator has taken pains to undercut this incipient dualism. The snake is only a creature, though the cleverest of the animal kingdom (3:1); and for his misuse of his powers he is demoted to the lowest of the wild animals (3:14).

46. The threat in 2:17 (*běyôm 'ăkolkā mimmennû môt tāmût*, "on the day you eat of it you shall surely die") does not mean "you shall become mortal." It has the common form of a death penalty and assumes prompt execution, but without specification of the means or agent (Westermann, *Genesis*, 224–25). The nonoccurrence is interpreted in different ways; see below.

sentences of punishment are delivered to each of the three actors. Although independent in origin, the judgments function now as a transmutation of the death sentence. Death is averted, not because it was a hollow threat, but because God has chosen to respond to his rebellious creatures with mitigating punishment. In place of death, the couple is offered life under changed conditions. They do not get the punishment they deserve; rather, God provides for life to continue where human action would have cut it off. Thus the sentences represent both judgment and grace.

The sentencing is preceded by interrogation of the human actors—not the snake—reinforcing the view that it is the humans alone who are finally responsible. The man and the woman are each required to account for their actions, and each passes blame before admitting "I ate" (3:12, 13). The punishments are etiologies of life's hardships, relating to the nature of the transgressors, not the transgression(s), and returning to the themes of Genesis 2: work, reproduction, and primary relationships. The man's punishment picks up the "ground" theme of the frame story and is the most elaborate. Here again we see that the base story concerned only 'ādām from the 'ădāmâ—creating a striking disjunction between crime and punishment; because the man listened to his *wife*, the *ground* is cursed (3:17)!

The woman's punishment has been constructed to correspond to the man's with a symmetry that is often missed by interpreters. As a consequence of their disobedience, both man and woman will now experience pain in their labor and estrangement in their relationship to the source of their existence (as both origin and means of livelihood/work). The man will labor in painful toil, and the ground from which he was taken and on which he depends for his work will become an enemy with which he must struggle (3:17-19). Correspondingly, the woman's labor will be painful and arduous, and the man, from whom she was taken and on whom she depends for her (reproductive) work, will become her ruler (3:16-17).

The punishments are parallel in structure and clearly meant to be comparable.[47] There is no disproportionate emphasis on the woman's punishment—and no mention of her crime. In fact, the weight of emphasis falls clearly on the man. Because the woman's work depends on relationship with the man, however, her punishment has a social dimension lacking in the man's. This etiology of life and work in a peasant agricultural society knows a fundamental social order characterized by patriarchy—and views it as a consequence and sign of sin, of human action that has altered God's original intention for creation.

47. See Bird, "Sexual Differentiation," 21 [1995: 15] and 31 [1995: 25] n. 32. Cf. Meyers, *Discovering Eve*, 99–109.

Traditional interpretation has focused on the woman's sentence, understanding it as a divine decree determining the conditions of women's life in every age and divorcing it from consideration of men's roles and the conditions of men's work. Few have observed that the woman's prominence in the temptation scene has no consequence in the judgment scene. Both woman and man have sinned and there is no weighing of guilt in the assignment of penalties. The sin is one, disobedience of a divine command, but the consequences differ according to circumstances of life.

I have argued that the woman in the temptation scene speaks for the pair, providing the only rationalization for the action that both take. Traditional associations with food, snakes, and initiation rites have thrust the woman forward as representative of the species in this fateful episode. But the man's eating of the proffered fruit signals assent to her reasoning. Although no speech is recorded between the woman and the man, the man's sentence opens with the indictment, "Because you listened to the voice of your wife" (3:17).[48] Thus whether the voice of temptation is the voice of another (snake or woman) or an inner voice is irrelevant to the final judgment. Both man and woman have heeded another voice over the voice of God, and that is their common sin. The gender-differentiated roles in the drama do not describe gender-specific patterns of sin, but they do illustrate differing responses to temptation, one involving active reasoning, the other unreflective acquiescence to another's leading. We may speculate about the motive,[49] but it has no place in the judgment. The man has chosen, whether by reason or not, to heed the voice of his companion over the voice of God.

Original Sin?

Should we speak of sin in characterizing the action of the woman and man in this passage, and what consequence does it have for interpreting subsequent accounts of transgression? We have noted that the Yahwistic narrator has transformed an etiology of the pain and limits of human life into a crime-and-punishment story, in which this condition is construed as a penalty for disobedience of a divine command. It is this juridical structuring that invites the interpretation of sin, together with the emphasis on the divine command. That interpretive construct is notably absent

48. This should not be construed as a general condemnation of men heeding their wives. It is prefaced to the main indictment, because the man has attempted to absolve himself by pointing to the woman—as God's gift to him (3:12). Since no speech is reported in the woman's offering of the fruit, the reference to her voice (3:17) appears to allude to her conversation with the snake, in the man's presence and hearing, not to a private communication.

49. Cf. Trible, *God*, 113.

from the concluding account of expulsion from the garden (3:22-24), which appears as a third consequence of eating the forbidden fruit.[50] This notice reaches back to the opening scenes of the creation story (2:4b-17), reverting to the solitary "human" and picking up the theme of immortality. Here the notion of human threat (3:22), rather than wrongdoing, is invoked to explain the divine action. Thus the concept of sin may be seen as the Yahwist's contribution to the story of origins.

Terminology for sin is lacking in the passage, but appears in the following chapter (4:7), which continues the Yahwist's narrative. There *ḥaṭṭā't* ("sin") is used in relation to murder, the prime sin against humanity, encoded in divine law (the Decalogue) and an apt example of the first sin. How then is the disobedience in the garden to be understood, for eating forbidden fruit surely does not stand in the same category as murder? There is no single term in the Hebrew Scriptures that represents our notion of sin, and the most commonly used terms describe particular offenses, rather than a state or disposition. The language of sin has its primary development in relation to the cult and sacrificial system, and it is not until relatively late that attempts are made to analyze the source or cause of such offenses and abstract a notion of sin as a state of opposition to, or separation from, God.[51]

The importance of Genesis 3 for such reflection is that it describes the first instance of human opposition to divine will, cast as disobedience of a divine command. Thus it points forward to an understanding of divine-human relations governed by divine commands/word (law and prophets). It serves in the Yahwist's history to identify the "root cause" of the sin that will henceforth mark human history with acts of violence, deceit, and corruption. But it does not and cannot answer the ultimate question about the source of the impulse to disobedience. What Genesis 3 affirms is that sin arises within creation, but is not a constituent element of created human nature or order. It appears in interaction, and thus has a fundamentally social character.[52] And although the preconditions are present in the structures of human existence, sin is actualized only in history.

50. This account stands in tension with the preceding in a number of ways, and must originally have constituted an alternate version of the passage from prereality into reality. In its present state, however, it provides a needed note of transition to the world "outside the garden" and expands the category of human limits by emphasizing mortality.

51. Condon, "Biblical Doctrine," 20–22; Robin C. Cover, "Sin, Sinners: Old Testament," *ABD* 6:31–40, esp. 33; Rolf Knierim, *Die Hauptbegriffe für Sünde im Alten Testament* (Gütersloh: Mohn, 1965) esp. 13–17.

52. I use the term "social" broadly to include the internal, or internalized, voices of conscience and reason as well as communal interaction. The interaction is not the cause, but creates the condition for sin to arise.

Consequently the Yahwist distinguishes "historical" sins, such as the sin of Cain, from the disobedience in the garden.

The traditional doctrine of original sin recognized this distinction, even though its classical formulation employed terms and concepts foreign to the Genesis account—and inadequate for modern theological reflection. Whether the doctrine can, or should, be maintained is not a question for an Old Testament exegete, although I find some such concept of a predisposition, or precondition, of sin indispensable—and compatible with modern critical readings of Genesis 3.[53] But it cannot be derived from this chapter alone, and preoccupation with the doctrine in reading this text has greatly narrowed and distorted its meaning.

53. Cf. Lohfink, "Böse," 185–99; Barr (*Garden*, 92) argues that for most of Christianity the garden story is not the *ground* of the idea of original sin, but the mode by which it was symbolized. For modern theological views, see Richard Robert, "Sin, Saga and Gender: The Fall and Original Sin in Modern Theology," in Morris and Sawyer, *A Walk in the Garden*, 244–60.

IV
HARLOT AND HIERODULE

9

THE HARLOT
AS HEROINE:

Narrative Art and Social Presupposition
in Three Old Testament Texts

Abstract

THE NARRATOR AS ARTIST WORKS WITHIN A HISTORICALLY DETER-
mined social world in which shared understandings of language, ges-
tures, roles, and so on create the repertoire of symbols and senses employed in literary creation. Full appreciation of narrative art consequently
requires both literary and social (historical) criticism. This essay attempts
to combine the two methodologies by examining the interrelationship of
narrative art and social presupposition in three texts having a harlot, or
assumed harlot, as a major actor (Gen 38:1-26; Josh 2:1-24; 1 Kgs 3:16-27).
Two questions guide the investigation: (1) What is the image of the harlot
assumed in the text? and (2) How does that image or understanding affect
the construction or narration of the story? The study argues that each of
the texts requires as its presupposition a view of the harlot as a marginal
figure in the society, tolerated but despised, and that fundamental ambivalence toward the harlot's role is not resolved by any action of the harlot,
in either literature or life.

Originally given as a paper in the Narrative Research on the Hebrew Bible Group at the
SBL Annual Meeting in Dallas, December 19–22, 1983; it was published after long delay in
Miri Amihai, George W. Coats, and Anne M. Solomon, eds., *Narrative Research on the Hebrew Bible* (*Semeia* 46; Chico, Calif.: Scholars Press, 1989) 119–39. Cross-references to articles
that are reprinted in this volume are indicated by an asterisk in square brackets following
the original page number.

A desire for brevity and alliteration in the title has led me to overextend the meaning of the term "heroine." It is intended here as a cover term for three cases in which a harlot (or assumed harlot) plays a major role in a biblical narrative. My aim in this article is to explore the role of social presupposition in narrative construction or storytelling, using the case of the harlot, or prostitute,[1] as an example. I am convinced that literary art and social presuppositions are so interrelated in any literary work that adequate interpretation requires the employment of both literary criticism and social analysis. Neither alone suffices. Each makes assumptions about the other, often leaving them unrecognized and uncriticized. Here I want to focus on their interrelationships.

Narrative art, in whatever form and whatever degree of sophistication, depends upon highly selective and purposeful use of language and images. The narratives of the Hebrew Bible, especially those contained within the Pentateuch and Deuteronomistic History, represent a particularly compressed and selective form of storytelling art, in which individual terms or figures must carry far more weight of suggested meaning than in the more expansive and nuanced prose of the modern novel, or even of the novella (ancient or modern). Thus, when a designation such as *zônâ* is attached to a name or a figure, a picture is called up in the reader's or hearer's mind and a range of meanings, attitudes, and associations on which the narrator may draw in constructing or relating the story. The twofold question I want to address in this article is (1) What was the image and understanding of the *zônâ* assumed in each of the narratives? and (2) How was that image or understanding employed by the narrator, or how did it influence the construction or narration of the story?

In my analysis I have set aside the question of historicity, insofar as this was possible without violating the terms of the narrative. That is, I have not made a judgment about the historical claims made by any of the narratives. Each of the narratives I shall examine is presented as the account of a historical event, and historical experience may dictate much of the terms of each narrative. But each is also clearly a literary work that has been shaped in its presentation by social and literary considerations. It is to these that I wish to direct my attention.

In the space alotted to me I can give neither a full literary analysis of each narrative nor a complete portrait of the harlot as she is presented in the biblical texts and other relevant records from the ancient Near East.

---

1. I use the terms interchangeably, adopting "harlot" because of its use by the RSV (on its misuse, see below). Cf. T. Drorah Setel, "Prophets and Pornography: Female Sexual Imagery in Hosea," in Letty M. Russell, ed., *Feminist Interpretation of the Bible* (Philadelphia: Westminster, 1985) 89–91, for usage that distinguishes the terms.

While I will draw from time to time on a broader study in progress,[2] I will concentrate my attention in this article on the information supplied by the three texts or required for their understanding. My procedure will be to comment on those features of the portrait of the harlot that have significance for the particular text under consideration and thus to compose and develop the picture as I move through the three texts. I will begin, however, with a brief preliminary sketch, summarizing those traits or elements that are essential to the portrait of the prostitute in Israelite society. My treatment of the individual cases will attempt to explain and defend that sketch.

First, definition and terminology. A prostitute, or harlot, is a woman who offers sexual favors for pay.[3] In the Hebrew Bible she is normally designated by the single term *zônâ*, a *qal* participle from the root *ZNH*, used either alone, as a substantive, or attributively.[4] Her social status is that of an outcast, though not an outlaw, a tolerated but dishonored member of society. She normally has the legal status of a free citizen; where she is a slave, or is otherwise legally dependent, it is not because of her occupation. As a free citizen she may seek the legal protection of the state, and as a woman who is not under the authority of a husband, she may

2. I am currently engaged in a book-length study of the harlot and the hierodule in Old Testament and ancient Near Eastern literature and society. (I use the term "hierodule" as a provisional class designation for all types of cult-related women, without regard to their particular duties, activities, or status.) While the two figures, or classes of women, are commonly identified and even exchanged in interpretive literature, beginning with the Old Testament's polemical treatment of Canaanite religion and culture, there appears to be little or no evidence of confusion or interchange in the primary ancient texts. In her popular treatment of the origins of prostitution, Gerda Lerner ("The Origin of Prostitution in Ancient Mesopotamia," *Signs: Journal of Women in Culture and Society* 11 [1986] 236–54) rightly criticizes the confusion of the two classes by most authorities as well as the attempt to derive secular prostitution from sacred sexual service (238–45); but she falls prey to the same confusion in her own treatment of *harimtu* ("prostitute") (244–46). This essay does not permit discussion of the important but complex question of the relationship between the harlot and the hierodule or assessment of Lerner's arguments, which are based on secondary sources and misconstrue critical Mesopotamian texts.

3. John H. Gagnon, "Prostitution," in David L. Sills, ed., *The International Encyclopedia of the Social Sciences* (New York: Macmillan and Free Press, 1968) 12:592; Cf. Paul Henry Gebhard, "Prostitution," in *The New Encyclopedia Britannica* (15th ed.; Chicago: University of Chicago Press, 1980) 15:75–81. Male prostitution, which was homosexual, appears to have been a limited phenomenon and is poorly attested in our sources. (Cf. Gebhard, "Prostitution," 80.) It is not considered in this article.

4. I have discussed the problems of the translation and use of this term and the related verbal forms in an unpublished paper ("'To Play the Harlot': An Inquiry into an Old Testament Metaphor," Perkins School of Theology, Southern Methodist University, Dallas, Texas, 1981 [expanded version published in Peggy L. Day, ed., *Gender and Difference in Ancient Israel* (Minneapolis: Fortress Press, 1989) 75–94] [*219–36]). Some of the issues are treated in the discussion of the Tamar story above.

have rights of legal action (e.g., signing contracts) not possessed by other women, except hierodules and widows without male guardians. She is typically contrasted to the "normal" woman, that is, the married woman, from whom she is separated spatially and symbolically, through distinctive dress[5] and habitat. The places and times of her activity maintain distance between her and the married woman. She is a woman of the night, who appears on the streets when honorable women are secluded at home. She approaches strangers and businessmen by the roadside and in the public squares, and she lives in the shadow of the wall, on the outskirts of the city, where the refuse is dumped.[6]

Prostitution is not a universal phenomenon, nor can it properly claim to be the world's oldest profession.[7] But it *is* characteristic of urban society, and more specifically of urban patriarchal society. It is a product and sign of the unequal distribution of status and power between the sexes in patriarchal societies, which is exhibited, among other ways, in asymmetry of sexual roles, obligations, and expectations. This may be seen in the harlot's lack of a male counterpart. Female prostitution is an accommodation to the conflicting demands of men for exclusive control of their wives' sexuality and for sexual access to other women. The greater the inaccessibility of women in the society due to restrictions on the wife and the unmarried nubile women, the greater the need for an institutionally legi-

---

5. See Gebhard, "Prostitution," 76; Cf. also the following texts:

> She is not a wife, she is a ḫarimtu [prostitute]. (JEN 666:14, Nuzi [*CAD* H:101b])

> A qadištu [hierodule] whom no husband has married (must go) bareheaded in the street, must not veil herself.
> A ḫarimtu [prostitute] must not veil herself. (KAV 1 v 66, Ass. Code §40 [*CAD* H:101b; cn. G:152b]*)

In the latter case, both the harlot and the unmarried hierodule are prohibited from wearing the veil, which is the distinguishing garb of the married woman. The preceding clause requires the married hierodule to veil herself on the street.

CAD H:101b mistakenly connects the two clauses cited, understanding the qadištu as a class of ḫarimtu. Cf. Theophile J. Meek, trans., "The Middle Assyrian Laws," *ANET*, 183.

6. On the harlot's habitat, note the following:

> If a man's wife has not borne him children (but) a harlot (from) the public square. (Lipit-Ishtar Law Code §27 [Samuel Noah Kramer, trans., "Lipit-Ishtar Lawcode," *ANET*, 160; cf. §32])

> If someone regularly approaches a ḫarimtu at a streetcrossing. (CT 39 45:30, SB Alu [*CAD* H:101b])

Cf. also Gideon Sjoberg, *The Preindustrial City, Past and Present* (New York: Free Press, 1960) 133–37, and A. Leo Oppenheim, "Mesopotamian Mythology II," *Orientalia* 17 (1948) 41.

7. Gebhard, "Prostitution," 76.

timized "other" woman. The harlot is that "other" woman, tolerated but stigmatized, desired but ostracized.

A fundamental and universal feature of the institution of prostitution wherever it is found is an attitude of ambivalence. The harlot is both desired and despised, sought after and shunned. Attempts to show changes in attitudes toward prostitutes over time or from one culture to another founder on this point. Despite considerable historical and cultural variation in attitudes, the harlot is never a fully accepted person in any society.[8] What a man desires for himself may be quite different from what he desires for his daughter or wife. One of the earliest and clearest expression of that fundamental attitude of ambivalence toward the harlot is found in the Gilgamesh Epic. As Enkidu is about to die, he looks back over his life in the civilized world, recalling its pain, and he curses the harlot who initiated him into that world from his former carefree life among the beasts of the steppe. The curse is an etiology of the harlot as outcast and despised.[9]

> Come, prostitute,[10] I shall establish (your) status,[11]
> a status that shall not end for all eternity.
> . . . .
> May [your lovers] discard (you) when sated with your charms,
> [May those whom] you love [despise(?) . . .] your favors(?).
> . . . .
> [Dark corners] of the street shall be your home,
> The shadow of the city's wall shall be your station.
> [Men shall piss there in front of] your feet,
> The drunken and thirsty shall slap your face.

8. Attempts to compare attitudes and incidence of prostitution in Canaanite and Israelite society or in different periods of Israelite history are futile, because the data do not permit statistical comparison and because the different literary genres in which the references are preserved display quite different pictures of the harlot and attitudes toward her (e.g., Proverbs offers practical advice to men, stressing the pocketbook, while Priestly legislation is concerned with the harlot as ritually unclean and her contacts as defiling).

9. The translation and interpretation of the following texts from the Gilgamesh Epic (VII, iii.6–22 and iv.1–10) is based on Oppenheim, "Mesopotamian Mythology," 40–41, and Ephraim A. Speiser, trans. and ed., "Akkadian Myths and Epics," *ANET,* 86–87. Cf. Jeffrey H. Tigay, *The Evolution of the Gilgamesh Epic* (Philadelphia: University of Pennsylvania Press, 1982) 170–72.

10. The term *šamḫatu,* which is interchanged with *ḫarimtu* ("prostitute") in the texts relating to Enkidu and the harlot, is treated as a proper noun by Tigay (*Evolution,* 171). Speiser translates "harlot-lass" ("Akkadian Myths," 74–75) or simply "lass" (86), noting the etymological meaning "pleasure girl" (74 n. 23).

11. Oppenheim's rendering of the phrase *ši-ma-tu lu-šim-ki,* conventionally translated "I will decree (your) fate."

But Shamash, overhearing Enkidu's curse, chides him, reminding him of the fine clothes and food that he had enjoyed and of his companionship with Gilgamesh. All this was the harlot's gift, for which he should be grateful. Enkidu acknowledges the right of Shamash's argument and counters his curse with a blessing. The blessing is an etiology of the harlot as desired.

> May [your lover(?)] (always) return(?) (to you)
> [even from far away places]
> [Kings, prin]ces, and nobles shall love [you].
> None shall slap his thighs (to insult you)
> [Over you the old man will] shake his beard.
> [. . . the young(?)] will unloose his girdle for you.
> [So that you shall receive from him(?)] lapis and gold.
> [May he be paid] back (who) pissed in front of you,
> [May his home be emptied(?)], his filled storehouse.
> [To the presence of] the gods [the priest] shall let you enter.
> [On your account] a wife will be forsaken, (though) a mother
> of seven.

Genesis 38:1-26

Let us turn now to the biblical narratives. Genesis 38 stands as an independent tradition unit within the Joseph story. It recounts a complex story concerning Judah, with a number of etiological motives. The centerpiece of the chapter, however, and the bulk of the narrative is a fully developed story in itself with its own internal dynamics in which etiological elements are lacking or play a minor role.[12]

The scene is set in the Judean Shephelah in the period before the Israelite settlement, a time when Israel's ancestors lived side by side with the people of the land and intermarried with them, apparently without censure. "At that time," the narrator informs us, "Judah went down from his brothers" and sojourned with an Adullamite named Hirah, marrying a Canaanite woman, who bore him three sons (vv. 1-5). For the eldest, Er, Judah selects a wife named Tamar,[13] a woman of the region. But Er dies at the hand of God as does the second son, Onan, who refuses to fulfill the

12. Cf. John Skinner, *A Critical and Exegetical Commentary on Genesis* (2d ed.; ICC; Edinburgh: T. & T. Clark, 1910); Gerhard von Rad, *Genesis: A Commentary* (trans. John H. Marks; rev. ed., OTL; Philadelphia: Westminster, 1972); E. A. Speiser, *Genesis* (AB 1; Garden City, N.Y.: Doubleday, 1964); Claus Westermann, *Genesis 37–50: A Commentary* (trans. John J. Scullion; Continental Commentary; Minneapolis: Augsburg, 1986).

13. Heb. *tāmār* means "palm," a fertility symbol. The symoblism in the text is far richer and the literary art more subtle and complex than my limited analysis is able to convey.

duty of the levirate toward his brother's widow (v. 8). Judah, now fearful of losing his only remaining son, sends Tamar home to her father's house, instructing her to remain a widow until the third son, Shelah, grows up. And as a dutiful daughter-in-law she goes, a widow, yet "betrothed" and therefore not free to remarry. Judah in his anxiety has sealed her fate, for he intends her widowhood to be permanent.

With Tamar's dismissal, attention is turned to Judah. Years pass and his wife dies. And when his mourning is over, he sets out with his friend Hirah to attend to the shearing of his flocks at Timnah in the hill country (v. 12). The report of Judah's journey is a signal to Tamar, who has perceived her father-in-law's design and is unwilling to accept the fate he has determined for her. His journey provides an opportunity for Tamar to act. But the meaning of her action and her intention in it is not spelled out by the narrator, who simply reports as an observer and thus elicits the reader's speculation. "She put off her widow's garments," he says, "covered herself with a 'veil' and wrapped herself in it (*wattĕkas baṣṣā'îp wattit'allāp*) and sat at the entrance to Enaim, which is on the road to Timnah" (v. 14).[14]

The language is deliberately opaque and suggestive. The narrator does not say that Tamar dressed as a harlot. That is the inference that Judah makes—and is intended to make—but the narrator leaves it to Judah to draw the conclusion. "When Judah saw her, he thought her to be a harlot because she had covered her face (*wayyaḥšĕbehā lĕzônâ kî kissĕtâ pānêhā*)" (v. 15).[15] His action is presented as following naturally from that inference: "[So] he went over to her by the roadside" and propositioned her. And Tamar, in keeping with her assumed role, asks what her favors are worth to him (v. 16). Judah offers her a kid from his flock, but Tamar demands a pledge until he is able to send it, specifying his signet, cord, and staff, which he gives her. With the essential negotiation completed, the critical action begins: "He lay with her and she conceived by him" (v. 18b). The scene concludes with the note that she departed, removing her veil and resuming her widow's garments (v. 19).

How are we to understand this scene of entrapment and why does it succeed? Tamar, the victim of her father-in-law's injustice, has been denied the means of performing her duty toward her deceased husband and for achieving a sense of womanly self-worth in bearing a child. Her bold

14. The location is uncertain (cf. ancient versions, and commentaries), but unnecessary for our analysis.

15. The "veil" may have been understood immediately by hearers as a harlot's apparel, but it is more likely that the term is meant to be more general in its application and more ambiguous in the author's use. By suggesting, but not specifying, a harlot's garb, the narrator makes of her act both an act of concealment and an act of invitation.

and dangerous plan aims to accomplish that end by the agency of the man who has wronged her.[16] It satisfies both duty and revenge. It is not a husband she wants, but an heir for Judah, and so she approaches the source. It is intercourse she wants, not marriage. Her plan works because of the role she has chosen to accomplish this end. The features of the story that make it work involve commonly held presuppositions concerning the prostitute, some peculiar to the Israelite/Canaanite setting of this story, others widely shared.

Judah is needy and therefore vulnerable. At the point where the critical action begins, he is depicted as recently bereaved and hence in need of sexual gratification or diversion. The notice about his wife's death is certainly meant to provide this motivation. He is also a traveler, away from home, desiring entertainment and free to seek it in a strange place. Prostitution is typically offered (and often organized) as a service to travelers, a tourist attraction. Attention is directed to the activity rather than the actor(s). The act is basically anonymous; anyone can provide the service. In this case, that common aspect of anonymity is reinforced by a custom of concealment of the face, at least in public, and apparently also in the execution of the encounter. (A dimly lit room would have aided concealment, though it is unclear from this account just where the union took place.) The harlot's veil is a specific feature of this story and an essential prerequisite for the construction of the tale, or at least for this plan of action. It cannot be universalized, however.[17] Tamar's position is probably just as telling as her garb. A lone woman sitting by the road without apparent business would probably be enough to suggest the wares she was selling.

The climax of the narrative comes, as the text says, "about three months later" (or, at the end of the first trimester), when it is reported to Judah that his daughter-in-law Tamar has "played the harlot" (*zānĕtâ*) and "moreover . . . is with child by harlotry (*hārâ liznûnîm*)" (v. 24). Now the English translation which I have quoted from the RSV contains a word-play that is absent in the Hebrew, or it sharpens a wordplay that is not focused in the original. The translation of the verb *zānâ* as "play the harlot" is, I think, mistaken,[18] but it points to an important sociolinguistic

---

16. Tamar is legally helpless; therfore she must move outside the law to accomplish what duty (for her the higher "law") demands of her.

17. It is useless to argue from the Middle Assyrian Laws (cf. n. 5 above) to practices in Canaan/Israel, since dress is a matter of local or regional custom. Restrictions or prescriptions in dress are generally meant to distinguish the married or betrothed woman from all other classes of women, saying, in effect, "hands off!" That the harlot is not always veiled in Israel is suggested by Jeremiah's reference to the "harlot's brow" (Jer 3:3).

18. Bird, "To Play the Harlot."

consideration in the language employed to describe Tamar's disguise and her crime. The English translation acknowledges that Tamar "played the harlot" when, in fact, no one but the reader knows that that is literally true. What the Hebrew means in its use of the verb and the qualifying noun *zěnûnîm* is that Tamar, who is bound by her situation to chastity, has engaged in illicit intercourse, the evidence of which is her pregnancy. The Hebrew word *zānâ*, like its Arabic cognate, covers, I believe, a wide range of extramarital sexual relations, including both fornication and adultery, although its biblical usage appears focused on the activity of the unmarried woman.[19] In any case, when Judah hears this report of his daughter-in-law's unfaithfulness, his response is an immediate uncondi- tioned sentence: "Bring her out and let her be burned!" (v. 24).

If the wordplay in the English translation is overdrawn, the Hebrew use of the common root *ZNH* in two critical scenes of the narrative is still worthy of note and explanation. A striking contrast is created through use of the same root to describe two situations which occasion very different reactions from Judah. When he perceives that the woman by the road is a *zônâ*, his response is a proposition; when he hears that his daughter-in- law has *zānâ*-ed, his response is a sentence of death. He embraces the whore, but would put to death the daughter-in-law who "whored." The irony on which the story turns is that the two acts and the two women are one, and the use of etymologically related terms as the situation-defining terms strengthens the irony. The essential difference between the two uses is the sociolegal status of the woman involved. In the first instance, the term *zônâ* describes the woman's position or profession (prostitute) as well as the activity on which it is based. Thus, it serves as a class or status designation. In the second instance, the verb describes the activity of one whose sociolegal status makes it a crime. The activity is the same in both instances, as the common vocabulary indicates, namely, nonmarital inter- course by a woman. In one case, however, it appears to be licit, bearing no penalty; in the other it is illicit, bearing the extreme penalty of death.

This anomaly is explained by the differing social positions of the actors. What is outlawed for the one by her status as a "married" woman is al- lowed to the other by her status as an unmarried but nonvirgin woman,

---

19. According to Hans Wehr (*A Dictionary of Modern Written Arabic* [ed. J. Milton Cowan; Ithaca, N.Y.: Cornell University Press, 1961]), Arabic *zanā* has the meaning "to com- mit adultery, fornicate, whore." Cf. *zinan*: "adultery, fornication;" *zināʾ*: "adultery, fornica- tion;" *zānin*: "fornicator, adulterer;" *zāniya*: "whore, harlot, adulteress." See Fatima Mernissi, *Beyond the Veil: Male-Female Dynamics in Modern Muslim Society* (New York: John Wiley & Sons; Halstead, 1975) 24–25. While the activity designated by this root is usually understood as illicit, that description does not give adequate account of the differences in attitudes and sanctions related to the sex and status of the actors. See below.

but not without penalty. The harlot's *act* is not penalized, I would argue, because her *role* or occupation is. The harlot is a kind of legal outlaw, standing outside the normal social order with its approved roles for women, ostracized and marginalized, but needed and therefore accommodated.[20] A stigma is always attached to her role and her person, however desired and tolerated her activity. But she does not bear the stigma alone, although only she is legally ostracized; she passes a measure of it on to her patrons. The cost to the man is admittedly slight and may be understood in different ways, from contamination to humiliation or intimidation. For the harlot not only demands a price, she controls the transaction, as is so well illustrated in our narrative (is this to be understood as a reversal of the normal sex roles?). There is a degree of opprobrium about the whole affair, and a degree of risk for the man, who may be trapped, duped, or "taken." Thus, ambivalence pervades the whole relationship and is, as I argued earlier, a fundamental feature of the institution.

In my analysis of the narrative plot and of the harlot's role within it I omitted a scene which has heavily influenced most discussions of this chapter and is frequently made the central point. The scene is important to our understanding of the narrative, and of the harlot, but it has been overinterpreted and misinterpreted, I believe, precisely because insufficient attention has been given to narrative art in its analysis.

When Judah sends back the kid by his friend the Adullamite and attempts to reclaim his pledge, the friend cannot find her and so inquires of the men of the place (MT: "her place"): "Where is the *qĕdēšâ* who was at Enaim by the wayside?" They reply, "There has been no *qĕdēšâ* here" (v. 21). Hirah then returns to Judah, repeating their answer verbatim.

---

20. Susan Niditch ("The Wronged Woman Righted: An Analysis of Genesis 38," *HTR* 72 [1979] 147 n. 13) has explained this anomalous position of the prostitute by using the term "liminal," as employed by Victor Turner: "That which is liminal is that which is betwixt and between nearly [*sic*] defined categories. A harlot falls between the two allowable categories for women. She is neither an unmarried virgin, nor a non-virgin wife." As a liminal character, outside the social order, Niditch argues, the harlot "belongs to a special class of women who can 'play the harlot' without being condemned." "In effect," she continues, "one could fall between the proper categories and survive, once that outside betwixt-and-between status was itself institutionalized and categorized" (147).

While Niditch's analysis of women's roles and of the harlot's status in ancient Israel society corresponds closely to my own (made independently in an unpublished paper [Phyllis A. Bird, "Harlot and Hierodule: Images of the Feminine in Old Testament Anthropology and Theology," Bunting Institute Colloquium, Radcliffe College, Cambridge, Mass, 1980], I have retained my original characterization of the harlot as a "legal outlaw," because I want to emphasize the ambivalence or conflict in attitudes toward the prostitute and the fact that she is both freed and constrained by her position.

What are we to make of this shift in terms? Have we misread Tamar's action? Did she intend to represent herself as a hierodule, a cultic "prostitute," who might be understood to have some particular association with festivals of the yearly cycle such as sheepshearing? I think not, though it is conceivable that at some stage in the development of this story such an association might have been made. The substitution of terms in this passage is not accidental, and the interchange must indicate some kind of association between the two figures. But there is no justification for the common collapse of the two nor for assuming that the word "hierodule" is the determining designation for understanding Judah's action.[21]

The term qĕdēšâ is confined to the interchange between Hirah the Adullamite and the men of the place. Two possible factors might affect this usage: first, the designation of the woman as a hierodule[22] might reflect the narrator's view of Canaanite usage, for it occurs only in the conversation of non-Israelites; second, it is language used in public speech. Judah's original action was prompted by a private assessment: "he thought her to be a harlot" and acted accordingly. But the search for the shady lady requires public inquiry. The decisive clue to the substitution of terms is given, I believe, in Judah's response to Hirah's report. "Then let her keep the things as her own," he says, "*lest we be laughed at*" (lit. "lest we become an object of contempt"). But what might be the reason for contempt or ridicule? A sacred act of lovemaking with the hierodule of a Canaanite cult? Hardly, for the people of the place are understood to be Canaanites and would find no cause for contempt in that. Being outwitted, and more specifically "taken," by a common prostitute? Surely.

Here the issue of opprobrium surfaces. Judah, a man of standing, who has surrendered his insignia to a prostitute in a moment of weakness, does not go back in person to retrieve his goods, but sends a friend, a man of the region, to inquire discreetly of the local inhabitants. Hirah knows how to handle the situation; he uses a euphemism—comparable to our substitution of the term "courtesan" for the cruder expression "whore" (a substitution of court language in the latter instance, cult language in the former). Here we have an example, I think, of a common contrast between private, or "plain," speech (which may also be described as coarse) and

---

21. Von Rad's interpretation is, unfortunately, typical of this type of reasoning, which invariably appeals to Herodotus: "Tamar . . . does not pretend to be a harlot as we think of it, but rather a married woman who indulges in this practice [sacrifice of chastity in the service of the goddess of love], and Judah too thought of her in this way" (von Rad, *Genesis*, 354–55). Cf. Michael C. Astour, "Tamar the Hierodule: An Essay in the Method of Vestigial Motifs," *JBL* 85 (1966) 185–96.

22. There is no justification for RSV's translation of "harlot" here.

public, or polite, speech (which may also be described as elevated).[23] Such
an interchange of terms does not require that the two have identical meanings, especially since euphemism is a characteristic feature of biblical Hebrew usage in describing sexual acts and organs. A foot or a hand is not a
phallus, though both terms are used with that meaning. And a *qĕdēšâ*, I
would argue, is not a prostitute, though she may share important characteristics with her sister of the streets and highways, including sexual intercourse with strangers.[24]

Joshua 2:1-24

The story of Rahab in Joshua 2, like the story of Tamar in Genesis 38, is a
distinct literary unit, with its own tradition, clearly set off from the surrounding material. While the history of the Rahab story, in both its literary and preliterary stages, is more complex than the Tamar story, and
while an attempt has been made to integrate the tale into the now dominant account of the miraculous fall of Jericho, the narrative in Joshua 2
can still be analyzed as a discrete literary unit, and the apparent duplication or displacement in the narrative which has taxed many interpreters
does not substantially affect my analysis. Only the Deuteronomistic editing, which is both obvious and limited, constitutes a reinterpretation of
the tradition that represents a significant literary variant.[25]

The account opens with the sending of two spies from the Israelite
camp at Shittim and closes with their return. The spies are instructed by
Joshua in the first verse of the chapter to "see the land"[26] (i.e., the land
west of the Jordan), which Israel is poised to attack. In the concluding

---

23. Speiser (*Genesis*, 300) is one of the few commentators who has recognized this. See
now Robert Alter, *The Art of Biblical Narrative* (New York: Basic Books, 1981) 9.

24. Whatever the reasons for the identification of these two marginal classes of women,
it is essential to maintain the linguistic distinctions made in the Hebrew. See n. 2 above.

25. The analysis of Martin Noth (*Das Buch Josua*, 2d ed.; HAT 1/7; Tübingen: J. C. B.
Mohr (Paul Siebeck) 1953]) remains basic. See also Robert G. Boling, *Joshua* (AB 6; Garden
City, N.Y.: Doubleday, 1982); J. Alberto Soggin, *Joshua: A Commentary* (trans. R. A. Wilson;
OTL; Philadelphia: Westminster, 1972); John Gray, *Joshua, Judges, and Ruth* (NCB; Green-
wood, S.C.: Attic, 1967); and Hans Wilhelm Hertzberg, *Die Bücher Josua, Richter, Ruth* (ATD
9; Göttingen: Vandenhoeck & Ruprecht, 1953). On the question of sources, see further Gene
M. Tucker, "The Rahab Saga (Joshua 2): Some Form-Critical and Traditio-Historical Obser-
vations," in James M. Efird, ed., *The Use of the Old Testament in the New and Other Essays:
Studies in Honor of William Franklin Stinespring* (Durham, N.C.: Duke University Press, 1972)
66–86; and Sigmund Mowinckel, *Tetrateuch-Pentateuch-Hexateuch* (BZAW 90; Berlin:
Töpelmann, 1964) 13–14, 33–34.

26. Omitting "and Jericho" with LXX, Noth (*Josua*, 24), and NEB, as displaced from the
following clause (where LXX reads it) or secondarily introduced to explain the following
account, which concerns only Jericho.

verse, the returned spies report that "Yahweh has given the whole land into our hands; and moreover all the inhabitants of the land are faint-hearted because of us" (RSV; NEB "panic-stricken," v. 24).

That language, augmented by the Deuteronomistic editor in the reference to the peoples' response,[27] presupposes the institution or ideology of holy war, in which an assurance of victory is required from Yahweh before the battle can take place. But the assurance which the spies offer is given without consultation of a priest or other oracle, by spies whose mission has been simply to spy out the land. We might assume then that the assurance of victory is an inference from what they have seen. But what lies between the opening and closing sentences is no account of a secret reconnoitering of the land, as commissioned, but the account of a single encounter in Jericho, the spies' first stopping place across the Jordan, an encounter from which they escape only by the skin of their teeth, or more precisely, by a lie and a cord. The key figure in their escape and in their knowledge of the land and its inhabitants is the harlot Rahab. In the present form of the story, she is both savior and oracle.

Commentators invariably discuss the role and reputation of Rahab. Two questions shape that discussion: (1) Was Rahab a hierodule? and (2) Why would the Israelites consort with a prostitute, who is portrayed as a heroine, without apparent censure of her profession or role? Some commentators claim to find a cult legend at the root of the tradition, an etiology of a sanctuary or of a class of sacred prostitutes which persisted in later Israel.[28] Even those who can find nothing in the present story to support a cultic identification feel constrained to observe that the term zônâ may designate either a sacred or a secular prostitute and is thus ambiguous, leaving either interpretation as a possibility.[29] The question of Rahab's profession is prompted in part by wonder at her role in the tradition, in which the stigma normally attached to prostitutes is perceived as lacking. Either, it is argued, she cannot have been a common prostitute, or the status of the prostitute must have been higher in Canaanite society, for she appears in the story as a fully accepted member of the society.

In contrast to these opinions, I shall argue that nothing in the story

27. wĕgam nāmōgû kol-yōšĕbê hāʾāreṣ mippānênû (v. 24b) is a Deuteronomistic phrase that picks up the words of Rahab's speech: wĕkî nāmōgû kol-yōšĕbê hāʾāreṣ mippĕnêkem (v. 9bβ), the main piece of Deuteronomistic composition in the chapter (Tucker, "The Rahab Saga," 70).

28. Inter alia, Hugo Gressmann, Die Schriften des Alten Testaments in Auswahl I/2 (Göttingen: Vandenhoeck & Ruprecht, 1922) 136; Gustav Hölscher, "Zum Ursprung der Rahabsage," ZAW 38 (1919/20) 54–57; and Mowinckel, Tetrateuch, 13–15.

29. E.g., Soggin, Joshua, 36; Boling, Joshua, 144; J. Maxwell Miller and Gene M. Tucker, The Book of Joshua (Cambridge Bible Commentary; Cambridge: Cambridge University Press, 1974) 31.

suggests a hierodule and that, conversely, an understanding of Rahab as a harlot is essential to the story. I shall also argue that her portrayal as a heroine in no way cancels the negative social appraisal attached to her role as a harlot.

The narrator begins the account of the spies' mission with a deliberately suggestive lead sentence. "Go, view the land," the spies are instructed, and the report of their action immediately follows: "and they went and came to Jericho[30] and entered the house of a harlot (*bêt-ʾiššâ zônâ*), whose name was Rahab, and slept there (*wayyiškĕbû šāmmâ*)."[31] The place should probably be understood as an inn or public house, but the narrator clearly wishes to focus attention immediately on the connection with Rahab and especially on her occupation. Thus the designation *ʾiššâ zônâ* precedes the name as the determining expression following the noun "house." The language is obviously meant to suggest a brothel, and the following verb, *šākab*, reinforces the suggestion.[32]

The association of prostitutes with taverns or beer houses is well attested in Mesopotamian texts,[33] and it may be surmised that a similar association is assumed in our passage.

> As a prostitute he took her in from the street (and) supported her,
> as a prostitute he married her but gave her back (as separate property) her tavern. (*Ana ittišu* VIII, ii.23–25 [*CAD* Ḫ:102a])

30. See n. 25. Cf. LXX, which reads Jericho here, but also has a longer text.

31. There is no justification for RSV's "lodged," which eliminates the double entendre in the Hebrew. It rests, however, on ancient precedent; the Old Greek eliminated the sexual intimation by employing *kataluein* (LSJ), a verb that normally represents the Hebrew root *LWN/LYN* in LXX and is used only here to translate *ŠKB* (Hatch-Redpath).

32. *bêt zônâ* may be a technical term for a brothel. Cf. Jer 5:7, "they committed adultery and trooped to the harlot's house (*bêt zônâ*)"; Ezek 16:41, *wĕśārĕpû bāttayik bāʾēš . . . wĕhiš-battîk mizzônâ*: "they shall burn your houses . . .; I will make you stop playing the harlot" (the whole section, beginning in v. 35, is addressed to Israel as a harlot). If *bêt zônâ* is a technical term, then the insertion here of the word "woman" into the construct may represent a weakening of the term in the direction of an individual's house: it was the house of a woman who was a harlot—or a promiscuous woman. It is difficult to judge the force of *ʾiššâ zônâ*, which appears as a frequent variant of *zônâ* used alone. But however the compound term is interpreted, its use to identify the house can only be understood as provocative. See vv. 3 and 4 and n. 35 below.

The qualifying term *zônâ* is not used again in chap. 2. This is in keeping with the author's style in describing the roles of the main figures when they are first introduced (*ʾănāšîm mĕraggĕlîm* and *ʾiššâ zônâ*, v. 1) and thereafter referring to them simply as "the men" and "the woman." The qualifying role designations are employed again in chap. 6, where the characters are reintroduced.

33. See Thorkild Jacobsen and Samuel N. Kramer, "The Myth of Inanna and Bilulu," *JNES* 12 (1953) 176, l. 106, and 184 n. 68. Cf. also Eugen Bergmann, "Untersuchungen zu syllabisch geschriebenen sumerischen Texten," *ZA* 56 (1964) 2–3; A. Falkenstein, "Sumerische religiösche Texte," *ZA* 56 (1964) 118–19; and *CAD* A/II:473 (*aštammu*).

When I sit at the entrance of the tavern I (Ishtar) am a loving prostitute.[34] (SBH 106:51–53 [*CAD* Ḫ:101b])

Indirect testimony to this association comes from §110 of the Laws of
Hammurabi, which decrees death for the *nadītu* who enters a tavern.[35]
Since the *nadītu* belonged to a class of hierodules who were bound by a
rule of chastity and normally cloistered, the kind of activity associated
with the place is apparent. In our passage, the "house" is identified as
Rahab's and is clearly not her family home, since her parents and siblings
must be brought into *her* house in order to be saved (v. 18).[36] In view
of her profession, then, it is reasonable to view the house as her place
of business.

The narrator's words about the spies' approach to their task tantalizes
the reader and elicits speculation about the spies' motive and plan. How
is this action meant to serve their mission? What exactly do they think
they will do there? Do they hope to obtain information by sleeping with
a loose and, presumably, loose-tongued woman? Do they mean to bargain
for intelligence from a businesswoman who will sell anything for a price?
Or do they simply hope to overhear the talk of local citizens and travelers
who have gathered there or engage them in unguarded conversation over
a pitcher of beer? Whatever their precise plan of action may be, they have
chosen a natural place to begin their reconnaissance of the land. For the
inn, or public house, or brothel, provides them both access and cover. It
is a resting place for travelers and a gathering place for all sorts of persons
seeking diversion and contacts; strangers will not be conspicuous here and
motives will not be questioned. The proprietor's status also makes the
harlot's house a logical point of entry, for, as an outsider in her own community, the harlot might be expected to be more open, perhaps even sympathetic, to other outsiders than would her countrymen.

But if the spies have chosen their point of entry wisely, they have not

34. *ḫa-ri-im-tum raʾimtum.* A variant, written as a gloss, *šarraqitum:* "a female thief,"
gives testimony to the low repute of the place and of the classes associated with it.

35. The term here is *É-KURRUN(NA)* = *bit-kurrunim*(?): "tavern, ale-house" (cf. G. R.
Driver and John G. Miles, *The Babylonian Laws* [2 vols.; Oxford: Clarendon, 1955]), which
may be distinguished from the *É-EŠDAM* = *aštammu,* "inn." Jacobsen and Kramer ("Inanna
and Bilulu," 184–85 n. 68) argue that the latter should be understood as "Gasthaus mit Her-
berge" rather than "bordello," even though it was typically frequented by and owned by the
ḫarimtu (prostitute). They see it as "the social center of the state or village . . . a place in
which the inhabitants would typically gather for talk and recreation after the end of work"
(185 n. 68).

36. I take the references to her *bêt-ʾāb* in 2:12, 18 as ancient expansions of the basic story,
belonging to the etiological motif that comes to expression now in 6:17, 22-23, 25. A distinction must be made between her house and her "father's house" (= family or lineage). The
latter survives, the former does not.

gone unobserved. The king of Jericho has been informed of their entry and whereabouts and sends immediately to Rahab, requesting that she hand over the men who have entered her house. Instead, she hides the spies and shrewdly diverts the king's men with a false report. Here again the ambiguous language of entry/intercourse is employed, first by the king's messengers who command: "Bring out the men who were going in to you (*habbā'îm 'ēlayik*), who entered your house" (v. 3); and then by Rahab, who acknowledges: "They did indeed come in to me (*bā'û 'ēlay*)" (v. 4).[37] Thus sexual innuendo is not confined to the opening verses but pervades the whole first scene as an element of narrative intention. Rahab's action, however, contradicts the expectations aroused by the suggestive language, leaving the reader to speculate about her intentions.

At the end of the opening sentence the reader is meant to ask: Why did the spies go to a harlot's house and what did they do there? At the end of the first scene the reader is left with the question: Why did Rahab do what she did? The story has given us no reason to believe that there was any previous relationship between the two parties. What then can explain her action? The reader must speculate—and is invited to do so by the construction of the narrative. But the modern reader must speculate without the "feel" for the situation possessed by the ancient audience. Multiple motives and factors may be involved, either originally or as the result of editorial reinterpretation. Rahab's response may represent hostility to the king and his cohorts. Perhaps she has been harassed before about her establishment and its clients. If dangerous aliens are found on her premises, she will surely be penalized. Her action may then be interpreted as self-interest, an effort to save her own neck, and/or her business and reputation. Or is a connection to be seen in class affinity or class interest? Are we to understand her act as that of a social outcast among her own people protecting the representatives of an outcast people, an outcast people on the move, that may offer her a new future? I must admit that I find no element in the story to suggest the latter understanding, but I will leave the matter open.

In the present form of the narrative, the question of Rahab's motivation is answered in the following scene. In an eloquent speech, enhanced by the Deuteronomist, Rahab reveals to the spies, whom she has concealed on the roof, the meaning and purpose of her action. She has come to strike a bargain, and now she presents her terms; ḥesed for ḥesed, she requests, my life for yours. By her act of protection, here described as an act

---

37. The Old Greek lacks the suggestive first clause in v. 3. MT may be conflate, but the echoing language of v. 4 is assumed by all of the versions and thus is firmly fixed in the tradition.

of *ḥesed*, she has established a bond of obligation with the spies. Now she seeks their protection when they shall be in a position to give it, an act of *ḥesed* on their part, since they are now morally obligated, though not legally bound.[38] Her speech begins with a confession of Yahweh's mighty acts toward Israel and concludes with a request for an oath of assurance from representatives of Yahweh's people.[39] The scene ends with the spies' oath.

In the final scene, Rahab enables the spies to escape by letting them down through a window in the wall, in which she ties a scarlet cord as a sign to the attacking Israelites, so that they will recognize and spare her house. The outcome of this encounter—viz., the saving of all who were in the harlot's house—is reported in chapter 6, with the etiological note that Rahab "dwelt in Israel to this day" (6:25).

This account supplies us with further information about the harlot in Israel's understanding and corroborates features noted in other ancient Near Eastern texts and in comparative studies. She lives on the outer periphery of the city, where other outcast and low-caste groups or professions are commonly located in the ancient city. Her house in the wall (near to the city gate?) would be readily accessible to travelers and easily located. Was the red cord a permanent sign of an ancient red-light district, or only specific to this narrative?[40]

It has been argued on the basis of this story that no censure or stigma was attached to the harlot in early Israel—or in Canaanite society—in contrast to later Israel. But this argument misreads the story. The entire account depends upon Rahab's marginal status, in both Canaanite and Israelite societies. Her descendants, persisting in later Israel, form a distinct group, the strange tolerance of which is "explained" by the etiology of the harlot's loyalty. And it is only because she is an outcast that the men of Israel have access to her (an "honorable" woman would not meet alone with strange men). The narrator has drawn upon popular understanding of the harlot's profession and reputation in the construction of the story

38. Katharine Doob Sakenfeld, *The Meaning of Hesed in the Hebrew Bible: A New Inquiry* (HSM 17; Missoula, Mont.: Scholars Press, 1978) 64–70.

39. The oath has been commonly understood in recent literature as a covenant oath (e.g., Boling, *Joshua*, 147 n. 12). But there is no reference here, or in chap. 6, to a covenant, despite recognizable similarities between this story and the story of the Gibeonites. The oath here functions as a guarantee that the spies will honor their promise to Rahab to spare her family when they take control of the city.

40. The initial reference to the cord in the phrase, "a strand of *this* scarlet cord" (v. 18), suggests that it is already known and associated with the house (though it could also be understood as something brought by the spies). One may surmise that a sign, ordinarily associated with the house in one capacity, has been reinterpreted in the story, giving it a new meaning and function.

and deliberately elicits that understanding in his opening words, which place the whole of the subsequent action in a harlot's house. The associations that operate in this story are many and complex, and may never be fully determined by the modern reader, but understanding requires some attempt at specification.

The prostitute's low social status and low reputation are essential, and related, features. The reader does not expect anything from her, or at least not anything of moral strength, courage, or insight. For she is the lowest of the low and, as Jeremiah's search illustrates, Israel did not expect much from the lowly (Jer 5:4-5). The harlot is viewed as lacking in wisdom, morals, and religious knowledge. Her low status and despised state must be due either to unfortunate circumstance or personal fault, and neither, I think, would elicit much sympathy or charity from an ancient audience. The harlot may be a victim, but she is commonly viewed as a predator, preying on the weakness of men, a mercenary out for her own gain, an opportunist with no loyalty beyond herself, acknowledging no principle or charity in her actions.

These attributes in an enemy may serve the Israelite spies well, though the game they would play with her is a risky one. The story requires no positive assessment of the harlot, no counter to the common portrait, to explain the initial action of the spies nor, I have suggested, to explain Rahab's action in saving them. For although the harlot lacks wisdom in the popular view, she lives by her wits. She is a shrewd and calculating operator, and men must beware her tricks. Self-interest (here broadened to include her kindred) still plays an important role in the final form of the story and may have played a larger role in the pre-Deuteronomistic version. But while essential to the construction of the tale, it is not the decisive motive. The present form of the story builds on a reversal of expectations. The negative presuppositions are required precisely for their contribution to that reversal.

Rahab does not act as we expect her to act when she protects the spies. Self-interest alone cannot explain her commitment, for the risk of siding with an unknown force against one's own people is too great to ascribe solely to that motive. Either faith or discernment, or both, is required to explain such unproved loyalty (*ḥesed*), and for that there is no place in the ruling stereotype of the harlot. But if the harlot as heroine involves a conflict of expectations, it is also a recognizable subtype of the harlot in literature (and presumably also in life), a romantic antitype to the dominant image: the whore with the heart of gold, the harlot who saves the city, the courtesan who sacrifices for her patron.[41] Her action, which is praise-

---

41. The motif is widespread. I have seen examples from Chinese as well as European literature. For a parallel from classical literature, see below.

worthy in itself, is the more so for being unexpected and unsolicited. In her display of loyalty, courage, and altruism, she acts out of keeping with her assumed character as a harlot and thus reveals her true character as a person. But this does not normally lead to a change in her status, or a change in attitudes toward harlots. The determining negative image of the harlot is not fundamentally challenged by the counterimage, but maintained. For the harlot is never allowed to become a good wife, but only a good harlot, a righteous outcast, a noble-hearted courtesan, the exception that proves the rule—just as Robin Hood does not define the type of the bandit, but only the antitype.

Rahab is a heroine because she protects the Israelite spies and, as a consequence, contributes to Israel's victory. If the LXX preserves an original variant, she may have been credited originally with enabling the Israelites to breach the wall and hence with handing over her city to the invaders, a motif which is closely paralleled in two classical texts pointed out by Hans Windisch.[42] In the present form and setting of the story, the deliverance of the city to Israel is attributed to Yahweh's miraculous action, and Rahab's role is that of an oracle rather than an instrument of that action (her deliverance of the spies may be taken as a kind of proleptic sign of Israel's victory). The Deuteronomistic redaction of the chapter has made Rahab's speech the center of the story. Rahab is here the pagan confessor, the one who discerns what others fail to see, and the one who commits her life to the people of Yahweh. She is wiser than the king of Jericho, and also more clever. Like the lowly Hebrew midwives, she outwits the king. Like them, she is bold in rejecting an unrighteous command. Like them, she is given a house and a name in Israel and a story to perpetuate her memory, while the king she opposed remains nameless and forgotten.

The Israelite author has made of the harlot of Jericho a hero of faith and a friend of Israel. I have assumed that the story depends on a reversal

---

42. Hans Windisch, "Zur Rahabgeschichte (Zwei Parallelen aus der klassischen Literatur)," *ZAW* 37 (1917/18) 188–98. Windisch argued that the Rahab story should be seen as one example of a type in which a city is delivered from its enemies (external or internal) by a prostitute and the memory of her action is perpetuated by etiological legend. His two classical parallels include a Roman and a Greek legend, the former concerning a prostitute of Capua who remained loyal to Rome when the city fell to Punic invaders, the latter a hierodule of Abydos (referred to as both *hetaira* and *pornē* in the account) who enabled her countrymen to retake the city from enemy occupation.

Windisch notes a common attitude displayed in the transmission of the two stories that honor a common prostitute. As Christian and Jewish interpretation have traditionally shown embarrassment over Rahab's profession and the absence of censure in the biblical narrative, a similar attitude is evident in the Roman tradition in which wonder was expressed at the Senate's action (granting freedom and restoration of possessions) on behalf of a woman of low repute. In the case of Rahab, tradition elevated her by suppressing knowledge of her occupation or making her a convert, allowing her to be a heroine only as an ex-harlot (Windisch, "Rahabgeschichte," 188–92).

of expectations. Others have argued that it could also be explained by
unnoted affinities, by positive expectations that might serve to qualify the
predominantly negative expectations of the harlot. A parallel might be
drawn by the narrator—and an affinity recognized—between the low or
outcast estate of the harlot of Jericho and the low and outcast estate of the
band of escaped slaves beyond the Jordan. While Israel's petition to the
kings in the Transjordan was met only by uncomprehending belligerence,
their approach to the harlot of Jericho elicits immediate reception and a
pledge of support. Rahab knows what the kings do not know, that the
Lord is with this outlaw band and no power can stand against them. And
so the wise harlot sides with the outcasts whose day is dawning on the
eastern horizon. I find that construction theologically appealing, but I
cannot now find historical or literary evidence that would convince me of
its plausibility.

The story of Rahab depicts a figure identified with a Canaanite milieu,
and a group identified by her name, persisting, anomalously, in later Israel. I find no suggestion of cultic identification either in the narrative of
Joshua 2 or in the etiological note of Joshua 6. It is a clan legend, not a
cult legend, memorializing an individual and her family, not a sanctuary
or cultic institution. An Israelite lineage, not a class of hierodules, traces
its ancestry to this heroine. The harlot designation of its eponym suggests
an outcast status for the group, which requires explanation. The story
provides the explanation: it was because of the *ḥesed* of Rahab toward our
ancestors that her clan dwells among us today.

1 Kings 3:16-27

If the harlot of Joshua 2 and the supposed harlot of Genesis 38 are depicted
in Canaanite settings, the existence of prostitution as a recognized institution in Israel is also well attested.[43] Relative incidence is impossible to
judge and so are changes in attitudes. If Israelite religion censured the
institution, it was still accompanied by the same attitudes of ambivalence
displayed in cultures more open to its acceptance. And the basic stereotypes and presuppositions still hold, as we can see from various biblical
witnesses. An instructive example from the period of the monarchy is
found in the famous story of Solomon's judgment (1 Kgs 3:16-27).[44]

43. The term *zônâ* is used in the following texts relating to the period of the monarchy
or later: Lev 21:7, 14; Deut 23:19; 1 Kgs 3:16; Isa 1:21; 23:15, 16; Jer 3:3; 5:7; Ezek 16:30, 31, 33, 35,
41; 23:44; Hos 4:14; Joel 4:3; Mic 1:7 (bis); Nah 3:4; Prov 6:26; 7:10; 1 Kgs 22:38; Prov 23:27; 29:3.
44. This story has long been recognized as having the character of popular tradition or
folktale and constituting a distinct literary unit. See Hugo Gressmann, "Das Salomonische
Urteil," *Deutsche Rundschau* 130 (1907) 212-28; John Gray, *I and II Kings: A Commentary* (2d

The story concerns a case of rival claims brought by two harlots (*nāšîm zōnôt*, v. 16) who are described as living together in one house, probably to be understood as a brothel because of the reference to "strangers" in v. 18.[45] Both give birth, according to the story, within three days of each other. The women are alone at the time with no others[46] in the house—an unlikely situation in a normal household, but one essential to the story and the case it presents; for as they are harlots and as they are alone, there are no witnesses to the incident they describe, and no husbands or kinsmen to defend the claims of the women or to arbitrate for them. Thus it is a case of one woman's word against another, and more specifically, one harlot's word against another, that is, the words of women whose word cannot be trusted. For the harlot is characterized in the ruling stereotype as a woman of smooth and self-serving speech. One does not expect truth from such as these. And so the case that is presented to Solomon is a case to test the wisest judge. The harlot plaintiffs assure that.

As the case is laid out before the king, the child of the one dies and she substitutes the child of the other for it. Each now claims the living child as her own, and Solomon must judge whose claim is true. Here Solomon's wisdom is displayed, for he does not attempt to discern the truth through interrogation—a hopeless approach with habitual liars. His wisdom lies in recognizing a condition that will compel the truth. The story—and Solomon's action—appeals to another stereotype of the woman, that of the mother, who is bound by the deepest emotional bonds to the fruit of her womb. That bond will not lie. And so Solomon orders a sword to be brought and the child to be divided between the two claimants. At this the true mother reveals herself by relinquishing her claim in order to spare her child.

Again I would argue that the story does not reveal a generally accepting

---

ed.; OTL; Philadelphia: Westminster, 1970) 114–16, 127–29; Martin Noth, *Könige* 1 (BKAT 9/ 1; Neukirchen-Vluyn: Neukirchener Verlag, 1969) 44–48; and James A. Montgomery, *A Critical and Exegetical Commentary on the Books of Kings* (ICC; Edinburgh: T. & T. Clark, 1951) 108–10.

45. Presumably prostitutes withdrew from active work during advanced stages of pregnancy. Unfortunately, we know virtually nothing about the working conditions of prostitutes in ancient Israel, means of contraception that may have been employed, or arrangements for raising (or disposing of) children. From the story of Jephthah we learn that although he was the son of a harlot, he was apparently raised in his father's household or was at least recognized by his father as a son and potential heir (Judg 11:1-2). The prohibition of priests from marrying harlots (Lev 21:7, 14) implicitly recognizes the practice by others. One may surmise that a man might marry a harlot who had borne him a child, especially a son.

46. The Hebrew *zār* (v. 18), meaning "stranger," one outside the family. It may be assumed from the fact that they were harlots living together that there would be no husbands present, or other members of a normal family. The use of the word "stranger" here refers, presumably, to clients.

attitude toward harlots, as some have argued, but depends, rather, on their marginal status and their reputation for lying and self-interest. It is these commonly held presuppositions about the harlot that make this case an ideal test, one by which extraordinary wisdom might be demonstrated. For the audience is meant to see only two prostitutes, but Solomon in his wisdom sees what is hidden by that stereotype, namely, a mother. In this case two counterimages operate, which are normally distinct but are here combined in a single figure. The case is built on the one and resolved on the other.

What I have tried to do in these three examples is to draw out the picture of the prostitute that was operative in each and show how it functioned in the narrative. The author has reckoned in each case with the attitudes and presuppositions that would be called forth from his audience by the use of the term *zônâ*. These presuppositions are, for the most part, subtle and complex and are commonly missed or misread by modern readers who mistake narrative interest for social status, and role in the story for role in life. The harlot heroine, or protagonist, remains a harlot. She is lifted for a moment, as an individual, into the spotlight by the storyteller, but her place remains in the shadows of Israelite society.

10

"TO PLAY THE HARLOT":

An Inquiry into an Old
Testament Metaphor

THIS ESSAY EXPLORES A NUMBER OF PROBLEMS RELATED TO THE translation and interpretation of the Hebrew root *ZNH*, with particular attention to its metaphorical or figurative use.[1] It is prompted by problems in translation and definition, difficulties in determining the boundary between literal and figurative uses, and interest in the use of a metaphor drawn, apparently, from female behavior to characterize the behavior of collective Israel.

The translation "play the harlot" is RSV's conventional rendering of the Hebrew verb *zānâ*, in both literal and figurative uses, replacing the familiar but archaic "go awhoring" or "commit whoredom" of KJV. Unlike the "whoring" language which may describe either male or female activity

Originally published in Peggy L. Day, ed., *Gender and Difference in Ancient Israel* (Minneapolis: Fortress Press, 1989) 75–94. Cross-references to articles that are reprinted in this volume are indicated by an asterisk in square brackets following the original page number.

1. It presents preliminary and abbreviated arguments from a larger study in progress, titled provisionally "Harlot and Hierodule in Israelite Anthropology and Theology." In many cases the length and format of the present essay do not permit full argumentation or documentation of critical points, for which the reader is referred to the forthcoming work.

The only major study of the root is the unpublished Ph.D. dissertation of Oral E. Collins, "The Stem *ZNH* and Prostitution in the Hebrew Bible" (Brandeis, 1977; University Microfilms International 77-13364), which, in my view, has serious flaws in literary-linguistic and sociological analysis. A superior, though less exhaustive, treatment is given by M. Hooks in chap. 3 of his dissertation, "Sacred Prostitution in Israel and the Ancient Near East" (Hebrew Union College, 1985) 65–151. The best summary treatment is that of Seth Erlandsson, "*zānāh*," *TDOT* 4: 99–104; cf. J. Kühlewein, "*ZNH*, huren," *THAT* 1: 518–20. See also articles on prostitution or "sacred prostitution" and commentaries, especially Friedrich Hauck and Siegfried Schulz, "*pórnē, pórnos, porneía, porneúō, ekporneúō*," *TDNT* 6: 579–95; W. Kornfeld, "L'adultère dans l'Orient antique," *RB* 57 (1950) 92–109; and Jes Peter Asmussen, "Bemerkungen zur sakralen Prostitution im Alten Testament," *ST* 11 (1958) 167–92.

("to have unlawful sexual intercourse *as* or *with* a whore"),[2] the "denominative" rendering of RSV defines the behavior by reference to a female model. Both translations, however, share an orientation toward the professional prostitute. Is this a peculiarity of English idiom or does it represent the Hebrew understanding? A primary question for investigation must be the relationship of verbal uses to the noun *zônâ* ("prostitute"). Another question concerns the meaning of the verb when used with a masculine subject.[3] Most of the examples represent clearly metaphorical uses, describing pursuit of other gods (Judg 2:17; 8:33; Deut 31:11) or participation in illicit cultic activity (Lev 20:5; 17:7; Judg 8:27). In Num 25:1, however, the usual cultic and metaphorical interpretations are strained and the translation of RSV appears ludicrous: "While Israel dwelt at Shittim the people (*hā'ām*) began to play the harlot (*wayyāḥel . . . liznôt*) with the daughters of Moab." Is the usage here figurative or literal, or does it represent some other type of extended use?[4]

A further question is raised by the common identification of prostitution and "sacred or cultic prostitution." The assumption of such an institution as a pervasive and constitutive feature of Canaanite religion is fundamental to most interpretations of the root *ZNH* and discussions of "fertility cult religion."[5] Although the institution is construed in different ways, the term by which it is designated is never called into question. Yet the concept expressed by combining words for "sacred" (or "cultic") and "prostitution" is not found in the Hebrew Bible or in any ancient Semitic language.

From biblical Hebrew and Akkadian sources we know only of "prostitutes" (Heb. *zônâ;* Akk. *ḥarîmtu*) and "sacred/consecrated women" (Heb. *qĕdēšâ;* Akk. *qadištu*) along with other classes of female cult functionaries (*ēn/ēntu, nadītu, ugbabtu, ištarītu, kulmašītu*).[6] While prostitutes *may* have functioned at times in the cultic sphere (in which case the circumstances

---

2. *Webster's Seventh New Collegiate Dictionary* (Springfield, Mass.: G. & C. Merriam, 1972).

3. The examples cited below are all of the *qal* (basic) stem. The *hiphil* (8 times, all masc.) functions in most cases as a causative of the *qal;* on its use in Hosea see below.

4. Collins saw the problem of determining literal and figurative uses as one of the primary methodological problems in previous treatments of the root ("The Stem *ZNH*," 13–17).

5. See Hooks, "Sacred Prostitution," for a comprehensive review (survey of theories, 1–4) and critique of this assumption.

6. The functions of the women designated by these terms (which have limited geographical and chronological distribution) are still poorly understood. See J. Renger, "Untersuchungen zum Priestertum in der altbabylonischen Zeit," *ZA* 58 (1967) 114–87; R. Harris, "The NADĪTU Woman," in *Studies Presented to A. Leo Oppenheim* (Chicago: University of Chicago Press, 1964); and Hooks, "Sacred Prostitution," 10–23.

require careful attention) and while hierodules[7] *may* have had functions
or duties involving sexual activity (here too the circumstances require
careful attention), the terms used in the indigenous languages to describe
these two classes never connect the sacred sphere with prostitution or
prostitution with the cult.[8] It is only through association that the interpretation arises, and it is only in the Hebrew Bible that the association is
made in a deliberate manner. It would appear then that the identification
is the result of a specifically biblical and, I shall argue, polemical interpretation.[9]

In the limited scope of this essay it is impossible to give attention to all
of the interlocking issues that affect interpretation of this root and its
unique metaphorical employment in the Hebrew Bible. I shall begin with
a summary treatment of the primary meaning(s) of the root and then
move to a detailed examination of selected texts in the book of Hosea,
which appear to represent the earliest metaphorical usage.

ZNH/zônâ

The basic meaning of the root as expressed in the verb *zānâ* is "to engage
in sexual relations outside of or apart from marriage,"[10] activity that is
normally understood as illicit; hence the primary definition of BDB:
"commit fornication."[11] In relation to *N'P*, "commit adultery," with which
it is often associated and may at times coincide, *ZNH* is the more general
or inclusive term. Cognate usage (Aramaic, Ethiopic, and Arabic) exhibits
a similar broad meaning, especially evident in Arabic *zanā* "to commit

7. I use the Greek term, meaning "temple slave," as a convenient and arbitrary class term
for all nonpriestly cultic personnel, since the languages in question lack a single designation.
8. Cf. Collins, "The Stem *ZNH*," 33–34; Hooks, "Sacred Prostitution," 10–45 and 152–85.
9. The idea may also have arisen independently in classical sources. It has certainly been
nourished by the sensationalist accounts of Herodotus (*History* 1.199) and Lucian (*De Dea
Syria* §16) describing the strange religious and sexual customs of the Babylonians and Phoe-
nicians. Neither, however, uses the expression "sacred prostitution" in their descriptions of
practices, which they refer to the general female population, not to professional prostitutes
or hierodules. See Hooks, "Sacred Prostitution," 32–36, 40–41.
10. So also Erlandsson, "*zānāh*," 100; followed by Hooks, "Sacred Prostitution," 70.
11. BDB also gives as a second basic meaning "be a harlot." In its classification of uses,
however, it lists as 1. "*be or act as a harlot*," offering the alternative "commit fornication" only
for Num 25:1, specified as a "man's act." Further categories are 2. "fig. *of improper intercourse
with foreign nations*," 3. "*of intercourse with other deities*, considered as harlotry, sts. involving
actual prostitution," and 4. "*zwnh* of moral defection" (only Isa 1:21). The *pual* and *hiphil*
uses are all defined in terms of "fornication," further classified as "sexual" or "religious." Cf.
HALAT, 1:263–64.

adultery, fornicate, whore" (cf. *zinan* and *zinā'*, "adultery, fornication"; *zānin*, "fornicator, adulterer"; *zāniya*, "whore, harlot, adulteress").[12]

As a general term for extramarital sexual intercourse, *ZNH* is limited in its primary usage to female subjects, since it is only for women that marriage is the primary determinant of legal status and obligation. While male sexual activity is judged by the status of the female partner and is prohibited, or penalized, only when it violates the recognized marital rights of another male, female sexual activity is judged according to the woman's marital status. In Israel's moral code, a woman's sexuality was understood to belong to her husband alone, for whom it must be reserved in anticipation of marriage as well as in the marriage bond. Violation of a husband's sexual rights, the most serious of sexual offenses, is signified by the term *N'P*, "adultery"; all other instances of sexual intercourse apart from marriage are designated by the term *ZNH*.[13] These include premarital sex by a daughter, understood as an offense against her father or family (Heb. *bêt 'āb*, "father's house"), whose honor requires her chastity (Deut 22:13-21; Lev 21:9; cf. Gen 34:31); or sex by a levirate-obligated widow (Gen 38:6-11, 24-26), understood as an offense against her father-in-law or her deceased husband's family.[14]

It also includes the activity of the professional prostitute, who has no husband nor sexual obligation to any other male. Herein lies a critical distinction. Whereas the promiscuity of a daughter or levirate-obligated widow offends the male to whom each is subject, and is penalized accordingly, the harlot's activity violates no man's rights or honor, and is consequently free from the sanctions imposed on the casual fornicator. Strictly speaking, her activity is not illicit—and neither is her role.[15]

The distinction between the two classes of activity (fornication and prostitution) described by the common root *ZNH* is strikingly illustrated by the account of Judah's reaction to Tamar in two episodes of the narra-

12. Hans Wehr, in J. Milton Cowan, ed., *A Dictionary of Modern Written Arabic* (Ithaca, N.Y.: Cornell University Press, 1961). See further Collins, "The Stem *ZNH*," 4–12; Hooks, "Sacred Prostitution," 67–69.

13. *ZNH* is not used for incest or other prohibited relationships, such as homosexual relations or bestiality. It focuses on the absence of a marriage bond between otherwise acceptable partners.

14. Although Tamar is living in her father's house as a widow (Gen 38:11), she is identified as Judah's daughter-in-law in the critical scene when she is accused of "playing the harlot" (v. 24). For a fuller discussion of this case, see my article, "The Harlot as Heroine: Narrative Art and Social Presupposition in Three Old Testament Texts," in Miri Amihai, George W. Conts, and Anne M. Solomon, eds., *Narrative Research on the Hebrew Bible* (*Semeia* 46; Atlanta: Scholars Press, 1989) 119–39 [*197–218].

15. On the legal and social status of the prostitute, see below and Bird, "The Harlot as Heroine"; cf. Susan Niditch, "The Wronged Woman Righted: An Analysis of Genesis 38," *HTR* 72 (1979) 147.

tive in Genesis 38. In the first, he embraces a woman whom he identifies as a *zônâ* (v. 15, RSV: "he thought her to be a harlot"); in the second he condemns to death a woman whose activity is identified by the verb *zānâ* (v. 24, RSV: "your daughter-in-law has played the harlot [*zānĕtâ*]"). The irony of the situation, on which the story turns, is that the two women are one, and so too is their action. But it is construed differently according to the perceived circumstances, more particularly, according to the sociolegal status of the woman involved. In the first instance, *ZNH* describes the woman's profession ("he thought her to be a harlot"), and consequently her status—as an ostracized but tolerated purveyor of sexual favors for men. In the second, *ZNH* describes the activity of a woman whose sociolegal status ("your daughter-in-law" [*kallātĕkā*]) makes such activity a crime.

Hebrew linguistic usage links the fornicator and the prostitute, but it also distinguishes them, by syntactic and contextual means. A proper understanding of the root *ZNH* and its usage in the Hebrew Bible requires careful and discriminating attention to linguistic, literary, and sociological factors that determine meaning.

The Hebrew term for "prostitute," *zônâ*, is the *qal* feminine participle of the verb *zānâ*, used as a noun of profession either alone (*[haz]zônâ*, "[the] prostitute") or in apposition to *'iššâ* "woman" (*'iššâ zônâ*, "a prostitute woman").[16] Thus in Hebrew conception the prostitute is "essentially" a professional or habitual fornicator, a promiscuous or unchaste woman, whose role and profession are defined by her sexual activity with men to whom she is not married. The noun represents a special case of the activity denoted by the *qal* verb. Despite this apparent relationship of dependence, however, virtually all discussions of the root reverse the order of influence, pointing to prostitution as the determining content of the verbal usage and thereby perpetuating the fixation on the professional model exhibited in the common English translations "play the harlot" and "go awhoring."[17] Is such a shift justified, and under what conditions?

The semantic relationship between the verbal and nominal uses of the root is, in fact, complex, affected in part at least by the figurative usage which dominates in the Hebrew Bible and invites interchange. Once the

16. Cf. Benjamin Kedar-Kopfstein, "Semantic Aspects of the Pattern *qōtēl*," *Hebrew Annual Review* 1 (1977) 158, 164–65.

17. A major problem with Collins's study ("The Stem *ZNH*") is his understanding of the root in its "primary, literal sense" as referring to "actual prostitution" (13). As a result, he can only ask what *kind* of prostitution (secular or sacred) it designates and whether it is literal or figurative. Cf. Hooks, "Sacred Prostitution," 70. Francis I. Andersen and David Noel Freedman (*Hosea* [AB 24; Garden City, N.Y.: Doubleday, 1980] 160) appear to be alone in challenging the common English interpretations.

participle has become the identifying term for the prostitute, this specialized usage may exercise a secondary or "reverse" influence on the verb.
The verb may be understood to describe the exercise of the profession
(Amos 7:17), or it may acquire connotations and associations that were
originally peculiar to the noun. Nevertheless, the basic meaning of the
verb as describing fornication or illicit extramarital relations should be
the starting point for interpreting any given use.

Another factor contributing to the problems of determining the meaning of the root is inadequate sociological analysis of the phenomenon of
prostitution. The figure designated by the Hebrew participle *zônâ* represents a recognized institution, known throughout the ancient Near East
and most urban cultures, whose relatively constant features can be described and analyzed quite apart from the terminology used for it in any
given language or culture.[18] Thus while Hebrew linguistic usage gives important clues to Israel's understanding of prostitution, it does not suffice
to describe the nature of the institution or how it functioned. It is the
historically functioning institution, however, with all of its associations,
that supplies the content of the term *zônâ*, not the etymology. What is
needed is a sociologically adequate account of the institution as it functioned in ancient Israel. This is especially urgent in view of the widespread
assumption of an analogous or allied institution in the sacred sphere likewise identified by the term "prostitution."

In lieu of that needed account a few words of analysis must suffice.
Prostitution shares with fornication, as defined in Israel, a fundamentally
female profile,[19] despite the fact that both activities require active male
participation and may involve male initiation (cf. Gen 38:15-16). This
asymmetry of conception and description is a characteristic feature of patriarchal societies, reflecting a general pattern of asymmetry in gender-
related roles, values, and obligations (a phenomenon recognized in a more
limited way by the notion of the "double standard"). The anomaly of the
prostitute as a tolerated specialist in an activity prohibited to every other
woman is a particular feature of patriarchal society, representing an
accommodation to the conflicting desires of men for exclusive control

18. See Bird, "The Harlot as Heroine," 120–21 [*194–201]; John H. Gagnon, "Prostitu-
tion," in David L. Sills, ed., *The International Encyclopedia of the Social Sciences* (New York:
Macmillan and Free Press, 1968) 12:592–98; Paul Henry Gebhard, "Prostitution," *The New
Encyclopedia Britannica* (15th ed.; Chicago: University of Chicago Press, 1980) 15:75–81; and
Vern L. and Bonnie Bullough, *Women and Prostitution: A Social History* (Buffalo, N.Y.: Pro-
metheus, 1987).

19. The prostitute has no male counterpart; male prostitution, which was homosexual,
was a limited phenomenon and is poorly attested in our sources. There is no masculine
noun corresponding to *zônâ*, which is paired with *keleb*, "dog," in Deut 23:19.

of their wives' sexuality (and hence offspring)[20] and, at the same time, for sexual access to other women. The greater the inaccessibility of women in the society as a result of restrictions on the wife and unmarried nubile woman, the greater the need for an institutionally legitimized "other woman." The prostitute is that "other woman," tolerated but stigmatized, desired but ostracized. As I have attempted to show elsewhere, attitudes toward prostitution are characterized by ambivalence in every society, and the biblical evidence does not support the notion of a sharp distinction between Israelite and Canaanite society with respect to the prostitute's legal or social status.[21]

In my analysis, neither the verb *zānâ* nor the noun *zônâ* in their primary uses refers to cultic activity or has cultic connotations. Where then does the cultic interpretation arise, and under what conditions? Does it represent Israelite understanding or is it an interpreter's imposition? I shall limit attention to three linked texts in the book of Hosea, which represent, I believe, the primary literary and religio-historical context for the development of the figurative usage. The discussion must remain partial and tentative, since the key texts contain multiple interlocking problems of interpretation, some unresolved and others incapable of summary treatment. I have chosen, nevertheless, to begin with these texts, because I believe they are critical and because they illustrate a number of different interpretive problems.

The Birth of a Metaphor: ZNH in the Book of Hosea

The opening words of the book present a sign-action that introduces the governing metaphor of chapters 1–3 and the theme of the collected oracles, articulated by use of the root *ZNH* (1:2).[22] Hosea is commanded to get a "woman/wife of promiscuity" (*'ēšet zěnûnîm*) and "offspring/children of promiscuity" (*yaldê zěnûnîm*), "because the land is utterly promiscuous (turning) away from Yahweh" (*kî-zānōh tizneh hā'āreṣ mē'aḥărê yhwh*). The prophet is to represent by his marriage and family life Yahweh's relationship to Israel as a relationship subverted by Israel's promiscuous behavior. The use of *ZNH* in the interpretive *kî* ("for, because") clause is clearly figurative, with the land (grammatically feminine) replacing the

---

20. Collins emphasizes male concern for legitimacy of offspring as the primary motive in identifying activity by *ZNH* ("The Stem *ZNH*," 263).

21. "The Harlot as Heroine," cn: 121–22, 125, 130–31 [*199–201, 206, 213–14].

22. For basic literary and historical analysis, see Andersen and Freedman, *Hosea;* James Luther Mays, *Hosea* (OTL; Philadelphia: Westminster, 1969); and Hans Walter Wolff, *Hosea: A Commentary on the Book of the Prophet Hosea* (trans. Gary Stansell; Hermeneia; Philadelphia: Fortress Press, 1974).

usual female subject. Although the underlying metaphor is that of marriage, the use of *ZNH* rather than *N'P* serves to emphasize promiscuity rather than infidelity, "wantonness" rather than violation of marriage contract or covenant. The connotations of repeated, habitual, or characteristic behavior are reinforced by the emphatic verbal augment (*zānōh*) and by repetition of the noun *zĕnûnîm* ("promiscuity, fornication") to characterize both the wife and the children.

The woman is not described as a *zônâ*, although most commentators speak inaccurately of Hosea's marriage to a harlot.[23] Rather, as an *'ēšet zĕnûnîm* she is characterized as a woman of loose sexual morals, whose promiscuous nature is exhibited in her "fornications" (*zĕnûnîm*). The use of the abstract plural noun points to habitual behavior and inclination rather than profession (cf. *rûaḥ zĕnûnîm*, "spirit of promiscuity," 4:12; 5:4). It is also open to extended or figurative meanings. In fact, the pairing of "woman of promiscuity" with "children of promiscuity" would appear to point in that direction, since, as we have seen, fornication normally describes a woman's activity. What sense can it make applied to the children?

Although *zĕnûnîm* can be understood to refer to the woman in both expressions and thus to characterize the children as the product of her promiscuous activity ("children [born] of promiscuity"), the mimicking construction of the paired terms and the linkage without an intervening verb suggest that the author intended to claim for the children the same nature as their mother. The message of the sign-action, enunciated in the following *kî* clause and elaborated in chapter 2, is that the land "fornicates"—and so do its inhabitants (children). The identification and interchange between mother and children, land and people is clear in chapter 2, where the mother's pursuit of her lovers is equated with cultic activities of the general population—and especially males. Thus mother and children should not be sharply differentiated.

What then does *zĕnûnîm* mean when applied to the children? I suggest that the term be read in its incongruous "literal" (but abstract) sense. The function of the sign-act is to shock, and intimate, and confound—and more particularly to point forward to the explanation that follows. As in other prophetic sign-actions, the sign depends on the interpretive word for its meaning and is chosen and/or formulated in the light of the intended message. The message in this case is that the land is unfaithful to Yahweh—like a promiscuous wife and promiscuous children. The charac-

---

23. Cf. JB "marry a whore, and get children with a whore"; NAB "a harlot wife and harlot's children." In contrast, Wolff argues that the term describes activity in the popular sex cult of the day and thus characterizes the woman as an "average, 'modern' Israelite woman" (*Hosea*, 14–15).

terization of the wife by *zĕnûnîm* makes sense as literal description (even if it raises questions of plausibility), but the duplicate characterization of the children must be heard as strange and enigmatic, raising a question about the meaning of both uses. That, I think, is exactly what it was meant to do, opening the way to the explanation that follows. But the explanation is as enigmatic as the action it interprets. What does it mean to say that the land "fornicates"?

The meaning of the charge is revealed only in chapter 2, to which it points and on which it depends.[24] The implication, however, is clear: the land (people) has relations with other lovers in place of (*mē'aḥărê*, lit. "from after/behind") Yahweh. The logical supposition is that the "affairs" are with other gods, although 1:2 does not identify the object(s) of Israel's affections. It points, rather, to the aggrieved husband, with a construction that is unique to Hosea. The sequence *zānâ + min/mē*, "(away) from," occurs only in Hosea and Ps 73:27, and appears to be dictated by the marriage metaphor to which Hosea has adapted his usage. Normally *zānâ* does not carry the notion of infidelity, which is supplied by the context and made explicit here by Hosea's inventive construction. In each of the three occurrences of the sequence in Hosea (1:2; 4:12; 9:1) the *min* is compounded with another preposition that serves to connect the statement to a following expression. In the case of *mē'aḥărê* the expression that explains the usage is found in 2:5 (cf. v. 13),[25] where the charge of fornication (*zānĕtâ 'immām*, "their mother ZNH-ed") is interpreted by the quotation, "For she said, 'I will go *after* (*'aḥărê*) my lovers.'" The preposition "after" belongs to the idiom *hālak 'aḥărê*, "walk after," "follow." Hosea has appropriated it to describe, in a privative construction (*zānâ min*), the relationship to the one abandoned.

The charge of fornication that opens the book is elaborated in an extended allegory in 2:2-13 (Heb. 4-15), which develops the figure of the promiscuous bride and points to the activity underlying the metaphor. The opening accusation employs the mother-children metaphor and *zānâ/ zĕnûnîm* language of 1:2, and likewise identifies mother and land (2:3; cf. v. 12). In v. 5b the summary charge of promiscuity (v. 5a) is substantiated with a quotation from the accused:

> For she said, "I will go after my lovers,
> who give me my bread and my water,
> my wool and my flax, my oil and my drink."

24. Cf. commentaries and Gale Yee, *Composition and Tradition in the Book of Hosea: A Redactional Investigation* (SBLDS 102; Atlanta: Scholars Press, 1987).
25. Heb. 2:7, 15. To avoid cumbersome double notation, only the RSV numbering is given for verse references in chap. 2.

The picture presented in these words is that of a woman who seeks lovers for their gifts, called specifically "hire" ('etnâ)[26] in v. 12. Here the metaphor points to the figure of the professional prostitute, who is distinguished from the casual fornicator by her mercenary motive and multiple partners (pl. "lovers"). But she is also depicted as a wife (vv. 2, 7, 13) and mother (vv. 2, 4, 5), who has "behaved shamefully" (hōbîšâ // zānĕtâ, "committed fornication," v. 5a), and it is her status as wife that is reflected in the punishment envisioned in vv. 3 and 10.[27] It appears that the author has drawn upon the full range of images and attitudes associated with the root ZNH to create his portrait of wayward Israel. It also suggests that the distinction between fornication and prostitution was essentially a legal one and that popular opinion regarded the behavior as essentially the same.

But what is represented by the metaphor, and to what extent are the terms of the figure dictated by the activity it describes? It is clear from the nature of the gifts mentioned in v. 5 that they are, directly or indirectly, the products of the land (cf. vv. 8, 9, 12) which depend on the life-sustaining gift of rain. Israel thinks they come from her lovers, whom she pursues (vv. 5, 7), adorning herself to win their favor (v. 13); but they are in fact the gifts of her husband Yahweh (v. 8), who will take them away, exposing her nakedness (vv. 9, 10, 12; cf. v. 3). The allegory is transparent: Israel has turned to the Canaanite rain god Baal (pejoratively represented as plural lovers) when her covenant lord, Yahweh, is the true God of fertility; the means of her lovemaking is the cult (vv. 8, 11, 13). The allegory is consistent, and daring in its appropriation of the basic fertility myth of the earth mother wed to the rain god.

The fundamental issue, in Hosea's view, is still the same as in the days of Elijah, viz., Who is the true god of fertility, Baal or Yahweh?—but now there is no contest. The battle of rival deities for national homage and state support has been won. What Hosea attacks is a Yahweh cult perverted by practices derived from the old (Baal) religion of the land, so that, in effect, it is really Baal that is worshiped ("courted") in these practices, not Yahweh.[28] The plural reference to the object of Israel's promiscuous devotion ("lovers," vv. 5, 7, 10, 12, 13; "the baals," v. 13; cf. v. 17) is, I suggest, an

---

26. Apparently a variant of 'etnān (9:1; Deut 23:19; Mic 1:7; etc.), "a harlot's wages."

27. Wolff, Hosea, 34; cf. John Huehnergard, "Biblical Notes on Some New Akkadian Texts from Emar (Syria)," CBQ 47 (1985) 433–34.

28. The emphasis is on cultic practice rather than on rival/foreign gods. Hosea never directly identifies the "lovers" with "the baals." The expression "other gods" ('ĕlōhîm 'aḥērîm) occurs only in 3:1, with pōnîm 'el- ("turning toward") as in Deut 31:18, 20. I regard 3:1-5 as a redactional composition that does not reflect Hosea's own usage here. Cf. commentaries.

intentional device for "belittling" Baal, denying him a proper name and the status of a true rival. It also serves to identify the deity with the local cult places, and reinforces the impression of feverish cultic/sexual activity suggested by reference to multiple feasts (vv. 11, 13). Despite the innuendo of chapter 2, the suggestion of cultic sex remains just that. The sexual language belongs exclusively to the allegory, while the cultic activity to which it points is represented in terms elsewhere descriptive of normative Yahweh worship: pilgrim feast (*ḥag*), new moon, and Sabbath—every appointed feast (*kōl môʿēd*) (v. 11 [Heb. 13]).[29] It is only in chapter 4 that sexual language is employed in a nonmetaphorical way in conjunction with cultic language—and the key term is *ZNH*.

Hosea 4:11-14 is a judgment oracle framed by short proverbial sentences (vv. 11 and 14b).[30] The indictment begins in v. 12 with a condemnation of oracular practices, followed by an explanatory *kî* clause employing the root *ZNH*, which functions as a leitmotif in the pericope, uniquely combining literal and metaphorical uses:

> My people[31] inquires of his [= its] "tree"
> and his "rod" gives him answer,
> For a *spirit of fornication* (*rûaḥ zĕnûnîm*)
> has led (them) astray,
> and *they have fornicated* (*wayyiznû*)
> from under (*mittaḥat*) their God.

The charge of seeking oracular guidance by illicit means is couched in language that suggests both idolatry/apostasy ("tree" and "rod" as cult objects associated with other gods or illicit cult)[32] and sexual activity ("tree" and "rod" as phallic symbols). The sexual innuendo of the opening

29. The clue to the condemnation is not in the names of the feasts, which represent a catalogue of Israel's traditional, and mandated, days of offering, but in the qualifying personal pronouns ("*her* pilgrim feast," etc.) and the cover term, *mĕśôśâ* "her rejoicing." The feasts commanded by Yahweh have become occasions for Israel's pursuit of her own pleasure or gain; and so Yahweh condemns them as "(feast) days of the baals" (v. 13).

30. For literary and textual analysis see commentaries and my forthcoming work. I take the people (*ʿammî*, v. 11) to be the subject throughout and view *zĕnût* of v. 11a as secondary and belonging to v. 10.

31. Reading with MT, followed by RSV and Mays, *Hosea*, 72; cf. NJV; Wolff, *Hosea*, 72; and Andersen and Freedman, *Hosea*, 343, 364–65 (who read "my people" with the preceding verse). My translation is literal where necessary to bring out features of the Hebrew lost in a more idiomatic rendering.

32. The terms suggest the Asherah pillars and standing stones (*maṣṣēbôt*) associated with open-air sanctuaries in numerous texts (e.g., Deut 16:21; Judg 6:25); for idols, see Jer 2:27; 10:8.

bicolon is reinforced by the use of *ZNH* in the following sentence. The language is strongly reminiscent of 1:2 in its combined use of *zānâ* and *zĕnûnîm* and in the syntax of the verb (with *min* + a preposition of position, here *taḥat*, "under"). As in 1:2, the language functions metaphorically to characterize the nation as promiscuous in its inclination (*rûaḥ zĕnûnîm*) and activity (*wayyiznû*). Here, however, the appeal to a female interpretive model cannot be explained by the grammatical gender of the subject. There is no personification of the land as mother; instead the people themselves (*ʿammî*) are the subject, represented throughout the pericope by male-defined activity as well as masculine gender. NJV reflects this shift to a masculine subject by employing male-oriented or gender-neutral terminology ("a lecherous impulse," "they have strayed"). Yet the model for the usage continues to be the promiscuous bride, as reference to the wronged partner implies—employing a preposition (*taḥat* "under") that is even more sexually suggestive.[33]

The indictment of cultic practice continues in vv. 13-14aβ in a quatrain whose first and final lines form an *inclusio* marked by parallel syntax, rhyming Hebrew verb forms and identical opening and closing verbs.[34]

1. (13aα)   On the mountaintops they "perform sacrifices,"
            and on the hills they "make offerings,"
2. (13aβ)   Under oak and poplar
            and terebinth—because its shade is good.
3. (13b)   That is why their[35] daughters fornicate
            and their daughters-in-law commit adultery;

33. It might be argued that the metaphor of the promiscuous wife is lost altogether here, with the root becoming simply a figurative term for illicit cult and/or cultic sex. Or one might view this usage as drawing on a broader root meaning describing male as well as female involvement in extramarital sex. Attempts to "defeminize" the usage are made difficult, however, by *mittaḥat* and by the possessive pronoun ("*their* God"; cf. Num 5:19, 20, 29). The remaining occurrence of *zānâ min/mē* in Hos 9:1 (*kî zānĕtâ mēʿal ʾĕlōhêkâ*, "for you have fornicated from upon your God") clearly has a female model in mind although the verb is masculine, as here, addressing collective Israel. The accusation of fornication is followed immediately in 9:1 by the amplification, "you loved (a harlot's) hire (*ʾetnān*) upon (*ʿal*) all grain-threshing floors," recalling the figure of the prostitute and repeating other key terms (*ʾHB*, "love," and *dāgān*, "grain") of chap. 2. We must conclude then that collective Israel is personified as female in each of these uses of *ZNH* and accused of "acting like a promiscuous woman/prostitute."

34. My reconstruction of the quatrain omits v. 14aα as a later addition. The notion of punishment, even when negated, is out of place here, and the inclusion of this line obscures the symmetry and interconnections of the original oracle. The force of the argument is not substantially altered by the deletion. See commentaries.

35. MT (Hebrew) has second masc. pl. suffixes ("your") on both nouns, which may be original, occasioned by a shift in the argument at this point to draw the consequences of the indictment for the listeners, addressed now directly (cf. Mays, *Hosea*, 73). The shift to second person may also have been introduced when the secondary "no punishment" statement was

4. (14aβ)[36] For they themselves "divide" with the prostitutes
and "perform sacrifices" with the hierodules.

The first two lines describe cultic activity in literal but suggestive terms. The verbs, which resume the present tense (imperfect) of the opening indictment, represent the primary terms for cultic action, ZBH, "to sacrifice," and QTR, "to burn incense" or "present offerings,"[37] but both are given an unusual vocalization (*piel*) used elsewhere only of illicit cultic activity.[38] Introductory prepositional phrases place emphasis on the locus of the activity ("*on* the mountaintops" and "*on* the hills"), making location a key to the interpretation. This emphasis is underlined in the second line by a list of tree names introduced by a new preposition, without an additional verb. The preposition *tahat* "under" creates a complementary pair with the *'al* ("upon") of the preceding line, but also picks up the *tahat* of the *mittahat* ("from under") in v. 12: the people have ZNH-ed *from under* their God by "offering" *under* trees—because their shade is "good"![39]

The accented terms of location (*on* the heights and *under* shady trees) suggest what this "offering" really involves. As in the opening indictment, the message of sexual activity is carried by innuendo, without the use of explicitly sexual language; and as in v. 12, it is followed by an interpretive word employing the verb *zānâ*—only this time the usage is literal. Line 3 (v. 13b) describes the consequences of the activity condemned in lines 1 and 2: "That is why their (your) daughters fornicate and their (your) daughters-in-law commit adultery."[40] The structure of the argument is

---

added. Wolff (*Hosea,* 85) and Andersen and Freedman (*Hosea,* 369) see different groups addressed by lines 3 and 4. I have translated as third person to enable English readers to connect the male subjects, whom I believe to be the same throughout, whether addressed directly or indirectly.

36. See n. 35 above.

37. The paired terms constitute a *merismus* intended to cover all forms and occasions of cultic activity. Cf. Wolff, *Hosea,* 86.

38. I have used quotation marks in translating all four of the *piel* verbs in the first and final lines as an attempt to duplicate the Hebrew use of a system of vocalization which suggests that something else is intended by these terms than they usually convey. None of these verbs is normally used in this stem. Cf. Wolff, *Hosea,* 35. This polemical use of the *piel* is characteristic of Hosea, who provides the earliest examples of the usage and may well be its originator.

39. Cf. 14:7-8 (Heb. 8-9), where Yahweh is likened to an evergreen cypress (the largest of trees) and his protecting "shade" (RSV "shadow") is described by the same term used here (*ṣēl*).

40. "Daughters" (*bānôt*) and "daughters-in-law" (*kallôt,* lit. "brides," here = "son's brides") are paired for purposes of poetic parallelism. They are to be understood as a single class, viz., sexually mature young female dependents. Cf. Andersen and Freedman, *Hosea,* 369; Wolff, *Hosea,* 86–87.

clear: what the men do has consequences in their daughters' behavior. But what kind of consequences? That is the central interpretive problem of the pericope.

It is commonly understood to mean that the women engage in some form of "cultic prostitution" and that this activity represents the female side of the male activity alluded to in v. 13a, and spelled out in v. 14aβ. Both context and syntax require a literal reading, but does this include a specialized cultic meaning? The following considerations, point, I believe, to a noncultic interpretation, at least as the "first reading."

1. The pericope as a whole envisions the worshiping community as a body of males, although in the author's mind they represent collective Israel ("my people," v. 12). The description of the daughters' behavior is not one of the series of charges against Yahweh's "people." It is, rather, an argument directed at the men themselves, aiming to bring home to them the consequences of their actions.

2. The function of the statement, as indicated by the initial ʿal-kēn ("therefore," "for this reason"), is to draw a connection between two sets of circumstances that had not previously been linked (cf. 4:3). The revelatory force of the statement is in the correlation, not in the description of the activity itself, which must be clearly abhorrent. If the young women had been engaging in sexual activity at the sites of the men's "worship," the connection would be obvious and there would be no need for the ʿal-kēn.

3. The intention of the ʿal-kēn clause is best realized when the verbs are understood in their "plain sense," as describing the loose sexual conduct of those women for whom the men addressed bear responsibility. Fornication and adultery will be immediately recognized as the most serious of women's offenses; attributed to female dependents (daughters and daughters-in-law, not wives), these sexual improprieties also constitute an attack upon the men's honor.[41] The statement assumes a concern for the women's sexual morals; its message consists in linking their sexual activity to the men's cultic activity, a link that is dramatically substantiated in the climactic final statement (v. 14aβ).

To summarize, the men are accused of cultic impropriety, the women of sexual impropriety. (The women's offense is obvious; the men's is "under cover.") It may be sexual activity that defiles the men's worship, but it is worship that is the central concern of the pericope, as the verbs show. The men's worst offense is to dishonor God by their perverted worship. The women's worst offense is to dishonor their fathers and fathers-in-law

41. Deut 22:21; Lev 21:9; cf. Gen 34:31.

by their sexual conduct. The men dishonor their Lord (metaphorical use of *zānâ*, v. 12b); the women dishonor their lords (literal use of *zānâ*, v. 13b). This differential assessment of male and female behavior, as well as the overall male orientation of the pericope, illustrates the asymmetry of roles, activities, and values noted earlier as a characteristic of patriarchal societies. A further example is found in the concluding line.

Line 4 (v. 14aβ) of the reconstructed quatrain is linked to the preceding line (v. 13b) by repetition of the root *ZNH* (*tiznênâ*, "fornicate," *hazzônôt*, "prostitutes"), which carries the decisive meaning in both lines, and by a focus on paired classes of women. It is tied to line 1 by parallel construction and repetition of the initial verb to form an *inclusio*. Line 4 resumes (with emphatic *hēm* "they themselves") the third masculine plural subject of the first two lines, continuing the description of the men's activity and extending the series of prepositional phrases that define and condemn their action by reference to the circumstances in which it is performed. Here, however, for the first time, an explicitly sexual term (*zônôt*) appears, revealing what lay behind the earlier veiled references; the "sacrifices" *on* the mountaintops and hills and *under* the trees were performed *with* (*ʿim*) prostitutes and hierodules. The final statement sharpens the charges by focusing on a single determining feature of the activity which correlates the men's behavior with that of the women in the preceding line.

The correlation achieved through the use of *ZNH* does not equate the two pairs of women, nor describe the same activity; rather it points to an underlying connection between the activities of the fathers and the daughters. Each line makes a single, and distinct, statement: line 3, the men's female dependents are promiscuous; line 4, the men perform their "worship" with promiscuous women.

It is usually argued that the pairing of *zônôt* and *qĕdēšôt* means either that the *zônôt* are "sacred prostitutes," at least here, or that the *qĕdēšôt* are (simply) prostitutes.[42] Neither argument fits the requirements of the passage. The classes must be distinct in order to be identified, and the *qĕdēšôt* must be understood as having an essentially cultic identity, as indicated by the etymology of the term and by the use of *ZBH* ("sacrifice") to describe the activity performed with them. They represent a cultic role, but one associated in Israelite (prophetic) thought with "Canaanite" worship, not Yahweh worship. Thus the placement of the term *qĕdēšôt* in final

---

42. So Mayer I. Gruber ("Hebrew *Qĕdēšāh* and Her Canaanite and Akkadian Cognates," *UF* 18 [1986] 133–48), who argues that the etymology points to a basic meaning of "set apart," in this case "for degradation," in other Hebrew uses and in Akkadian "for exaltation" (133, 148). Hooks ("Sacred Prostitution," 187) arrives at a similar conclusion, drawing on the notion of "taboo."

position serves as the climactic revelation that these cult sites and cultic activities really belong to Baal, not Yahweh.[43] The meaning of the paired terms, however, is given in this context by the initial *zônôt*. Through this pairing and ordering the reader is meant to understand that *qĕdēšôt* are equivalent to prostitutes. But this directed reading is clearly polemical; it tells us what the prophet thought about the *qĕdēšôt*, but it does not give us any reliable information about the function or activities of these women, except that they must have been a recognized presence at the rural sanctuaries in Hosea's day. There may also be shock value in mentioning the *zônôt* first. While *qĕdēšôt* belong in a cultic context, though not a Yahwistic cult, *zônôt* do not. They belong in public squares and inns and along the highways (Josh 2:1; Gen 38:15; Jer 3:2; Isa 23:16; Prov 7:10-12), not at sanctuaries. Naming them as the company with whom the men conduct their worship tells us that this is perverted worship; naming *qĕdēšôt* as the men's companions says that it is "Canaanite"/ Baal worship.

Zônôt are defined by their sexual activity, *qĕdēšôt* by their cultic association. It is impossible to determine the nature of their cultic service from the biblical sources, which are too fragmentary and polemical. It is clear, however, from the limited Old Testament references that the Israelite authors understood their role to include some form of sexual activity, which they identified with prostitution. Through juxtaposition with *zônâ* the term *qĕdēšâ* acquired the sense of "sacred prostitution." Neither the assumption of sexual activity nor its equation with prostitution, however, can be taken at face value. Since Israel appears to have recognized no legitimate role for women as cult functionaries during the period in which *qĕdēšôt* are attested,[44] it would be easy for Israelites to assume that the presence of women at a sanctuary involved sexual activity. It is possible then that the charge of "sacred prostitution" has no base in cultic sex, but is rather a false inference.[45] It is also possible to understand the charge as a polemical misrepresentation of a cultic role that did involve some form of sexual activity, but was not understood by the practitioners as prostitution; the identification of the hierodule's role with the prostitute's would represent a distorted, outsider's view of the institution. A final possibility is that the isolated biblical references to *qĕdēšôt* represent a perverted rem-

43. Cf. the placement of "days of the baals" in the final verse of 2:2-13 to reveal the identity of the previously mentioned "lovers" (vv. 5, 7, 10, 12) and feast days (v. 11).

44. See my essay, "The Place of Women in the Israelite Cultus," in Patrick D. Miller, Jr., Paul D. Hanson, and S. Dean McBride, eds., *Ancient Israelite Religion: Essays in Honor of Frank Moore Cross* (Philadelphia: Fortress Press, 1987) 405–8 [*93–99].

45. This is the burden of Hooks's argument, for Israel and for the entire ancient Near East ("Sacred Prostitution," 203–7).

nant of an earlier Israelite or Canaanite cult, perpetuated in a perverted Israelite cult.[46] That is suggested by the presence of *zônôt*. The text offers no justification for viewing the *zônôt* as cultic functionaries. It does suggest that prostitutes found the rural sanctuaries an attractive place to do business, quite possibly by agreement with the priests. The verb (*PRD*, "divide, separate") offers little help in determining the role of the *zônôt* at the sanctuary, since it has been conformed to the series of polemical *piels* and occurs nowhere else in this vocalization or in connection with *zônôt*. Does it designate a cultic action as the other verbs of the series do?[47] The usage appears to be deliberately veiled and avoids the common verbs of sexual encounter.

The *zônôt* and *qĕdēšôt* of the rural sanctuaries must be viewed as a small, specialized class and therefore not descriptive of the general female population, whose younger generation is represented by the daughters and brides of v. 13b. They are not the daughters, or wives, of the men addressed by the oracle.[48] The argument of the concluding lines, which compares male to female activity, is not based on the identity of the actions or of the actors (strictly speaking, it is not a condemnation of the "double standard"). Rather it uses a case of transparent guilt in the secular sphere (*zānâ* of the daughters) to engage the male subjects and then exposes their involvement in similar activity in the sacred sphere (association with *zônôt*), insisting that the men's behavior is equally reprehensible, *or more so*, since it defiles worship with sexual activity.[49] In the final analysis such "worship" amounts to a rejection of Yahweh for other love objects (metaphorical *ZNH*, v. 12b). The fact that Hosea does not use the verb *zānâ* to describe the men's activity in line 4, despite his attempt to compare male and female behavior, confirms the interpretation of its use in v. 12 as metaphorical.

To summarize, in the primary texts of Hosea the root *ZNH* has the same basic meaning exhibited elsewhere in historical-legal usage, namely,

46. What Hosea describes is an *Israelite* fertility cult, not a Canaanite cult. Survivals, and/ or revivals, of older, pre-Yahwistic practices (among them the role of the *qĕdēšôt*) must be assumed, but it is impossible to learn from the biblical sources what role these may have played in the earlier cult or how the practices were understood by the practitioners.

47. The term is usually understood to mean something like "go aside" (so RSV; NJV; Wolff, *Hosea*, 72; Mays, *Hosea*, 72), with the idea of joining (sacred) prostitutes in groves adjacent to the sanctuaries. Andersen and Freedman (*Hosea*, 370) suggest, however, that it may refer to the dismembering of the sacrificial victim. Might it suggest a division of the priestly portion with the prostitute?

48. The professional women should probably be understood as recruited from the general Israelite population, but they are treated here as "other women." On the father's role in causing or permitting a daughter's promiscuity, whether casual or commercial, see Lev 19:29 and commentary by Collins, "Sacred Prostitution," 103–5.

49. Cf. the argument employed in the judicial parables, 2 Sam 12:1-7 and 14:2-20.

"to engage in illicit/extramarital sexual activity, to fornicate"; and as a professional noun (*zônâ*), "a prostitute." The subject is always female[50] and the activity has, in itself, no cultic connotations. Alongside this basic meaning and corresponding to it in its primary images is a metaphorical usage created by Hosea to characterize and indict Israel's worship. In its original(?) form, Israel (represented as the land, mother of the inhabitants, but interchanging with the inhabitants themselves, always conceived as male) is depicted as a promiscuous wife who abandons her husband for lovers, behaving like a common prostitute in pursuit of hire. The activity represented by the metaphor is cultic activity, which the metaphor reveals to be in effect service of "the baals" rather than Yahweh. It exhibits the character of "nature worship" in its aims, location, and means, including activity of a sexual nature, which Hosea represents as "simply" fornication.

The metaphorical use of *ZNH* invokes two familiar and linguistically identified images of dishonor in Israelite culture, the common prostitute and the promiscuous daughter or wife. As a sexual metaphor, it points to the sexual nature of the activity it represents. Its female orientation does not single out women for condemnation; it is used rather as a rhetorical device to expose men's sin. By appealing to the common stereotypes and interests of a primarily male audience Hosea turns their accusation against them. It is easy for patriarchal society to see the guilt of a "fallen woman"; Hosea says, "You [male Israel] are that woman!"

50. In addition to the texts treated, cf. 3:3 *tiznî* (*qal* with feminine subject and literal meaning). Three instances of the *hiphil* occur in the book (4:10, 18; 5:3), all involving some textual problems. A provisional survey of these occurrences suggests that the *hiphil* is meant to represent the male activity in fornication, much as the male activity in giving birth to a child (*YLD qal* with female subject) is normally represented by the *hiphil*, although in metaphorical usage the *qal* can have a male subject (e.g., Deut 32:18, of God).

V

HERMENEUTICS AND
THE AUTHORITY OF
THE BIBLE

11

TRANSLATING SEXIST LANGUAGE AS A THEOLOGICAL AND CULTURAL PROBLEM

I APPROACH THE QUESTION OF SEXIST LANGUAGE[1] IN SCRIPTURE AS a feminist Christian drawing on a particular Protestant understanding of Scripture and faith that I would characterize as liberal evangelical. I have chosen to accept this heritage, in critical appreciation, as a faith tradition that has prepared me for and, I believe, compelled me to my present understanding.

The overwhelming androcentrism of biblical language presents contemporary communities of faith with a serious and unavoidable theological problem, which is made more acute by their understanding of the Bible as the primary or exclusive source of revelation and norm for belief and practice. It presents a theological problem because it misrepresents to

Originally given as part of the "Biblical Jubilee" program of Union Theological Seminary, April 8–9, 1987; it was subsequently published in *USQR* 42 (1988) 89–95.

1. By "sexist language" I mean language that employs masculine terms and images inappropriately to describe human and divine reality. It is the product of patriarchal society and serves to perpetuate androcentric perspectives. Not all uses of exclusively male terms are sexist, however. When "fathers" describes male ancestors, the language is not sexist. On the other hand, many terms that appear to be inclusive may have exclusively male referents. Householders, redeemers, and elders in ancient Israel were male, and in Hebrew the term for "people," 'am, often designates an exclusively male body, more specifically, the army. The problem of grammatical gender in Hebrew contributes further complications, especially in the case of plurals and collectives, where the gender of the word is often not a reliable clue to the gender of the referents. This paper does not attempt to deal with the technical problems of translation, but aims rather to explore broader theoretical issues. The analysis is necessarily and regrettably oversimplified.

the modern hearer both the nature of God and the nature of humanity by its preponderant use of male reference.[2]

But the problem it signals cannot be solved, in my view, by translation, because it is essentially a hermeneutical problem. Attempting to solve the problem of the Bible's sexist language through translation alone may only serve to mask the deeper problem and prevent critical engagement with the underlying issues.

The Bible's androcentric language is a sign of the androcentric and patriarchal world in which the biblical writings were composed and transmitted. The fundamental problem, for me, is the way in which the Bible's anthropology and theology have been limited and distorted by the pervasive sociocultural bias of patriarchal androcentrism, which affects thought as well as speech and shapes experience as well as expression. Male bias in Scripture is far deeper and more pervasive, I think, than most appeals for inclusive language translations generally recognize.

Sexist language is but one sign of a deeper problem, which is the sexist nature of the Bible's social world and thought world. But the problem that this sexist distortion presents to the translator and interpreter of Scripture is not a new one. It is simply one instance of the more general and widely recognized problem of cultural specificity with which all translators and interpreters of ancient or foreign literatures must contend. And in my view, it should be treated in exactly the same manner as in other ancient or foreign literatures. Neither appeal to the concept of inspiration or canon nor to the expectation of contemporary hearers for an authoritative contemporary word should exempt the Scriptures from the demands placed upon other foreign literatures. What makes the Bible a special case, and an especially difficult case for translators, is the heavy existential investment of its users in it, its status as a holy book, its broad distribution, and its great variety of interpretation and use. It is also unique in that it is known before it is translated. For most readers, a new translation is simply an alteration of what tradition has given them, a tradition that has fixed and sanctified the received translation as the "word of God."

The problem of sexist language in Scripture is but one instance, I have argued, of a more general problem in transcultural communication, but it may well be the most critical and illuminating instance in forcing us to clarify our understanding of the nature and authority of Scripture and the way Scripture communicates to us. That is because it permeates the entire Bible and is not confined to removable segments, and because it touches

---

2. This modern judgment must raise the question whether androcentric language also misrepresented human and divine nature to the ancient hearer, but respect for the historical nature of language and of truth does not allow collapse of these two judgments.

every reader at the point of his or her self-understanding and self-image and at the point of our primary representations of God. The problem of androcentric language is essentially the same problem that Bultmann addressed in his attempt to free the gospel from the bondage of its mythological language and worldview.[3] But it requires a more comprehensive response, because it identifies a broader and subtler limitation or distortion, one that persists in large segments of the contemporary world, supported, in part, by biblical tradition. And just as Bultmann's program of demythologizing failed, in my view, to give adequate resolution to the problem he identified, so too, I believe, any attempt to separate the message of Scripture from its patriarchal matrix must also fail.

For me, the Bible's sexist language, insofar as it accurately represents the authors' own thought world and linguistic and social conventions, has an important sign value in alerting the reader to a deep and persistent underlying cultural bias that is less easily recognized. It forces us to consider the more fundamental question of how the Bible as a historically and culturally limited document is to be understood as a source of religious authority for contemporary believers. In what way does the Bible constitute or convey revelation or truth? How does it function in communities of faith to inform, instruct, and inspire? How is it read, studied, and heard? These are the questions that are of primary concern to me and they are questions that the problem of biblical androcentrism can help us answer; but they are not, in my view, questions for the translator.

I am not trained in translation theory, and my remarks at this point may be woefully inadequate, but I have been forced by the occasion of this panel to formulate, in a preliminary way at least, my understanding of what I am about as a translator of Scripture and my obligations in translation, in order to address the more specific question of translating androcentric language.

I

I am fully aware that no sharp line can be drawn between translation and interpretation. I understand translation as a form of interpretation, but one that operates under a fairly narrow set of conditions. While interpretation is concerned with a wide range of historical and cultural obstacles to understanding, translation focuses on the obstacle of language. Its aim is the transfer of a message from one language to another. But it is never

---

3. Mary Ann Tolbert makes the same comparison in "Defining the Problem: The Bible and Feminist Hermeneutics," in idem, ed., *The Bible and Feminist Hermeneutics* (*Semeia* 28; Chico, Calif.: Scholars Press, 1983) 115.

a purely linguistic operation. Since language is both a product and a bearer of culture, translation always involves a transfer from one cultural sphere and one cultural medium to another. And since it concerns the transfer of messages, not simply words, it requires attention to meaning and intention. Thus it is always subjective, and it always demands an effort to determine both the speaker's intention and the anticipated response of its audience.

What controls govern this subjective art, and to whom is the translator obligated? What special demands are laid upon the Bible translator by the nature of the text and by the audience of the translation? In my view, the Bible translator has no special obligation, or license, that is not shared by every other translator. Bible translation should be viewed as similar to the translation of any other ancient literature. But the nature of the Bible translator's audience dictates special care and concern to anticipate and minimize misunderstanding arising from audience expectation or demand.[4]

The translator serves both the author and the audience, but in distinction from the preacher or expositor, the translator's obligation is to the author exclusively. The translator serves the speaker[5] by rendering the speaker's message in the receptor language in such a way that it reproduces as fully and faithfully as possible the sense of the original, including its style, tone, level of discourse, and effect. Anyone with any experience in translation knows the difficulties of achieving such multileveled correspondence and recognizes the need in any given instance to sacrifice one demand to another. But the goal remains valid and applies equally, I believe, to the biblical text. The fact that the Bible is the product of multiple and unknown authors (addressing multiple and often unspecified audiences) does not remove the fundamental obligation to the speaker; it simply makes the effort to discern the author's intention more complex and the assurance of a correct (i.e., faithful) interpretation less certain.

The translator's final obligation, I have argued, is to the speaker, but

---

4. The problem of audience demand is especially acute not only because of the fact, noted above, that the Bible is already known to its readers, but because it is understood by a large segment of the church as belonging to the people and as intelligible to any reader by the direct gift of the Holy Spirit.

5. I use the terms "author" and "speaker" interchangeably to designate the originator of the message, assuming the situation of oral, face-to-face communication as my model. While this is modified in various ways, by distance in time and space and by means of mass distribution (whether by manuscript, print, or other media) that vastly expands the audience, I do not think that the basic model is fundamentally altered by the qualifying circumstances; a speaker/writer always has some audience in mind and a hearer/reader always imagines some speaker. Nor do I think the model is invalidated by the notion of a collective author, such as represented by a tradition (e.g., the legal tradition represented by the earliest stratum of the Covenant Code).

that obligation can only be fulfilled by attention to the audience. The translator must anticipate how an audience will hear what is said and choose from the available words and constructions in the receptor language those that will enable the speaker's words to be heard as the speaker intends. For the Bible translator, however, there are always a minimum of two audiences for any given word, the audience of the author or redactor and the audience of the translator. While it may often be possible for the translator to unite the two audiences, enabling the contemporary audience to hear the words as those originally addressed, this is not always possible or desirable. In cases where the two audiences do not converge, it is the ancient audience that should determine the rendering. The aim of the Bible translator, in my view, should be to enable a modern audience to *overhear* an ancient conversation, rather than to hear itself addressed directly. Paul's letters to the Corinthians should be translated with the Corinthian church in mind, and the book of Amos as addressed to eighth-century Israelites—and seventh-century Judeans, as determined by internal analysis of the text.

It is not the translator's duty to make her audience *accept* the author's message, or even identify themselves with the ancient audience, except in the sense that any literary work invites identification with its subjects. I am not certain that the translator is even obliged to make the modern reader *understand* what is overheard. Much of an ancient work may remain enigmatic and uncomprehended because the experience and thought world of the ancient audience is foreign (as we recognize when we encounter such terms or usages as "firmament," "leprous houses," "teraphim," or "bride price"). No translation, or paraphrase, can carry the full burden of interpretation required by any ancient and foreign literature. The Scriptures are not self-interpreting and no translation can make them so. They require explanatory notes, study, exegesis, and exposition to be understoood—and that has been so since the beginning of the formation of the canon.

I have argued that translation, in the strict sense in which I use the term, is characterized by obligation to the ancient author, with attention primarily to the dynamics of communication with the ancient audience(s). I distinguish this translation from the "translation" that occurs in preaching, paraphrase, hymnody and metrical psalms, lectionary readings, litanies, prayers, and responsive readings. All of these are determined in much greater degree by the interests and needs of contemporary audiences, and all move in varying measure out of the category of translation into that of interpretation, whether this occurs in a single action (such as the preacher's or lector's own interpretive rendering of the original text) or in a two-stage action dependent on a published translation.

Both types of translation/interpretation are valid and necessary, I think, and I practice both. I change the text in order to gain a hearing for an ancient word from a modern audience or in order to re-create, emphasize, or extend what I believe to be the essential thrust of the text. But I do this as an interpreter, not as a translator. I cannot agree with Phyllis Trible's argument that the postexilic substitution of the spoken term *Adonai* for the divine name represented by the tetragrammaton constitutes "theological warrant for changing the text."[6] She is right in maintaining that this substitution altered the *meaning* of the text, at least for those dependent on oral proclamation (or on translations that fail to preserve evidence of the disparity between the written and the spoken word). But it is not a precedent for changing the meaning of the text through translation. In fact it illustrates the extreme care that was taken to preserve the original text (and sense) even when theological motives made it no longer acceptable. The eventual fixing and closing of the canon initiated a new phase in the interpretation of sacred tradition.[7] Once its structure and content were determined, it was no longer possible to make the sacred writings speak to new audiences by recomposition or redactional activity. From that point on its meaning could be altered only through midrash and other forms of commentary, that is, by supplements to the text, not by altering the text itself. With the fixing of the canon, translation and interpretation take different forms.

II

Moving now from general considerations to specific problems, I want to consider a number of cases involving issues of masculine language. The first is the case of the Hebrew slave law in Deut 15:12-18, which begins by specifying the subject of its interest as "your brother, a Hebrew man": ʾāḥîkā hāʿibrî, but immediately modifies this with the addition, ʾô hāʿibrîyâ: "or a Hebrew woman," so that the lead sentence refers the whole of the following paragraph to both men and women: kî-yimmākēr lĕkā ʾāḥîkā hāʿibrî ʾô hāʿibrîyâ. The RSV translates literally, treating each of the identifying terms separately in turn: "If your brother, a Hebrew man or a Hebrew woman, is sold to you."

In view of the fact that the paragraph in its present form clearly intends to be inclusive, should one not replace the now dissonant "your brother" with "your fellow Hebrew," "your fellow citizen," "one of your kindred," "your brother or sister," or the like? I think there are cases where this should be done and where one could argue that the masculine singular

---

6. Phyllis Trible, "Postscript: Jottings on the Journey," in Letty M. Russell, ed., *Feminist Interpretation of the Bible* (Philadelphia: Westminster, 1985) 148.

7. Cf. James A. Sanders, "Hermeneutics," *IDBSup*, 404–5.

formulation of the following clauses is meant as generic langauge, in accordance with conventions of Hebrew legal style that need not be duplicated in an English rendering. In this instance, however, the case description concludes in v. 17b with the words, *wĕʾap laʾ ămātĕkā taʿaśeh-kēn:* "And to your female servant you shall do likewise," creating an *inclusio* with the supplement to v. 12, directing the reader to understand the case inclusively. In view of the manner in which this inclusive reading has been accomplished in the Hebrew, by redactional supplements rather than recasting the original, I would preserve the dissonance of the Hebrew gender references in the English translation, allowing the English reader to see with the Hebrew reader a process of reinterpretation in the text that is not fully realized in the language. This case raises a further question, however, about the assumed generic use of the masculine singular in Old Testament legal sentences, since it shows that where unambiguous extension of a case to both men and women is intended, explicitly inclusive language is used.

The second case I want to consider concerns the provisions in Joshua 20 for cities of refuge to which a *rōṣēaḥ,* translated in RSV by "manslayer," may flee for protection from the "avenger of blood" (*gōʾēl haddām*) in cases of unintended homicide. The first problem concerns the victim of the homicide. Since the victim is described by the noun *nepeš:* "living being," "soul," in the qualifying phrase *makkēh-nepeš bišgāgâ:* "killer-of-a-person unintentionally," *man*slayer is clearly inappropriate as a contemporary English rendering of *rōṣēaḥ.* One might opt simply for "slayer," or "homicide" (which duplicates *makkēh-nepeš* with a Latin compound). But what of the gender of the slayer, who is identified by a masculine singular participle from the root *RṢH:* "murder" or "kill"? Duplicating the participle (with "murderer," "killer," or the like) creates no problems of gender reference in English, but the resumptive pronouns required by English do. In this case, I believe we are dealing with a situation governed by particular social, economic, and legal customs that pertained peculiarly to males. Asylum was an institution designed to preserve the family and property rights of an endangered male, and its provisions as described in Josh 20:1-6 would make no sense for a woman in ancient Israel. The differential value placed on men's and women's lives in the case of vows suggests a principle that appears to have been operative here as well. This prescription exhibits a concern for the male citizen typical of patriarchal societies. In my view, it should not be transformed into a general principle through translation. The contemporary reader should be allowed to abstract the principle and ponder the possibility of its extension or general applicability on the basis of the male-formulated case as it is presented in the Hebrew. Consequently, I would retain the masculine pronouns that identify the slayer in the RSV.

But if this represents a special case, what about the more general laws, such as those found in the Covenant Code? Is the typical casuistic formula, "If a man ('*îš*) . . . ," meant to represent any occurrence of the situation described or only occurrences involving males? It is apparent, I think, that this formulation is dictated by a legal tradition in which the cases are meant to be exemplary and extendable to other situations with comparable conditions, so that the masculine language alone cannot be the decisive criterion for interpretation or translation. A similar convention still operates in American legal practice. I have no objection in principle to treating clauses of this type as potentially inclusive of women and translating them accordingly, but a close look at the examples provided by this collection suggests that these cases were framed with men in mind: owners of slaves, animals, lands—and women. That impression is confirmed by the occasional use of explicitly inclusive formulations ('*îš wě'iššâ*, "a man or a woman," Exod 20:28, 29) and by the use of the same formula *wěkî-*[verb] '*îš*, "if a man [does X]," to introduce the case of borrowing (an animal) (Exod 22:13 [Eng. 14], *wěkî-yiš'al 'îš*) and the case of seducing a virgin (Exod 22:15 [Eng. 16], *wěkî-yěpatteh 'îš*), both in the same series. It would appear that this whole corpus of laws was constructed primarily with the intention of clarifying the rights and duties and protecting the life, honor, and interests of the males in the community, or of the male-ordered community.

My preference is to retain the masculine formulation of the original, as reflecting the sociohistorical situation in which the laws were constructed and operated. This does not prevent extension to include women (the case of the slave law in Deuteronomy shows that just such an extension happened during the period of the formation of the canon), but it preserves the ambivalence and exhibits the bias of the original for the contemporary audience, forcing them to consider the setting and the purpose of the laws.

I come to a different conclusion in the case of the Psalms, where such expressions as '*ašrê hā'îš*, "blessed/happy is the man," are, I believe, intended to be broadly inclusive; and so I would translate with inclusive formulations, such as "blessed are those" or "blessed is the one." A male perspective—and male experience—still dominates the Psalter, however, even in such personal expressions of "common" religious sentiment. Psalm 128 may serve as an example. Although its initial words appear to be emphatically inclusive: '*ašrê kol-yěrê' YHWH:* "blessed are *all* who fear the Lord," the content of the promised blessing, expressed in v. 3, betrays a more limited target of these words: '*eštěkā kěgepen pōrîyâ*, "Your wife will be like a fruitful vine." Like the Decalogue, the psalms too envision a congregation of males. But here I would allow the audience to discover this bias from the content of the petitions and blessings, rather than impose it upon them by the use of masculine language that will sound more exclusively and emphatically male-oriented to the contemporary American audience than to the ancient Hebrew congregation.

I return then to my original point. As a feminist interpreter of Scripture I prefer to expose the androcentric and patriarchal nature of the biblical text and of the world in which it was formed. Only then can we begin to deal at all adequately with the problem of how revelation can be conveyed through such flawed vehicles of grace as our Hebrew ancestors and our own prophets and teachers.

12

BIBLICAL AUTHORITY
IN THE LIGHT OF
FEMINIST CRITIQUE

THIS ESSAY REPRESENTS THE CONCLUDING LECTURE IN A SERIES
of four on the topic "Feminism and the Bible: A Critical and Constructive Encounter."* Originally entitled "Living Waters: Biblical Authority Reappraised," it begins with a summary of the first three lectures:
1. "Broken Cisterns: Biblical Authority in Crisis"; 2. "Root Damage: Feminist Critique"; and 3. "The Lord's Planting: Feminist Hermeneutics."

In my first lecture I argued that society today is facing a crisis of morals
and meaning and that the church in attempting to respond to this crisis
is experiencing its own crisis. At a time when many both inside and outside the church look to it for a clear word of guidance, it seems to have
lost its direction and its voice. It is rent by internal controversies, many
involving protest over the erosion or abandonment of traditional beliefs
and practices. For many, the crisis in the church is a crisis of authority,
for others a crisis of identity. I believe that it is both, and that they are
related. For Protestants, authority for belief and action has been vested

---

* The 1993 J. J. Thiessen Lectures, Canadian Mennonite Bible College, October 19–20,
1993; published under the title *Feminism and the Bible: A Critical and Constructive Encounter*
(Winnipeg: CMBC Publications, 1994). The published form of the lectures retains the style
of oral delivery, with only minor revisions and the addition of footnotes. The issue of biblical
authority, which is the focus of these lectures, is treated more fully in my article, "The Authority of the Bible," in Leander E. Keck, ed., *The New Interpreter's Bible* (Nashville: Abingdon, 1994) 1:33–64. Much of the thought presented in these lectures was developed in a
series of lectures on "Feminist Theology and the Bible" presented at the Triennial Translators
Workshop of the United Bible Societies, Victoria Falls, Zimbabwe, May 15–20, 1991, and in
the Francis B. Denio Lectures on the Bible, "Biblical Authority in Crisis," delivered at Bangor
Theological Sseminary, January 20–21, 1992.

traditionally in the Bible and appeals to Scripture. Today both the rhetoric of biblical authority and the content of biblical faith are under attack or have fallen into disuse.

In my second and third lectures I looked at feminist attitudes toward the Bible, beginning with the nineteenth century, in which the Bible played a prominent role in American culture and in public debate. The women's movement from its inception was forced to define itself in relation to a book that was widely recognized as supporting the subordination, and oppression, of women. Feminists could not remain neutral to claims of biblical authority and truth, and the test of truth was their own experience—which gave them mixed messages, for compelling moral judgments and spiritual insights were combined in the Bible with narrow vision and hurtful restrictions. A persisting tension is evident within the women's movement between the belief that the Bible as the word of God *must* support the equality of male and female, and insistence that the Bible as a primary source and sanction of women's oppression (perhaps *the* primary source) cannot be accorded the status of divine revelation—or reveals a God who is not worthy of reverence.

Contemporary feminism has largely relegated that problem to the church. In a religiously plural culture in which religion has become primarily a private affair and in which the Bible, as a sectarian document, has undergone a general crisis of authority and use, feminists outside the church have little reason to struggle with biblical patriarchy and androcentrism. The Bible stands confirmed in their view as a document of female oppression. Thus the dilemma for feminists within the church is intensified.

Feminist theologians and biblical scholars have not for the most part softened the nineteenth-century critique of biblical patriarchy; rather they have shown the Bible's patriarchal bias to be deeper and more pervasive than earlier thought. Androcentrism characterizes every stage of the composition, canonization, and interpretation of Scripture, and it cannot be removed by excising particular passages. As Rosemary Ruether summarizes it,

> The Bible was shaped by males in a patriarchal culture, so many of its revelatory experiences were interpreted by men from a patriarchal perspective. The ongoing interpretation of these revelatory experiences and their canonization further this patriarchal bias by eliminating traces of female experience or interpretating them in an androcentric way. The Bible, in turn, becomes the authoritative source for the justification of patriarchy in Jewish and Christian society.[1]

1. Rosemary Radford Ruether, "Feminist Interpretation: A Method of Correlation," in Letty M. Russell, ed., *Feminist Interpretation of the Bible* (Philadelphia: Westminster, 1985) 116.

How can such a work claim divine sanction, and how can women find an authoritative word in a book that systematically distorts the truth of women's nature and experience, making it conform to men's or setting it apart as "other," alien, unclean? Katharine Sakenfeld opened her 1985 survey of feminist uses of the Bible with the question, "How can feminists use the Bible, if at all?"[2] The answer she gave on the part of religious feminists, was, for the most part: painfully and selectively.[3]

Why then do women seek to hold on to a book that has historically enslaved them? There is no single answer to this question, but two essential components of an answer include the following. First, the Bible, especially in Protestantism, is essential to articulation of Christian faith and thus essential to Christian identity. That is why the modern loss of familiarity with Bible content is so serious for the church; it represents a dangerous amnesia that threatens loss of identity. For Protestants, however, the Bible is not only an historical source; it is a means of communication with God, a mediator of the divine word to contemporary believers, a source of present contact with the living Word—available to all believers.[4] Christian faith without the Bible is unthinkable. Where personal identity has been shaped as Christian identity, any threat to a primary source and sustainer of that identity may be too great to bear without fundamental and wrenching revision of the image of self. In assessing the threatened loss, one must consider the emotional as well as the cognitive aspects of traditional faith.

Loss of community is also critical for women who reject a patriarchal Bible and the religious community that bears it. That is why alternative communities, and alternative symbols and sources of revelation, are so important for feminist critics of patriarchal religion, whether "women-church" or Wicca, or other forms of Goddess/female-centered religion. That is why "sisterhood" is essential, first for women—and then for men, who must learn as outsiders to find themselves named and claimed by circles centered in women's experience.

2. Katharine Doob Sakenfeld, "Feminist Uses of Biblical Materials," in Russell, *Feminist Interpretation*, 55.

3. Her conclusion is worth citing, since it identifies the question of authority as the critical underlying issue: "Thus no feminist use of biblical material is finally immune to the risk of finding the Bible hurtful, unhelpful, not revealing of God, and not worth the effort to come to grips with it. Regardless of approach, feminists may find that the Bible seems to drive them away from itself (and sometimes from God), rather than drawing them closer. *At the heart of the problem lies the issue of biblical authority*" (ibid., 64; emphasis added).

4. On this aspect of biblical use and the particular dilemma this creates for Protestant feminists, see Mary Ann Tolbert, "Protestant Feminists and the Bible: On the Horns of a Dilemma," in Alice Bach, ed., *The Pleasure of Her Text: Feminist Readings of Biblical and Historical Texts* (Philadelphia: Trinity International, 1990) 5–23.

But there is another reason for feminists to maintain the painful tie to a patriarchal text beyond the threat of lost community and the threat to identity, and that is that this source of bondage is at the same time a source of liberation, and, in my view, the primary source of feminist critique of patriarchal oppression. I am a feminist because I am a Christian, and I am not alone. For the critique of oppressive systems (economic, political, and ideological) and of idols, and the demand for justice are fundamental to the biblical message. When feminists turn that critique and that demand on systems of patriarchal power and ideology, they are simply actualizing in our day an old message, whose radical implications had not fully been realized. Ruether and Russell are right, I believe, when they identify the fundamental message of the Christian Bible, and Christian faith, as a message of liberation, wholeness, and healing, governed by principles of love and justice.

Different generations, groups, and individuals will hear that message in different texts and in different terms, and they will translate it in terms appropriate to their own contexts and experiences—as a word of release from bondage for African-American slaves in nineteenth-century America, as a critique of oppressive political systems in Latin America, as a rejection of racist social policies in South Africa and twentieth-century America, and as judgment on women's oppression in patriarchal societies around the globe. But the critique of patriarchy is far more difficult to carry through on biblical grounds, for the very texts that carry the liberating message are often cast in exclusively male terms: "brotherhood" symbolizing the egalitarian ideal and a community of equals whose rights and duties are mutually binding—but only on other men (more specifically, freemen, natives, and property owners). The feminist critique turns back on the very texts that have sparked and preserved the message of justice and the vision of wholeness. Do the terms of debate, identity of the speakers, or limits of the vision invalidate the message? When does the weight of patriarchal culture become too much for the word to bear; when does it crush those who attempt to wield it for new battles?

Different feminists assess the tension between patriarchal word and liberating message in different ways and use different means to locate and retrieve a feminist message. I will sketch some of those responses shortly, but first I want to return to the fundamental question of allegiance to the book and to the community that has transmitted and interpreted it. I spoke of the Bible as shaping and sustaining Christian identity and community. These are in fact primary ways in which the Bible exercises authority. But biblical authority is more commonly identified with assent to propositions concerning the Bible's reception as the word of God: verbal assent to propositions concerning the Bible's divine origins, rather than life conformed to its teaching. And it is this claim of divine origin and order that is at the center of feminist critique. For a great many feminists today, perhaps the majority, recognition of the Bible's complicity in patriarchal oppression (in its origins as well as its use) requires rejection of the Bible as a source of revelation or norm for belief and action, and more specifically, as "word of God." Patriarchal texts must be divested of idolatrous claims to divine authority, they argue. The words of men must be unmasked in their attempts to represent themselves as the words of God.

Such an attack on the Bible as a human creation and a tool of patriarchy appears blasphemous to believers who reverence the Bible as the word of God. Many women, torn by this attack on a book by which they have lived, choose to trust its words as they have received them and submit to its authority as interpreted by the church, reasoning that it is better to serve God than "man" (more specifically, other women)—to follow God even against their own experience and will. I repeatedly encounter women struggling with new options for their lives, who believe that they must submit to male authority (even abusive authority) because it is God's way, revealed in Scripture. People who work with battered women report this as a common argument.[5] To forsake, or even question, a way that has been identified as God's way is too great a risk. For many both inside the church and out, the view of the alternatives is the same: accept the Bible as the word of God and submit to it, or reject it as the word of men.

It is a tragic dilemma, with tragic results for those who elect either option, because it rests on a false understanding of Scripture and scriptural authority. False beliefs hurt, and false or inadequate understandings of the nature of biblical authority are hurting the church today. I understand the appeal—especially in uncertain and tumultuous times—of a system that offers security, even if it pinches at places. And I am not ready to reject altogether the notion of submission of the will, or the metaphor of struggle, or even hierarchical models of authority, all of which have biblical sanctions and all of which have come under feminist attack. But I do reject idolatrous identification of human systems of order with divine plan or will. It is here, I believe, that feminism has an indispensable contribution to make. What is widely perceived as a threat to faith (namely, feminist critique of patriarchy) is, I believe, God's gift in our time—to the church and to the world—to save us from the false idols to which we cling and to lead us forward to the wholeness envisioned in creation, or revisioned as new creation.

Feminists insist that the Bible is the words of men—and further, of

5. See Susan Brooks Thistlethwaite, "Every Two Minutes: Battered Women and Feminist Interpretation," in Russell, *Feminist Interpretation*, 96–107.

men who have misconstrued the nature of our sexually bifurcated (dimorphous) humanity, creating systems of oppression for women, which operate at both the political and ideological level. Feminist critique of the Bible is the most penetrating and comprehensive of all modern critiques of the Bible's culturally determined limits and perversions, because it leaves no place of safe retreat. In my own view, which corresponds at this point to the most radical critique, there is no pure remnant, no untainted core, no tradition, or set of texts, or sayings behind the text, that has escaped the imprint of patriarchal culture—which is to say that the Bible is a human book, and it partakes of the limits, and the sinful distortions, of human existence.

But that is no reason whatever to deny authority to this book, authority even as the word of God; for we have heard God speaking here, God's words in human speech and thought. In fact we do not hear that word in any other way. The heart of the gospel message by which we live, and to which this book testifies, is that God has chosen to dwell among us, as one of us, and that we know God because we have seen God in our own likeness. And if God is not bound to that appearance and time, if I can see God in the prophet of Montgomery and Memphis, Martin Luther King, or in the compassionate friend of the dying, Mother Teresa, it is because I have learned to see Her in a Jewish teacher of first-century Palestine, a male leader in the tradition of his ancestors, who assembled an inner circle of men to further his mission, a teacher rejected by those to whom he came, but whose death gave life to a new community that would encircle the globe, embracing and challenging all of the kingdoms and cultures of this world.

Word of God in human words: that is the mystery and power of our affirmation about the Bible, and that is the source of its authority for us. But how does it operate? How do we identify the divine within the human, distinguish eternal truth from transient and fallible human claims? How do we apprehend the Spirit in a work of ink and paper, papyrus and parchment? That is the problem of every generation and of every reader, and every solution is partial and fleeting. Every effort to separate Spirit from flesh, the timeless from the time-bound, falls short and cannot escape the trap of its own time, absolutizing the forms of a particular age and culture or abstracting a Spirit that cannot be recognized or apprehended under the actual conditions of life.

It is here that feminism helps us so profoundly, by showing us how deeply imbedded our cultural constructs, and our gender-determined consciousness and needs, are in our sacred writings—and in the revelatory experiences and religious practice out of which they grew. Feminists insist that this partial view cannot stand for the whole; it requires a constructive effort to bring the feminine into view and into the shaping and substance of future discourse about the divine. Feminists are divided, however, on whether the androcentric tradition preserved within the Bible can give access to a source of truth capable of comprehending and addressing female experience and female ways of knowing, or whether it is bound to its male origins in a manner that excludes incorporation of female experience and representation of the divine.[6]

Feminists who continue to hold on to the Scriptures of Judaism and the early church find a significant measure of continuity between the faith articulated in those writings and the faith expressed in feminist dreams and hopes. They find the link in different ways and in different places, as I noted in my treatment of Rosemary Ruether, Letty Russell, Phyllis Trible, and Elisabeth Schüssler Fiorenza,[6a] and with different understandings of the nature of biblical authority.

Before I attempt concluding generalizations on feminist hermeneutics and biblical authority, I want briefly to expand my sketch of the options pursued by various feminist biblical scholars, drawing on Sakenfeld's 1988 survey.[7] Sakenfeld presents a typology of feminist positions on biblical authority, focusing on the role of women's experience (and definition of experience) in appropriating the biblical witness. Nearly all would agree, she says, that experience cannot be ignored in interpreting Scripture, but from that point of agreement three lines of thought diverge. At one extreme is Schüssler Fiorenza, who makes experience, and more particularly "the personally and politically reflected experience of oppression and liberation," the criterion of appropriateness for biblical interpretation and evaluation of biblical authority claims.[8]

---

6. I have argued elsewhere ("The Authority of the Bible," 61–63) that contemporary feminist critique is similar in many ways to the Marcionite critique in the early church, with similar consequences. As early Christians found much within the Jewish Scriptures morally and intellectually incompatible with their faith in Christ, so feminists today find much within the two-part canon morally offensive and incompatible with the message of the gospel as they have come to understand it. And as early Christians took different paths in responding to the perceived defect of the Scriptures, so too do feminists today. Those in the early church whose position ultimately received the stamp of orthodoxy insisted that the witness to God's activity in the ages prior to Christ was essential to Christian understanding. In order to retain that witness they developed various means of interpretation that subordinated, reinterpreted, or dismissed as no longer relevant passages that appeared incompatible with later belief. A similar approach is taken by those feminists today who believe that the Bible, despite its defects, contains a message of liberation and critique that is essential to the feminist agenda. They are struggling in various ways to free that message from the constricting matrix in which it has been transmitted.

[6a. Bird, *Feminism and the Bible*, 54–66.]

7. Sakenfeld, "Feminist Perspectives on Bible and Theology: An Introduction to Selected Issues and Literature," *Int* 42 (1988) 5–18.

8. Elisabeth Schüssler Fiorenza, *In Memory of Her: A Feminist Theological Reconstruction of Christian Origins* (New York: Crossroad, 1983) 32; Sakenfeld, "Feminist Perspectives," 7.

At the other extreme Sakenfeld places the literature of the evangelical wing of American Protestantism, illustrated by essays from the Evangelical Colloquium on Women and the Bible held in 1984.[9] While she notes diversity of opinion within that collection and cautions against generalizing, she finds that most of the authors seek a canonical check on "destructive subjectivism," while struggling with the question of "how Scripture itself can adjudicate debates between competing interpreters."[10] For example, Letha Scanzoni and Nancy Hardesty appeal to the Wesleyan "quadrilateral" (Scripture, tradition, experience, and reason) in asserting that while Scripture must be the first source of theology, the three other sources always come into play. They recognize the unavoidable subjectivity of the interpreter, but formally subordinate experience to Scripture. They also define experience differently from Fiorenza, identifying it as "our own personal religious experiences and those of people we know,"[11] in contrast to Schüssler Fiorenza's specific focus on the struggle for liberation. For Scanzoni and Hardesty as well as Schüssler Fiorenza, however, it is women's experience that is decisive.[12]

Sakenfeld finds a middle ground, or another angle of vision, in Letty Russell's understanding of authority and experience. Russell insists that authority, as "legitimized power," "accomplishes its ends by evoking the assent of the respondent."[13] Speaking in personal terms, she says:

> The Bible has authority in my life because it makes sense of my experience and speaks to me about the meaning and purpose of my humanity in Jesus Christ. . . . Its authority in my life stems from its story of God's invitation to participation in the restoration of wholeness, peace, and justice in the world.[14]

"Somehow," Sakenfeld comments, "the Bible for Russell evokes consent through the power of God's Spirit despite its many sexist, racist and triumphalist texts whose viewpoint must be rejected."[15] Mary Ann Tolbert

---

9. Sakenfeld cites a number of different works as representing this position, including the essays from the colloquium, edited by Alvera Mickelson, *Women, Authority & the Bible* (Downers Grove, Ill.: InterVarsity, 1986); Letha Dawson Scanzoni and Nancy A. Hardesty, *All We're Meant to Be: Biblical Feminism for Today* (rev. ed.; Nashville: Abingdon, 1986); and Reta H. Finger, "The Bible and Christian Feminism," *Daughters of Sarah* 13 (1987) 5–12.

10. Sakenfeld, "Feminist Perspectives," 7–8.

11. Scanzoni and Hardesty, *All We're Meant to Be,* 31; cited by Sakenfeld, "Feminist Perspectives," 8.

12. Sakenfeld, "Feminist Perspectives," 8 n. 8.

13. Letty M. Russell, *Household of Freedom: Authority in Feminist Theology* (Philadelphia: Westminster, 1987) 21; Sakenfeld, "Feminist Perspectives," 8.

14. Letty M. Russell, "Authority and the Challenge of Feminist Interpretation," in Russell, *Feminist Interpretation,* 138.

15. Sakenfeld, "Feminist Perspectives," 9.

describes the paradox as a tension between "God as enemy and God as helper."[16] Both Tolbert and Russell propose new paradigms of authority, with Tolbert emphasizing partnership in place of domination, and Russell speaking of "the authority of the future," described as "God's intention for a mended creation."[17]

Sakenfeld goes on to discuss the variety of ways in which the Bible functions as a resource for constructing feminist theologies, identifying three principal options. The first focuses on reinterpretation of texts traditionally read as requiring women's subordination within a patriarchal system and the highlighting of hitherto ignored texts that present women in more "positive" light. This approach, which attempts to show that the texts either meant something else[18] or refer to special circumstances of the time, seems to be especially important to evangelical feminists, Sakenfeld notes.[19] The second option involves recognition of general themes in the Bible that offer the possibility of a theological critique of patriarchy and is exemplified by Ruether's appeal to "prophetic principles" and Russell's appeal to the biblical vision of a "mended creation" or "household of freedom." The third involves "approaching texts about women to learn from the intersection of experience of ancient and modern women living in patriarchal cultures," an approach represented by Trible and Fiorenza.[20]

Before I return to the question of authority in Christian faith, I want to elaborate briefly on an earlier emphasis in my treatment of feminist theology, viz., its links to a broader movement.[20a] That movement has affected biblical studies in the academy as well as the church, and it has impacted Jewish as well as Christian interpretations of Scripture. While a survey of this broader arena lies outside the scope of these lectures, some account of these new interpretive efforts is necessary to illustrate the scope of the movement and the issues it has identified. Its most important contribution to academic inquiry, I noted earlier, has been its identification of gender as a critical variable in every field of study involving human subjects.

Attention to gender need not involve a specifically feminist perspective, although it is a consequence of feminist interests. Gender study has now become a recognized subdiscipline of anthropology, and gender analysis belongs to the core of current anthropological theory.[21] In biblical studies,

16. Mary Ann Tolbert, "Defining the Problem," in Tolbert, ed., *The Bible and Feminist Hermeneutics* (*Semeia* 28; Chico, Calif.: Scholars Press, 1983) 120.

17. Russell, *Household,* 18; Sakenfeld, "Feminist Perspectives," 9.

18. E.g., mutual submission instead of simply women's submission in Eph 5:21-33.

19. Sakenfeld, "Feminist Perspectives," 10.

20. Ibid., 11.

[20a. Bird, *Feminism and the Bible,* chaps. 2 and 3, esp. pp. 21–25, 28–33, 42–54.]

21. Henrietta Moore, *Feminism and Anthropology* (Cambridge: Polity, 1988) vii.

an important contribution has been made to the discipline by a collection of essays edited by Peggy Day under the title *Gender and Difference in Ancient Israel*.[22] The volume exhibits a variety of approaches by female scholars to gender-nuanced interpretion of Hebrew Bible texts and related ancient Near Eastern literatures—some with sociological or historical interest, others with primarily literary interests. Many of these essays employ social science methods and data to interpret gender roles and relationships in the biblical texts. Day's introduction to the volume provides a helpful discussion of the role of female experience in feminist historical interpretation.[23]

More recently we have begun to see sociologically oriented studies of women and gender roles in the Bible, such as Naomi Steinberg's work on the patriarchal narratives and their genealogical frame.[24] Steinberg focuses on the role of inheritance and kinship in the accounts, interpreting women's roles and strategies in terms of these dual concerns. Literary representations of gender are the focus of Athalya Brenner and Fokkelien van Dijk-Hemmes's volume, *On Gendering Texts: Female and Male Voices in the Hebrew Bible*.[25]

Two recent works by Jewish feminist scholars make important contributions to current debate concerning the nature and extent of patriarchy in the Hebrew Bible—and in the social order and religious conceptions behind the text. Carol Meyers, in *Discovering Eve*, criticizes the concept of patriarchy as employed in contemporary feminist analysis and especially its use in analyzing ancient Israelite society. It fails, in her view, to recognize the complex dynamics of male-female relations, especially in situations where women exercise significant power, but have no formal authority; and it makes inappropriate equations between ancient Israelite and modern Western society.[26]

22. Peggy L. Day, ed., *Gender and Difference in Ancient Israel* (Minneapolis: Fortress Press, 1989).

23. Ibid., 1–11.

24. Naomi Steinberg, *Kinship and Marriage in Genesis: A Household Economics Perspective* (Minneapolis: Fortress Press, 1993).

25. A number of biblical scholars, as well as popular authors, have suggested that portions of the Hebrew Bible may have been authored by women, at least at an oral or precanonical stage. See, e.g., Edward F. Campbell, Jr., *Ruth* (AB 7; Garden City, N.Y.: Doubleday, 1975); S. D. Goitein, "Women as Creators of Biblical Genres," *Prooftexts* 8 (1988) 1–33; and Harold Bloom, *The Book of J* (New York: Grove Weidenfeld, 1990). While women appear to have been the creators of certain types of songs, proverbs, and stories, the Bible, as a literary production, must be understood, I believe, as a male creation, dominated by male interests and perspectives, even in the incorporation of traditions originating in female circles. On the question of "voice," in contrast to authorship, see Athalya Brenner and Fokkelien van Dijk-Hemmes, *On Gendering Texts: Female and Male Voices in the Hebrew Bible* (Leiden: Brill, 1993) 1–13.

26. Carol Meyers, *Discovering Eve* (Oxford: Oxford University Press, 19) 24–45.

Meyers's critique of feminist theologians has an unspoken target in the tendency of Christian feminists to identify patriarchal oppression with ancient Israel and the Jewish Scriptures, either by characterizing Christianity as a liberating alternative for women or by criticizing the failure of New Testament Christianity to repudiate this oppressive legacy. Meyers acknowledges an oppressive misogynist stream within Judaism, observable in the latest stages of composition and redaction of the Hebrew Scriptures, but she attributes this primarily to Hellenistic influences (i.e., late, pagan/non-Jewish influences) and to fundamental social changes occasioned by the institution of the monarchy. Premonarchic Israel was an egalitarian society, she insists, in which women had equal status with men, and it is this period that is normative for her.[27] In her command of current anthropological literature and her use of this to illuminate the life of village Israel as the ethos in which Israelite theology was born, Meyers is without peer and has contributed significantly to an understanding of gender relations in the context of family life and economic relations in ancient Israel—even if her interpretation and dating of key texts must be rejected, as I believe they must.

Tikvah Frymer-Kensky's book, *In the Wake of the Goddesses*,[28] targets the divine realm as the source for ancient Israelite views of gender roles and relationships. In contrast to the surrounding nations, whose gods reflected and at the same time legitimated the gender roles of the society, Israel's sole, sexless God provided no gender models for its citizens, but encouraged an anthropology that de-emphasized sex and gender and prescribed behavior without acknowledgment of gender. Frymer-Kensky recognizes a gender-specific, and misogynist, strain in the textual tradition, but argues that the great majority of texts address readers without attention to gender, and hence equally.[29] Although I think this argument involves a fundamental misunderstanding of the nature of androcentric generic representation, it brings renewed attention to the discrepancy between ideal constructions (formulated or construed as inclusive) and practice. Frymer-Kensky also draws attention to the problems of a sole deity and of gender representation in conceptions of the divine.[30] Her

27. Ibid., 40–45, 165–96. Meyers uses the expression "functional nonhierarchy" (43 and passim) to describe the relationship between the sexes in ancient Israel. And although she acknowledges that "functional nonhierarchy of at least some peasant societies is not synonymous with equality" (43), she concludes that "male dominance did not exist in the formative stages of Israel" (187). Thus her argument parallels Fiorenza's in ascribing a gender-egalitarian impulse to the origins (= normative period) of the community/faith.

28. Tikvah Frymer-Kensky, *In the Wake of the Goddesses: Women, Culture, and the Biblical Transformation of Pagan Myth* (New York: Free Press, 1992).

29. Ibid., 118–43.

30. It is worth noting that the question of biblical monotheism has received scant attention in the hermeneutical discussion of American feminist exegetes, in contrast to their Euro-

treatment of goddesses in ancient Mesopotamian religion and culture is a major contribution—and the only reliable popular introduction.[31]

Both Meyers and Frymer-Kensky aim through historical argument to support traditional affirmations of the Bible's authority, although neither identifies this aim, and both seek to accomplish this by minimizing female oppression. They may both be right in attributing a greater degree of gender equality, or indifference, to ancient Israel, but I do not think that historical argument of egalitarian intent is sufficient to ground a feminist affirmation of the authority of the Bible. Patriarchal bias and androcentrism remain in the text—as distortions, intended or unintended, of the image of God and of humankind.

I return now to the general question of biblical authority, taking Letty Russell's statement as an example of a contemporary formulation. In the fuller form of the statement cited above Russell says:

> The Bible has authority in my life because it makes sense of my experience and speaks to me about the meaning and purpose of my humanity in Jesus Christ. In spite of its ancient and patriarchal worldviews, in spite of its inconsistencies and mixed messages, the story of God's love affair with the world leads me to a vision of a New Creation that impels my life.[32]

I note the following points:

1. The statement does not appeal to particular texts, but to the Bible as a whole. The Bible carries authority as a single, complex composition.

2. The claim is personal, anchored in individual experience. Here Russell speaks only for herself. This characteristic feature of feminist theology, which rests final authority in personal experience, has been heavily criticized by those who are wary of subjectivism, and I shall return to this point.

3. The source of the authority is a message. The authority is not merely formal, but rests on content. Meaning and authority are intimately linked.

4. Although the content of the message, as Russell identifies it, is formulated in distinctively modern terms, it is recognizable as the recapitulation of an old story, a story told and retold by the church. It points to a

---

pean counterparts. See the pointed observation by Marie-Theres Wacker, "Feministisch-theologische Blicke auf die neuere Monotheismus-Discussion: Anstösse und Fragen," in Marie-Theres Wacker and Erich Zenger, eds., *Der Eine Gott und die Göttin: Gottesvorstellungen des biblischen Israel im Horizont feministischer Theologie* (Freiburg: Herder, 1991) 32 n. 36.

31. As far as I know, this is the only overview of the subject available to a general audience that is written by a scholar familiar with the original texts in their original languages and ancient cultural context.

32. Russell, "Authority and Challenge," 138.

history of interpretation, and a locus for that interpretation (the church),
even as it reaches behind this tradition to the Bible itself for a fresh reading—a reading in conversation with the concerns of a new day.

5. The message is centered in Jesus Christ, who is seen as revealing
God's intention for the world and God's means of relating to the world.
This message contains as essential components a word about God, myself,
Jesus, and the world. The authority of Scripture is exhibited and tested in
what is primary and central to its message, rather than what is secondary
or peripheral. Discerning the center is therefore essential.

6. The authority is future-oriented, even as it is anchored in the past.
It offers a vision that proclaims that God's business with the world is not
yet finished. What has been is meant to prepare us for what will be, to
chart the direction and invite us to participate in this project.

7. The Bible energizes those who hear its message. Its vision impels. It
brings readers and hearers into contact with the source of its power.

Russell's statement does not meet the usual tests for affirming the authority of Scripture that have been devised by those most concerned to
safeguard it, but it touches virtually all of the essential points of the doctrine. Russell's choice of contemporary idiom is no more culture-bound
than "traditional" or "orthodox" formulations, which have frozen the language of an earlier age, employing it, however, to clothe distinctively
nineteenth-century ideas. As critics of fundamentalism have noted, this
defense of a threatened tradition is a modern phenomenon shaped in response to a modern crisis. The crisis remains, and it remains unsolved
by new assertions of authority. It remains because it is ultimately a crisis
of meaning.

I have considerable sympathy for the argument of David Clines when
he proposes to discard the notion of authority altogether.[33] I agree with
his complaint that the concept of an authoritative text has frustrated our
ability truly to hear what the text has to say, and that it has constrained
and misdirected biblical interpretation. I spend too much energy trying
to get students past the preconceptions they bring to the text and their
anxieties over the "right" interpretation, so they can encounter the text
afresh, on its own terms. But I do not think we can read the Bible as
Christians without raising the question of its authority for us, and I think
Clines misunderstands the meaning of authority.

His argument surfaces in a critique of Phyllis Trible's reading of Genesis 2–3, a text which he views as "persist[ing] in its androcentric orienta-

33. David A. J. Clines, "What Does Eve Do to Help? and Other Irredeemably Androcentric Orientations in Genesis 1–3," in idem, *What Does Eve Do to Help? and Other Readerly
Questions to the Old Testament* (Sheffield: JSOT Press, 1990) 47–48.

tion, from which it cannot be redeemed despite the constructive pro-
gramme of second-generation feminists among Biblical scholars."[34] The
text (as irredeemably androcentric) is in conflict, he asserts, with a principle (viz., the equality of the sexes) which he cannot give up without a
loss of personal integrity.[35] Posing the dilemma as a reader's choice between faithfulness to the teachings of the Hebrew and Christian Scriptures
or faithfulness to her/his own integrity as a whole human being,[36] Clines
rejects the option of ascribing the sexism of the text to the primitive world
of the Old Testament and denying its authority, as well as the option of
"accept[ing] the authority of the Bible in matters to which the heart and
mind can clearly consent" while rejecting it when it conflicts with our
deeply held convictions.[37]

For Clines, the notion of authority points interpreters in the wrong
direction, focusing on the nature of the text, rather than its function. He
does not want to maintain that the Bible is "right" (or even wrong), "but
that it impacts for good upon people." Identifying authority with dogma
and the plundering of the Bible for proof texts for theological warfare, he
chides feminists for failing to see that "'authority' is a concept from the
male world of power relations" and that a more inclusive language of influence, encouragement, and inspiration would be more acceptable.[38]

Clines misunderstands the nature of authority, I believe, although he
does describe a popular use of the term (which William Countryman defines as "tyranny").[39] And he rightly sees that the question of authority
directs attention away from the living word to its credentials, away from
encounter with the text to external tests of its truth or trustworthiness.
Those who press the question of authority think to assure the purity of
the Bible's precious contents, but they have constructed humanly devised
cisterns that cannot hold living water. What we need now is not more
cement to plaster the cracks of our broken cisterns, but a way to drink—
a path to the living waters that spring up from the depths in an ever-
flowing stream.

The path to the waters of life has been strewn with obstacles—obstacles that define the object of our search in misleading terms and narrow
the path we must walk by setting up preconditions on what we must believe and how we must read. Our fundamental problem with the Bible

---

34. Ibid., 37.
35. Ibid., 45–46.
36. Russell's formulation of the dilemma, in "Authority and Challenge," 137.
37. Clines, "What Does Eve Do," 46–47.
38. Ibid., 47–48.
39. William Countryman, *Biblical Authority or Biblical Tyranny? Scripture and the Christian Pilgrimage* (Philadelphia: Fortress Press, 1981).

today, I believe, is a problem of understanding—and authority rests ultimately on understanding. Old understandings have been challenged by modern conceptions and experience. But we are reluctant to set aside past formulations so that the words can speak afresh to us. Changing times require changing concepts and changing assessments—not simply new translations. Our conversation with the ancient texts must reflect the changing circumstances of our world, but it must also honor the integrity of the ancient speakers.

I do not think there is *one* right way of using or understanding the Bible. That is what most doctrines of authority attempt to assure. The result is a straitjacket on the reader/believer—and on the Spirit, which usually manages to escape anyway and manifest itself in strange places, like the feminist movement. I do want to plead, however, for an approach to understanding the Bible and to understanding its authority that is consonant with the character and content of the Bible itself and with the diverse needs and abilities of its users. We speak different languages of faith that are both genetically and culturally conditioned. I do not think these differences can be dismissed as "merely" semantic. But however real our differences and however deeply rooted in our individual and collective psychosocial histories, we belong to the same household of faith, united in allegiance to Christ, and confession of that allegiance requires us to engage in conversation.

The primer for that conversation is the Bible, providing us with a vocabulary of faith, and a pattern for our discourse. And it is a pattern of dialogue. What is most striking about the Bible as a written document is its pluriform and multivocal character. A collection of writings of different genres, ages, subject matter, and theologies, the Bible spans more than a millennium of time in its own internal witness and represents hundreds of voices. It presents us with the conversation of a community over time, a conversation about the source and meaning of its life, its destiny, and its vocation. It is a conversation that adopts new language for new occasions, a conversation that is filled with conflict and passionate argument as different voices present their visions and their claims to truth.[40] It requires us to enter into that conversation and to test those claims. We cannot stand by as onlookers, nor can we respond only through aesthetic appreciation. These voices claim to speak the truth about the nature of our existence, our destiny, our world. Conservatives rightly stress that the Bible makes ultimate claims.

To respond appropriately is to test those claims—not simply accept

40. See further Phyllis A. Bird, *The Bible as the Church's Book* (Philadelphia: Westminster, 1982).

them. For the Bible is the first word in the Christian's journey, not the last, the primer for our theological reflection, not a ready-made theology for our day. If we have rightly understood the conversation within the canon of Scripture, we must continue it. For it is a conversation about a God who is alive and not dead, and about a world that is God's creation and the place of God's encounter with humankind. And it is a world of change—for good and for bad. We cannot return to the biblical world, nor can we make it speak our language or endorse our concerns. It has no feminist message, in my view, but it does have a message about the nature of our humanity and the requirements of justice that in our day must be translated into terms of full equality of women in order that the image of God may be fully revealed.

I return to the question of authority. I reject notions of biblical authority that link it to a particular theory of divine agency or impute a special supernatural character that removes its writings from the constraints of human nature, history, and culture. I reject identification of its authority with particular theological formulations—or with a particular trajectory or core within the writings. Although I agree essentially with Letty Russell and Rosemary Ruether and other liberation theologians in recognizing a prophetic/visionary stream of tradition within the Scriptures that describes their central message, and message for me, I am uneasy about resting a notion of the Bible's claim on me on such a selective principle. I reject the notion of a canon within the canon, or a canon behind the canon (whether Fiorenza's *ekklēsia* of women or Schubert Ogden's "earliest apostolic witness"), even as I acknowledge the functional necessity of such a concept. I want to insist that the notion of biblical authority be distinguished from meaning-for-me, and at the same time insist that when the Bible ceases in significant measure to have meaning for me, its authority is dubious or null. I reject the criterion of meaning-for-me, or even meaning-for-my-group, because the Bible, in contrast to other books, is a communal document—created and transmitted through communal processes. Because the Bible is the church's book, that is where I must work out my understanding of it and its meaning for my life, in conversation with others there—even as I draw upon and contribute insights into its meanings derived from other sources, including academic study in the company of men and women of other faiths and of no religious faith. But where I give account of my understanding is in the church.

When I speak of a concept of biblical authority that does not rest (exclusively) on my consent, it is because as a Christian I come to the Bible with a presumption of what I shall find there that is shaped by my experience in the church. In the church, I live in a Bible-shaped world of liturgy and prayer, of song and story and sermon topics, of admonitions and exhortations. The Bible comes to me through family use and church school with credentials that I will only later test. In short, by the church's testimony of use and honor, the Bible comes to me as having authority. But it can retain that authority only as it is confirmed in my own experience—which may require discarding arguments on which it originally rested. Ultimately the Bible's authority rests on its ability to reveal its Author in a way that enables us to recognize Her in our own day. Only as it directs our attention away from itself to the living God may we proclaim it as the "word of God."

The authority of the Bible does not rest in the infallibility of its statements, but in the truth of its witness to a creating and redeeming power, which can and must be known as a present reality. The Bible as the word of God in human words exhibits the cultural limits and sinful distortions of humanity in every age, witnessing thereby to the central affirmation of Christian faith that God is most fully and truly revealed in assuming this same human nature. The Bible shares the incarnational character of the One to whom it bears witness. It proclaims by its composition as well as its declarations that the Creator has chosen to be revealed in creation, even coming among us as one of us. But that manifestation does not exhaust or circumscribe the divine presence or power, and the word by which that action is recalled and re-presented is only the servant of the living Word. The words of God spoken to prophets and poets are essential to Christian faith and carry the authority of their Speaker, but the word of God cannot be contained in any document; nor can it be comprehended apart from the Word made flesh, which is both the center and the norm of Scripture.

SCRIPTURE INDEX

Old Testament

New Testament

SUBJECT INDEX

n. 37, 199 n. 2, 220, 228, 233–35
Religion, cross-cultural studies, 5, 100, 106–109, 111, 112, 114, 115 n. 34, 117–18, 119 n. 44, 172; definition and theory, 103, 104–6, 111, 113–19; magic and folk r., 101, 112–13; role of gender in, 104–6, 114–20
Religion, Israelite (general), 5, 13 n. 1, 19, 27, 81–85, 101, 103–4, 105 n. 4, 106, 110, 112 n.26, 113, 119–20, 216; family r. and ancestor cult, 81, 92, 99–100, 110–11. *See also* Cult: ancestor c.; mediums, magic and sorcery, 101–2, 112–13, 118; reconstruction of, 84–86; women's place and practice, 5, 27, 42, 44–45, 56, 60, 62–63, 65, 81–102, 104–6, 109–14, 119–20. *See also* Women in ancient Israel: distinct patterns, practices, and perceptions, 87–88, 91 n. 28, 100–102, 104, 106, 113–14, 118–20; marginalized in a male-oriented cult, 27–28, 30, 42, 44–45, 81, 91, 93 n. 34, 98, 105; relation to foreign/heterodox cults, 42, 56, 81, 92, 99, 100, 119. *See also* Asherah, Fertility figurines, Hierodule, Queen of Heaven, Tammuz; religious specialists and cultic personnel, 42, 81, 91, 93–99. *See also* Dancer(s), Hierodule, Prophet, Singers, Women: serving at the Tent of Meeting
Religion, Western; contemporary, 2, 6, 106 n. 6, 241, 249–50, 255, 263; historical, 2, 9, 175–76

Ruth. *See* Women . . ., named

Sacrifice, 18, 27 n. 34, 43 n. 78, 84 n. 12, 88, 90–93, 95 n. 37, 97 n. 41, 99, 118, 230–31, 233; as a male prerogative, 93 n. 34
Sanctuary (central/state and local), 20, 87, 91, 93, 95 n. 37, 96–97, 114, 118, 209, 216, 234–35. *See also* "High places" (*bāmôt*); s. attendants (female), 96. *See also* Women: serving at the Tent of Meeting
Sarah. *See* Women . . . , named
Serpent. *See* Snake
Sex (as activity), 20 n. 11, 25 n. 25, 32, 52–53, 61, 151–53, 170, 174, 185 n. 35, 222. *See also* Sexual: activity, drive, knowledge, intercourse, relations; extramarital s., 23–24, 25 n. 25, 61, 230 n. 33; "s. cult"/cultic sex, 226 n. 23, 230 n. 33
Sex(es) (as classification: male and female), 27, 28 n. 35, 29, 33, 42, 43 n. 79, 44, 47 n. 87, 48, 51, 58, 59, 126, 128 n. 12, 145, 149, 151–53, 156, 161–63, 165, 167, 171, 183, 200, 205 n.; 19, 258 n. 27. *See also* Gender, Sexual: differentiation, distinction
Sexism, 1, 2, 261; sexist Scripture/language in Scripture, 9, 83, 239–47 (esp. 239–40), 255. *See also*; Androcentrism
Sexual; access/encounter/relations, 62, 200, 205, 225, 235; activity/acts, 98, 172, 189 n. 43, 208, 221, 223, 231–36; allusions/connotations/innuendo,187

n. 43, 210 n. 31, 212, 229–30; attraction/drive/energy, 24, 58, 164 n. 26, 165–66; attributes, 31, 32, 44, 47, 58; constitution, 142, 156, 156; differentiation/distinction, 2, 7, 89 n. 24, 127–29, 140, 142, 143, 145, 151–53, 158, 160–63, 170; discrimination, 29; division of labor, 86, 94 n. 35, 95 n. 38, 181; equality, 145, 151, 161, 261; favors, 199, 223; infidelity, 25; intercourse, 22 n. 16, 24, 25 n. 25, 28, 29, 48 n. 89, 185, 187 n. 43, 208, 220, 222; knowledge, 187–88 n. 43; language/terms, 229, 231, 233; morals, 226, 232; partner, 25, 31, 39; pleasure/gratification, 25, 31, 204; (sexually determined) roles, relationships, status, 9, 29, 30, 44, 51, 71, 87, 93, 98, 149, 162, 200, 206. *See also* Female, Gender, Male; reproduction, 128, 158, 160–61; transgressions/offenses, 20, 23, 25, 30, 222; union, 25 n. 26, 38 n. 6, 171. *See also* Bisexual, Homosexual
Sexuality/sexual nature (biological and psychosocial), 2, 7, 23, 24, 38, 49 n. 89, 61–62, 71, 94 n.; 35, 97, 127, 129, 142, 144 n. 53, 146, 151, 155–56, 160–63, 167–73, 188 n. 34, 200, 222, 225
Sin, in the Genesis creation accounts, 2, 48, 153, 165–666, 191n. 16, 174–75,188 n. 43, 191–93; identification with woman, 174–75; "original sin," 174–75, 176 n. 9, 185 n. 38, 191–93; term lacking in Genesis 3, 192; traditional inter-

pretation, 174–75, 179, 188, 192. *See also* Creation in the J account: Gen 3:1-24

Singers/singing; entertainers, 43, 96 n. 39; female cultic s., 42, 91, 94 n. 35, 96; male cultic, 96 n. 39

"Sisterhood," 250

Slave(s), 69, 71–77, 90 n. 25, 95 n. 38, 216, 251; as member of a man's household/possessions, 21 n. 12, 23, 37, 38 n. 61, 64, 77, 246; associated with other landless classes in Deuteronomy, 76; distinct terms for male and female slaves, 73 n. 22; female slave, 21, 25, 26, 27 n. 33, 28 n. 36, 30, 39, 43, 52, 63, 72–74, 199, 244

Slavery/enslavement, 20, 28 n. 36, 72–73, 75–76

Snake, in Genesis 3. *See also* Creation: Gen 3:1-24; and the woman in Genesis 3, 179, 182–85; as voice of inner debate, 189; associations with life and death, 184

Sorceress, 30, 42, 43 n. 78; sorcery, 43 n. 78, 92, 101, 112

Spinning, as woman's craft, 43 n. 80, 59, 95 n. 36

Subordination of woman to man; as primary sign of "fallen" creation, 165. *See also* Creation in the J account: Gen 3:1-24

Subjugation of the earth; as distinct theme from dominion, 146–47. *See also* Creation in the P account

Tamar. *See* Women . . ., named

Tammuz, women weeping

for, 42 n. 77, 92, 100, 114 n. 33. *See also* Relgion

teraphim, 92, 111

Theology; feminist, 127 n. 11, 256. *See also* Feminism, Feminist; t. of sexuality, contemporary; contribution of Genesis 1–3, 155–73; J's theological anthropology, 152–53; P's theological anthropology, 150–51

Theophany; women as recipients, 100

Tombs; women's visits and rituals, 108–110. *See also* Cult: ancestor

Translation; as form of interpretation, 241–43; of Scripture, 240, 242; of sexist/androcentric language in Scripture, 239, 241–46. *See also* Sexism

Unclean(ness), 16, 27, 28, 42 n. 76, 201 n. 8, 250. *See also* Impurity

Virgin (*bĕtûlâ*), 16, 52, 61, 65, 91, 97, 206 n. 20, 246. *See also* Woman: young; virginity, 24, 114 n. 33

Vows, 23, 28, 30, 35 n. 52, 44, 57, 64, 87–88, 91, 98–99, 100–101, 109

Weaving, as woman's craft, 59, 95; as male profession, 58, 95 n. 36; women weaving for Asherah, 92, 95 n. 36, 114 n. 33

Widow, 21, 26, 27, 30, 34, 35, 40, 54, 60, 64, 73, 76–77, 88 n. 22, 200, 203, 222

Wife (= "woman of MN"), 16, 17, 21, 25–27, 31, 32 n. 44, 33–34, 36, 37–40, 49 n. 92, 52, 56, 58, 74, 89, 95 n. 37, 98, 145 n. 55, 149, 162, 190, 191, 200

n. 5, 201–3, 215, 232, 235. *See also* Husband; as sexual partner, 23, 24, 25, 31, 61–62, 200, 224–25; as stranger/outsider in husbands family, 39, 56; as subject to husband's authority, 30, 64; a dependent, not chattel or property, 21, 23, 33, 37, 38, 64; "bad w.," 31; barren w. *See* Barren woman; foreign w. 37, 56; "good w.," 17, 31, 33, 38–39, 58; as key to man's success, 33; in Prov 31 (RSV = *'ēšet ḥayil* "woman of valor/ worth") 17, 31, 58; hidden behind male addressees and subjects, 27 n. 12, 62, 76, 89, 246; multiple wives, 34, 36 n. 56, 38 n. 60, 60, 75 n. 29, 109. *See also* Concubine, Polygyny; primary image and vocation as mother, 23, 25, 35, 37, 41, 57–60, 88. *See also* Mother; promiscuous w. (in prophetic metaphor and rhetoric), 40, 225–28, 230 n. 33, 236; slave w., 39, 72–74; terminology, 37, 52

Wife, identified by husband; Manoah's w., 93, 100; Noah's wife, 58, 145 n. 55

Wisdom, 32, 53, 184, 188, 214, 217–18, as exhibited, sought, and transmitted by women, 31, 33, 34, 44, 58, 187 n. 41; as god-like, 186–87; personified as f., 32, 65

Witch, witchcraft. *See* Medium, Sorceress, sorcery

Woman. *See* Women.

Womb, 31, 59; as opened by God, 16, 26; as term for

woman (RSV "maiden"),
15; compassion as "w.-
feelings," 60; woman's
bond with fruit of her w.,
35, 60, 217
Women in the ancient Near
East; harlot, 184, 186–87,
199 n. 2, 201–2, 210, 213,
215 n. 42; hierodule/
"priestess" (*qadištu, ēn/
ēntu, nadītu, ugbabtu, ištarītu, kulmašītu*), 89, 94
n. 35, 97; n. 41, 118, 211,
220; other, 98, 112–13
n. 29
Women in cross-cultural
studies, 5, 86–88, 106–11;
religious practice and experience, 106–9
Women/woman in the He-
brew Bible/Old Testa-
ment (textual representa-
tions), general features,
2–4, 7, 13–51 passim,
52–66 passim; as clues to
women behind the text,
52–53; as largely invisible
and without voice, 5–6,
13, 56, 64–65; as male
constructions/repre-
sentations, 53; as meta-
phor or symbol, 4, 6, 16,
51, 236.; diversity of representations, 14, 18–19; in
the creation accounts, 18.
See Creation accounts; in
the "historical" writings
(and prophets), 33–45,
251; in the legal traditions
(including religious law),
20–30, 244–246. *See also*
Women in Israel: legal
status; cultic impurity occasioned by menstrua-
tion or childbirth, 27–28;
inheritance of women,
26. *See also* Inheritance;
sexual offenses, 23–25; in
Proverbs, 30–33. *See also*
Adulteress, Mother: as

teacher/counselor,
Woman: contentious,
"strange"/"foreign" (*zrh*),
Wife: "good" ('*št ḥyl*); in
the Song of Songs, 32
n. 46. *See also* Women in
Israel
Women in Israel (women
behind the text), general
features; authority,
power, and influence, 45,
56–57, 64–66, 257–58. *See
also* Authority; economic
status and roles, 31, 43–
44, 55, 57–59, 62. *See also*
social status and roles;
home as woman's prov-
ince: site of primary
work, worship, authority,
and power, 27 n. 34, 44;
n. 81, 57, 60, 86, 86; legal
status, 21, 23. *See also*
Women: in the legal tra-
ditions; generally subject
to male authority within
the family, 23. *See also*
Authority, Prostitute,
Widow; religious life and
place in Israelite religion.
See Religion, Israelite:
women's place and prac-
tice; social status and
roles. *See also* economic
status and role; deter-
mined by roles within
the family, 97; roles
within the family, 31, 55,
57–60, 169 n. 34. *See also*
Concubine, Daughter,
Daughter-in law, Family
(Israelite), Mother, Slave:
female, Wife, Women in
the Hebrew Bible; roles
and activities outside the
family, 62, 97. *See also*
Dancer, Hierodule,
Keener, Medium/; necro-
mancer, Midwife,
Prophet (female), Prosti-
tute, Religion: women's

place and; practice,
Singer, Slave: female,
Widow, Women: "wise
w."; sources and prob-
lems of reconstruction,
83, 103–4. *See also*
Women in the Hebrew
Bible/Old Testament
Women/woman in Israel/
Hebrew Bible, particular
roles, conditions, and attributes; as authors of
biblical books or genres,
257 n. 25; as contentious,
17; as craftswoman, 43
n. 80, 59, 95. *See also*
Crafts, Spinning, Weav-
ing; as help(er). *See*
Help(er), Creation in the
Yahwist's (J) account; as
lover, 31, 32 n. 46; as
mother. *See* Mother; as
mourner. *See* Mourner;
as partner, 45; as prop-
erty, 14; as protector of
the dead, 60; as sexual
object, 44; as under-
handed, 44, 45 n. 83; as
victim of oppression or
violence, 71; as wise, 15,
31, 43 n. 80, 58, 215–16.
See also "wise w."; barren
w. *See* Barren; Canaanite,
202; dancer, *See* Danc-
er(s)/dancing; divorced.
See Divorce; foreign w.
(*nokrīyâ*), 34, 37, 39, 54,
56, 98. *See also* "strange
w.," Wife: foreign; "He-
brew w." (*hā'ibrīyâ*), 244;
w. in childbirth/labour,
as image of helplessness,
35, 60. *See also* Child-
birth/childbearing;
"loose w" (['iššâ] *zārâ*).
See "strange w."; old(er)
w., 60; "w. of worth." *See*
Wife: "good"; poor w.,
67–69, 72–74, 76–77;
post-menapausal w., 60;

AUTHOR INDEX

Abusch, T., 113 n. 29
Albright, W. F., 42 n. 77,
Alexander, P. S., 175 n. 3
Alter, R., 208 n. 23
Amihai, M., 4 n. 10, 61
n. 15, 103 n. 1, 197, 222
n. 14
Anderson, B. W., 123 n. 2,
129 n. 13, 131 nn. 16 and
19, 134 n. 26, 145 n. 54,
148 n. 65
Andersen, F. I., 223 n. 17,
225 n. 22, 229 n. 31, 231
nn. 35 and 40
Asmussen, J. P., 219 n. 1
Astour, M. C., 207 n. 21
Atkinson, C. W., 66

Bach, A., 250 n. 4
Bailey, J. A., 185 n. 35
Bailey, J. S., 48 n. 91
Bal, M., 65 n. 22, 176 n. 10,
177 n. 11
Balch, D., 8 n. 19
Banton, M., 105 n. 5
Barr, J., 123 n. 2, 134 n. 24,
147 n. 63, 178 n. 12, 184
n. 34, 187 n. 41, 188 n. 43,
193 n. 53
Barth, K., 124 n. 3, 125, 126,
126 nn. 8 and 9, 127, 127
n. 10, 128, 128 n. 12, 143
n. 51, 144 n. 53, 158, 158
n. 8
Barthélemy, D., 164 n. 25
Barufaldi, L. L., 128 n. 12

Bassler, J., 175 n. 5
de Beauvoir, S., 83 n. 10
Becking, B., 5 n. 11, 67
Beer, G., 82 n. 7
Benzinger, I., 81 n. 3, 82 n. 5
Bergmann, E., 210 n. 33
Betteridge, A. H., 114 n. 32,
119 n. 44
Binford, M. B., 112 n. 28
Bird, P. A., 5 n. 14, 6 n. 16,
61 n. 15, 62 n. 16, 63 n. 18,
66, 104 n. 2, 106 nn. 6
and 7, 110 n. 22, 112 n. 27,
117 n. 38, 118 n. 39, 157
n. 4, 158 nn. 5 and 7, 159
n. 10, 161 n. 15, 162 n. 19,
163 nn. 20 and 21, 169
n. 31, 170 n. 35, 181 nn. 22
and 23, 182 n. 25, 190
n. 47, 204 n. 18, 206
n. 20, 222 n. 15, 224 n. 18,
254 n. 6a, 256 n. 20a, 262
n. 40
Blank, S. H., 43, n. 80
Blenkinsopp, J., 74 nn. 24,
26 and 27, 75 n. 30
Bloom, H., 257 n. 25
Böhl, F. M. T., 137 n. 36, 138
n. 37
Boling, R. G., 208 n. 25, 209
n. 29, 213 n. 39
Bonhoeffer, D., 126 n. 8
Børresen, K. E., 2 n. 4, 156
n. 3, 175 nn. 3, 4 and 6,
176 n. 8, 181 n. 22
Bourguignon, E., 85 n. 14
Braulik, G., 179 n. 18

Brenner, A., 66, 257, 257
n. 25
Brown, J. K., 86 nn. 16 and
17
Brown, P., 110, 110 n. 20
Brubaker, P., 67 n. 1
Brueggemann, W., 10
Buchanan, C. H., 66
Bullough, B., 224 n. 18
Bullough, V., 224 n. 18
Burns, R. J., 63 n. 20
Bynum, C. W., 105 nn. 4
and 5

Cahill, L. S., 168 n. 30
Cameron, A., 112 n. 29
Camp, C. V., 66
Campbell, E. F., 257 n. 25
Carmichael, C. M., 176 n. 9,
178 n. 12
Carrez, M., 164 n. 25
Chaney, M., 15 n. 5
Charles, R. H., 18 n. 6
Childs, B., 32 nn. 45 and 46
Clark, E. A., 175 n. 5
Clements, R. E., 66
Clines, D. J. A., 182 n. 24,
260, 260 n. 33, 261, 261
n. 37
Coats, G. W., 4 n. 10, 61
n. 15, 103 n. 1, 129 n. 13,
147 n. 63, 197, 222 n. 14
Collins, A. Y., 53 n. 2, 65
n. 24, 177 n. 10
Collins, O. E., 219 n. 1, 220
n. 4, 221 n. 8, 222 n. 12,

Keel, O., 96 n. 39, 184 n. 33
Knierim, R., 192 n. 51
Koehler, L., 123 n. 2, 125
    n. 4, 133 nn. 23 and 24
König, E., 81 n. 4, 140 n. 43
Kornfeld, W., 219 n. 1
Kraemer, R. S., 112 n. 28
Kramer, S. N., 200 n. 6, 210
    n. 33, 211 n. 35
Kraus, H-J., 104 n. 4
Kühlewein, J., 219 n. 1
Kuhrt, A., 112 n. 29
Kutsch, E., 179 n. 18

Lambert, W. G., 135 n. 31,
    138 n. 38
Lamphere, L., 85 n. 14, 86
    nn. 16 and 17
Landy, F., 177 n. 11
Langland, E., 86 n. 15
Lehmann, P., 126 n. 9
Lemaire, A., 186 n. 39
Lemche, N. P., 72 n. 22
Lerner, G., 199 n. 2
Lesko, B. S., 54 n. 4, 103 n. 1
Lewis, I. M., 87 n. 20, 112
    n. 28
Lewis, T. J., 110 n. 21
Locher, C., 66
Lohfink, N., 69 n. 13, 75
    n. 32, 76, 76 n. 36, 124
    n. 2, 147 n. 62, 148 n. 70,
    193 n. 53
Löhr, M., 82 n. 7
Long, B. O., 129 n. 13
Loretz, O., 124 n. 2, 125 n. 4,
    134 n. 24, 135 n. 27, 142
    n. 49
Lussier, E., 164 n. 25

Maag, V., 130 n. 13, 134
    n. 24, 138 n. 37, 141 nn. 44
    and 46
Majonet, J., 188 n. 43
Martin, M. K., 85 n. 14, 86
    nn. 16 and 17
Maturin, H. J., 66
Mays, J. L., 70 n. 18, 72
    n. 20, 225 n. 22, 229 n. 31,
    230 n. 35, 235 n. 47

McBride, S. D., 5 n. 12, 63
    nn. 18 and 19, 81, 103 n. 1,
    113 n. 30, 234 n. 44
McCarter, P. K., Jr., 109
    n. 18
McDonald, E. M., 82 n. 7
McEvenue, S. E., 130 n. 15
McKane, W., 32 n. 44
Meek, T. J., 200 n. 5
Mendelsohn, I., 43 nn. 78
    and 79, 72 nn. 21 and 22,
    75, 75 n. 28
Mernissi, F., 108, 108 n. 15,
    205 n. 19
Mettinger, T. N. D., 124
    n. 2, 125 n. 5, 132 n. 22,
    136 n. 34
Meyers, C., 53 n. 1, 54 nn. 3
    and 5, 56 n. 6, 57 n. 9, 59
    nn. 10 and 12, 62 n. 17,
    106 n. 7, 166 n. 28, 176
    n. 10, 190 n. 47, 257 257
    n. 26, 258, 258 n. 27, 259
Meyers, J. M., 74 n. 25, 75
    n. 30
Mickelson, A., 255 n. 9
Miles, J. G., 211 n. 35
Miles, M. R., 66
Millard, A. R., 138 n. 38
Miller, J. M., 124 n. 2, 130
    N. 15, 132 n. 22, 133 n. 23,
    209 n. 29
Miller, P. D., Jr., 5 n. 12, 63
    nn. 18 and 19, 81, 103 n. 1,
    113 n. 30, 166 n. 28, 169
    n. 34, 234 n. 44
Minault, G., 86 n. 17
Moberly, R. W. L., 174 n. 1
Montgomery, J. A., 41 n. 73,
    217 n. 44
Moore, H. L., 116 n. 37, 256
    n. 21
Moore, R. L., 105 n. 5
Moran, W. L., 123 n. 1, 135
    n. 31, 136 n. 33
Morgenstern, J., 97 n. 40
Morris, B., 105 n. 5
Morris, P., 175 nn. 3 and 6,
    176 nn. 7, 8 and 9, 177
    n. 11, 179 n. 16, 193 n. 53

Mowinckel, S., 208 n. 25,
    209 n. 28
Moye, R. H., 177 n. 11

Naidoff, B. D., 164 n. 24
Nelson, J. B., 156 n. 1, 168
    n. 30
Neusner, J., 113 n. 29
Niditch, S., 178 n. 13, 184
    n. 31, 206 n. 20, 222 n. 15
Nöldeke, T., 125 n. 4
Noth, M., 20 n. 9, 21 n. 11,
    23 n. 20, 37 n. 58, 112
    n. 26, 208 nn. 25 and 26,
    217 n. 44
Nowack, W., 81 n. 3, 82 n. 5

O'Connor, M., 166 n. 28
Ogden, S., 263
Oppenheim, A. L., 200 n. 6,
    201 nn. 9 and 11
Ortner, S. B., 86 n. 15, 87
    n. 18
Otto, E., 135 nn. 27, 28 and
    29
Otwell, J., 66, 82 n. 9
Otzen, B., 186 n. 39

Pagels, E., 174 n. 2, 175 n. 5,
    179 n. 16
Papanek, H., 86 n. 17
Parpola, S., 136 n. 32, 137
    n. 36
Patai, R., 22 n. 14, 25 nn. 27
    and 29, 26 n. 30, 28 n. 36,
    39 n. 67, 40 n. 71, 42 n. 77
Patte, D., 177 n. 11
Paul, S. M., 70 n. 18
Pedersen, J., 22 nn. 14 and
    17, 24 n. 21, 25 n. 26, 26
    n. 30, 36 n. 54, 38 n. 62,
    39 n. 63
Peritz, I., 82 n. 7
Pleins, J. D. 68, 68 nn. 4, 5
    and 9, 69 n. 14, 76 n. 35
Porter, S. E., 179 n. 16
Pritchard, J. B., 63 n. 19